NEGOTIATIONS

Cultural Memory
in
the
Present

Mieke Bal and Hent de Vries, Editors

NEGOTIATIONS

Interventions and Interviews, 1971–2001

Jacques Derrida

Edited, Translated, and
with an Introduction
by Elizabeth Rottenberg

STANFORD UNIVERSITY PRESS

STANFORD, CALIFORNIA

Stanford University Press
Stanford, California

© 2002 by the Board of Trustees of the
Leland Stanford Junior University

Printed in the United States of America
on acid-free, archival-quality paper

ISBN 0-8047-3891-2 (alk. paper)
ISBN 0-8047-3892-0 (pbk: alk. paper)

Original Printing 2002
Last figure below indicates year of this printing:
11   10   09   08   07   06   05   04   03   02

Typeset by Publication Services 11/13.5 Garamond

Contents

Introduction: Inheriting the Future   I
Elizabeth Rottenberg

PART I. NEGOTIATIONS

Negotiations   II

Letter to Jean Genet (Fragments)   41

Declarations of Independence   46

What I Would Have Said . . .   55

Economies of the Crisis   69

Events? What Events?   74

"Pardon me for taking you at your word"   77

The Deconstruction of Actuality   85

Taking Sides for Algeria   117

For Mumia Abu-Jamal   125

Open Letter to Bill Clinton   130

Derelictions of the Right to Justice   133

PART II. THINKING AT ITS LIMITS

Politics and Friendship   147

The Aforementioned So-Called Human Genome   199

Nietzsche and the Machine   215

"Dead Man Running": Salut, Salut   257

PART III.   ETHICS AND POLITICS TODAY

Ethics and Politics Today   295

On the "Priceless," or the "Going Rate" of the Transaction   315

The Right to Philosophy from a Cosmopolitan Point of View   329

As If It Were Possible, "Within Such Limits" . . .   343

Globalization, Peace, and Cosmopolitanism   371

Notes   387

NEGOTIATIONS

Introduction: Inheriting the Future

Elizabeth Rottenberg

> This is one of the possible definitions of deconstruction—precisely
> as legacy.
> —Jacques Derrida

I. No sleep

Negotiations, the volume, has a long and complex history. Originally
conceived by Deborah Esch and Tom Keenan more than ten years ago,
the volume set out to articulate the never-ending, unrelenting "il faut" of
deconstruction or justice with Jacques Derrida's very singular political engagements of the moment. However, the projected volume grew to such
monstrous proportions over the years that its publication was endlessly
deferred. Indeed, even at 404 pages, the reader may still find that the volume shows signs of its difficult birth. And yet this excessiveness, this im-
moderation, this impossibility of just stopping or settling with a selection
of texts (of just saying "no"—no more texts . . .) was perhaps less the
symptom of a compulsion on the part of the editors than it was a response
to an impossible demand: Keep negotiating! You must always negotiate
further!

The impossibility of stopping: this means, as *Negotiations* will propose to show, the necessity of reading and analyzing constantly not only
our whole conceptual machinery but also its interestedness. From where
does a given discourse draw its authority and its legitimacy? Who is behind

it, who is mediating it, by what means, and to what ends? What and who (individuals, groups, nations, languages, discourses) will have been excluded from it ("Pardon me for taking you at your word")? Who is talking about "crisis" and in view of what effects and what interests ("Economies of the Crisis")? What is being pushed into the shadows by that which appears under the official title of "event" ("Events? What Events?")? Where does the value of objectivity come from ("Politics and Friendship")? In every situation, in every context, questions that address (or do not address) the origins of one's concepts and the weight of tradition are not simply discursive or theoretical: they are also political.

And never will a just politics arise from a limitation on thinking. On the contrary, Derrida argues: the questioning of a conceptual legacy already demonstrates a certain readiness to change; it shows that transformation is already beginning to take place or that it is at least possible. It is imperative (indeed urgent) that one further refine and differentiate one's concepts: on every occasion, one must explain why one is acting in a particular way, why one believes it is better to do this than that, why a particular act in a given context is more likely to achieve this than some other act. And to make such evaluations, one must pass through thought: "these evaluations are *actions of thought*" ("Nietzsche and the Machine"). Hence, infinitely close reading is nothing other than the condition of political responsibility. Political responsibility requires that one read events, that one analyze situations, that one pay attention to the rhetoric of the demagogues and the media. Constantly. For one always risks falling back into a new dogmatic slumber (even, and perhaps especially, with terms such as "ethics," "morality," "responsibility"). Negotiation is an "enervating mobility" that "prevents one from ever stopping": this means "no thesis, no position, no theme, no station, no substance, no stability, a perpetual suspension, a suspension without rest" ("Negotiations")—no sleep: anything less and one acts irresponsibly. "I repeat: responsibility is excessive or it is not responsibility."[1]

On the other hand, however, one must negotiate. Negotiation is passive: there is no "outside" negotiation. One is thrown into negotiation. From the outset, and even when one thinks one is not negotiating—that there is something that cannot be negotiated, that there is something nonnegotiable—one negotiates. Not negotiating is a way of evaluating. It is "a way of handling the problem so as to calculate the coming of a new politics, of another politics, of a future chance" ("Ethics and Politics Today"). This is what is so terrifying about negotiation, says Derrida: negotiation must always negotiate the nonnegotiable.

[N]egotiation does not negotiate between negotiable things, by exchanging negotiable things, negotiation—and this is what makes it terrible—must negotiate the nonnegotiable, to save its being nonnegotiable. ("Negotiations")

There is no negotiating negotiation: negotiation is passive from the standpoint of an affirmation that it does not control. "As soon as I open my mouth, there will have been affirmation" (p. 27). Affirmation says "yes"—"yes" to the other, "yes" to negotiation—even when one refuses to negotiate. In fact, this "yes" is what makes refusal possible in the first place, for this "yes" is first a response, a response that is "originary," and nothing precedes this response. Response or responsiveness is already presupposed wherever one addresses oneself to the other, that is to say, everywhere, were it "to deny, to argue, to oppose" the other (p. 355). One will always have had to say "yes" in order to say "no."

If, however, any given discourse can and should be analyzed, if it is deconstructible—which is to say it can be taken as a historical artifact worthy of analysis and deconstruction—"that *in the name of which* one deconstructs is not in the last instance deconstructible" (pp. 229–230, my emphasis). Derrida will call this irreducibility "justice." Although justice, in this sense, is outside the law of negotiation (it transcends negotiation), it nonetheless requires negotiation and the strategies of negotiation. What is foreign to the process of negotiation nonetheless requires the process of negotiation. What is radically heterogeneous to negotiation is indissociable from negotiation. This is because "justice" and "negotiation" are not symmetrical terms. Justice is above negotiation. But even if it always remains above negotiation, justice needs negotiation. This exigency is itself constitutive of justice, for justice could not remain nonnegotiable—one could not "*save* its being nonnegotiable"—were its nonnegotiability not predicated on a limit, the boundary line of negotiation. A "justice" that was not bound to negotiation in this way would be flat, abstract, quixotic, illusory, and perfectly inhuman—it would have no positive reality, no life.

II. Substitution versus enumeration: seriature

And there is another word. . . . I used it only once in a text on Levinas.[2] The word is "seriature." The etymology leads back to *cord, rope.* "Seria" is also the idea of a series, that is, the necessity of a proliferation of gestures, particular each time. I cannot reconstitute this text here. It talks about the necessity of linking. In a chain, thus, there is always the same metaphor of rope, chain, shuttle. The necessity of linking gestures or moments that do not let themselves be linked, which are absolutely singular every time. And one has to link singularities, that is, put in a series things that do not let themselves be put into series. This can be a definition of negotiation. Why one must repeat and put into a series, in a kind of serial generality, things that do not let themselves be serialized, which are singular and nonnegotiable every time. ("Negotiations")

Hence negotiation is the necessity of linking singularities, of putting into series—"in a kind of serial generality"—what is absolutely singular and nonnegotiable every time. But how can what is absolutely singular be put into a series in which its very singularity becomes replaceable? How can a singularity be both irreplaceable *and* universalizable in its singularity? To be replaceable in its very irreplaceability: this, says Derrida, is the predicament of every singularity. The stakes of this predicament are prodigious, moreover, for the possibility of singularity grounds the fact of moral law in modern moral theory. At the heart of *Negotiations*, thus, lies not only the question of singularity but the grounding of all political and moral thought.

Indeed the very concept of singularity appeals to what Derrida calls the *principle of neutralization* (indifference, equivalence, substitution). In the moral realm, says Derrida, this repetition-serialization takes the form of an absolute indifference, an indifference to all particular characteristics: "two human beings *for example* have an equal moral, juridical, political *dignity* whatever their differences in all other respects (social, economic, biological, sexual, psychical, or intellectual, etc.)" ("On the 'Priceless,' or the 'Going Rate' of the Transaction"). Without this universalizing principle, without this neutralizing indifference, dignity itself, that is, the possibility of singularity, responsibility, decision—everything we call *politics* and *ethics*—would be obliterated.

But Derrida's concept of "seriature" raises not only the question of singularity: it also introduces the concept of seriality. If every singularity has an absolute worth or dignity, if every singularity is by definition an end in itself, then the very concept of singularity points to an infinite chain of objective and independently existing ends, an abyssal possibility of enumeration. Is there a difference between substitution (repetition) and serialization (enumeration)? Or to ask the same question differently, what is the relation *between* one singularity and the other in this chain? If all singularities or ends in themselves are literally replaceable in their irreplaceability, that is to say, *interchangeable, exchangeable* in their dignity and absolute worth, are they invariably and therefore also immediately recuperated by a system of exchange and substitution—the economy of the marketplace? Would there not exist an absolute difference *between* singularities? And how does one *pass*—indeed can one pass—between singularities without at the same time immediately reducing an absolute worth to a comparable worth, and without assimilating an intrinsic and irreducible difference to precisely the "*same* difference"?

III. A double legacy: Kant-Derrida

Since this bond between singularities, as well as the promise it carries, is what I call *spectral*, it cannot be made into a community; the promise of the bond forms neither a national, linguistic, or cultural community, nor does it anticipate a cosmopolitan constitution. It exceeds all cultures, all languages, it even exceeds the concept of humanity. ("Nietzsche and the Machine")

Derrida calls the bond between singularities—the bond that links what will not be linked—*spectral.* To be spectral is to be neither present nor absent; it is neither to be nor not to be. Indeed the spectral, says Derrida, is what exceeds all ontological oppositions between absence and presence, visible and invisible, living and dead ("The Deconstruction of Actuality"). A bond that is spectral, therefore, is something that cannot be contained within any traditional concept of community. It is a protest against citizenship, a form of political solidarity that is opposed to the border politics of the nation-states: it is what Derrida calls *the democracy to come.* In other words, the spectrality of the bond affects the very essence of the possible. It makes possible the impossible, the coming of the other, the invention of the future.

The spectral bond carries the present beyond itself; it haunts every moment of apparent presence. It not only makes the future possible (as impossible), it also makes possible the ghostly return of the past. This ghostly return or "revenance" conveys what Derrida calls a *legacy*. Because it is spectral, this legacy always retains an undecidable reserve:

[W]hoever inherits chooses one spirit rather than another. One makes selections, one filters, one sifts through the ghosts or through the injunctions of each spirit. There is legacy only where assignations are multiple and contradictory, secret enough to defy interpretation, to carry the unlimited risk of active interpretation. It is here that a decision and a responsibility can be taken. ("The Deconstruction of Actuality")

An act of inheritance requires decision and responsibility, and whoever inherits must pass through the undecidability in which Derrida grounds every decision qua decision. For an act of inheritance to take place, there must be a moment or space that is absolutely heterogeneous to knowledge (all knowledge and the knowledge of all). Indeed this passage through undecidability to which every responsible decision owes its possibility is exactly that moment or space of passivity (a passivity that is not in the least incompatible with freedom and autonomy) in which a legacy must remain suspended, hovering between a mode which is that of cognition and a mode which is no longer that of cognition.

Whoever inherits, says Derrida, selects one specter rather than another. Indeed one might go so far as to say that the specter haunting *Negotiations* is the specter of Kant. Not only does Derrida return to Kant repeatedly in the volume, but it is on the basis of Kant's notion of dignity—precisely against it in its name—that Derrida takes up the question of singularity. More surprising, however, is Derrida's return to a very Kantian notion of legacy. For Kant as for Derrida, an act of inheritance remains an extraordinary act; on the one hand, because it elicits from the heir a response to a chosenness; on the other hand, because a true act of inheritance always implies momentous decisions and responsibilities. Until there is a decision on the part of the heir, in other words, a legacy remains suspended; it hovers between acceptance and rejection.[3]

But Derrida's concept of legacy will not be that of Kant. For Derrida the question of legacy is no longer simply a question that is left to the other: rather it is *the* question that *must be* left to the other. One might say that Derrida reads Kant with new emphasis, and that it is this shift, this change of voice, this accentuation that changes everything. In other words, Derrida remains faithful to the legacy of Kant by breaking with the particular *modality* of Kant's thinking of legacy.[4] To inherit, as Derrida does here, is to insist on another modality, the modality of the other. Although the bond between singularities may be something that exceeds the "concept of humanity," it cannot be opposed to the human: on the contrary, it would seem, it is neither reducible to nor separable from what is called *the human* ("Taking Sides For Algeria," "Derelictions of the Right to Justice").

The absolute alterity of the other resists all subjectivation, all internalization. The other is non-reappropriable, and in a certain way, says Derrida, nonidentifiable. And yet the obligation to protect the other's otherness is not merely a theoretical imperative. Indeed, how are we to read the "bond between singularities, as well as the promise it carries"? If the promise and the bond are "spectral," if from this bond and this promise we can expect no community or constitution, if the promise of the bond "exceeds all cultures, all languages . . . the concept of humanity," who is to say that this bond, that this promise is/will be in the last instance acceptable, that is to say, tolerable? It would seem, rather, that no singularity as such ever recovers from this bond and that this bond, as well as the promise it carries, are the intolerable price we pay for moral and political possibility: we cannot accept, it would seem, a bond to that which in the other remains utterly solitary and unresponsive. And yet it is perhaps only because it carries with it something unacceptable that this legacy remains the legacy of the future. And of future *Negotiations*.

NEGOTIATIONS

Negotiations

D.E.: Maybe we can just begin with the dictionary. Specifically with the etymology of this term "negotiation" that is our focus—the etymology being neg-otium, not-ease, not-quiet—

J.D.: . . . no leisure . . .

D.E.: . . . no leisure . . . and try to get at the character of this un-ease, this lack of leisure, or, to use a word that comes up again and again in your texts, the difficulty of negotiation, perhaps the impossibility of negotiation. And I thought, just to begin with an example—and there would be many examples possible as a beginning—but to take one that is autobiographical on your part, in that interview with Geoff Bennington, which you have not seen, but I will just cite, because I think it raises at least two questions that I would like to talk about. The context is that you are responding to a question about your role in the founding of the Collège [International de Philosophie]. "First, even if I have been involved with the Collège from the beginning, it does not represent anything especially attached to me, and I have tried to do all I could to avoid using the Collège as a place for representing any group to which I am attached, or representing myself. I remain at a distance in the Report, insisting that the Collège should not express a special philosophy, and, of course, should not represent deconstruction. That is my ethics in the situation. It is very difficult because, at one and the same time, I want to defend what I think is 'truth' and not to influence the evolution of the Collège. It is very difficult, and I have to negotiate this every day." Now, two points. I will just begin, or you can begin if you have a thought, but just to take them in the order in which they arise there: the question of ethics, the question of the ethical-political dimension when you say, "this is my ethics in this situation." Does the concept of negotiation, if it is a concept, and if we need a concept for it (this is a further question as well), does negotiation enable one to avoid certain constraints, certain inadequacies in traditional ethical discourse, for example, or in traditional political discourse? Is it more appropriate, more effective in contexts where the traditional discourse is not tenable as such, and in order to negotiate (and we still have to specify what we mean), to take account of, respect, be responsible to those traditional modes, traditional ethical modes, traditional political modes? If that seems like a good beginning?

J.D.: Yes. Let us return to the etymology of the word "negotiation". On the one hand, you have chosen it as a theme, as a guiding thread, because you felt, just as I do, that the word imposed itself on me. I did not really choose it, it has imposed itself on me in a recurrent way for a very long time. Why? This word is no more perfect and no more univocal out of context than any other: therefore, I also had to *negotiate* its usage, bend it according to its folds, so to speak, but also bend it to my writing, to another writing in any case. I appropriated the etymology for this new writing (ethical or political). Un-leisure is the impossibility of stopping, of settling in a position. Whether one wants it or not, one is always working in the mobility between several positions, stations, places, between which a shuttle is needed. The first image that comes to me when one speaks of negotiation is that of the shuttle, *la navette,* and what the word conveys of to-and-fro between two positions, two places, two choices. One must always go from one to the other, and for me negotiation is the impossibility of establishing oneself anywhere. And even if in certain situations one thinks one must not negotiate, that there is a nonnegotiable, say, the categorical imperative, one must nonetheless negotiate the relation between the categorical imperative and the hypothetical imperative. We will perhaps return to the problem of the hypothetical, but if there is an ethics of negotiation, it is as much in the sense of moral law as it is in the autobiographical dimensions you alluded to earlier; it is a feeling, an affective relation I have to myself of being someone who cannot stop anywhere. This can be both the feeling of a *duty* when one thinks one can settle in the categorical imperative but also a passivity without which one could not be certain that one might not settle in it. For one thing is certain, I am certain that one must get out of it, that one must negotiate with the situation, with hypothetical imperatives.

One must calculate. Thus, there is a feeling of duty—a respect for the law. Here one might naturally insert a reflection of the Hegelian sort on the critique of the categorical imperative that betrays morality by abstraction. But we cannot engage in this direction. Thus this necessity to calculate a kind of supplement, duty, imperative, ethicity. In my own behavior, and here the word "ethical" will not have the sense of moral obligation but the sense of *ethos*, of manner of being, of *habitus*, I feel this reference to negotiation to be as much of a moral tyranny that weighs on me as I do a style or a manner of treating the *double bind* in order to avoid it, of passing very quickly from one pole to the other of the double bind. One cannot separate this concept and this practice of negotiation from the concept of the *double bind*, that is, of the double duty. There is negotiation when there are two incompatible imperatives that appear to be incompatible but are equally imperative. One does not negotiate between exchangeable and negotiable things. Rather, one negotiates by engaging the nonnegotiable in negotiation. And I have the feeling that, both in my work and in my political-institutional engagements, but also in my manner of being that is the most, how shall I say it, personal, affective, the style is what imposed itself on me: I cannot do otherwise. Thus, when I think negotiation, I think of this fatigue, of this without-rest, this enervating mobility preventing one from ever stopping. If you would like to translate this philosophically, the impossibility of stopping, this means: no thesis, no position, no theme, no station, no substance, no stability, a perpetual suspension, a suspension without rest. There is no rest in suspension and, furthermore, suspension, if you were to translate it philosophically, is the phenomenological *epochè*, the Skepsis, etc. But a suspension that is not theoretical, a suspension that is precisely not the Husserlian *epochè* or the Skepsis or the kinds of suspension that Husserl and Heidegger discuss, which still belongs to the order of seeing: one suspends judgment, one sees. The suspension of negotiation I am talking about, on the contrary, is a suspension that cannot be theoretical; theory is not possible, or rather, theoretism is not possible.

This is why I prefer the word "negotiation" to more noble words. As I have already said in one of the texts you invoked, there is always something about negotiation that is a little dirty, that gets one's hands dirty. Once one negotiates, something is being trafficked, something in the order of a traffic, or the relations of force. It is a question of style, of social connotation: I prefer the word "negotiation" because it does not disguise the anxiety, about which I am speaking, with nobility. As a result, it seems more mediocre; one thinks of force, one thinks of compromise, one thinks of impure things.

Negotiation is impure. And this is precisely what I mean: impurity, the contamination of pure things, naturally, in the name of purity. The formal logic implied here is that, if you do not negotiate, the thing will be even more impure. We will be even dirtier [*salaud*] if we do not negotiate. Thus, in all the noble discourses about how "one does not negotiate," I quickly learned to recognize the danger of the worst sort. One could therefore say that it was a supplement of morality on my part. I still want to negotiate in the name of purity. This is another proposition that must be negotiated.

Good, enough about philosophical generalities on the etymologies of the word. I come now to the example, to the Collège. I would like to add a remark to the passage you have cited, from the point of view of negotiation. On the one hand, I thought it only fair to let people who wanted to enter the Collège remain free to give the college the orientation that seemed necessary to them, a diverse, critical orientation. From this point of view, my choices always take on a liberal appearance. I am a liberal. It was fair to leave this institution its openness, even if the orientations that it was to take on were not my own. I thought it fair but also smart. I calculated. If in the Report, for example, I marked the project of the Collège with my own opinions from the start, the project would have been less successful, not only among colleagues or other teachers but also with the government. Thus one needed (and this, too, is negotiation, and not only liberalism and a spirit of tolerance, this is also a political tactic) to present an acceptable project. But not acceptable at any price. It needed to be made acceptable to others, but there also needed to be room for what interests me. This situation is paradigmatic of all the situations in which I have been involved with institutions in the past. The problem of GREPH[1] was a similar problem, and a few were surprised to find that someone who spends his time deconstructing philosophy, etc., protests when one tries to destroy philosophy. Why do I do this? I can give at least two reasons: the first is that I thought the attacks, not only on the part of the government but also on the part of, let us say, a techno-capitalist society, were trying to reduce the field of philosophy and that these attacks, in fact, represented a philosophy. It was not only a destruction of philosophy, but the attack itself was made in the name of a certain unformulated philosophy that also became a matter for me to deconstruct. It made sense to oppose that philosophy, represented at the time by a certain "Haby" project of destruction of philosophy. At the same time, I find it necessary, vital that the philosophical debate remain open. For what interests me in the name of deconstruction to be possible, philosophical culture must remain alive and well. Deconstruction inhabits it and is inseparable from it. Philosophical teaching must continue to develop, one must continue to read, the relation to tradition must be as cultivated as possible: from this point of view, let it be said in passing, those who see deconstruction as a threat to culture and even to academic culture and to its canon, those who try to denounce its "barbarism," are the barbarians: most often, you know, it is they who have not read enough, especially the so-called deconstructive texts. Deconstruction presupposes the most intensely cultivated, literate relation to the tradition. Thus, it is a matter of keeping the field of tradition open, of making things such that the access to philosophy remains open to the greatest number of people: one must pursue the critical project of philosophy as far as possible; and one must also understand that there is no deconstruction without this critique, even if deconstruction is not simply critique.

The strategy was thus to keep philosophy open and in lively debate. It was the same thing for the Collège. For what interests me to have a chance of working, not only of being of interest but of working in the sense of negotiating (negotiation is work), the institution had to be open, pluralistic, liberal in style. And thus, for my part, it was not simply, as I say it in the phrase that you cited, a kind of ethical retreat, a respect for others. There is that, as well, of course. But it was also what I thought would be the best calculation, so that what interests me has room to breathe in the Collège. Thus, even there, negotiation, the relation of the act of negotiating with ethics, is very complicated. On the one hand, I erase myself and I erase what interests me the most to let others speak, out of respect for others. Deconstruction must not impose itself. But at the same time, obviously, this respect is a calculation; it is contaminated by calculation.

As for determining what it is the calculation works toward, this is the most difficult task, perhaps even impossible, impossible to accomplish or to define, I mean precisely as a task. For why would I want deconstruction to be understood or to be effective? Why would I identify myself with it? If I were pushed a little too far, one would see that I myself ("I," "me"—I do not know what I mean in saying this) do not have an absolute interest in something like deconstruction succeeding.

My relation, then, to the logic of deconstruction is rather complicated. Here, too, one has to negotiate. If deconstruction cannot simply be radical, there is a negotiation inside deconstruction. The latter cannot be radical because the value of radicality itself must be deconstructed; it communicates with all sorts of values, such as the values of fundamentality and the origin. If one associated the value of radicality with deconstruction, it would do away with itself, would destroy itself, or would destroy all the securities we still need, which, for example, I still need. So negotiation is constantly under way, the negotiation which is none other than deconstruction itself. It is not a matter of a negotiation between deconstruction and something else. There is negotiation in deconstruction, between the values, themes, meanings, philosophemes that are deconstructed and a certain maintenance, or survival, of their effects.

Well, this is very abstract, I will give an example—the value of presence, because its role is just as important in this context. It is evident that the deconstruction of this value does not prevent us from counting on it at all times. If deconstruction were a destruction, nothing would be possible any longer. The least desire, the least language would be impossible. Thus, within deconstruction, if one can speak here of an inside, there is this negotiation. In *The Post Card*, the signatory of the dispatches says somewhere, "In the end, I deconstruct" (and I will quote from memory) "the things I love." One could also say that deconstruction "involves the structures" or the constructa, the things constructed that make life or existence possible. Deconstruction makes the constructed character appear as such, which is not artificial in opposition to the natural (precisely this opposition needs to be deconstructed) but constructed or structured in view of making possible—of making possible . . . what? Not only consciousness, the person, the ego, the unconscious. Even if I said Dasein, I already have questions in reserve against Dasein.

Thus, to "make possible"—whence the paradox—that on the basis of which, now, deconstruction is engaged. One can take, for example, all the themes that have been privileged until now by deconstructive strategy: that is, presence, consciousness, sign, theme, thesis, etc. One cannot imagine oneself alive renouncing all consciousness, all presence, all ethics of language: and yet this is precisely what must be deconstructed. One must try to think what it is that makes us unable to "do without." Thus, on the one hand, the very menacing character of deconstruction. But, at the same time, it does not threaten anything because it is not a question of destroying what there is to deconstruct. Although phantasmatic, the threat is not, however, imaginary, and this explains the affective charge, the terrorized violence of the resentment and reactions against "deconstruction." Negotiation operates in the very place of threat, where one must [*il faut*] with vigilance venture as far as possible into what appears threatening and at the same time maintain a minimum of security—and also an internal security not to be carried away by this threat. This, too, is negotiation.

An essential aspect of negotiation is that it is always different, differential, not only from one individual to another, from one situation to another, but even for the same individual, from one moment to the next. There is no general law, there is no general rule for negotiation. Negotiation is different at every moment, from one context to the next. There are only contexts, and this is why deconstructive negotiation cannot produce general rules, "methods." It must be adjusted to each case, to each moment without, however, the conclusion being a relativism or empiricism. This is the difficulty. That there is something like an absolute rule of negotiation that can only be adjusted to political, historical situations.

Let us take a few examples. For example, what I was led to do in a micro-environment at the institutional moments to which you are alluding (the Collège, or GREPH) cannot be immediately translated or transposed to another moment in France or to another country or to another academic situation. This is obvious, and one can derive no general rule from this example. And yet there is no relativism, no empiricism. A law permits one to escape relativism and empiricism. The latter, like all the associated values of psychologism and historicism, represents a determined philosophy. The "law," "before" which what I call deconstruction is determined, commands one to think philosophy itself. It no longer belongs to philosophy. No longer simply. And it is only contextualizable insofar as this thinking, open in its context, this opening of context is not saturated by the determination of a context.

I think I have implicitly responded to something you asked me when you emphasized the everyday. I think that this is very important. Every day: for me this means negotiation cannot stop. One must always readjust. We have isolated global situations, called the Collège International de Philosophie, or GREPH. But this is too global. Inside the Collège, negotiation has also always been very complicated. My attitude has been very different: sometimes very harsh, strict, sometimes very flexible. In the Report the strategies are multiple. Some phrases are unconditional, others propose something like potential compromises to the government or other potential readers of the Report. Negotiation is constantly in a state of micro-transformation. *Every day*: this means it does not stop. This also means that, between politics—that is, public life—and private life (interests, desires, etc.), the communication is never broken. I do not believe in the conceptual value of a rigorous distinction between the private and the public. There can be the singular and the secret, but these resist the "private" as much as they do the "public." In what I write one should be able to perceive that the boundary between the autobiographical and the political is subject to a certain strain. Its rigor is never ensured. Between, let us say, the opening of *States General of Philosophy* and *The Post Card* there is a transition. Moreover, *The Post Card* discusses *States General of Philosophy* if I remember correctly. Thus, every day negotiation is under way; one cannot distinguish between one day and another, one cannot distinguish between day and night.

I return to the example of the Collège International de Philosophie. Although it is still an institution of modest dimensions, it is obviously a very privileged example. It is an open place and not exclusively French. How does one negotiate a relation—which I call, for convenience and brevity's sake, deconstructive—to philosophy in a philosophical place but also a place where philosophy will be put into question? The Collège International de Philosophie was defined not only as a place of learning and philosophical research but also as a place of learning and research on the subject of philosophy. Thus, for me, this was a particularly serious and critical moment of the negotiation. I would have experienced it differently, I would not have apprehended it in the same way had the Collège been an already existing university where philosophy was merely one department among others. Here, without wanting to give in to exaggeration or pathos, the matter concerned a place for philosophy in the world today, a college open to philosophical internationality where, in principle, if everything worked out, we were going to discuss what philosophy is to become, and should become, in the future. It was to be a crucial place for the fate of philosophy, for what we were going to do with philosophy, not only in Paris or in France but in the world at large. Thus, the gestures of negotiation in this case were particularly weighty, charged. One had to negotiate with who-knows-how-many partners at the same time. One could say that negotiation is always necessary and impossible at the same time, because one must always negotiate with more than one person, more than one partner. There are several addressees in a negotiation. Perhaps it is already impossible when there is just one, but if there is more than one, it is terrible. In the case of the Collège, one had to—I will broadly define the instances— negotiate with a socialist government represented by several agencies difficult to locate, difficult to isolate outside of a ministry that looked on things from above and assigned civil servants to us, functionaries who were intellectuals, "academics" in the ministerial offices at that moment. They were going to decide whether or not the Report was acceptable. Thus, one had to negotiate with a governmental power represented by a large number of people, all of whom had be considered, along with the addressees of the Report who—one could tell oneself in addition—might not read it in any true sense. This is what happened. Instead of paying attention to the "philosophical" project, they were attentive to the economic and architectural aspects. But one had also to think of one's philosopher-colleagues, especially in France, although not only in France; these were other virtual addressees. One had to think of the students, of people who were not entirely "academic," and also of other interlocutors immediately present and pressuring. Four of us worked on this Report, and I was in charge of organizing and coordinating the project. The most difficult thing in the end was to negotiate all of this with people as diverse in their interests as François Châtelet, Dominique Lecour, and Jean-Pierre Faye. We will not get into this, but you cannot imagine—unless you knew all three of them—how difficult this was. In writing the first draft of the text, I had to make an effort precisely not to mark the text in a personal way. Moreover, I was advised or asked in a friendly way to avoid the word deconstruction and the word différance, with the "a." In this kind of situation, similar to some that occurred in GREPH, I enter into the ranks, I melt into the multiplicity. There are things that interest me in the multiplicity of positions, but sometimes what happens is that I am the most repressed of all. I am made to understand that, above all, one must not speak of this. The situation is familiar to me: there I am (I could generalize) in a group of people who are friends, allies, or at least people who are not enemies, and I am made to understand that, if there is something that must be passed over in silence, it is I.

T.K.: I wanted to pick up on something. This difference between the values of positioning and taking a stand and making a decision (all of which are associated with a certain kind of presence and which is a very powerful tradition in political theory and in political practice), the necessity of taking a position, and this other value of mobility and of the shuttle, and of a kind of guerrilla tactics: this is interesting, because it is not purely a theoretical question. It is a tactical one of how to achieve certain effects in certain situations. But its implications are extreme and two examples occur. One is—at numerous points in the discussion of GREPH and here in the discussion of the Collège—you have talked about the importance of not structuring it hierarchically, of not structuring an institution hierarchically, not structuring it centrally—and not out of some sort of aesthetic aversion to hierarchy but from a serious political necessity . . .

J.D.: But there is also an aesthetic operation.

T.K.: O.K., well, I . . .

J.D.: I would not define it as aesthetic, but the two are connected.

T.K.: O.K. That negotiation is interesting, but also in the discussion on women's studies ("Women in the Beehive," in any case) you talk about the necessity of putting the very existence of a women's studies program at stake . . . in this kind of calculation, as a way of better ensuring its survival. And likewise it seems that, for any traditional political theory, the thought that, say, GREPH should be organized nonhierarchically and nonauthoritatively, would be the kiss of death for an organization. But that is what I meant about its not being simply a sort of perverse aesthetics that leads you away, or leads one away from hierarchy, or a kind of romanticization of the guerrilla, or something, but that there is, that it could be a better political strategy and a better political tactics, to adopt these unconventional methods, in this distinction between the . . .

J.D.: . . . the nonhierarchical . . .

T.K.: Right, in the distinction between position and mobility.

J.D.: Yes, what is important in an interview such as this one is that I say things precisely in a way that is the least calculated possible, naked; that I try to say things in a form in which I do not usually say them; and that I try to untangle things without trying to justify or defend myself. Take, for example, the problem of hierarchy or authority. In a certain way, I have, what you yourself called an *aesthetic aversion* to a certain form of authority, to the *manifestation* of authority, but I am not satisfied with the word *aesthetic*. We will keep it to designate what appears to be a spontaneous movement of taste. I have, it seems, a quasi-aesthetic aversion to authority and hierarchy. But not for every kind of authority or every kind of hierarchy. The aesthetic aversion has to do with the fact that, most often, the most common forms of authority and hierarchy, of power and hegemony, have something in them which I find vulgar, insufficiently refined, or insufficiently differentiated: thus my aversion to authority, in this case, is also an aversion to what is still too homogeneous, insufficiently refined or differentiated, or else egalitarian. Most often leaders (or those who have the authority) are people who establish themselves in positions of authority or hierarchy, who establish themselves in positions of power, and it is this installation that I find *disgusting*. It is a question of taste. I do not like it. Nor do I have a marked taste for the homogeneous generality to which some would like to reduce democracy.

But I am not speaking of political positions right now. The emphasis of what I am saying is rather Nietzschean, that is, in a certain way I am for hierarchy, I am for a certain type of hierarchization, for differentiation, for qualitative difference. If I am opposed to certain forms of political hierarchy, to certain forms of power, it is precisely insofar as they tend to neutralize differences for lack of taste, for lack of refinement. And from this point of view, I would put the imposition of hierarchical authority and democratism (which I distinguish from democracy) on the same side. In a given institution—you chose the example of GREPH—when I insist on the necessity of a nonhierarchical structure or the necessity of an unstable hierarchy, I do not think that there are nonhierarchical structures. I do not think they exist. There can be nonhierarchy according to certain codes. The erasure of a certain coded hierarchy always gives rise to a more subtle, more symbolic hierarchy, the code of which still remains in formation. I do not believe in the erasure of hierarchy. What I am opposed to is always a certain stabilizing or stabilized coding of hierarchy. Given certain situations (you cited the example of GREPH) I propose that one not give oneself a constitution, statutes that permit hierarchy to be stabilized; I say this both for the reasons I have already explained and because I see in this a more astute calculation at a particular moment. It interests more people and is concerned with breaking given hierarchies. For the same reasons, it is necessary to open the Collège to people who do not have an academic title or to people who teach in high schools in France; this is very important—and it is necessary that secondary school teachers not be subordinated to those who teach at higher levels. This is not a way of nullifying the hierarchy but a way of destabilizing the given hierarchies and codes and of answering to the expectations, to the desire and motivation of people who are oppressed, who cannot work. But, in any case, I am not an enemy of hierarchy in general and of preference nor even of authority. I am simply impatient before the given, stabilized, installed, that is to say, vulgar and dormant forms of hierarchy.

T.K.: Well, the other side of it is that women's studies example. And the question of whether the lack of stability in the traditional sense would put the existence of the institution at stake and the necessity of doing that, of taking that risk.

J.D.: Yes, but it seems to me that in this interview I have said that there are two things. On the one hand, there is a danger for women's studies in reconstituting classical programs and institutions, in modeling itself and its struggle on the given political models dominated by men and marked by phallocentrism. But at the same time, it seems to me that they [*elles*] cannot simply give this up without risk of death, for women's rights or for women's studies; thus both are needed at the same time. Here again, negotiation and . . . shuttle.

D.E.: Yes.

J.D.: This would lead us back to the examples of GREPH and the Collège, where the question of women's studies was also at stake. One of the first seminars of GREPH (the first even, the first seminar that worked very well as a seminar) was about the question of women, teaching, and philosophy. Many women, students, and colleagues, participated. Thus, the questions about women's studies and all the questions of GREPH were very quickly articulated among these women. At the Collège they were also very quickly articulated, and I think this is what I say in the Report; we organized seminars devoted to problems, let us say, of the "women's studies" type. And the seminar that was (and still lasts) the longest from the start of the Collège is Hélène Cixous's seminar. Many American women, many foreigners, participate in it. Thus, this rather Franco-American seminar will have been the most stable at the Collège.

Therefore, in neither of these institutions—GREPH and the Collège—did I propose that there be no hierarchy at all, that there be no authority. The object was to propose structures where hierarchies would not stabilize and would be without a lasting appropriation of power; but there are hierarchies. I do not think that an institution can function without hierarchy. There are elections, there is a director, I was the first director elected to the Collège for a year. And I assure you that this was also an everyday negotiation. But every time I felt I should mark my authority I did just that. This is another way of treating hierarchy and authority, but it is not at all an anarchism. I am not an anarchist, from this point of view, nor am I an anarchist in negotiation. Deconstruction is undoubtedly anarchic; it would be in principle, if such a thing could be said. It puts into question the archē, the beginning and the commandment, but the anarchism of deconstruction must constitute [*composer*] an authority with the necessity of hierarchy. And must help in thinking as well as in regulating this negotiation.

D.E.: The example of women's studies . . . since I have the text at hand, we can read it into the record, as they say, because it brings up Tom's questions but also something else that I wanted to talk about, at the beginning. In response precisely to the question of political strategy, you say, "One way of dealing with these problems, not necessarily in women's studies, but on the whole, is to try to do both things at the same time, to occupy two places, both places. That is why deconstruction is often accused of being conservative and not conservative, and both are true. We have to negotiate, to maintain, for instance, women's studies as a classical program now, a now-classical program, and at the same time to ask radical questions that may endanger the program itself" (which was what you were talking about). "And what is the measure? You must check every day, what the measure is. There is no general device." And so on. Just to add to what Tom was saying . . . the question of the temporality of negotiation that underlies this *à la fois*, which you have addressed in part. But you talk, on the one hand, about the double bind and the double strategy, but then, in what you were just saying, it seems like it is more a multiplicity. And this, what you call in some of the remarks around the Prague incident "a difficult coincidence," this kind of simultaneity, *à la fois*. Is that one of the ways that you think, one of the ways in which you think this?

J.D.: Yes. It is extremely enlightening to do what you have just done, to focus on the question of time: two things at once, every day, at the same time. Obviously, one cannot do two things at the same time. It is not possible.

T.K.: Not to mention more than two.

J.D.: Not to mention more than two. It is not possible. What does it mean to say "it is not possible"? First, it means that *I*, that *I* cannot. Supposing that *I* were a simple instance—me—I cannot make two gestures at once. I am not saying that this is true, that I cannot make two gestures at once, I am saying that this is what appears to be the case, that usually for common sense (which is sometimes philosophy) one cannot make two different gestures and especially two contradictory gestures at once. One cannot do this at the same time. It is not possible. Thus, if it were possible it would mean that the unity of *at the same time* was dislocated, did not exist, that there is no *at the same time*. That is to say that the affirmation according to which one cannot do two contradictory things in a single moment, in a single place, this affirmation presupposes that something like a moment, an instant, a place, and an *I* that is ruled by this unity exist. This moment and this place would have an indivisible identity and in this indivisible identity I could not do two contradictory things. But this is not certain. Because, first of all (I am trying to improvise the principle of this analysis) the imperative so to speak, the *il faut* in my text does not concern what *I*, what I must do, what an individual alone must do. All the actions we are discussing are collective actions—of a differentiated, diverse community with heterogeneous times and rhythms. In women's studies there is a director who does what has to be done to run the institution, to legitimate it, and at the "same time" there is someone else—her ally—who is asking radical questions that may threaten what the other does. The *at once* decomposes. And because all of this also takes place through marks and acts of language, symbolic acts, there is never indivisibility. There is no indivisibility of the "at once." In every word, in every phrase, and more radically, in every mark the *at once* explodes. One sentence can have two meanings and two effects. The context is open and mobile. For this reason, on the one hand, I need to give up a philosophy of the moment, the indivisibility of the *at once*, and I have to give up the purely egological initiative of the political subject as sole master of what he does and of deciding what is done. The ego itself is divisible. This is also why there are delegations, why there is différance with an "a," why contradictory things happen at the same time, why conflictual things cohabit the same institution for example, in the same country, in the same society. The unity of this time is not ensured. There is no experience of this unity of time, no individual experience. One does not know where this "same time" is.

Nonetheless, for the egological subjects that we also are, the temptation is great to assemble, and think in, a system. System: this means to assemble in a theme. To think these contradictions, or this *double bind* in a system, as the individual subjects that we are: we perceive it as a painful impossibility. That each of us be responsible for all at once: this is what must be given up, but we cannot give it up. Nevertheless, driven as I am by the desire to assemble, which is an indestructible desire, I force myself—if I cannot do everything in the same instant—to produce forms of action or forms of givens, where two contradictory things are as close to each other as possible.

This has its effects on rhetoric, on the way we construct phrases, on a style of behavior. I am seen simultaneously as an extremely conservative and extremely unconservative person. I have an image that trembles. In the end, negotiation is at work in every word. At least I try to make it work in every statement. A microscopic attention would make this trembling appear in writing. The first example of it that comes to mind is the introduction to

States General, the discourse on philosophy in *States General*, where now and then there are short, very short phrases or two or three words, which cause the authority of the discourse to crumble . . . the confidence, the reliability of what I am saying—which is a discourse—for unconditional philosophy, the affirmation of unconditional philosophy. At one point, I say something to the effect of "the unconditional affirmation of philosophy, if there is one." But no one heard the "if there is one." What we were calling negotiation earlier is, for me, not simply a diplomatic operation that takes place in political-institutional contexts. It is an operation that takes place in every sentence: no, in every word, practically, that I publish.

T.K.: That is the page we were on in *States General*. And I wondered if there was a link that could be made between the difficulty of the temporality of negotiation and the strange temporality that you analyze in the founding of an institution. Particularly . . . if we could talk about it in terms of language, because it always seems to involve this future anterior tense, this hypothesis of a future. And that is the gesture you make at the end of the *States General* speech in discussing the problem of negotiating the nonnegotiable and associating it with this necessity of affirmation, and of an absolutely intractable, positional gesture.

J.D.: Not positional, affirmative . . . I distinguish here.

T.K.: O.K., well then, that's the question. What is the difference between the positional gesture of the founding of an institution and the affirmative gesture of the negotiation?

J.D.: Let us begin by distinguishing affirmation and position. I am very invested in this distinction. For me it is of the utmost importance. One must not be content with affirmation. One needs position. That is, one must create institutions. Therefore, one needs position. One needs a stance. Thus, negotiation, at this particular moment, does not simply take place between affirmation and negation, position and negation: it takes place between affirmation and position, because the position threatens the affirmation. That is to say that in itself institutionalization in its very success threatens the movement of unconditional affirmation. And yet this needs to happen, for if the affirmation were content to—how shall I say it—to wash its hands of the institution in order to remain at a distance, in order to say, "I affirm, and then the rest is of no interest to me, the institution does not interest me . . . let the others take care of that," then this affirmation would deny itself, it would not be an affirmation. Any affirmation, any promise in its very structure requires its fulfillment. There is no promise that does not require its fulfillment. Affirmation requires a position. It requires that one move to action and that one do something, even if it is imperfect.

At the same time, as we well know—it is what we always experience—because the position is not the affirmation, the very positivity of the institution will threaten, corrupt, cover over the affirmation. And the shuttle of negotiation is precisely between affirmation and position, that is, between the nondialecticity of the affirmation and the dialecticity of the position. My suspicion regarding position is really a suspicion regarding the dialectic—the thesis-synthesis, position-antiposition, synthesis-system, etc. Thus, negotiation, if we really want a formality here or a formal definition, negotiation for me is a negotiation between the non-dialectic and the dialectic. There is a totally dialectical concept of negotiation, the standard concept of negotiation. I would shift it: the worst, the most necessary, or the most difficult in negotiation is the negotiation between what does not negotiate (and which is nondialectical, nondialectizable) and the dialectizable.

But the dialectic (a Hegelian would say) is precisely the dialectic of the nondialectic and the dialectic. So what is the dialectic? Is it that against which I raise the value of an affirmation, that is, a conventional Hegelianism or else another Hegelianism? This is an open question for me. When I say Hegelianism, I also say Marxism. From this point of view, in any case, there is not much difference. Thus, the concept of negotiation that we discussed earlier can sometimes seem nonphilosophical, that is, non-Hegelian, non-Marxist, etc., precisely in its acute specificity, or it can carry a Hegelianism or a Marxism to its fulfillment, for with Hegel there is always plenty to say: the dialectic is not the dialectic: the dialectic is the dialectic of the nondialectic and the dialectic. So here I do not have an answer. What I am doing is perhaps still very Hegelian or very Marxist or perhaps radically non-Hegelian, non-Marxist.

D.E.: But I think that gesture is one that makes some things possible for your students . . . this sentiment of never finishing. You deploy it in your pedagogy somehow. It is an impulse for more work . . . do you want to talk more about *States General*?

T.K.: No, but I still want to talk about the future. The future anterior.

J.D.: Oh yes, that's right.

T.K.: And for instance, in the analysis of "Declaration of Independence," there is the complicated relation between the backward of the *après coup* and the forward of the future anterior. And the temporal paradox there seems to be not exactly reproduced, but there is a similar tension in this practice of negotiation. And I am still interested in this strange relation between negotiation and institution. And I thought that maybe the timing problem, the problem of rhythm, the problem of a certain kind of speed, of trying to go too fast and too slow at the same time seems to affect both of those structures.

J.D.: The affirmation that becomes foundational does not belong to the time of foundation; it is always already presupposed, always prior. It is what allows for the future anterior, but it is itself *irrecuperable*, so to speak, in every sense of the word. *Irrecuperable* in the vulgar sense, for it is untreatable, and irrecuperable for memory, because the "yes" of the affirmation is not the "yes" that I say. It is always already presupposed by any language. The affirmation is always prior to its formulation, to its explicitation, to the positional gestures it engenders. What I am doing when I speak of *affirmation* is to recall it. I recall. There had to be affirmation. There will have to have been affirmation.

In the negotiation I am talking about, and which always refers to this affirmation, there is always something passive. And this will complete the formal definition of negotiation. I insisted on the work of negotiation previously; negotiation is a constant activity. But at the same time negotiation is passive. It is passive from the standpoint of an affirmation it does not control. The affirmation is before me. I am not the one who affirms. I am not the one who says "yes." What I say, as soon as I open my mouth, as soon as I do something, as soon as I desire something is that there has been affirmation. There had to have been affirmation and promise and a "yes." And in relation to this *there will have been* [il y aura eu], or *there will have had to have been* [il y aura fallu], the activity remains passive, however overwhelming, enervating, and ceaseless it may be; this is a certain kind of passivity. It is not incompatible with activity. One could cite a word of Blanchot or Levinas to say that this passivity is more passive than passivity. It is not symmetrical to activity. They are two heterogeneous orders of temporality.

The second response concerns, more particularly, what you said about rhythms, differences of rhythm, differences of speed. Do you remember what we said earlier of "at the same time"? There is not an "at the same time," there is not, period . . . there are simply differences, multiplicities of rhythm. In the phenomenon, or in what has the appearance of "at the same time," there are already differences of rhythm, differences of speed. In political or institutional action one must not only make several speeds cohabit with each other, one must also enable the multiplicity of speeds (there are not only two, there are more than two speeds) to be rendered not only possible but necessary and enable diversities to cohabit in an institution.

And when one writes a text, what does one do? When one writes a text, one tries to write in such a way that the reading is *immediately* affected by it, and also—something irrecuperable—in such a way as to produce long term effects, a kind of *short run–long run*. But what probably serves as my rule (which does not mean that I am able to follow this rule) is the attempt to have the two rhythms, the multiplicity of rhythms and speeds potentially assembled in as economical a space or time possible. To enable a phrase to have an immediate effect and also a reserve, to say other things to others, later on.

What I am saying about a phrase also applies to an institution. This is what an institution is. Think of our earlier examples, GREPH, or the Collège: an institution is something that responds in the present to an urgency and at the same time builds toward the future. Rhythms are knotted in a body: here, the body of an institution in unimaginable, unrepresentable, unobjectivizable forms. If one wanted to give oneself an objective representation, objectivized of what an institutional body is, one would need—and I think this is made impossible precisely by objectivity, by the order of representation—one would need to be able to represent a body made up of knotted speeds or rhythms, of knotted differences of rhythm. A knot that represents the vibrations of different speeds. It is not representable, but this is what an institution is, nonetheless. Every institution is this. Language is this. A phrase is this. A phrase is a knot where, on one hand, there is something that is immediately legible or visible, and on the other, there are already vibrations enabling a phrase of Heraclitus, for example, to still vibrate today and to produce effects. I cite Heraclitus because his writing is aphoristic. But one could cite Plato.

T.K.: There is a kind of negotiation between the necessity to go fast and the necessity to wait, as well, but, there is a . . .

J.D.: . . . necessity to what?

T.K.: . . . to wait. Necessity in politics is both about immediately speaking and taking a stand, making a decision, and knowing when is the right time to do that; a kind of drawing out or waiting.

J.D.: Yes.

D.E.: It is impatience and patience—a kind of alternation. I wonder whether this is something you look for in the texts you read, also . . . one example that comes to mind is in the letter to Genet. You talk about the temporality of [George] Jackson's letters, and the temporality of their history— you say: "the time of their history takes place between the precipitation of the absolute impatience of immediate pleasure and the endless work of preliminary mediations . . ."

J.D.: One thinks of negotiation as a work of mediation. I would say that negotiation is a to-and-fro between impatience and patience. There must be impatience. A patient negotiator is not effective. It does not work. One must make use of impatience and patience. But one must have absolute impatience. This is not to say "a little more" impatience; the impatience must be absolute. One can put patience in relation with what I said earlier about passivity. What gives one patience? Patience is not something that one chooses. One does not play at being patient. One must be patient; first of all, because in any case, one is forced to wait. Until death. One is there, dependent on it, and thus, in any case, one is patient. One *really must* be patient. Even in impatience one is patient.

Thus, between the passivity I mentioned previously and patience, there is a relation or an essential affinity, but between passivity (the "yes" we are discussing) and impatience there is too. The "yes" is unconditional—it does not wait. The "yes" does not wait and we will always wait. Patience and impatience both sign this "yes." They contradict each other but they do not contradict each other.

There is a word that keeps coming back to me, and the image of the knot. Negotiation as a knot, as the work of the *knot*. In the *knot* of negotiation there are different rhythms, different forces, different differential vibrations of time and rhythm. The word *knot* came to me, and the image of a rope. A rope with an entanglement, a rope made up of several strands knotted together. The rope exists. One imagines computers with little wires, wires where things pass very quickly, wires where things pass very slowly: negotiation is played along all of these wires. And things pass, information passes, or it does not pass, as with the telephone. Also, cables that pass under the sea and thousands of voices with intonations, that is, with different and entangled tensions. Negotiation is like a rope and an indeterminable number of wires moving or quivering with different speeds or intensities.

This image came to me spontaneously, but in fact it has often come to me in different contexts, that of the knot, of the *bind*, of the ligament, of obligation. In *Glas*, in particular, in which the concept of stricture was never—how shall I say it—received. There are at least two words from this point of view that did not arrive, so to speak. These two words have to do with the same motif. First there is the word *stricture* that had a very important and nondialectical role in *Glas*. The difference of stricture is something other than a dialectical opposition. It consists in differences of force, of tightness. It is more or less tight. *Stricture* is an English word that exists in English and that does mean exactly the same thing as what I make it mean in French. *Stricture* means being tight, more or less tight. It is more or less tight, more or less strict. I would speak of a stricture of negotiation, rather than of a dialectic of negotiation.

And there is another word of same type which has also gone unnoticed. I used it only once in a text on Levinas. The word is "seriature." The etymology leads back to *cord, rope*. "Seria" is also the idea of a series, that is, the necessity of a proliferation of gestures, particular each time. I cannot reconstitute this text here. It talks about the necessity of linking. In a chain, thus, there is always the same metaphor of rope, chain, shuttle. The necessity of linking gestures or moments that do not let themselves be linked, which are absolutely singular every time. And one has to link singularities, that is, put in a series things that do not let themselves be put into series. This can be a definition of negotiation. Why one must repeat and put into a series, in a kind of serial generality, things that do not let themselves be serialized, which are singular and nonnegotiable every time.

T.K.: There is another knot that we could talk about, which would be necessity. If you translated it into German . . .

J.D.: *Notwendigkeit?*

T.K.: Right.

J.D.: The stricture about which there is much discussion in *Glas*—although I also say it in *Truth in Painting*—is that what is more or less attached-detached is never detached, absolute, absolved. It is never attached or detached. Thus, neither free nor attached, it is more or less attached, more or less tight.

D.E.: The locus classicus is the Gordian knot and the story that Alexander, lacking the patience to untie it, cut it. So, there is the temptation to cut it.

J.D.: But I think the negotiation we are talking about does not prevent us from cutting. One must also cut. But one is never sure of the right time, there is always a risk. A negotiation that is certain of its strategy is not a negotiation, it is a bad negotiation. In negotiation there is an element of absolute "yes," of absolute uncertainty, of risk, there is the incalculable. The negotiation I am discussing is not simply a calculation. One calculates as much as possible, but there must also be a nonintegratable, incalculable part. The decision to cut or not to cut the Gordian knot is never certain. If one were sure of the calculation, it would not be an action or a decision; it would be a programming. There must be decision, there must be absolute risk, and thus there must be the undecidable. There is no decision without the undecidable. If there are no undecidables, there is no decision. There is simply programming, calculation. There must be political, ethical decisions, but these decisions are possible only in situations where the undecidable is a necessary dilemma [*épreuve*], the law. Without this dilemma, one is content to apply a program, to deploy a causality. But at the moment of the undecidable, decision is not possible, either. I am explaining in an altogether informal way the necessity of an experience that should not only be mine in ethical, political, or other, even private, situations. I do not believe in the radical distinction between public and private.

T.K.: That is almost a definition of the political, though. If it were not, if it did not have that incalculability, then it would just be a technical, computer-oriented problem. You would not need politics.

J.D.: Yes, yes, absolutely. But let us say, if, for us to need politics, we have to refer to some radical undecidability, then we also risk having no politics. Everything seems possible: tyranny, democracy, anarchy, hierarchy. At the same time, when one wants to think the political radically, one must cross these situations of undecidability, always maintaining the "possibly" open (for it is not merely a phase, a moment), all the while engaging in a consistent decision. Consistent with what? With—as much as possible—the most radical affirmation that led to the indecision: to the possibility of the future, to the coming of the event, to the gift, to the promise, to memory, to as many themes as need be put to the test of deconstruction in view of politics. Without which one merely repeats stereotypes; one leaves dogmatic presuppositions in abeyance; one lets the machine work, which works very well or very badly.

T.K.: . . . or compromise.

D.E.: It does not dissimulate the nondiscursive forces. So language on the one hand, and you . . . in the readings . . . of Descartes, Kant, Kafka, Mandela— all of those texts—there is an insistence on the linguistic, on the linguistic structures, as with the structure of the name in "Geopsychoanalysis" . . .

T.K.: the promise . . .

D.E.: the promise . . .

T.K.: the affirmation . . .

D.E.: . . . the performative . . . and the way these are linked to political and institutional stakes . . .

J.D.: I am beginning to repeat what I have already said. I prefer the word *negotiation* to the word *dialog*. It takes into account the relations of nondiscursive forces. This is not the only reason I am bothered by the word *dialog*. It is not simply because it reminds one of spoken communication, but because, in the pathos, precisely, or in the implicit ideology of this word, there is the idea of irenism, pacifism, ecumenicalism, and often a hint of parish-pump Christianity. The word connotes a kind of pacifist religiosity that seems too facile and leads one to believe that, with dialogue, one will rediscover transparency and what is equivocal will be made clear. This optimism, which is a little religious, also bothers me in the Habermasian ideology of communication. I am not speaking of a *dialogical* order that could function in other contexts but of an alleged ethics of dialogue.

And there is also, more profoundly, the idea of symmetry and reciprocity. In all of the structures we have described until now, it was their asymmetrical character that seemed inevitable to me. I do not believe there is symmetry in intersubjective relations. And dialog is also a relation between two "subjects." All the questions raised by the concept of "subject" also concern the concept of dialog. Thus, no symmetry, not only because there are relations of force (and that sometimes even weakness is a force, that one can play weakness as a force) but also because of what we said earlier about affirmation; all of this makes affirmation into something which is not to be found in dialog, which is not accounted for in the structure of dialog. This affirmation is not simply discursive. Previously you said that the appeal to affirmation takes its point of departure in language. In this you touched on a very difficult problem for me—a problem of strategy. On the one hand, I always think it necessary to recall the dimension of language, and, at the same time, essentially what I do and what begins with a deconstruction of logocentrism consists in, and calls for, a beyond-language, or an outside-language. Often my work is interpreted as the work of someone who says, in the end, everything is language, there is only language, there are no things, there is nothing beyond language; this is an absolute linguisticism. A very paradoxical reception of work that begins by doing the opposite. But I think that the two need to be done. One must constantly recall a certain ir-reducibility of the textual or discursive dimension of language, and, at the same time, recall that there is in the textual something that is not discursive, a trace that is not linguistic.

I return to the problem of the affirmation. The "yes," the affirmation, is not simply the "yes" pronounced or verbalized. I recalled this regarding Joyce. The affirmation is not to be confused with the proffering of a "yes." The "yes" is a particular phenomenal manifestation of an affirmation prior to language. Not prior to language in general, to the trace or to the mark, but prior to discursivity. And the unconditional affirmation that has always already taken place at the moment I begin to speak makes it nondialogical; it is not yet engaged in a dialog.

When Heidegger says, for example, that *die Sprache* is in a certain sense a monologue. What does he mean by this? He certainly does not mean, naturally, that *die Sprache*—language, speech—is a kind of autism, of enclosed relation to oneself. He means that there is no metalanguage, and that, whatever one does, *die Sprache spricht*. It is language that speaks. *Die Sprache spricht* means that if one wants to say something about language, one must already be in language. In *Of Spirit* I showed this movement with which Heidegger, in a very late text, complicates his discourse on the ques-tion. "Before" the question (which always presupposes language) there is a kind of consent to language, which belongs to it without truly belonging to it. And this he calls *Zusage*. *Zusage* is a manner of consenting, of saying "yes," to language, to the call. There is a "yes" there (which is a kind of con-sent, of *Gelassenheit*) more originary even than the questioning. To question, one must already be in language. And to interrogate oneself on the essence of language, to ask what *die Sprache* is, one must already be in language. And one must already have said "yes" to language.

Thus, this "yes" to language allowing one to truly speak to the other is monolingual, strange in a sense; it is language speaking of itself. Language speaks of itself. I would not say this of spoken language. I would say this of the mark in general, in order not to limit things of language to language itself. And thus, there is a "yes" of the mark that (furthermore) can be erased, and this "yes," or erasable mark, is before language; it is presupposed by any language; it is not yet a dialog. Nor is it identical to itself, nor enclosed in itself, because it is already difference. But this difference, this affirmation in difference, is not yet dialogical.

T.K.: At one point, in discussing what is different about GREPH with regard to other available political organizations, you say: "What we are looking for in GREPH and in the articulation between the practice of GREPH and philosophical work is a new political language, philosophical-political, which has not yet discovered its own language and is constantly forced to negotiate with other existent or dominant political languages." There is, first of all, this question of a new language and GREPH's marginality, or whatever, with relation to existing political codes, or the desire not to have what GREPH does be immediately translated into the available political codes. Then, at another point, in this same set of discussions, you analyze some particular situation, some political situation, in terms of right, it is the question about the militancy of GREPH, whether GREPH is a militant organization, whether you and the others are militants. And you provide an analysis of this in terms of language, and then you say: "This is the first aspect, that this new demand that I analyze in insufficient terms of language, codes, receptivity, communication, translations, etc., . . . but nothing could be explained if one were to go by this formal analysis of receptivity and communication." So it seems that there is always this double relation of an interest in avoiding traditional codes and in forging a new code, and even a code that is marked essentially by an emphasis on language, or text, or marking, and then, on the other hand, the gesture that says: and even that code is insufficient.

J.D.: On the one hand there are codes. A mark is immediately coded, because it can be repeated, and thus it is immediately codable and coded, even a nondiscursive mark, even a gesture. There are, thus, nondiscursive codes. There are nondiscursive, gestural codes of decision in strategy, dance, politics, etc. Thus, what I am doing in this gesture, and in this movement that you cite, is to say: I translate into the discursive code possibilities of codes that are not discursive and that we no not know yet, the code of which is not yet formalized. Every time one speaks of what is meta-discursive, nondiscursive (but not meta-textual, you understand, in the sense I give to the words *text, mark, trace,* etc.)—what we have been doing the entire time with the word *negotiation,* in other words—one is speaking of force. A multiplicity of forces, conflicts of forces.

The word *force* is indeed very obscure. Force is the common but always different possibility of the "movement" of "life," of "desire," of impulses, of as many metonymies as you like. *Force* is basically a very common name for designating that for which we do not have a clearly expressible concept in a given philosophical code. In philosophy, the value of force has always been in representing what resisted conceptual analysis. Hence the risk.

However, what gives me a kind of confidence (perhaps too much confidence) in the word *force* is a truly Nietzschean axiomatic: force is always a "difference of force." Force is differential, there is not a substance of force. When one says that force is differential, what one is really saying is that force is not something. It is not a substance, it is not something that is stabilizable, which would fall under phenomena.

So when I name *force* I am thinking of a differentiality, which thus, as differentiality, is also immediately trace or writing, a network of marks, and marks that are codable, like any mark, in iterability, and at the same time inscribe and erase themselves or inscribe and can erase themselves. What is "proper" to any mark is the power to erase itself. If a mark has a structure such that—as I often say—*it succeeds only* by erasing itself, it succeeds only by erasing itself. Or it occurs through an erasing . . . erasing itself. At that moment force is itself also a weakness. It is a manner of not appearing. When one says force is a weakness and that sometimes, well, there is more force in weakness or that weakness is revealed to be stronger than force, at that moment one is engaged in a discourse on force that no longer has the coherence of classical logic and is no longer *reliable.*

And in fact this is what I am always referring to, at least vaguely, when I say *force;* force is not power, finally. It is not something; force is always inscribed in a space where a ruse (not a subjective ruse but a ruse of structure) is possible, making the weakest strongest. And this can be translated into political terms. Always to put oneself on the side of the weakest and the most oppressed is also a kind of confidence in the future. One says to oneself, one knows that in the end true force is on the side of the oppressed, that this is true force, and conversely.

Every time I use the word force, all of these difficulties are in reserve: the reference to Nietzsche, the impossibility of substantializing force, the reversibility of relations of force, not merely the Nietzschean idea of genealogy that sees the weak as those who prevail in the end but also the idea of force being a weakness. To return to what we previously said of hierarchy: when I put myself on the side of those who protest against an established and oppressive or repressive authority, one could say that I put myself on the side of the weak. But at the same time those who hold the power are also very weak. Take, for example, South Africa. Mandela is the weakest, he is in prison, and at the same time it is clear that he is much stronger—not he himself, but what he represents is much stronger. Perhaps, for these very reasons, one should no longer use the word force. It is not stable. In another context and at another moment, I will no longer use the word force. What imposes it on me is a certain given of discourse, certain discursive situations.

D.E.: The other thing about that passage, that response, the way you conclude it—you say that it is a question of pathos, which I take to be a question of avoiding pathos, or of resisting pathos.

J.D.: Not avoiding pathos in general, avoiding this pathos.

T.K.: Dialog.

J.D.: Yes, dialog full of pathos. But . . . in view of another pathos, because I do not think I would avoid all pathos.

D.E.: I guess that was also a question we had thought about in terms of the relation between pathos and ethos. And what I had in mind there, maybe just an example of a way that resistance to some pathos brings us back to some new and more difficult thinking of ethics is, de Man. De Man's understanding of allegory, of the displacement from pathos to ethos in allegory, in his reading of Julie.

J.D.: I do not remember it very well.

D.E.: Well, he says—I can just cite something very quickly, just as a reminder—he says: "Allegories are always ethical, the term ethical designating the structural interference of two value systems. In this sense, ethics has nothing to do with the will . . . of a subject, nor *a fortiori*, with a relationship between subjects. The ethical category is imperative (that is, a category rather than a value) to the extent that it is linguistic and not subjective. . . . The passage to an ethical tonality does not result from a transcendental imperative but is the referential (and therefore unreliable) version of a linguistic confusion. Ethics (or, one should say, ethicity) is a discursive mode among others." O.K.? And that ethics, that understanding of ethics involves some sort of displacement from pathos.

J.D.: If by pathos you understand some subjective mood or . . .

D.E.: Right. You think there is another way of understanding pathos? Because it seems like an important question in thinking about the potential pathos attached to some of your examples, such as Mandela, such as Jackson, such as, maybe to some extent Prague. Is there some thinking of pathos that does not fall prey to those thinkings that you resist, or that you . . .

T.K.: Especially the way that pathos is often associated with a tragic scheme, a sort of sacrifice of the oppressed, and so on . . .

J.D.: Yes. I do not know that I would want to save pathos at any price. It seems to me that I do not look to avoid it in any case, at any price. So the question would be that of the choice between a given pathos and another. I also try not to give in to it . . . not too much. But when I do give in to it (and I think one must in general), I try to make it such that the pathos is not too easily translatable into terms of subjective affectivity. Also, I do not know if this is what Paul de Man is saying—the text you cited is complex—if what he is saying of ethicity is, or is not, an affair of language. I do not know if it could be said of the pathos about which I am thinking, which is not subjective nor simply discursive, either. I do not know how far I would agree with all of the propositions of Paul de Man on the subject of what would be simply discursive. One would have to spend time on the meaning of each word. This is an extremely complex text. Thus, I do not know if, when I say discursive, I mean it in the same sense as does Paul de Man. This is a problem.

Thus, I would put pathos in the same structure, in the same series with what we said earlier about patience and passivity. It is something that is before the subject, that is before what we call affectivity in the usual sense. And yet there is suffering . . . there is suffering. Nor do I really believe in the possibility of a language that is absolutely apathetic, neutral. I do not believe it exists. There are ways of controlling the pathos, of making it as discreet as possible, almost neutralized, but this creates yet another pathos. Paul de Man writes texts that have very little pathos in them but which have pathos all the same. It is a very limited, a very discreet pathos, which is there for those who are sensitive to it but in a way that is perhaps even more marked than cries or tears.

T.K.: It sounds to me related to what, in *Philosophy of the States General*, you describe in terms of joy, of gaiety. Right at the moment where the word "intraitable" or "nonnegotiable" comes up, it is in the sentence about the necessity of combating simultaneously and joyously, without accusation, without trial per se, without nostalgia, with an "intraitable gaieté."

J.D.: So is gaiety pathos or not?

T.K.: Certainly not something associated with the customary political rhetoric of pathos and mourning for the imprisoned Mandela or the assassinated Jackson or the tortured Argentinean political prisoners.

J.D.: But there, well . . . I do not know what impression my texts give from this point of view, but I do not feel them as filled with pathos.

T.K.: No, not at all. And that is what is interesting. That is what seems to me to make them different from the typical condemnations and denunciations and accusations.

J.D.: For example, the text on Mandela. One could do a reading, not a perverse one but a reading of the text, that would show that it is in fact yet another trial of Mandela. A way of showing that he remains caught in the system to which he is opposed . . . that is, to a certain degree—not totally— but still there is something in him which should have been negotiated, which also lets itself be imprisoned in Western discourse, in Protestant discourse, in discourse in short. Thus, here I tried to destroy the pathos, a certain pathos, by coldly analyzing Mandela's discourse. I tried to show the logic, the program to which he had to submit. And then there is a moment where this verges on the pathetic once again: it is the moment where I say— one does not know who Mandela is. One does not know yet where Mandela is . . . This may or may not be felt as pathos, one does not know . . .

D.E.: Yes, I think it was in the context of remarking a certain resistance. The reason I said "resistance to pathos" initially was, there is a resistance—

for example in that text on Mandela—to the pathos of liberation, or the politics conceived as liberation, which is something that you scrutinize.

T.K.: While at the same time it is a text demanding that Mandela be liberated . . . likewise for Jackson.

J.D.: But there— I know that there are at least two postures or two gestures. There is the one which, even when taking sides, continues to coldly analyze the ideology of the bias, that is, the analysis of the revolutionary of emancipation, I would say, of liberation, in which I do not believe without reservation; and then, I know that I myself can personally be very sensitive to the emotion attached to revolutionary pathos. This does not prevent me from also trying to *scrutinize* at the same time. But it sometimes happens that I experience moments of classic left-wing pathos—never of right-wing pathos. This is true: I am unable to have moments of right-wing pathos. Moments of a classic left-wing pathos that cohabit with a cold analysis, this is my history. I am still, as they say, viscerally left-wing. Thus, when I hear— even today when it has gone out of fashion—when I hear the International, I may sing along and tears come to my eyes.

Both affects are to be found in the texts in question. There is a cold movement of taking sides. Taking sides, nevertheless, but coldly. And then a movement of sympathy, or of "sympathos," for the oppressed. *Sym-pathos* at that moment is truly sympathy.

T.K.: But there seems to be an argument in the first text on South Africa, for instance, that a political discourse, posed in terms of liberation and human rights at a certain point, stops being sufficient to analyze and understand and change the South African situation. So it is not just . . . so there is a certain political necessity in extending . . . extending the vocabulary, or giving up a certain vocabulary at a point.

J.D.: How does one isolate the moment of pathos? I can, for example, without illusion as to the future of a given political strategy of liberation, desire to participate in a revolt, even if it is badly calculated and remains a chant or a demonstration of a despairing mass. In the pathos of indignation, of revolt, of revolution, of liberation even, there is something to which I remain very sensitive and with which I associate myself. It is almost aesthetic, one might say, aesthetic. The *aesthesis* of this pathos is the moment of passive sensibility. There are such moments. I do not like crowds. I do not like mass movements. But sometimes there are pacifist mass movements full of indignation, processions to which I am easily able to associate myself, descending into the streets, as they say; where I like to be in the middle of an anonymous crowd protesting against some terrible thing. This moment of pathos is not hindered by analysis. And it does not limit analysis. In the texts there are even moments of this type, they are very discreet, rare, furtive, but of this type. In any case, I am on that side, and this is not without relation to the unconditional affirmation we discussed previously.

D.E.: That is irreducible, somehow?

J.D.: Yes.

D.E.: This is a good place to stop.

Letter to Jean Genet (Fragments)

20 August 1971

. . . . . . implies that we must not make of it simply a *case* or an *affair*. For the reasons you already know:

1) If Jackson's "story" remains exemplary, it is not because it is absolutely singular. Everything that would confer on it the fascinating—and thus abstract—character of an exception would serve the interest of the adversary. There are more "Jacksons" than anyone can count. Their prison is also in France, as you know. And elsewhere. The "testimonials" and "protests" that we might send to the United States must not distract us from this fact. Jackson: "*I don't recognize uniqueness, not as it's applied to individualism, because it is too tightly tied into decadent capitalist culture*" (p. 4).

2) Second, it is not a *case*, because the juridical and formal development of the problem, though it must not be overlooked (on the contrary), constitutes only its hollow and derivative representation. Another alibi. Jackson is aware of this. As his analysis progresses, less and less attention is paid to the police *scandal*, to the *form* of the illegality, however savage and "ferocious" it might be. Through what might be called juridical *zigzagging*, in a society that is so particular about its legalism, so jealous of its formalism, a general violence (a differentiated violence, but indissociably racist-sexual-economic-political) can unfold with practically no limits, always knowing how to find its way, constructing its way in the figure of the zigzag in order to explode in a single direction and with no return. To combat only the zigzag, or in the zigzag, is also

to recognize that the adversary has "grounds," to consolidate them and to paralyze oneself without any hope. "*Ferocious cunning*" of a "*system.*"

3) Finally, if one denounces only a *case* or an *affair* (in the sense that, in France, the implications of these *scandals* have always been buried beneath the form of ritualized or fetishistic debates), is there not a risk of closing up the wound of everything that has been broken open by the letters you presented, of reducing these enormous stakes to a more or less literary, or even editorial, event, to a French, or even Parisian, production that an intelligentsia, busying itself with its signatures, would have staged for itself? That is why I am still hesitant to participate in the collective action you described to me; and that is why I worry about the emphasis that could one day be placed on what you call the "literary talent" of Jackson the "poet" (which must *also* be recognized, of course you are right, and you are not the one I suspect of anything here; which must *also* be used, I agree). And other similar traps. Will one ever know who is laying a trap for whom in this scene?

. . .

With the best intentions in the world, with the most sincere moral indignation in the face of what, in effect, remains unbearable and inadmissible, one could then lock up again that which one says one wants to liberate. Domesticate a breakout. In one sense (but let us not forget the other), this breakout has already taken place: the black, controlled and enslaved by the white (the white-racist-capitalist), once again *becomes something other* than the reduced, direct, or inverted image of his master. He exceeds the gaze of the jailer and frees himself from his condition as pupil. What is exorbitant—and here is another dissymmetry—is that the black escapes from the white without being on the run: no longer able to be pursued, condemned, an ex-con, nor, likewise, can he be acquitted, proved innocent, rehabilitated. Having become black again in the most irreversible fashion, he is out of reach of the white, being no longer the same (a kind of white, a little or poor white) nor the opposite (another white, a white other). He is also a "dirty red" ("*they already are informed that I am a dirty, real dirty red, and they have already made their plans to stone me*" [p. 292]). Thus racism, always strangely linked to this return of same to same, has *totally disappeared* for Jackson; see, for example, the letter to Angela Davis (21 May 1970).

. . .

. . . . . . Yes, you are right, what is most important here, most "new," is that black spirituality, traditional religiosity has been unmasked or, in any case, reduced to silence: precisely as the ethereal element of slavery ("neo-slavery" says Jackson), an internal slavery—thanks to which one could pretend to have abolished the other—an ideal servitude, an invisible chain of identification, a sublimation of black into white, a symbolic law enforcement. The theories of nonviolence that Jackson analyzes in such a rigorous and differentiated fashion (for example in the letter to his mother from March 1967) are the best examples of this. That is why blacks are *divided,* and why Jackson's struggle, which returns incessantly to this motif of division, is so painful, his explanations so endless, his pedagogy directed at other blacks (and first of all, of course, at his mother and father—"*The conflicts and contradictions that will follow me to the tomb started right there in the womb*" [p. 4]) so patient and so impatient. He must constantly *reckon with* this division, and his letters carry all the marks.

. . .

. . . . . . In a cold and more and more analytic manner, a "system" finds itself taken apart in these letters, with that gesture of a prisoner who has all his time and no more time. *System* is Jackson's precise word. More and more frequent. "Political and economic system," "capitalist system," but also "system" of "Western ideas," of "Western culture." In a prison— this one and others—where it thought it had put its outside in chains, the system of (Western-white-capitalist-racist) society has made possible, *by this act,* the analysis of its functioning, a *practical* analysis that is at once the most implacable, the most desperate, but also the most *affirmative.* There is nothing fortuitous about this. Along the same lines would also be found that "unconscious death wish" that Jackson talks about somewhere.

. . .

. . . . . . "system": Jackson, to be sure, never minimizes the specifically racial aspect of the problem [*black* problem, therefore sexual: "all true freedom is black and is invariably confused with sexual freedom, which is also black. . . . Sex is dark," says Artaud, speaking of the plague. The black is the United States' other plague, the plague of the other and perhaps the same one Freud was talking about when he got off the boat. Jackson sees the link between prison and "*the necessity to repress sexual needs*"; this is a region of the analysis he never misses. With the result that, when he says he is "*a Black who wants to be black*," we are already a far cry from the themes of authentic negritude, etc.], but he never reduces the whole system to it. He avoids this trap as well. He is not content to relate this racial-sexual problem to all other manifestations of racism in the world (a constant appeal to the "international solidarity" of the oppressed, so many references to Dachau—he signs from Dachau—to "concentration camps," to "Germany in the '30s," to all forms of colonialism and neo-colonialism), to all other forms of censorship and repression. He also articulates it more and more rigorously after the structures of economic processes. "*Slavery is an economic condition*" (p. 251). In the United States, of course and first of all, but also on the scale of worldwide contradictions (among capitalist societies, among capitalist and socialist societies, among socialist societies). This revolutionary accuses both the system of capitalism and that of "Western culture" *at the same time*: this explains why the exorbitant can also be this eye turned with more and more insistent steadiness, as you have remarked, from out of the closed-off inside of this prison in the direction of China.

. . .

. . . . . . Jackson's letters are not only cries, although they remain that as well ("*I am uneasy thinking that you may be attracted to the tragedy of me*" [p. 271]), nor are they only writings of political theory. The time of their history is worked out *between* the precipitation of absolute impatience, of immediate bliss, and the endless work of preliminary mediations. In both cases, everything can be lost. Which is why there is the strange calculation, Jackson's mortal strategy ("strategy" is his word), that economy of loss which makes him declare so often that he accepts his death and yet. . . . That is what I meant earlier when I wrote, I believe, the word *affirmation* or *affirmative*. Which is also where the two questions, which he asks of two women, come from. It would be necessary to quote the whole thing, but to be brief, I will extract two passages that I want to recopy now. These are, as I said, two questions to two women. I put them side by side:

By the time I've solved these minor [problems] that temporarily limit my movements, we'll have also settled whether or not it is selfish for us to seek gratification by reaching and touching and holding; does the building of a bed precede the love act itself? Or can we "do it in the road" until the people's army has satisfied our territory problem? That is important to me, whether or not you are willing to "do it in the road."

You dig, I'm more identifiable with Ernesto than with Fidel. When this is over I immediately go under. (To Z., 11 April 1970)

"One doesn't wait for all conditions to be right to start the revolution, the forces of the revolution itself will make the conditions right." Che said something like this. Write me and let me have it straight. (To Angela Davis, 21 May 1970)

. . .

. . . . . . One must therefore struggle for Jackson's "liberation." Overlook nothing to accomplish it. But also, without making of it a pretext and without whitewashing a guilty party, know that the prison, over there, with its miradors, its speculum, its spectaculum, its televisions of every kind, cannot totally close him in, keep watch on him. "Justice" must be forced to record that. . . .

. . .

. . . . . . Where (who) are we now, who are exchanging these words like words to the wise? In the place where, however much or little it may be, they have the chance to penetrate that other scene in which Jackson wrestles with his chains, so far from and so close to us, also in the chain of all those who struggle with him, *"who have stepped across the line, into the position from which there can be no retreat"* (p. 282), *everywhere,* wherever this struggle lives on.

Translated by Peggy Kamuf

Declarations of Independence

It is better that you know right away: I am not going to keep my promise.

I beg your pardon, but it will be impossible for me to speak to you this afternoon, even indirectly, about what it was that I was engaged to discuss. Very sincerely, I would have liked to be able to do so.

But, because I would rather not simply remain silent about what I should have spoken to you about, I will say a word about it in the form of an excuse. I will speak to you, then, a little about what I will not speak to you about and about what I would have wanted—because I ought—to have spoken about.

Still, it remains that I fully intend to discuss with you—at least you will be able to confirm this—the promise, the contract, the engagement, the signature, and even that which always presupposes them in a strange way: the presentation of excuses.

In honoring me with his invitation, Roger Shattuck proposed that I try (here of all places) a "textual" analysis, at once philosophical and literary, of the Declaration of Independence and the Declaration of the Rights of Man. In short, an exercise in comparative literature, one that would treat unusual objects for specialized departments in this improbable discipline of "comparative literature."

At first I was astonished. An intimidating proposition. Nothing had prepared me for it. No previous work had led me along the path of such analyses, whose interest and necessity obviously impose themselves.

Upon reflection, I said to myself that, if I had the time and the strength to do it, I would like to try the experiment, at least to put to the test here those conceptual schemes—such as a critical problematic of "speech acts," a theory of "performative" writing, of the signature, of the contract, of the proper names of political and academic institutions—that had already proved useful elsewhere, with what are called other *objects*, whether "philosophical" or "literary" texts. Basically, I said to myself: if I had the time or the strength, I would have liked, if not to try a juridical-political study of the two texts and the two events that are marked in them—(a task inaccessible to me), then at least to sharpen, in a preliminary way and using these texts as an example, many questions that have been elaborated elsewhere on an apparently less political corpus. And out of all these questions, the only one I will retain for the occasion, this afternoon at a university in Virginia—that has just celebrated, more appropriately than anywhere else, the bicentennial of the Declaration of Independence (already setting the tone for the celebration of another anniversary or birthday around which we will turn shortly[1])—is this one: *who signs, and with what so-called proper name, the declarative act that founds an institution?*

Such an act does not come back to a constative or descriptive discourse. It performs, it accomplishes, it does what it says it does: this at least would be its intentional structure. Such an act does not have the same relation to its presumed signer—to whatever subject (individual or collective) engages itself in producing it—as a text of the "constative" type, if in all rigor there are any "constative" texts and if one could come across them in "science," in "philosophy," or in "literature." The declaration that founds an institution, a constitution, or a state, requires that a signer engage him- or herself. The signature maintains a link with the instituting act, as an act of language and an act of writing, a link that has absolutely nothing of the empirical accident about it. This attachment does not allow itself to be reduced—not as easily, in any case, as it does in a scientific text, where the value of the utterance is separated, or cuts itself off, from the name of its author without essential risk, and, indeed, must be able to do so in order to lay claim to objectivity. Although in principle an institution—in its history and in its tradition, in its offices [*permanence*] and thus in its very institutionality—must render itself independent of the empirical individuals who have taken part in its production, although it has in a certain way to mourn them or resign itself to their loss, even and especially if it commemorates them, it turns out, precisely by reason of the structure of instituting language, that the founding act of an institution—the act as archive as well as the act as performance—*must maintain within itself the signature.*

But just whose signature exactly? Who is the actual signer of such acts? And what does actual [*effectif*] mean? The same question spreads or propagates itself in a chain reaction through all the concepts affected by the same rumbling: "act," "performative," "signature," the "present," "I" and "we," etc.

Prudence imposes itself here, as does attention to detail. Let us distinguish between several instances within the moment of your Declaration. Take, for example, Jefferson, the "draftsman" of the project or draft of the Declaration, of the "Draft," the facsimile of which I have before my eyes. No one would take him for the true signer of the Declaration. *By right,* he writes but he does not sign. Jefferson represents the representatives who have delegated to him the task of drawing up what they knew *they* wanted to say. He was not responsible for *writing,* in the productive or initiating sense of the term, only for *drawing up,* as one says of a secretary that he or she draws up a *letter,* of which the spirit has been breathed into him or her, or even the content dictated. Moreover, after having thus drawn up a project or draft, a sketch, Jefferson had to submit it to those whom, for a time, he *represented* and who are themselves *representatives,* namely the "representatives of the United States in General Congress assembled." These "representatives," of whom Jefferson represents a sort of advance-pen, will have the right to revise, to correct, and to ratify the project or draft of the Declaration.

Shall we say, for all that, that they are the ultimate signers?

You know what scrutiny and examination this letter, this literal Declaration in its first state, underwent, how long it remained and deferred, undelivered, in sufferance between all those representative instances, and with what suspense or suffering Jefferson paid for it. As if he had secretly dreamed of signing all alone.

As for the "representatives" themselves, they do not sign, either. In principle at least, because the right is divided here. In fact, they sign; by right, they sign for themselves but also "for" others. They have been delegated the authority or the power of attorney to sign [*ils ont délégation ou procuration de signature*]. They speak, "declare," declare themselves and sign "in the name of . . .": "We, therefore, the representatives of the United States of America in General Congress assembled, do in the name and by the authority of the good people of these . . . that as free and independent states. . . ."

By right, the signer is, thus, the people, the "good" people (a decisive detail because it guarantees the value of the intention and the signature, but we will see further along on what, and on whom such a guarantee is founded or founds itself). It is the "good people" who declare themselves free and independent by the relay of their representatives and of their representatives of representatives. One cannot decide—and this is the interesting thing, the force and "coup de force" of such a declarative act—whether independence is stated or produced by this utterance. We have not finished following the chain of these representatives of representatives and doing so further complicates this necessary undecidability. Is it that the good people have already freed themselves in fact and are only stating the fact of this emancipation in [*par*] the Declaration? Or is it rather that they free themselves at the instant of and by [*par*] the signature of this Declaration? It is not a question here of an obscurity or of a difficulty of interpretation, of a problematic on the way to its (re)solution. It is not a question of a difficult analysis that would fail in the face of the structure of the acts involved and the overdetermined temporality of the events. This obscurity, this undecidability between, let us say, a performative structure and a constative structure, is *required* to produce the sought-after effect. It is essential to the very positing or position of a right as such, whether one is speaking here of hypocrisy, of equivocation, of undecidability, or of fiction. I would even go so far as to say that every signature finds itself thus affected.

Here, then, are the "good people" who engage themselves and engage only themselves in signing, in having their own declaration signed. The "we" of the Declaration speaks "in the name of the people."

But these people do not exist. They do *not* exist as an entity, the entity does *not* exist *before* this declaration, not *as such*. If it gives birth to itself, as free and independent subject, as possible signer, this can hold only in the act of the signature. The signature invents the signer. This signer can only authorize him- or herself to sign once he or she has come to the end—if one can say this of his or her own signature in a sort of fabulous retroactivity. That first signature authorizes him or her to sign. This happens every day, but it is fabulous—every time I evoke this type of event I think of Francis Ponge's "Fable": "By the word *by* commences then this text / Of which the first line states the truth [*Par le mot* par *commence donc ce texte / Dont la première ligne dit la vérité*]."

In signing, the people say—and do what they say they do, but they do so by differing or deferring themselves through [*différant par*] the intervention of their representatives, whose representivity is fully legitimated only by the signature, thus after the fact or belatedly—henceforth, I have the right to sign, in truth I will already have had it since I was able to give it to myself. I will have given myself a name and an "ability" or a "power," understood in the sense of power- or ability-to-sign by delegation of signature. But this future perfect, the proper tense for this "coup de droit" (as one would say, "coup de force"), should not be declared, mentioned, taken into account. It is as though it did not exist.

There was no signer, by right, before the text of the Declaration, which itself remains the producer and guarantor of its own signature. With this fabulous event, with this fable that implies the structure of the trace and is indeed only possible by means of the inadequation of a present to itself, a signature gives itself a name. It opens *for itself* a line of credit, *its* own credit for itself *to* itself. The *self* rises forth here in all cases (nominative, dative, accusative) as soon as a signature gives or extends credit to itself, in a single "coup de force," which is also a stroke [*coup*] of writing, as the right to writing. The "coup de force" makes right, founds right or law, gives right, *brings the law to the light of day, gives both birth and day to the law* [donne le jour à la loi]. Brings the law to the light of day, gives both birth and day to the law: read *The Madness of the Day* by Maurice Blanchot.

That this unheard-of thing should also be an everyday occurrence should not make us forget the singular context of this act. In this case, another state signature had to be erased by "dissolving" the links of colonial paternity or maternity. This is confirmed in reading: this "dissolution," too, involves both constation and performance, indissociably mixed. The signature of every American citizen today depends, in fact and by right, on this indispensable confusion. The constitution and the laws of your country somehow guarantee the signature, as they guarantee your passport and the circulation of subjects and of seals foreign to this country, of letters, of promises, of marriages, of checks—all of which may be given occasion or asylum or right.

And yet. And yet another instance still holds itself back behind the scenes. Another "subjectivity" is still coming to sign, in order to guarantee it, this production of signature. In short, there are only countersignatures in this process. There is a differantial process here because there is a countersignature, but everything should concentrate itself in the *simulacrum of the instant*. It is still "in the name of" that the "good people" of America call *themselves* and declare *themselves* independent at the moment at which they invent (for) themselves a signing identity. They sign in the name of the laws of nature and in the name of God. They *pose* or *posit* their institutional laws on the foundation of natural laws and by the same "coup" (the interpretive "coup de force") in the name of God, creator of nature. He comes, in effect, to guarantee the rectitude of popular intentions, the unity and goodness of the people. He founds natural laws, and thus the whole game that tends to present performative utterances, *as* constative utterances.

Do I dare, here in Charlottesville, recall the *incipit* of your Declaration? "When in the course of human events it becomes necessary for one people to dissolve the political bands which have connected them with another, and to assume among the powers of the earth the separate and equal station to which the laws of Nature and Nature's God entitle them, a decent respect to the opinions of mankind requires that they should declare the causes which impel them to separation. We hold these truths to be self-evident: that all men are created equal; that they are endowed by their creator with inalienable Rights. . . ." And finally: "We therefore the Representatives of the United States of America, in General Congress assembled, appealing to the Supreme Judge of the world for the rectitude of our intentions, do in the Name and by the authority of the good People of these Colonies solemnly *publish* and *declare*, that these united Colonies are and of right ought to be *free and independent states.*"

"Are and ought to be"; the *and* articulates and conjoins here the two discursive modalities, the *to be* and the *ought to be*, the constation and the prescription, the fact and the right. *And* is God: at once creator of nature and judge, supreme judge of what is (the state of the world) and of what relates to what ought to be (the rectitude of our intentions). The instance of judgment, at the level of the supreme judge, is the last instance for saying the fact *and* the law. One can understand this Declaration as a vibrant act of faith, as a hypocrisy indispensable to a po-litical-military-economic, etc., "coup de force," or more simply, more economically, as the analytic and consequential deployment of a tautol-ogy: for this Declaration to have a meaning *and* an effect, there must be a last instance. God is the name—the best one—for this last instance and this ultimate signature. Not only the best one in a determined con-text (such and such a nation, such and such religion, etc.), but the name of the best name in general. Now, this (best) name *ought to be* a proper name. God is the best proper name, the very best proper name [*Dieu est le nom propre le meilleur*]. One could not replace "God" with "the best proper name [*le meilleur nom propre*]."

Jefferson knew this.

Secretary and draftsman, he represents. He represents the "repre-sentatives" who are the representatives of the people in whose name they speak: the people themselves authorizing themselves and authorizing their representatives (in addition to the rectitude of their intentions) in the name of the laws of nature that are inscribed in the name of God, judge and creator.

If he knew all this, why did he suffer so? What did he suffer from, this representative of representatives who themselves represent *to infin-ity*, up to God, other representative instances?

It would appear that he suffered because he clung to his text. It was very hard for him to see it, to see *himself* corrected, emended, "im-proved," shortened, especially by his colleagues. A feeling of wounding and of mutilation should be inconceivable for someone who knows not to write in his own name, his proper name, but *simply by representation* and in place of another. If the wound is not erased in the delegation, it is because things are not so simple, neither the structure of the repre-sentation nor the procuration of the signature.

Someone, let us call him *Jefferson* (but why not *God?*), desired that the institution of the American people should be, by the same token, the erection of his proper name. A name of state.

Did he succeed? I would not venture to decide.

You heard the story before I did. Franklin wants to console Jefferson about the "mutilation" (the word is not my own). He tells him a story about a hatter. He (the hatter) had first imagined a signboard for his shop: the image of a hat and, beneath it, an inscription: "John Thompson, hatter, makes and sells hats for ready money." A friend suggests that he erase "hatter": what good is it, anyway, since "makes hats" is explicit enough? Another friend proposes that he remove "makes hats," since the buyer could not care less who makes the hats as long as he likes them. This "deletion" is particularly interesting—it deletes the signing mark of the producer. The third friend—it is always friends who urge the erasure—suggests that he economize on "for ready money," because custom at the time demanded that one pay "cash"; then, in the same movement, that he erase "sells hats," as only an idiot would believe that the hats were to be given away. Finally, the signboard bears only an image and, under the iconic sign in the shape of a hat, a proper name, John Thompson. Nothing else. One might just as well have imagined other businesses and the proper name inscribed under an umbrella, or even on a pair of shoes.

The legend says nothing about Jefferson's reaction. I imagine it as strongly undecided. The story reflected his unhappiness but also his greatest desire. Taken as a whole, a complete and total erasure of his text would have been better, leaving in place, under a map of the United States, only the nudity of his proper name: instituting text, founding act, and signing energy. Precisely in the place of the last instance where God—who had nothing to do with any of this and, having represented God-knows-whom-or-what in the interest of all those nice people, no doubt could not care less—alone will have signed. His own declaration of independence. In order, neither more nor less, to make a state-ment of it [*en faire état*].

The question remains: How is a state made or founded, how does a state make or found itself? And independence? And the autonomy of one that both gives itself and signs its own law? Who signs all of these authorizations to sign?

I will not, in spite of my promise, engage myself on this path today.

Making it easier on myself, falling back on subjects that are closer, if not more familiar to me, I will speak to you of Nietzsche: of his names, of his signatures, of the thoughts he had for the institution, the state, academic and state apparatuses, "academic freedom," declarations of independence, signs, signboards, and teaching assignments [*signes, enseignes, et enseignements*]. Nietzsche today, in short, in Charlottesville, to celebrate some birthdays.[2]

Translated by Tom Keenan and Tom Pepper

What I Would Have Said . . .

I have kept silent throughout the colloquium, it is true, but one cannot therefore conclude that I was merely in attendance. I have also participated. Having been invited, I came here, thus signaling an approval and solidarity in principle. If I have remained silent, it is indeed because I have remained . . . constantly interested by what I was hearing and no less so by what I was observing. And yet I was not able to take the floor or thought I had better not, neither within the group "Creation and Changing Society" nor in the plenary session, even when I was explicitly invited to do so.

Why? Because I do not want my silence to acquire an equivocal meaning, I will try to give my reasons, also what I would have sketched out if I had spoken for the several minutes to which it was indeed reasonable (but that is a first problem) to limit the time of each presentation. I will thus take as my rule here that I must not exceed that dimension. Formal consequence: aphorism or ellipsis, the improvisation of a "sketch": in short, a telegram, ten words or ten minutes.

I

"We" were the hosts; therefore, we had to give the floor first of all to our foreign guests (moreover, this had been suggested to us, and it was a good idea). Something was thereby freed up—time, the margin, or the heart of hearts—for a teeming mass of questions about the place and time that, during these thirty-six hours, was named "France." Why was this happening in France? And why could it take place only in France? Why in today's France: a left-wing majority at this singular moment of its experience of "socialism à la française," placing the cultural project and "culture"— the name of a bottomless enigma for whoever tries to think about it today— at the center of its program? Why is France the only place capable of instigating and welcoming such a "demonstration"? I thus spent a lot of time, in parentheses, enumerating in a well-reasoned manner *all* the countries— more precisely, all the *states*—for which such a public demonstration would be unthinkable, undesirable, impracticable. If, after the subtraction, there remains only France, then *voilà*: offered up to many readings, a large symptom of world history, but also a singular responsibility, an event without common measure. Deciphering it remains difficult, but the strange and spectacular community assembled for thirty-six hours could not even begin to understand itself, to think about its responsibility, if it did not give every chance to all these possible readings and even to the most critical ones. Was it possible to do them justice in these conditions, and given the protocols, the speaking arrangements, the rules of an implicit deontology, the constraints of rhetoric and time? And how is one to affirm this French responsibility, while erasing any trace of nationalism?

II

Yes, it was a "public demonstration." A necessary limit in an initial moment, to be sure, but still a limit. It was first of all a matter of an act and an event: taking a position, affirmation and testimony here take precedence over work, adventurous research, real discussion. And that is also why (I said to myself) one's simple presence—I mean silent presence— counted no less than the speeches made. Or to put this in other terms that come down to the same thing: the fact of speaking could seem more essential than what was then being said, which, overall, followed a programmable logic without any surprises. Which leads to this paradox: all things considered, and heard with *a certain ear*, I ended up thinking that this public demonstration had been *silent*. It was strangely reserved—even mute— dignified and generous in a kind of silence; and this silence is difficult to situate, both on the side of the anticipated speeches as well as on the *other* side. "A certain ear": when one has an ear only for what could interrogate or disturb the depths of the consensus. It is in silence that the true questions take shape. Which ones?

In any case, dignified and generous, successful in getting people to show up and be counted, such a demonstration can receive its meaning only from the future. If it does not become the impetus for other experiences, for experiences that are *other* (difference in places, participants, languages, rhythms and procedures for work, for risks taken, etc.), this "premier" will have been empty, formal: a protocol. At the same time, it will be more easily reappropriated by old forces and old programs. Worse, people will suspect the host power (and perhaps the guests) of having merely counted on it for some surplus-value in a moment's calculation. . . .

III

In this silence (but where was it? where was I?) I was saying to myself, I would have said: if there is a responsibility for those who are called, in such a confused manner, "intellectuals," "artists," "men and women of culture," then today it can only be exercised on one condition, at least. The condition: never participate in a demonstration, whether it be organized by the state or by private organizations, without asking oneself—and especially without asking *publicly*—in one form or another (a certain silence for example), either "live" or "on tape," the following questions:

a) Who is really behind things, at every moment of the process?

b) Who is mediating it, by what means, in view of what?

c) Who is excluded from it? This last question is the most indispensable. It provides the most reliable guiding thread for the analysis of any socio-institutional or socio-cultural phenomenon. It does not necessarily lead to protest or condemnation. However transitory it may be, no community can *identify itself* without exclusion. But it is always better to bring the modalities, the mechanisms, and, each time, the singularities of this exclusion to light. What evaluations explain them and justify them? What implicit discourse? From where does it draw its authority and its legitimacy? In this regard, the colloquium offered a fascinating field of analysis: a very great concentration in time and space; a large representation: great diversity: a mixture of genres, disciplines, milieux, statuses, etc. Great success in this regard, but still another reason to ask oneself, in view of other experiences yet to come: who and what will have been absent or excluded (individuals, groups, nations, languages, discourses)? And why? And how? Whether or not one is able to determine today a concept of culture that is at the same time rigorous and in proportion with the times (which may be out of all proportion), one should be able to agree on this: an affirmation of culture *must* allow itself to be traversed, worked over by these questions. It must exhibit these analyses, and, without any careful precautions, recognize these limits.

d) In what way does it not simply translate the presumed interests (no doubt themselves largely overdetermined) of the organizers, of all those to whom the initiative may be attributed? One must take into account the "responses," or those responses that are also "non-responses," in France and abroad. There are those who responded (yes or no), those who did not respond, those who said "yes" but did not come, those who came and did not speak (not right away or not at all, not in the plenary session or not even in a "smaller group"), those who only came to the last session or to the receptions, etc. And then the enormous participation of the press and the "media," whether invited or not: no more than the other cultural powers, this participation was not only a theme to be dealt with—a major theme—it was also from the beginning a place of decision for the interpretation of the colloquium itself, for its repercussion and its significance. Take account here of the whole of the press in, and outside of, France. Why was it both inevitable and pathetic that so much attention be given to some primitive and malevolent reaction in the *Wall Street Journal*? This symptom may be read in many different ways. For example: at the same time as a great "anti-Dallas" cry is going up everywhere—and there would also be a lot to say about this—voices protesting a French influence judged to be excessive and dangerous have made themselves heard in a part of the North American intelligentsia and, notably, in a fairly powerful corner of academic society. They are demanding a new protectionism, not against goods of the market or the cultural industry but against French thinkers, theoreticians, and writers judged to be too popular on American campuses. A few months earlier in the same newspaper (is this just a coincidence?), the new Chairman of the National Endowment for the Humanities indulged in an attack that went by the book but also went beyond the crudest sort of caricature. He was attacking a certain movement of thought that had come from France and whose "popularity" threatened, he claimed, the health of literary studies, in particular the "Humanities" and "English studies."[1] This is only one sign among many others. They all call for a very stratified analysis. No more than those that have just been mentioned, this analysis should not derive only from a sociology, an economy, or a politics of culture. These are no doubt necessary and moreso than ever. But there is a point (or rather a line, one that is itself divisible—that is the difficulty) where the limits of these concepts (sociology, economy, politics and, especially here, culture) become *more than* problematic. Even if it is not incorrect, it seems to me insufficient to say that the axiomatics and the grounds of these sciences are "in crisis." But this cannot be put forward, and certainly not demonstrated, in the course of such a colloquium, or even in the "after-the-fact" telegram that I am risking here. This leads me to the next point.

IV

What discourses *could not* be put forth, what gestures *could not* be made in such a colloquium, neither in this one nor in the majority of gatherings of the "colloquium" type? I was asking myself this question the entire time, without thinking that this "could not" was the result of a deliberate foreclosure, censorship, or prohibition. The acts of authority were extremely polite and extremely liberal. The society which was thus formed for thirty-six hours remained very open, tolerant, attentive, and pluralistic; it exposed itself on occasion, up to a certain point, to the risks of improvisation. This "could not" did not arise merely from a powerful contract or an implicit consensus but rather from constraints that are linked simultaneously to the scenographic plan, the technical conditions governing interventions, and especially the imperatives for immediate translatability. Everything had to be immediately intelligible and thus, in every sense of the word, *receivable*, in the form of sequences lasting from three to five minutes. Given this, recourse to facile consensus and the established code becomes the rule—and the theme from which the variations do not stray very far. Any question about the dominant code becomes inaudible, unless it takes the form of an easy and symmetrical provocation in the same register, which never changes anything in the scene. It is this plan or device that one would have to transform if other meetings are to follow: the small group sessions should be well prepared in advance, to be sure, but presentations should no longer take place by advanced reservation only for several minutes at the beginning of the session. Time should be given—another time and not just more time—so that new questions can take shape and new languages be tried out.

V

I attended the sessions of the group gathered around the theme "Creation and Changing Society." Without even claiming to reconsider the whole history and the whole discourse that is at work in a word like *creation*, for example, and that inhabits it within some given, determined "culture," how can one avoid trying to *situate* at least the problem of what is being presupposed here? On what basis does one recognize today a "creation," whether one calls it *artistic, scientific,* or *technological*? How are they to be distinguished? How are they to be measured, evaluated in their relation to social structures and history? If, for example (it is only an example, but is it an example among others?), one recalls—as at least someone did—the theological dimension of any discourse on "creation," then one must draw all the consequences from this: they can be numerous and very concrete. And, going quickly, at least the following: if one holds to the word *creation*, whether or not one retains its expressly theological value, one would have to (1) make secondary, or minoritize, anything that is merely transformation or technological implementation, indeed production, anything that is not *pure* creation, and thus all the conditions (socio-economic, institutional, techno-scientific, etc.), indeed the supporting structures—the most novel as well as the most ancient—of so-called artistic creation. What about language in this regard? Is it only an example (enormous problems . . .)? And (2) one would also have to admit that what one wants to call *creation* could not be programmed, even indirectly, no matter what the modalities, auxiliaries, delays, or relays may be. In the classical sense of these words (but must one be held to that sense, is that possible today, is it serious?), there would not be any such thing as a politics of creation or of creative culture. Whatever little theological memory remains attached to the word *creation*, one would at least have to recognize that what seems to spring up *ex nihilo*, naturally, with genius—the rupture, the unforeseeable, surprise, irruption, mutation, in short, *the future*, the coming of the future in its most unruly aspect—ought to remove the said creation from any *program*. No anticipation of it is representable. Which is why it would remain *dangerous*: not only *critical*, as was said—which would be re-assuring rather than alarming—but dangerous, exposed or exposing to the worst threats. Someone suggested it, and this was the single fortunately dis-cordant note (thus not well-heard) of these exchanges. Whether one delights in the thought or not, it is not certain that "creativity" is simply favored by peace (internal, social, or international), by conditions of prosperity or techno-economic progress, by the political discourse or the philosophical consensus modeled on such conditions. The contrary is not certain, either. It would thus seem that the problem calls for another elaboration and other premises. A hurried conclusion: one must work at reinterpreting, translating, writing all of these languages differently; one must beware of whatever seems to go without saying; one must think and rethink beyond these axiomatics. In other circumstances and according to other plans, would it not be possi-ble to welcome *clashing* discourses (which does not mean noisy or messy ones, on the contrary, but discourses that would be capable of taking and speaking these risks, at another rhythm, in another "style")? This seems to me *possible* and *compatible* with what is most generous, rigorous, open, and co-herent in the "politics of culture" prompting this colloquium—at least as concerns what I perceive and appreciate of it. Does it suffice, moreover, to say "*possible* and *compatible*"? In fact, the only vital chance for whatever supports such a "politics of culture" is that it expose itself to discussion, to the most provocative, the least reassuring, the most intransigent kinds of thinking, that it expose there the very foundations of its discourse. Beginning here (to say nothing for the moment about the rest) with the concepts of *crisis* and *culture*.

VI

What is called *the crisis*? In the singular, armed with its definite arti-cle, passing very quickly from one sentence to another, the word was meant to evoke a commonplace, the empty or overloaded center of the colloquium. There would be no end to descriptions of things that "are going badly" today for man, for the humanity of man, and for the total-ity of humans. Ill-being and threat spare no *region*, whether one means by this the territory of cultures, nations, political regimes, etc., or the regions of being and meaning (technical, economic, political, ethical, religious, metaphysical, scientific, artistic—I deliberately amass these classical categories in great disorder so as to end up with the question: where is one to situate the specificity of the cultural here? I will come back to this below). Sparing no region, this ill-being and threat do indeed affect the destination of humanity, and, more than ever in the last fifty years, we are unable to localize them, assign them a proper place, so as to contain them. It would be a matter, rather, of an illness of the place. Now, whether one likes it or not, the *polytopia* or *polysemia* of the crisis was reduced in the course of the colloquium. Reduced in the final analysis and in its global effect, even if this is not true with regard to some deviation in detail. Reduced, then, to the correlation of two places: the *techno-economic*, despite its being so difficult to circumscribe, today more than ever, and the *cultural*, which ended up being the name of all the rest!

Here, *two questions* to hasten this simplifying improvisation toward its conclusion (I would already have spoken more than ten minutes, and much too quickly, the chair of the session would have signaled to me by now. How can one speak of these problems at this rhythm? Finally, the only sign of patience or impatience I would like to make heard is this: slow down!).

First question: Is there *a* crisis here, one that is *one*? Can one believe that this correlation of two places, however one interprets it (the "cultural" crisis as the effect or the accompaniment of the techno-economic crisis, or inversely, culture as the "means of getting out of the crisis," the chance for a new momentum or another world equilibrium, etc.), allows one to situate the unity and the assembled unicity of the critical? To explain rationally the qualitative dispersion of critical places, forms, and temporalities?

Second question: Is there a crisis here that is a *crisis*? A crisis is always suspended—it is this suspension itself—from the possibility of a *judgment* and of a *decision* of discernment: a choice, evaluation, election, dénouement at the end of a process, a final or penultimate phase. As the word indicates (*krisis, krinein*), one must always get out of a crisis by the decisional act of a judgment, the action taken of a dénouement, or still yet the resolution of a decree [*le tranchant d'un arrêt*, literally, the cutting edge of an arrest]. Now, despite the many heterogeneous crises that one may speak about today, what brings humanity together in the most common anguish may perhaps no longer allow itself to be thought of in the form of crisis. The latter would still suppose phase, period, pause, suspense, but also decidability, voluntarism, predictability, judgment, predictability, foreseeability, programmation, a principle of reason, as well as a whole network of

European philosophemes inseparable from the most foundational language of Western culture. If one calls all of that *crisis*, is one not "Europeanizing" again (or already)? For "thought"—which is not simply science, theory, or even philosophy—this is the moment to think beyond crisis, not that this will suffice to get out of it, but because it is indispensable if one wants to see or hear the crisis announce itself, and if the concept of crisis is to take form or become necessary in its very *horizon*—in other words, beginning from its *limits*. (Here, with a sudden deceleration, the fiction of an immense parenthetical colloquium. On the program, Husserl's *The Crisis of European Sciences and Transcendental Philosophy, The Crisis of European Humanity and Philosophy*, the great teleo-eschatological discourses of the nineteenth and twentieth centuries—one would follow here the genealogical thread of European socialisms and recognize in it a certain French specificity—the Heidegger of *The Letter on Humanism* and *The Principle of Reason*, his meditation on the relations between metaphysics and technical modernity, as well as so many others from yesterday and today who would not necessarily be philosophers but who, as "scholars," "writers," "artists"— just so many of yesterday's guises or disguises—"think" this beyond-of-crisis.) And then (resumption, acceleration): is it enough to say that culture never resolves the crisis, having instead the vocation of putting-into-crisis? No, no doubt one must begin by recognizing the crisis in the very concept of culture. Better yet, one must begin by recognizing that the concept is no longer able to measure what is happening to the value of "culture."

VII

From this comes the necessity (which has been obvious for a long time now and especially recently) to specify the contours of what is called *culture*. If no one knows any longer how to fix the limits of this concept or, consequently, the competencies and responsibilities of, for example, a cultural politics, then in the final analysis this condition cannot be ascribed to some penchant for vagueness, although this cannot be excluded from the analysis here and there. Where does the cultural begin? Is it not necessary to initiate once again a patient meditation on all the oppositions that construct the value of "culture"? Does it begin wherever nature leaves off? Not *physis* but nature, which happens much later. Does it follow the trajectory of that long chain of meanings (*nomos, thesis, technē*—often opposed to *physis*—and then society, spirit, freedom, history, etc.) that have, one after the other, fixed the limits of "nature"? But is the value of "nature" not itself a "cultural" phenomenon (of which the most recent example would be, to take just one , the modern form of the "ecological" watchword)? Does "culture" then cover the whole "field" of social phenomena (technical, economic, ecological, lifestyle, ethical, legal, religious, aesthetic, etc.), the whole domain of the politics of the institutional and the symbolic? Do science and philosophy belong simply and entirely to culture? Are they really "cultural phenomena"? This is not obvious if the relativity of "cultures" cannot dominate the universalistic project of science, of philosophy, of philosophy as a science. Is the truth a thing of culture? If I name these classical problems in such a summary fashion, it is not to re-scholasticize the debate in a big hurry but rather to point to the urgency of some of its stakes:

a) Beyond the traditional divisions that France's cultural politics puts in question again (arts and letters, fine arts and "minor" arts, classifications and hierarchies that originate in various places), art no longer seems to confer a guiding thread or principal measure to culture—and thus to something like a "politics," or indeed a "Ministry" of Culture. The reason is that it has been replaced in this role by language in the most extended senses of "information" and "communication." This language of information no longer has any limit, and the result is the extension of the cultural field, of cultural competence. What about information, then, and what about the interpretation of the essence of language as information? This interpretation does not go without saying, and it hides an enormous "history." If one fails to think through this history, then what happens to the most lucid, the most versatile, and sometimes the most generous discourses on culture? Do these discourses escape the effects of a powerful program, its relentless combinational schema, and its worldwide empire? This quasi-somnambulant efficiency affects the whole so-called cultural field today via the path of information (communication, archivization, informatization, new technologies and new potentials linked to informatization, etc.). One result is the apparent impossibility of fixing limits on this field, and thus of evaluating it, whether to exalt it or minoritize it.

b) It would be a mistake to see only aggressiveness in a gesture that consists in subtracting from culture—and from its authority or its competence— a certain number of possibilities: for example, science, philosophy (perhaps), "thought" especially if by the latter one understands, among other things, that which interrogates culture, its concept, its history, its destination. A certain aspect of this "thought" always belongs to culture and this interrogation is never off-limits—on the contrary—to whoever answers for culture (I mean whoever bears some part of the responsibility for it), but the essence of this thought, if there is one, could never be cultural. A still more difficult, but related, problem: that of the relation between culture and the "arts" whose language is not yet or no longer informative (instrumentalizable) . . .

c) As a protocol to all these questions, a rigorous genealogy of the concept of culture is essential, even if it remains insufficient. First axiom, a triviality that should never be forgotten: it is a Western concept. It was formed, "cultivated," in the course of an original history. The very concept of history belongs to this history, and the constitution of *cultura* passes at least by way of relays no less enigmatic than *skholè, paiedeia.* With the value of "colonization," "culture" colonizes and then lets itself be colonized by *Bildung, formation,* etc. It is European by virtue of this whole network; it can cease to be so only in a properly colonizing movement. It is not, therefore, as some so loudly proclaimed, a generous "international of the imaginary." Where it is not colonial, then it is its internationality that remains imaginary. To recall this overdetermining sedimentation and its enormous scope is not, of course, to refuse "culture" to non-Western "cultures." It is to do precisely the contrary: to begin to reflect on this powerful "acculturation" of the very concept of culture whose theme is globalized under this European category. This process of assimilation, of incorporation into the history of Europe is not an accident or the effect of a decision; it belongs today to the history of the world. A certain withdrawal of Europe back within its little economic, demographic, or simply territorial borders makes no difference here. Likewise, nothing is changed here by insisting on the necessity of recognizing different cultural identities. In the course of the colloquium, the affirmation, or even the claiming of identities—that is, of cultural differences—was, to be sure, self-assured, unanimous, and, one must say, very nice. It formed the unquestioned contract of this international community. But that did not prevent this consensus from taking form in an element that remains Western through and through (quite the contrary). It *translated* itself (not only because a dominant language offered its services for reasons that were not merely technical or diplomatic) into the idiom of Western culture. Into the system and the Western concept of "culture." This could be described in a very concrete fashion. For example: it had to happen that speakers affirmed in the most noble and rigorous fashion cultural independence; this they did in the language, the logic, the axiomatics, and the juridical forms of the West at the very moment that this autonomy was being demanded for non-European societies by their most eminent representatives and with the approbation of this whole international community. The same dissymmetry marked the discourse of women speaking in the name of women, and this is not altogether *another* problem. All of the problems addressed, the discussions undertaken, the agreements or disagreements (rather few in fact and always secondary) were able to be formalized in the discourse of Western man, whether traditional or modern: his empire is far more powerful, its bases go deeper than all the phenomena of "colonialism," "neo-colonialism," "ethnocentric acculturation," etc., because he conditions them and informs everything, including the most sincere and respectable denunciations of these kinds of violence. We must never disguise this undeniable truth. As a thinking beyond culture and crisis, it gives the measure of a responsibility. The responsibility, here, of any cultural politics, beginning with that of France. A singular responsibility: even as it favors in such a spectacular and demonstrative manner the international affirmation of cultural differences by seeking to displace the axes of techno-symbolic domination, by contesting hegemonies, at the same time France also risks—if it does not give the thought we are talking about here a chance, if it does not *respond* to it—playing the forced card of homogeneity, that is, the globalization of Western metaphysics and techno-science that is underway. Other meetings should allow for these questions and specify these responsibilities. At its inception, the Collège International de Philosophie (an institution planned in France, yet authentically international) should offer a privileged place for such debates. This was spelled out in the Report concerning the founding of such a Collège: all the questions I have just raised could anticipate certain of the essential missions of this original institution and the spirit in which they could, it seems to me, be carried out. But this would have to include a new thinking and a new deontology of the relations between "culture" and all institutional structures, whether private or public, as well as between culture, "civil society," and "state."

VIII

There is no state culture: this is a sentence we heard in the course of the colloquium. What it meant was: *there should be no* state culture. And everyone agrees, beginning with the official representatives of France for whom this is fortunately a declared conviction. We know better than ever today the evil, misery, and violence of "state cultures." But are things so quickly settled? Considering certain transformations and mutations, the very notion of state culture must be re-elaborated. The intervention of the state today passes by way of completely other paths. These must be recognized in the most vigilant fashion—which is not always easy, the trajectories are not always visible—but they do not always and necessarily have the negative effect of a takeover by the state. What France can demonstrate today may once again be exemplary in this regard. It can offer a unique field of innovation. Someone said that "culture," or perhaps it was "creation," has always been inscribed outside of institutions, even against institutions. This would be true only if one placed a severe limitation on the concept of institution. It is always in a counter-institution—at least a virtual one or one that is being formed—always in its name that such challenges to the establishment have taken place to seek in turn some new legitimacy. Too often the discourse of wild an-institutionalism—which is itself very coded—serves, whether it likes it or not, the more or less hidden interests of the market or of private institutions. One learns to detect these appropriations and their cunning mechanisms. In certain conditions that need to be defined (among which are a new reflection on the power and structure of the modern state, the processes of institutionalization and legitimation, etc.), the state can play the paradoxical roles of counter-institution and counter-culture. It can struggle against abusive appropriations or hegemonies of the market, correct the lethal mechanisms at work in access to culture and to the techno-economic conditions of "creation." This apparently paradoxical task is more necessary than ever because of the massive role assumed by new technologies and new "support structures," whether one is talking about the creation or the diffusion of the arts, about training, education, new relations between technology, science, and the "fine arts." The strategies of appropriation are very novel today, the risks of monopolization are more serious than ever—they reach a national and international scale. The presence of the state must be limited, but that presence can be vital. And it can take only a contradictory form in constant readjustment: to struggle against structures of violent and abusive appropriation, monopolization, and standardization, to defend the rights and potential of (national and international) culture, to liberate space and forces to that end, without, however, programming, inducing, orienting—in any case, as little as possible, if that is possible—and without forgetting that *there is violence and there is violence*, that the most irruptive "creation" can never be pure of any desire for mastery. A plan of appropriation is always at work in it, and its calculation may be hidden behind sublime appearances. This is to say that the state—and all its representatives—need to have the art, culture, and discernment necessary to *know* where new paths are beginning to be broken, where it is advisable to open up *still empty places*, to arrange blank spaces, and then to accept to withdraw from them, letting "creation" and "thought" write themselves there without any state control.

IX

This *utopia* is also a regulating idea for a new deontology. It calls for a new relation of "intellectuals," "artists," "scholars," "philosophers," "thinkers," but also of the whole cultural community, to the state. This relation is marked by the same paradox, the same adventure, and it exposes itself to the same risks. Staying outside or abstaining remain illusory options and in fact impossible ones. Yet, a concern for the most rigorous independence must be affirmed all the more strenuously. And respected by the state, in its own interest. (Here once again, a final parenthesis: anamnesis and reinvention of political philosophy. This is impossible at such a colloquium, even in its aftermath. The empty place I was just talking about is never empty. And it is also the place of time allowed, another time, rhythms to be invented, programs and imperatives of "productivity" to be undone, even abandoned. In this regard, a rallying cry such as "culture to get out of the crisis" would be not only powerless but also shocking if it were interpreted as the mission of a new auxiliary in the service of techno-economic finalities governed by the value of "production" or "growth." For this not to be the case, should we not think about the concept of production and the value of productivity from within their history and their limits? This task would incite us on occasion to *think* beyond culture, philosophy, and science—to which such thinking has never meant any harm and to which, moreover, it has never done any.)

Translated by Peggy Kamuf

Economies of the Crisis

QUESTION: Based on, but not limiting yourself to your own area, could you tell us (in two pages) what is represented for you by the idea that the present world is in crisis?

FIRST TIME.—No, impossible, especially in two pages. Too many premises that would have to be examined in turn within the very words of the question, in each one of them.

SECOND TIME.—What if, beyond all the good reasons one may always have for not answering such a question in a few lines, this apparently *economic* argument betrayed precisely the essence of the "crisis"? Perhaps we no longer have at our disposal a *principle of response*, a discourse sure enough of its legitimacy (foundation, axiomatics, certitude, or truth) that it could authorize the *response in principle*, the telegram: "In two words, to decipher the crisis, look in this or that direction; here is the master code, text follows."

Well now, we know all about that. Codes and programs, prolegomena to all possible discourse on the crisis, are even somewhat too familiar to us. In all "areas": philosophy, history of civilizations and religions, political economy, military geo-strategy, medicine, techno-sciences in general, etc. We are tirelessly eloquent about the end of philosophy, about the inability of the human sciences—including psychoanalysis—to ground themselves in their theories and their institutions, about the recession of Marxist or humanist dogmatisms and, along with this, of their political or theological-political models, about the return of the religious in its enigmatic and dispersed power, about uncontrollable "technological mutations" that no longer seem commensurable with what we still call *ethics, politics, culture, ecology, economy*, about the manipulations of the "monetary disorder," about the impossibility of distinguishing a politics of science from a military programmation, the West from its other, Europe from *its others* (the United States, Japan, etc.), about the new for-itself of a finite humanity that finally knows itself capable of a radical auto-destruction, etc. These things and a few others are true, of course. But do they help us name or situate what is most singular about our present time?

THIRD TIME.—*The* "crisis," *this one here*, affects in its possibility every one of the words I have just used: *name, place, singularity,* "us," the *present*, the *this*. We are speechless at this point, at this, the most acute moment of the *paroxysm*, the point at which this crisis recalls no earlier crisis. At least this is what we think we sense. There is no lack of interpretations or analogies—we have too many of them. They are pertinent but insufficient. In particular, they do not lend themselves to being *joined*: no unique or dominant discourse, no system, no arbitrating tribunal to decide on the unity or the unicity of the said crisis. Thus (since you ask me about my supposed "area"), no philosophy of crisis, not even a crisis of philosophy. In a moment, I will venture a suggestion as to why the word *crisis* deserted the philosophical vocabulary after Valéry and Husserl. This, then, is the most abyssal "crisis," the crisis of crisis: there is no more philosophy of crisis, whether philosophy is an "area" or a fundamental ontology, the discourse capable of dominating the diversity of "regions." There would thus be no more "world" and still less a "present world," whose common horizon would be able to delimit a *determinable* experience and, as a result, an assured competence (philosophical, scientific, economic-political). The anticipation of this unity, even its language, seems to us to be withheld. Which might lead one to say—and some will think that this is the worst: there is perhaps not even a "crisis of the present world." In its turn in crisis, the concept of crisis would be the signature of a last symptom, the convulsive effort to save a "world" that we no longer inhabit: no more *oikos*, economy, ecology, livable site in which we are "at home." One more try, the word *crisis* says to us (which is indeed one of our homemade words), one more try to save the discourse of a "world" that we no longer speak, or that we still speak, sometimes all the more garrulously, as in an emigrant colony.

FOURTH TIME.—The "crisis" of the value of "crisis" cannot be, then, just one crisis among others. Here I would like to take into account the precise terms of your question. If, as I have just suggested, one should no longer even speak of crisis, there is all the same, as you say, the "idea that the present world is in crisis."

This "idea" is experiencing its greatest inflation; it has its theater and its rhetoric. And in fact it is what "represents," as you correctly recall, something for each one of us. Us? Perhaps one should also ask (a classic preliminary, but always necessary): Who is talking about crisis? Who is talking the most about it right now? Where? To whom? In what form? In view of what effects and what interests? By playing on what "representations"? Who are the individuals, which are the interest groups, the countries that hold forth this discourse of the crisis, hold it forth or hold on to it? An enormous task: one can indicate only its principle. Let us stay with its most assured generality. The "representation" of crisis and the rhetoric it organizes always have at least this purpose: to determine, so as to limit it, a more serious and more formless threat, one which is, in fact, faceless and normless. A monstrous threat but one that holds some desire in suspense: a threat to desire. By determining it as crisis, one tames it, domesticates it, neutralizes it—in short, one *economizes* it. One appropriates the Thing, the unthinkable becomes the unknown to be known, one begins to give it form, one begins to inform, master, calculate, program. One cancels out a future.

FIFTH TIME.—What are, in fact, the features of a crisis, those that limit it and thus assure it of its delimiting virtue?

1. A crisis is provisional, accidental, unintelligible—*but in regard to an order*. It disturbs rules, laws, norms, but only *for a time*. One must suspect that this disorder affects what is essential (it is an essential accident!), but there must also be a reassuring belief in *rhythm*: "One can't do anything about it (you can't do anything about it!), but it's only a crisis. It's very serious but it will pass." No crisis without a dénouement and the worst outcome (death after a heart attack [*crise cardiaque*], world war after economic crisis) is after all still a dénouement. The reassuring thing is that there are only two possible solutions.

2. And this because an effect of crisis appears as such and is spoken about in a "binary" situation. To be sure, decision is impossible here, but impossibility and powerlessness derive their critical sense only from the horizon of some awaited decision. *Krisis*: judgment, choice, decision.

Crisis: a moment in which the *krisis* appears (is or is said to be) impossible, but in regard to an awaited *krisis*, to a necessary judgment, choice, and decision *between two terms*. The crisis is not just any form of the incalculable; it is the incalculable as a *moment* of calculation, the undecidable that is still determined as the relation of a voluntary subject to a possible decision, to a calculation with which he intends to reckon. "For the moment, we accept our impotence, but we should be able to decide, control, program," and so forth. A singular disavowal, a voluntaristic stiffening that can go so far as to spread tetanus throughout a culture. This *double discourse* leaves room for every sort of cunning maneuver. But its duplicity, its *disarming* strategies or manipulations are only possible in a "world" ruled by the values of judgment, decision, techno-scientific lucidity. Competence, voluntarism, knowledge and know-how, mastery of a subject over present objects, productivism—in short, all of techno-metaphysical modernity without which it would make no sense to speak of "crisis."

SIXTH TIME.—The modernity of the discourse-of-the-crisis would thus be Western. Through and through, but according to a paradoxical logic. This logic in fact proves neither the unity nor the existence of the West. What is called the *crisis* "represents" an accident of the West: what is happening *to it, to its subject* [à son sujet]. But the crisis is an essential accident and one that, on its behalf, calls for science, conscience, and will, finally inciting the West to a gathering of self that has perhaps never taken place.

At stake, in effect, is the "unity" of Europe and of so-called Western philosophy: has there ever been such a thing in the strictest sense? This question does not prevent the discourse of the crisis from referring (itself) to this Western project and subject. As it would to its paroxysm. And this, even though the interests of several Western subsets are at war there or are trying to arrange in a different manner the critical effects of antagonism. To say *crisis* is to appeal to the subject of Europe, to recall it to itself, to its unity, its "freedom," just as Valéry did at the end of *The Crisis of Spirit* (1919), at the point where he spoke precisely of the "European Spirit" and of a "*diminutio capitis* of Europe."

This was before the "crisis of 1929." After that, during the 1930s, what is then called *The Krisis* . . . by Husserl also speaks of "the crisis of European humanity," "the crisis of European sciences," once again in view of the transcendental freedom of the subject: a decided return to forgotten meaning and to the hidden ground of techno-scientific objectivity, reactivation of the origin, reawakening, an essentially voluntary *Selbstbesinnung*. It is a matter of saving philosophy, whose universality always announces itself by means of the origin and the *telos* of European reason. But as soon as one questions or exceeds this axiomatic configuration (subject/object, judgment, decision, will, consciousness, competence, etc.), then the most disturbing aspect of the Thing no longer appears on a *stage of crisis*. It thus seems to me that Heidegger, for example, even if he used it, would never have emphasized the word *crisis*—which is sometimes smuggled back in by his translators. What one reads in these "great texts" can also be deciphered in the political discourse of Western democracies. This discourse tries desperately to *situate* the crisis in one or two areas. If it is not "in your head," then in the last analysis it is economic. And despite the *essential* powerlessness or incompetence that would prevent overcoming it for the moment (because the driving forces of the crisis could be purely economic if the economy were a strictly determinable region—which it is not), the disturbance would still, in principle, be a matter of know-how, judgment, will, decision. What is more, within the vague confines of the economy, the so-called worldwide crisis signals perhaps a powerful movement of auto-regulation of world capitalism. I refer here to what Claude Julien titles "The Benefits of the Crisis" (*Le Monde Diplomatique*, July 1983). Whether it succeeds or not, the economy of this auto-regulation induces *to a certain degree* all the measures taken "to get out of the crisis," even if these gestures give some premonition of *another* logic, a beyond of the economic crisis: for example, watchwords such as *politics against economism, especially in its monetarist form* or *culture to get out of the crisis*. Could this paradoxical calculation, this economy of "the benefits of the crisis" not be transposed to all "areas"? Secondary benefits, no doubt, but always worth taking. To maintain at a respectful distance, to postpone something farther away or too close, at once older and newer than the crisis, more terrifying but also more inciting to movement—I dare not say more interesting.

Translated by Peggy Kamuf

Events? What Events?

QUESTION: 1964–1984 . . . twenty years have passed. What events have had the greatest impact on us, what figures have been key? How have they affected our behavior, our personalities, our journal?

Your question excludes so many things! First of all, it excludes whatever does not belong to the public, political, historical realms; and then it excludes whatever has its own rhythm, a rhythm that goes beyond the time of *Le Nouvel Observateur*, two decades; next, it excludes whatever is outside the limits of a supposed competence: here, I guess, philosophy; perhaps even, finally, it excludes whatever does not have the visible outline, the theatrical form, or the official title of what people call *events*: that which could be, or must have been, talked about.

Let us accept the rules of the game. Now I will suppose that for a moment philosophy becomes the chosen place for perceiving or evaluating such "events" and I will venture the following response: by law, philosophy has never allowed itself to be assigned a set place. Every event is of interest to it and can affect it; in any case, each event of a philosophical nature also intersects with the thinking of this question: What is an event? What is it that *comes*, and where, to whom, in the form called an *event*? What is put into play there and sometimes hidden by the commotion of the scene? If, for example (to answer your question), I cited some "great moments," those that carry memorable names and dates (in no particular order: '68, the landing on the moon, Vietnam, Cambodia, the retreat of the Marxist orthodoxies in the West, their hurried replacement by anti-Marxist dogmatics, sometimes within the same intelligentsia, the new right-wing movements, the renewal or reaffirmation of racisms, sometimes of declared theological-political nationalisms, the hopes that are born here and there—Poland, Spain, Argentina, or, something else yet again, the France of '81, etc.), don't you think that these "coups de théâtre" must have pushed something else into the shadows, being on occasion destined to do so? What? *Either* nonevents (for example the massive immobility in Eastern Europe or in Latin America, that which does not budge or gets worse in South Africa, etc.) *or* things that *come to pass without passing* onto the stage, without going through the filter of information or the codes of political discourse, without appearing under the title of "event."

One might think of quiet and microscopic movements as well as of slow and powerful displacements of "centers": economy, sciences and technical know-how, culture, demography. In Eastern Europe, for example, the most serious cracks are perhaps to be found elsewhere than under Polish soil; in Israel, the law of demography, even in twenty years, is perhaps a more determining factor than the military tragedies or the diplomatic chess games. In a landscape of worldwide war that is in fact neverending (the stockpiling of surplus arms + local conflicts + the millions of deaths from starvation + the U.N. + the I.M.F.), the earthquake can no longer be measured by the "crises" that people talk about so much, no doubt to drown out this already muffled background noise.

But you would prefer that I speak about philosophy and its works. I propose therefore a fable for these last twenty years. *First decade* (of *Le Nouvel Observateur*, if you like, moreover it has its role to play here, too): a violent putting-in-question of philosophical self-assurance, of its identity, its proper *home*. This happens *first* in France, then elsewhere, since nothing emigrates better. This necessary and (it seems to me) irreversible questioning comes from both inside *and* outside the philosophical community. *Second decade*, grosso modo: people try to assimilate, thus also to neutralize or cushion, this shock. Finally, as of recently, a second wind among those who make a claim to, and affirm, philosophy by trying, in the best of cases, not to lose the very ancient and the not-so-ancient memory, not to give up in new institutions the most rigorous and necessary things from yesterday's institutions and noninstitutions. Do not ask me for names or titles of works. We have understood better now perhaps that philosophical work can never again be linked to the apparent signature of an individual (whether a professor or not) and turned into the Great Book of a system. The most powerful attempts in the genre date from the 1920s. Their interruption certainly gives one more to think about than so many well-finished works. Finally, I believe that an act of thinking, whether or not it is philosophical, cannot be measured by the experience of twenty years, still less by the noise it makes at the time. Remember "truth comes on the feet of doves . . ." Unless it has also just come and gone.

Translated by Peggy Kamuf

"Pardon me for taking you at your word"

Pardon me for taking you at your word. I will not take advantage of it. You remind us that *La Quinzaine littéraire* "has tried to be and continues to try to be the reflection . . . of the present intellectual situation." Who could doubt that? If one must try to answer your questions, it is first of all as homage to what this journal has done in that regard, with a rigor and dignity that are rather rare, more and more rare.[1]

But this is to attempt the impossible—you knew that in advance—and the required brevity does not help matters. Let us suppose that someone accepts to reply, in fact *pretends* to reply to some of the questions, even though everyone knows in advance that it is impossible to do them justice under these conditions, especially when their very formulation remains problematic. What would happen then? The feint would mean:

1. I cannot answer *your questions*, but I am answering *you*. I am *doing* it on this notable occasion in order to tell you that and in doing so—yes, *doing so*—I am participating in this anniversary celebration, I am for the continued life of *La Quinzaine*, and, in the main, despite certain reservations or certain causes for impatience, I approve of its work and its requirements. There, that would be *done*. Not without risk: how can one say "Long live *La Quinzaine*!" without seeming to want to put oneself in its good graces?

2. This is an exercise in "pragmatics," an *example* has just been given of it. It is an example *in two senses*: a) Example of a series of sentences

whose effective value is determined first by the context, by the social gesture one adopts, by the obligation it signs, rather than by the strictly discursive content exhibited there (what one might say here, for example, about "intellectual life in France," which indeed "has seen a wealth of events," or about the "lines of force" for the "future"). The content is not unimportant, but what will matter first is the manifestation of a certain solidarity with *La Quinzaine*; b) Example in this other sense: a rule has been proposed, and one claims to present an *ethical-political* example. One has let it be understood that here is what one *must do*: not only support *La Quinzaine* today but, *in so doing*, refrain from hiding these "pragmatic" implications, from mistaking the genre, code, and complication of one's intervention, from dispensing with analysis. If the "intellectual" still has a responsibility or some dignity, these require that at every opportunity he try to analyze *publicly* the socio-political scene in which he is participating, in which he is inscribed even before subscribing to it, and which his analysis in any case contributes to changing. With enough time and space, one ought to say here everything of which one approves, and to what degree, by associating oneself with *La Quinzaine*, what one tends to fight against or to marginalize by agreeing to answer *you*, even if one does not answer *your questions* here, now. These, then, are two sorts of examples.

But even before beginning to answer, one has already done two other things.

1. In passing, one has underlined, and *by the very fact, by the doing itself* [par le fait même], one of the features that has perhaps marked "intellectual life" during these last twenty years. The growing interest in "pragmatics" is not directed only at a theoretical discipline, the one which, fastening on the performative dimensions of discourse or writing, has caused theoreticism, linguisticism, or logocentrism, in the particular forms that triumphed at the very beginning of the 1960s, to show their age both within philosophy and elsewhere. This pragmatics in the broad sense has sharpened *and* displaced the most urgent questions of "intellectual" ethics or politics. Earlier, these questions concerned *either* the external conditions *or* the intrinsic content of a text. These considerations are still necessary, but they have been complicated by a proximate (albeit completely other) question: what am I doing *by writing* in a given situation? What happens—comes, or does not come, to pass—

through these marks? Whether it is governed by the tradition of philosophies or by that of social sciences, external analysis of the situation is no more sufficient than internal analysis of the content. One would have to analyze the performativity of writing itself, always more cunning and inappropriable than one thinks; one must, if need be, criticize this or that presupposition in the theories of the performative, recall that they themselves put to work texts that are not only constative (or theorems) but also performative, etc. In one fashion or another, there are an increasing number of "intellectuals" who, in the last fifteen years or so, take these performative dimensions into account and do so under new conditions (historical-political, socio-institutional, media-technical, editorial, academic, etc.)—new for their utterances, their writings, the evaluation of their image, their name, their signature. Now, there are some who *for the most part* do this to assume better a responsibility—what they consider to be the ethic demanded by these new situations. There are others who *for the most part* do it to ensure better a certain promotional performativity of their "production" and to exploit better these new potentials. This distinction, which governs many others, must be retained, but if one had enough time and space, one could show *where* and *why* its pertinence reaches a limit.

2. He who would have given you such an answer would have already showed himself such as he is. For better or worse, he would have signed: here is the example of someone who does not know how to begin without getting tangled up in endless protocols. He jumps in (because finally he does jump in) by endlessly proliferating prior fictions and hypotheses about what it will have meant "to plunge," even when all the questions on this subject have yet to be settled. In short, he would have sent you a snapshot—no, a signed video cassette—without another word.

Well, yes, one more word if you still have room for me. Is there a "present intellectual situation"? I very much doubt that one can find—*wherever it may be*—a *reflection* of it. As you know, the most interesting thing *La Quinzaine* does is not to reflect, but to take sides, evaluate, hierarchize, exclude, legitimate, or delegitimate, as one says. By what it declares or what it silences. It belongs to a field of forces, but it affects that field as well with each one of its sentences, with its headlines, its page layout, the choice of contributors, and addressees. In offering its hospitality, *La Quinzaine* has an ethics, a politics, an axiomatics: this is, it seems to me, the rather stable figure, in the midst of the storm, of an intelligent transaction in the liberal style (good taste, sober costume, but never old-fashioned, taking care to erase all external signs of dogmatism; but we know very well that there is always some *doxa* in an evaluation and that even politeness and good liberal manners are never free of all violence), thus a constantly readjusted contract between, on the one hand, the most refined memory of a threatened culture, the best of which must be saved (everything that has to do with the patience of reading and the time of the book, the resistance to illiteracy, etc.) and, on the other, the irruption of the new (difficult to recognize and decipher by definition) for which new *readers* must be formed, by which I mean those who read *La Quinzaine* as well as those who write for it. This disruptive newness characterizes not only contents—some meaning or message—but the ways of writing and also the technical forms of production and circulation, the supporting media, the market, the networks of decision-making and evaluation. One ought to devote an ample and systematic study to the history of this transaction, which is dramatic at times. *La Quinzaine*, overall, manages the transaction successfully; it survives, sober and serene, without too many concessions in one direction or another. It figures thus as a good witness for a study that would not rely *only* on the sociology of intellectuals, literature, philosophy, or even *French* culture.

Even if such a "present intellectual situation" existed, must one hope to see it "reflected"? Could it be reflected? For convenience sake, let us keep the word "intellectual," even though it is very equivocal. But "the present situation"? What is it made of? In the first place, it is *made*: an artifact, a heterogeneous composition whose unity is nowhere brought together. Its body could not be reflected in an image. One can talk about it, but one never meets up with it, and when one talks about it, then one supposes it to have a principle of synchronization. Now, is it not the case that our experience is one of a *double anachrony*, which the scene of the so-called present situation can only either fail to recognize or disavow? Synchrony: that is the scourge, or the yoke, the scourge or the yoke of a scale, the fictive limit of an equilibrium, a temporarily stabilized relation, seemingly objectifiable, always accredited by force and on the basis of which one claims to measure the two anachronies. That which "reflects" the state of forces or the established, hegemonic evaluations—which are supposedly based on "consensus"— is at the service of whatever has already made its way, or even been institutionalized in one way or another. One knows (worn-out program, boredom, boredom, anachrony) more or less everything that one reads in the "news" devoted to the aforementioned present cultural situation. But there is no "one," the population of readers is parceled out, indeed is constituted, on the basis of this partition of anachronies. The anachrony of the hackneyed is necessary on the television screen or in the lead articles of the literary columns to the extent that it silences, and *in order to* silence, *another anachrony*, that of texts that do not conform to the expectations of the greatest number, to the demand passed on by most of the authorized mediators, thus the *doxa* in general, in the press and in universities, in journals and in publishing houses. Is this other anachrony, this anachrony of the other, not the untimely dimension of the "present situation," its unimaginable, unrecognizable, monstrous, unthought face? One must also consider the negative (I do not say "unconscious") lucidity that is shown by evaluations made in view of preventing *this* un-present situation from appearing: the latter would come along to disturb the norms that give the evaluators their authority and that they thus protect.

I am unable here to designate the "content" and the name of the "intellectual" events that may have been important to me over the last twenty years. I will limit myself to the following, somewhat vague cliché: the field of evaluation in which the artifact called the "present situation" is constructed and in the middle of which *La Quinzaine* is situated. Twenty years ago, this field was really a field, still strongly unified, with at least the representation of a center and a manageable heterogeneity. The illusions of synchrony had a better chance then. Disagreements, divisions, and numerous codes could still be deciphered by means of a kind of big socio-cultural dictionary. In short, a rather stable configuration, a limited number of places of legitimation: the "big" publishing houses, the nobility of their imprint, of their brand name; the "big" journals; a certain kind of university; a few academic circles, their system of rewards, a regular functioning of the tolerated avant-gardes that played along and added surplus value to the brand name, etc. In twenty years, this system has, to be sure, extended

its monopoly and its large commercial centers; it has often appropriated the strategic centers of promotional evaluation (television is not
the only one). But simultaneously, it is losing its cohesion, and it is incapable of deciphering, evaluating, assimilating, supporting, "selling"
at the pace now required by works that have gotten too fine for their
sieves, too overencoded in some way, overburdened with an unrecognizable memory, demanding another apprenticeship in reading, the
micromovements of a (supercultivated) counterculture that is now
pushed into the periphery of the large commercial centers—this is
what the professional evaluators often judge to be "unreadable," what
they cannot bear, or simply what they will not allow to get through.
Besides the manuscripts that no one will publish and that circulate in
a quasi-private manner, there is the proliferation of "little" journals,
"little" publishing houses: these are so many places where, from now
on, certain events—and among them the most irruptive of our time—
will be situated. This is not the era of samizdat or of "underground"
literature—let us not confuse everything—but a zone of growing
shadow, a sort of clandestinity, a new partition of the public from the
private. And all of this happening in a fine mess. The licensed evaluators are more and more powerful, yet they feel threatened; they see terrible laws coming into play, at once for them and against them: for example, the techno-economic constraints that urge one to support old
models—for instance, literary and philosophical models—because
they are more acceptable, at the very moment that these laws weaken
and marginalize their traditional supporting media, in particular the
book. A thousand paradoxes follow from this, and contradictory duties for whoever does not simply laugh at this spectacle. One must add
that, although it may sometimes be comical, the spectacle is the result
of this war between the spectacular and its shadow, between what arrives on stage and what does not. Example of a contradiction: the book
still remains the principal "support" of risky, discreet, and generous
thinking, of rigorously ventured writing, but this writing becomes in-
decipherable in the middle of the great cultural circulation, the one
that is still run by computers of the not-yet-first generation that are
stopped dead in their tracks in the middle of the intersection like deaf
and dumb old men. I am not talking here about persons, but machines
for reproducing promotional evaluations that, without realizing it, by

definition are relentlessly evaluated in their turn by the very thing that remains unreadable to them. The two anachronies are at work as much in the form of the "book" as in that of "new support media." Hence the difficulty of the partition. One could point to innumerable consequences of this. I merely wanted to say what I feel: in this impossible negotiation that cannot satisfy anyone, *La Quinzaine* plays its cards in a fairly dignified way. A good sign, the sign that one must continue. I just noticed that the word *dignified* has urged itself upon me twice. Yes, dignified: I mean it in a moral or political sense, but also in a social sense; the latter is not always compatible with the former, but it does not in principle exclude it.

For what are we now better trained than twenty years ago? To read the blanks, to understand them and to wonder: why will this or that never be published although it is so much more powerful, more essential, etc.? Why can one do nothing to see that this gets published, or, if it is published, that it gets talked about, or, if it is talked about, that it does not get made into something unreadable, submitted to rules of reading that immediately destroy it? Thus we read the blanks as if they were superimposed or printed over what is printed. Which is to say that they tend to efface the rest. Example: imagine a synopsis of Italian music, covering a specific period; in it, you look in vain for the names of two composers or two works that, you imagine, no amount of indecency, vulgarity, or hatred could have caused to be omitted. But there is not even the least mention of these names or titles! From that moment on, what you will retain of this panopticon, what organizes and what bestows on it its most interesting meaning, are the names of the two musicians to whom this blind spot or this monument of disavowal has just been offered. These two names are then superimposed in big letters. And one day people will say, if they still talk about it: you know, that thing that did not even mention XXX or XXX! The evaluator evaluated.

—You always speak in an indirect and fictional fashion. You mentioned no event, no work, no person by name.

—I would have been accused of using a forum, of giving into friendship, even of naming those close to me. No one would have believed me if I had said they are close precisely because, for twenty years, I have not been able to separate the "events" that, as you say, "seemed important" to me and seem to me to "prefigure the future" (I am speaking especially of philosophical thought or of literature) from certain figures of friendship, from those to whom I had to try to get close to hear and understand them. But tell me, what is that which is close? Is it a thing of the present situation, this abyss of memory and of promise?

Translated by Peggy Kamuf

The Deconstruction of Actuality

PASSAGES: In Bogotá and Santiago, in Prague and Sofia, in Berlin and Paris—one has the impression that your thinking is in touch with actuality. Do you share this feeling? Are you a philosopher of the present, or at least a philosopher who thinks his time?

J.D.: How could one be sure? Moreover, "to be in touch with actuality" and "to think one's time" are not the same thing. In both cases, one should *do* something, something more or other than establish facts or give descriptions: participate, take sides, join in. Consequently, one "is in touch with" and thus one transforms if only just slightly: one intervenes, as they say, in a time that is not in front of one and given in advance. There are never any preestablished norms that might guarantee that one is indeed "in touch with actuality" or, to stick to your expressions, that one is "thinking one's time." In the work of certain people, you often get one without the other. But I don't think I am capable of improvising an answer to these kinds of questions. We must reckon with the time of the interview—and this time is limited. Now more than ever, thinking one's time—especially when one runs the risk or chance of speaking in public—means acknowledging (and thus using) the fact that the time of this speech is itself produced artificially. It is an *artifact*. In its very event, the time of such a public gesture is calculated and constrained, "formatted" and "initialized" by the organizations of the media (to put it briefly). This would deserve an almost infinite analysis. Who could possibly think his time today, let alone speak about it, without first paying heed to the public space and thus to a political present transformed at every moment, in its structure and its content, by the teletechnology of what is confusedly called *information* or *communication*?

Your question referred not only to the "present" but also to what is called *actuality*. Very schematically, let me quickly mention just two of the most current features of actuality. They are too abstract to capture what is most specific of *my* experience or any other *philosophical* experience of the aforementioned "actuality," but they do point to what constitutes actuality in general. One could go so far as to give them two portmanteau terms: *artifactuality* and *actuvirtuality*. The first feature, therefore, is that actuality is *made*: it is important to know what it is made of, but it is just as important to know that it is made. It is not given, but actively produced, sifted, contained, and performatively interpreted by many hierarchizing and selective procedures—*false* or *artificial* procedures that are always in the service of forces and interests of which their "subjects" and agents (producers and consumers of actuality—who are sometimes "philosophers" and always interpreters) are never sufficiently aware. The "reality" (to which "actuality" refers)— however singular, irreducible, stubborn, painful, or tragic it may be— reaches us through fictional constructions [*facture*]. The only way to analyze it is through a work of resistance, of vigilant counterinterpretation, etc. Hegel was right to remind the philosophers of his time to read the newspapers every day. Today, the same responsibility also requires us to find out how the newspapers are *made*, and *who* makes them, the dailies, the weeklies, and the television news. We would need to look at them from the other side: from the side of the news agencies as well as from that of the teleprompter. And let us never forget what such a statement implies: whenever a journalist or a politician appears to be addressing us directly, in our homes and looking us straight in the eye, he (or she) is actually reading on the screen at the dictation of a "prompter" and reading a text that was produced elsewhere at another moment, possibly by other people or even by a whole network of anonymous writers.

PASSAGES: There is a duty to develop a systematic critique of what you call *artifactuality*. You say "il faudrait " . . .

J.D.: Yes, a critical culture, a kind of education. But I would never say "il faudrait," I would never speak of a duty one has as a citizen or even as a philosopher without adding two or three crucial precautions of principle.

The first concerns the *nation*. (To respond briefly to what your first question seemed to imply—it sounded as if, returning from abroad, you had found reason to extract it from a travel journal: "here's what they say about you abroad: so, what do you think of this?" I would have liked to comment on this gesture.) Among the filters that "inform" actuality—and in spite of the accelerated but all the more equivocal internationalization—there is this privileging of the national, the regional, the local, or indeed the "West," that still overdetermines all other hierarchies (sports in the first place, then "politicking"—though not the political—and then the "cultural," in decreasing order of supposed demand, spectacularity, and readability). This privileging renders secondary a whole mass of events: all those that are judged to be far from the (supposed public) interest and the interests of the nation, the national language, the code or national style. On the news, "actuality" is spontaneously ethnocentric. It will exclude the foreign, sometimes within the country, without passion, doctrine, or nationalist declaration, and it will do this even when the "news [*actualités*]" features "human rights." Some journalists make meritorious efforts to escape this law, but by definition these efforts are never enough, and all does not depend on professional journalists in the last instance. We must not forget this now, when old nationalisms are taking new forms by exploiting the most "advanced" media techniques (the use of both official radio and television in the former Yugoslavia is one very striking example). And let it be said in passing that some still found it necessary to challenge the critique of ethnocentrism, or, to simplify greatly, the deconstruction of Eurocentrism. This is still considered acceptable, even now: as if one they remained blind to everything that brought death in the name of ethnicity, right in the heart of Europe, within a Europe whose only reality today—whose only "actuality"—is economic and national, and whose only law, in alliances as in conflicts, is that of the market.

But the tragedy, as always, stems from a contradiction or a double postulation: the apparent internationalization of sources of information is often based on the appropriation and concentration of the sources of information and distribution. Remember what happened at the moment of the Gulf War. Although this may have represented an exemplary moment of awareness and, here and there, of resistance, it should not be allowed to conceal the generality and constancy of this violence in all conflicts, in the Middle East and elsewhere. At times, a "national" resistance may thus assert itself against this apparently international process of homogenization. This is a first complication.

Another precaution: this international artifactuality, this monopolization of the "actuality effect," this centralized appropriation of the artifactual powers to "create the event,"may be accompanied by advances in "live" communication or in so-called "real" time, in the present. The theatrical nature of the "interview" conforms, at least in fiction, to this idolatry of "immediate" presence, to "live" communication. The newspaper will always prefer to publish an interview with a photograph of the author, rather than an article that takes responsibility for reading, evaluating, and educating. But how can we make use of the new resources of "live" communication (video cameras, etc.) while continuing to critique its mystifications? And first by continuing to point out, and *demonstrate*, that "live" communication and "real time" are never pure: they permit neither intuition nor transparency, nor any perception unmarked by interpretation or technical intervention. And such a demonstration already calls for philosophy.

And finally—as I suggested all too briefly a moment ago—the necessary deconstruction of artifactuality must not serve as an alibi. It must not exaggerate the simulation and thereby neutralize all threats in what might be called the *delusion of delusion*, the denial of the event: "Everything," one might say then, "even violence, suffering, war, and death—everything is constructed, fictionalized, constituted by and for the media, nothing ever happens, there are only simulations and delusions." While taking the deconstruction of artifactuality as far as possible, one must therefore do everything to guard against this critical neo-idealism and recall not only that any consistent deconstruction is a thinking of singularity—and thus of the event, and what it retains that is ultimately irreducible—but also that "information" is a contradictory and heterogeneous process. Information can and must transform itself; it can and it must serve—as it often has—knowledge, truth, and the cause of the democracy to come, along with all the questions that follow from them. However artificial and manipulative it may be, we cannot help but hope that artifactuality will bend itself or lend itself to the coming of what comes, to the event that bears it along and toward which it is borne [*se porte*]. And to which it will bear witness, whether it wants to or not.

PASSAGES: Previously, you proposed another term related not to technology and artificiality, but to virtuality.

J.D.: Yes, if we had time I would want to insist on another feature of "actuality"—of what is happening today and of what is happening today to *actuality*. I would insist not only on the *artificial* synthesis (synthetic image, synthetic voice, all the prosthetic supplements that can take the place of real actuality) but also on the concept of *virtuality* (virtual image, virtual space, and thus virtual event), which certainly can no longer be opposed with philosophical equanimity to actual reality in the way one used to distinguish between power and act, *dynamis* and *energeia*, the potentiality of matter and the defining form of a *telos*, and hence of *progress*, etc. This virtuality is now inscribed in the very structure of the event produced; it affects both the time and the space of the image, the discourse, the "information"—in short, everything that connects [*rapporte*] us to the said actuality, to the implacable reality of its supposed present. Today a philosopher who "thinks his time" must, among other things, be attentive to the implications and consequences of this virtual time—both to the novelties of its technical uses, but also to what in what is new recalls possibilities much more ancient.

PASSAGES: Might we ask you to come back to an actuality rather more concrete?

J.D.: You think perhaps that I have been drifting or avoiding your question for some time now. I am not answering it directly. And some might say: he's wasting time, his time and ours. Or he's playing for time; he's putting off answering. And that would not be entirely false. The one thing that one cannot accept these days—on television, on the radio, or in the papers—is an intellectual taking his time, or wasting other people's time. Perhaps this is what needs to be changed about actuality: its rhythm. Time is what media professionals are not supposed to waste. Neither theirs nor ours. And in this they are often sure to succeed. They know the cost, if not the value, of time. Before imposing silence on the intellectuals as is regularly done, why not consider this new media situation? The effects of a difference of rhythm? Some intellectuals may be silenced by this difference of rhythm (those who need a little more time for analysis and will not agree to gear the complexity of things to the conditions under which they are made to speak); it may silence them or drown out their voices with the noise of others—at least in places that are dominated by certain rhythms and certain forms of speech. This other time, the time of the media, gives rise to another distribution, to other spaces, rhythms, relays, forms of speech-making and public intervention. What is invisible, unreadable, inaudible on the screen with the widest audience may be active and effective, either immediately or eventually, disappearing only in the eyes of those who confuse actuality with what they see, or believe they do see, in the window of the "superstore." In any case, this transformation of public space requires work, and I think the work is being done and is more or less well received in the places where one has become too used to expecting it. The silence of those who read, listen, or see the news, and also analyze it, is not as silent, it would seem, as the silence coming from the other side, the side from which the news appears, becomes, or makes one deaf to everything that does not speak according to its law. Consequently, the perspective should be reversed: a kind of media noise concerning pseudo-actuality falls like silence; it imposes silence on everything that speaks and acts. And it can be heard elsewhere or otherwise, provided one opens an ear to it. This is the law of time. It is terrible for the present; it always leaves one to hope or to count on the untimely. Here one would have to discuss the effective limits of the right of reply (thus of democracy): apart from any deliberate censorship, these limits point to the appropriation of time and public space, to their technical arrangement by those who exercise power in the media.

Still, if I allow myself this pause or this pose, a manner like any other, for these really are manners of thinking one's time, indeed it would be to the extent that I am trying to respond in all possible manners: responding to your questions, while being responsible for an interview. To assume this responsibility, one must at least know for what, and for whom, an interview is intended, especially when someone also writes books, teaches, or publishes elsewhere, at another rhythm in other situations, calculating his sentences otherwise. An interview must provide a snapshot, like a film still, a freeze-frame: this is how such and such a person, on such and such a day, in such and such a place, with such and such interviewers struggled like an animal in a difficult situation. This interview, for example: they speak to this guy about actuality, about what happens in the world every day, and ask him to say a few words about what he thinks: and off he goes, drawing back into his lair like a hunted animal. He multiplies the twists and turns, draws you into a labyrinth of precautions, of delays and relays, repeats in every possible way "slow down, it's not so simple" (which always scares people or causes them to snicker: fools for whom

things are always simpler than we think), or "we may sometimes complicate in order to avoid, but simplification is in fact a far more reliable
strategy of avoidance." So you get a virtual photograph: in the face of a
question such as the one you just asked, that is my most likely gesture. It
is neither purely impulsive nor entirely calculated. It consists in not refusing to respond to a question (or to a person), and because of this in trying to respect, as much as possible, the indirect conditions or invisible detours of the question.

For example, you distinguished between the "philosopher of the
present" and the "philosopher who thinks his time." And according to
you, I would be more of the latter. This can be understood in several ways.
Such and such a philosopher may concern himself with the present, with
what actually arrives, without asking himself endlessly about what the
value of presence signifies, presupposes, or conceals. Is this a philosopher
of the present? Yes—but no. Another may do the opposite: immerse himself in a meditation about presence or the presentation of the present without paying the slightest attention to what is happening now in the world
or around him. Is this a philosopher of the present? No—but yes. But I
am sure that no philosopher worthy of the name will accept this alternative. Like anyone who tries to be a philosopher, I want to give up neither
the present nor thinking the presence of the present—nor the experience
of what conceals them from us by giving them to us. For example, in what
we were calling *artifactuality* a moment ago. How are we to approach this
theme of presence and present? Under what conditions are we to inquire
into this subject? What do these questions *engage*? And is this pledge [*gage*]
not the law that should govern everything, directly or indirectly? I try to
respond to it. By definition this law remains inaccessible; it lies beyond
everything.

But this is just another manner of evasion, you will say, another
manner of not speaking about what you have called the *present* or *actuality*. The first question, the one I would have sent back to you, like
an echo, would be this one: but what does it mean to speak of the present? Of course it would be easy to show that, in fact, I have only ever
been occupied with problems of actuality, of institutional politics, or
simply of politics. One could then multiply (please do not ask me to do
this myself) the examples, references, names, dates, places. But I do not
want to give in to this mediagogical facility and take advantage of this
tribunal to indulge in self-justification. I do not feel I have the right to

do this, and whatever I may do not to shirk my political responsibilities, it is not enough, and I will always reproach myself for not doing enough.

But I also try not to forget that it is often the untimely approaches to what is called *actuality* that are most "occupied" with the present. In other words, to be occupied with the present—as a philosopher, for example—is perhaps to avoid the constant confusion of the present with actuality. There is an anachronistic way of treating actuality that does not necessarily miss what is most present today. The difficulty, the risk or chance, the incalculable, might perhaps take the form of an untimeliness that comes on time: precisely this one and not another, the one that comes *just on time, just* because it is anachronistic and out of joint (like justice itself, which is always measureless, oblivious to what is appropriate [*justesse*] or to the adaptive norm, heterogeneous even to rights over which it should preside), more present than the present of actuality, more in tune with the singular measurelessness [*démesure*] that marks the irruption [*effraction*] of the other in the course of history. This irruption always takes an untimely, prophetic, or messianic form; for this it has no need for clamor or spectacle. It can stay almost unapparent. For the reasons we discussed a moment ago, it is not in the daily papers that one speaks the most about this more-than-present of today [*ce plus-que-présent de l'aujourd'hui*]. Which is also not to say that it happens every day in the monthlies or the weeklies.

The response, a response that is responsible to the urgency of actuality demands these precautions. It requires discord, the disaccord or discordance of this untimeliness, the right [*juste*] disadjustment of this anachrony. One must, at the same time, defer, keep a distance, linger *and* rush. This must be done properly [*il faut le faire comme il faut*] to get as close as possible to what is happening by way of actuality. At the same time, every time and each time is another time, the first and the last. In any case, I like the gestures (rare as they are, no doubt even impossible, and in any case nonprogrammable) that bring together in themselves the hyperactual with the anachronous. And to prefer the alliance or the alloy of these two styles is not only a matter of taste. It is the law of response or responsibility, the law of the other.

PASSAGES: What relation would you see between this anachrony or untimeliness and what you call *différance*?

J.D.: This would perhaps lead us back to a more philosophical order of response, the one with which we began when we were discussing the theme of the present or of presence, that is, also the theme of différance, which is often accused of encouraging delay, neutralization, suspension, and therefore of relaxing the urgency of the present, its ethical or political urgency in particular. But I have never perceived an opposition between urgency and différance. Would I dare to say *on the contrary?* But that would again be to simplify things. "At the same time" that différance marks a *relation* (a "férance")—a relation to what is other, to what differs in the sense of alterity, thus a relation to alterity, to the singularity of the other—it also relates, precisely because of this, to what comes, to what arrives in a way that is both inappropriable, unexpected, and thus urgent, unanticipatable: precipitation itself. The thinking of différance is also, therefore, a thinking of urgency, of what I can neither elude nor appropriate because it is other. The event, the singularity of the event—this is what différance is about. (This is why I said that it meant something quite different from the neutralization of the event in that it is artifactualized by the media.) This is true even if—"at the same time" (this "at once," this "same time" in which the same disagrees with itself all the time, a time that is "out of joint," disturbed, dislocated, deranged, disproportionate, as Hamlet says)—différance also, and inevitably, contains within itself an opposite movement to reappropriate, divert, relax, in an effort to dull the cruelty of the event, or simply the death toward which it is bound. So différance is a thinking that tries to respond to the imminence of what comes or will come, to the event, and therefore to experience itself, insofar as experience also inevitably tends "at the same time" in view of the "same time" to appropriate what arrives: the economy and aneconomy of the other, both at once. There would no différance without the urgency, the imminence, the precipitation, the inevitability, the unforeseeable coming of the other, toward whom reference and deference are directed [*se portent*].

PASSAGES: What does it mean, for you, to speak of the event in that connection?

J.D.: It is another name for that which, in what arrives, one can neither reduce nor deny (or only, if you prefer, what one cannot deny). It is another name for experience itself, which is always experience of the other. The event does not let itself be subsumed under any other concept, not even that of being. The "il y a" or the "let there be something rather than nothing" arises perhaps from the experience of the event, rather than from a thinking of being. The coming of the event is what cannot and should not be prevented; it is another name for the future itself. This does not mean that it is good—good in itself—for everything or anything to arrive; it is not that one should give up trying to prevent certain things from coming to pass (without which there would be no decision, no responsibility, ethics, or politics). But one should only ever oppose events that one thinks will block the future or that bring death with them: events that would put an end to the possibility of the event, to the affirmative opening to the coming of the other. Thus, the thinking of the event always opens a certain messianic space, however abstract, formal, and barren, however un-"religious" it may be; hence this messianic adherence cannot be separated from justice, which I distinguish from rights [droit] (as I proposed to do in "Force of Law" and *Specters of Marx*, where it is perhaps the primary affirmation). If the event is that which comes [vient], comes to pass [advient], or supervenes [survient], it is not enough to say that this *coming* "is" not, that it does not belong [revient] to some category of being. The noun (the coming [la venue]) and the nominalized verb (the coming [le venir]) do not exhaust the "come [viens]" from which they come. I have often tried to analyze this sort of performative apostrophe, this call that yields to the being of nothing-that-is. Addressed to the other, this call does not yet simply speak—the desire, the order, the prayer, or the demand— that it nonetheless announces and may subsequently make possible. One must think the event from the "come [viens]," and not the reverse. "Come" is said to the other, to others who are not yet defined as persons, subjects, or equals (at least in the sense of calculable equality). Only if there is this "come" can there be an experience of the coming, of the event, of what arrives and therefore of what, because it comes from the other, cannot be anticipated. And there is no horizon of expectation for this messianic prior to messianism. If there were a horizon of expectation, of anticipation, of programmation, there would be neither event nor history (a hypothesis that, paradoxically and for the same reasons, can never rationally be ruled out: it is almost impossible to think the absence of a horizon of expectation). For there to be an event and a history, a "come" must be open and addressed to someone, to someone else whom I cannot and must not determine in advance—not as subject, self, consciousness, or even as animal, God or person, man or woman, living or nonliving (one must be able to *call* a specter, to appeal to it, for example, and I do not think this is just one example among others; there may be something of the "revenant," of the "reviens" at the origin, or at the end, of every "viens"). The one, *who*ever it is to whom "come" is said, cannot let him/herself be determined in advance. For absolute hospitality, he/she is the stranger, the one who arrives. I must not ask the absolute arrival [*arrivant*] to begin by declining an identity, by telling me who he/she is, under what conditions I am to offer him/her hospitality, whether he/she is going to integrate him/herself or not, whether or not I will be able to "assimilate" him/her into the family, the nation, or the state. If he/she/it is an absolute arrival, I must not propose a contract or impose any conditions. I must not; and furthermore, by definition, I cannot. Hence, what looks like a morality of hospitality goes well beyond any morality, and certainly beyond any law or politics. Indeed, birth itself, which is similar to what I am trying to describe, is perhaps unequal to this absolute "arrivance." Families prepare for a birth; it is scheduled, forenamed, caught up in a symbolic space that dulls the arrivance. Nevertheless, in spite of these anticipations and prenominations, the uncertainty will not let itself be reduced: the child that arrives remains unpredictable; it speaks of itself as from the *origin* of another world, or from an-*other* origin of this world.

I have been struggling with this impossible concept of messianic arrivance for a long time now. I have tried to detail the protocol in my forthcoming book on death (*Aporias*) and in a little book on Marx that I have just finished. What is most difficult is to justify, at least provisionally, pedagogically, the attribute "messianic." What is at issue is an experience that is a priori messianic, but a priori exposed, in its very anticipation, to what can only be determined a posteriori by the event. A desert within a desert (one signaling to the other), the desert of a messianic without messianism, thus without doctrine and religious dogma, this desolate anticipation deprived of horizon, retains from the great messianisms of the Book only the relation to the arrivant who may arrive—or who may never arrive—but of whom, by definition, I can know nothing in advance. Except that *justice*, in the most enigmatic sense of the word, is involved. And thus also revolution, because of what links the event and justice to this absolute rift in the foreseeable concatenation of historical time. The rift of eschatology in teleology, which must be dissociated from it, and this is always difficult. It is possible to give up the imagery or the revolutionary rhetoric, or even certain politics of revolution, perhaps even the politics of revolution altogether, but one cannot give up on revolution without giving up both the event and justice.

The event cannot be reduced to the fact that something arrives. It may rain this evening, or it may not, but this will not be an absolute event because I know what rain is, at least insofar as, and to the extent that, I know; and what is more, it is not an absolutely other singularity. What arrives in such cases is not an arrivant.

The arrivant must be absolutely other, other than the one I expect not to expect, that I do not expect, an expectation constituted by nonexpectation, without what in philosophy is called a *horizon of expectation*, when a certain knowledge still anticipates and prepares in advance. If I am sure there will be an event [*qu'il y aura de l'événement*], it will not be an event. It will be someone with whom I have an appointment—perhaps Christ, perhaps a friend—but if I know he is coming, and if I am sure he will arrive, then at least to that extent it will not be an arrivant. But of course the arrival of someone I am expecting may also, in some other way, surprise me every time as an unheard-of chance, a chance that is always new and can thus happen to me [*m'arriver*] over and over again. Discreetly, in secret. And the arrivant can always not arrive, as with Elijah. It is within the ever-open hollow of this possibility, namely the possibility of a noncoming, of absolute disappointment [*déconvenue*], that I refer to the event: it is also what may always not take place.

PASSAGES: For there to be an event, then, one must be surprised?

J.D.: Exactly.

PASSAGES: To take a recent example, were you surprised by the sudden discovery of an agreement between the extreme right and the thinking of the left?

J.D.: Brutal return to a "question of actuality"! But you are quite right, in the light of what we have been saying, we must not elude the question. The "agreement" you mention is complicated, though perhaps less improbable than it might at first appear. One would have to proceed with great care, and this is difficult to do when improvising. One would need to take account of many features or givens (which "extreme right," which "thinking of the left," etc., what "agreement," who, where, and when, within what limits, etc.?). Before considering the singular and atypical gestures, which are always the most interesting and the most innovative, here as elsewhere, one would have to recall those links of general intelligibility, of programs or logics that are not surprising. This is not the first time that positions of the far right have succeeded, on certain issues, in allying themselves with positions of the far left. Though based on different motivations and analyses, a certain kind of opposition to Europe may encourage strategies of a nationalistic bent on both the left and the right. Given the worries that one may find legitimate concerning economism or simply the economic politics, indeed the monetary politics, or simply the politics in which the states dominating in Europe are engaged, some of the left may suddenly find themselves in positions of objective alliance with the nationalism or anti-Europeanism of the extreme right. At this moment, Le Pen is insisting on his opposition to "free trade [*libre-échangisme*]" or "economic libertarianism." This opportunistic rhetoric may turn him into the "objective ally," to use an old expression, of those on the left who, with different motives, criticize the capitalist and monetarist orthodoxy into which Europe is sinking. Only vigilance and clarity of action and thought can dissolve such amalgams, or resolve them through analysis. The risk is constant, more serious than ever, and sometimes "objectively" irreducible: in an election, for example. Even if one sharpens the distinctions and cleavages (as one must always try to do) in analyses, in reports, in everything that might resemble an "explanation of the vote," in the places of publication, demonstration, and action, in the end, on the occasion of a given electoral conjuncture (given by whom, how, exactly?), the anti-European votes of left and right add up. As do the pro-European votes of the right and the left.

In much the same way, as you know, there have been left-wing revisionisms (I will be specific, as one must always be: the negationist revisionisms concerning the Shoah) that have slipped into antisemitism (if, indeed, they were not inspired by it). Some of these grew more or less confusedly out of an anti-Israelism in principle or, more narrowly still, out of a rejection of the de facto politics of the state of Israel in the long run, indeed throughout the history of Israel. Would these confusions resist an honest and bold analysis? One must be able to oppose such and such a politics of such and such a government of the state of Israel without being in principle hostile to the existence of this state (I would even say: on the contrary!), and without antisemitism or anti-Zionism. I would even go further with another hypothesis: to go so far as to ask oneself uneasily about the historical foundation of the state, its conditions and what followed from it, this need not, even on the part of some Jews, were they to espouse the idea of Zionism, imply any betrayal of Judaism. The logic of opposition to the state of Israel or to its de facto politics does not necessarily imply any antisemitism, or even any anti-Zionism, or certainly any revisionism in the sense I spoke of earlier. There are some very great examples one could cite (such as Buber, speaking of the past). But, to go no further than principles and generalities, don't you think that our duty today demands that we denounce confusion and guard against it from *two sides? On the one side*, there is the nationalist confusion of those who slip from left to right and confound every European project with the *fact* of the actual politics of the European Community today, or the anti-Jewish confusion of those who cannot recognize any dividing line between criticizing the Israeli state and anti-Israelism, anti-Zionism, antisemitism, revisionism, etc. There are at least five possibilities here, and they must remain absolutely distinct. These metonymic slips are all the more serious politically, intellectually, and philosophically, in that they threaten from *both sides*, so to speak: those who yield to them in practice and those who, *on the other side*, denounce them while *symmetrically* adopting their logic, as if one could not do this without doing that—for example, oppose the actual politics of Europe without being anti-European in principle; or question the state of Israel, its political past or present, even the conditions of its foundation and what has followed from it for over the past half-century, without thereby being antisemitic, or even anti-Zionist, or indeed revisionist-negationist, etc. This *symmetry* between adversaries links obscurantist confusion to terrorism. It requires relentless determination and courage to resist these hidden (occulting, occultist) strategies of amalgamation. To stand up to this double operation of intimation, the only responsible response is never to relinquish distinctions and analyses. I will say: never to relinquish their Enlightenment, which is also to say, the *public* display of this discernment (and this is not as easy as one might think). This resistance is all the more urgent now that we are in a phase in which the critical reworking of the history of this century is facing a dangerous turbulence. We will have to reread, reinterpret, exhume archives, displace perspectives, etc. Where will we go if all political critique and any historical reinterpretation becomes automatically associated with negationist revisionism, if every question about the past or more generally about the constitution of truth in history is accused of paving the way for revisionism (in *Specters of Marx* I quote a particularly shocking example of this repressive stupidity in a leading American newspaper)? What a victory for dogmatism, if a prosecutor rises at every moment to accuse of complicity with the enemy anyone who tries to raise new questions, to disturb good consciences or stereotypes, to complicate or reelaborate, in a new situation, the discourse of the left or the analysis of racism or antisemitism. Of course, to guard against such trials, one must be doubly prudent in one's discourse, one's analysis, and one's public interventions. And it is true that no absolute assurance can ever be promised, let alone given. Recent examples might again serve as a lesson if this were necessary.

I return to the letter of your question: "were you surprised," you asked me, "by this agreement?" I have proposed only a general, theoretical response: these are the schemas of intelligibility, these are the programs that make the agreement less surprising than it might at first appear, but this is also why one must not confuse everything. As regards the particular cases, the most interesting ones, we would need more time and a different context to analyze them. This is where one finds "surprises" and contretemps. Between the most general logic (the greatest predictability) and the most unpredictable singularity, is the intermediate schema of *rhythm*. Since the 1950s, for example, what discredited and caused the totalitarianisms of Eastern Europe to collapse was well known; it was the daily bread for people of my generation (along with the old "Fukuyama" style of discourse that has been reworked today on the supposed "end of history," the "end of man," etc.). What remained unpredictable was the rhythm, the speed, the date: for example, that of the fall of the Berlin Wall. In 1986–87, no one *in the world* could have had even the vaguest idea of it. Not that the rhythm is unintelligible. It can be analyzed belatedly, taking into account new causalities that escaped earlier experts (in the first place, through the geopolitical effect of telecommunication in general: indeed, the entire sequence in which a signal such as the fall of the Berlin Wall is inscribed would be impossible and unintelligible without a certain density of the telecommunications network, etc.).

PASSAGES: To develop your point in a different direction: immigration is no higher now than it was half-a-century ago. Yet today it takes people by surprise. It seems to have surprised the social body and political class, and it seems that the discourses of both right and left, by refusing illegal immigrants [*immigrés clandestins*], have degenerated into xenophobia in an unexpected way.

J.D.: In this respect, at least in the *discourse* of the two so-called "republican majorities," the differences are mainly differences of emphasis. The overt political line is more or less the same. The common axiom, the consensus, as they say, is always: stop illegal immigration, no excessive, unproductive, disruptive hospitality. The implementation of this consensus is more serious today, the atmosphere has changed, and this is not a negligible difference. But the principles remain the same: the national community must be protected against what might affect its body *too much*, that is, affect the consciousness that the national community should have, so one thinks, of its bodily integrity (an axiom on the basis of which, let it be said in passing, one should ban all biological or cultural grafts, and this would extend very far—unless it leads nowhere, straight to death). When François Mitterand spoke of the threshold of tolerance (some of us reacted publicly to this formulation that escaped him and that he subsequently had the notable merit, courage, or cleverness to retract), this careless lapse spoke the truth about a discourse shared by the republican parties of the left and the right, and even the far right: there must be no arrivants in the sense we talked about earlier; arrival must be controlled, and we must filter the flow of immigration.

I realize, of course, that what I was saying earlier about the arrivant is politically unacceptable, at least so long as politics is modeled, as it always is, on the idea of the identity of a body proper that is called the *nation-state*. There does not exist a nation-state in the world today that as nation-state can find it acceptable to say: "we throw open our doors to everyone, we put no limit on immigration." To my knowledge—and I don't know if you can give me a counterexample—every nation-state is constituted by the control of its borders, by the rejection of illegal immigration, and by the setting of strict limits to the right to immigrate and the right of asylum. This concept of the border constitutes, precisely as its very limit, the concept of the nation-state.

Given this, the concept can be treated in different ways, but these different politics, however important they may be, remain secondary with regard to the general political principle, namely, that the political is national. It is then used to justify the filtering of passages and the banning of illegal immigration, even though one recognizes that this is, in fact, impossible, and indeed, under given economic conditions, undesirable (a supplementary hypocrisy).

What I have said about the absolute arrivant will not give rise to a *politics* in the traditional sense of the word: a politics that could be implemented by a nation-state. While I realize that what I said earlier about the event and the arrivant was, from the point of view of this concept of politics, an apolitical and irreceivable proposition, I nonetheless claim that a politics that does not maintain a reference to this principle of unconditional hospitality is a politics that loses its reference to justice. It may retain its rights (which I again distinguish here from justice), the right to its rights, but it loses justice. Along with the right to speak of justice in any credible way. We cannot discuss this here, but one would have to try to distinguish between a politics of immigration and the respect for the right of asylum. In principle, the right of asylum (such as it is in France for the time being, the right of asylum is recognized for political reasons) is paradoxically less political, because it is not modeled in principle on the interests of the body proper of the nation-state that guarantees this right. But, apart from the fact that it is difficult to distinguish between the concepts of immigration and asylum, it is almost impossible to delimit the properly political nature of the motivations for exile—those that under our constitution justify a request for asylum. After all, unemployment in a foreign country is a dysfunction of democracy and a kind of political persecution. Moreover, the market plays a part in this; the rich countries always share in the responsibility (if only through foreign debt and everything it symbolizes) for the politico-economic situations that push people into exile or emigration. And here we touch on the limits of the political and the juridical: one can always demonstrate that, as such, a right of asylum can be null or infinite. Thus this concept is always without rigor, but one only ever worries about this at moments of global turmoil. The concept needs to be re-elaborated from the ground up if one wants to understand or change something in the current debate (for example, between constitutionalism on the one hand, and neo-populism on the other—the neo-populism of those who, such as Charles Pasqua, want to change the constitution's article on the right of asylum to accommodate the presumed wishes of the "French people," a new or very ancient people that would suddenly no longer be the one to have voted its own constitution). But let me return to the specificity of your question. It seems, you were saying, that today's "social body and political class" have been taken by "surprise." By immigration or by xenophobia?

PASSAGES: Xenophobia.

J.D.: What the political class has been adjusting to—the political class that has been in power since 1981 and the one that succeeds it today—is not so much xenophobia itself as the new possibilities of exploiting it or taking advantage of it by taking advantage of the citizen. One fights over an electorate, basically that of "les sécuritaires [the security-minded]" (the way one speaks of "les sanitaires [the sanitation-minded]"—since what is at issue, we are told, is the salvation and health of a social body around which one needs to maintain a cordon, also referred to as a "cordon sanitaire"): the Front National, dominated by a quasi-biological image of the health of the nation's body (*quasi*-biological because the nationalist phantasm, as with its politicking rhetoric, often passes by way of these organicist analogies). Take, for example, parenthetically, the rhetoric of a recent intervention by Le Pen (*Le Monde*, 24 August 1993)—remarkable, as always, for its somnambulistic lucidity. Rather than the classic idea of the territorial border as being a line of defense, Le Pen henceforth prefers the figure (both timely and antiquated) of "a living membrane permeable to what is favorable, but not to what is not." If a living organism could calculate this filtration in advance, it might perhaps achieve immortality, but it would also have to die in advance, let itself be killed or kill itself in advance, for fear of being *altered* by what comes from the outside, by the other. Whence this theater of death with which many forms of racism, biologism, organicism, eugenics, and sometimes philosophies of life, so often agree. Before closing this parenthesis, let us return again to something that will please no one: whoever, whether on the left or on the right, and "like-everyone-else," advocates immigration control, excludes illegal immigration and claims to regulate legal immigration, subscribes, in fact and by right, whether he likes it or not—and with more or less elegance or distinction—to Le Pen's organicist axiom, which is none other than that of a national front (the front is a skin, a selective "membrane": it only lets in what is homogeneous or homogenizable, what is assimilable or at the very most what is heterogeneous but presumed "favorable": the appropriable immigrant, the proper immigrant). We must not close our eyes to this inevitable complicity: it is rooted in the political insofar as the political is, and will be, linked to the nation-state. And whenever we are forced to recognize, as with everyone else, that we cannot do otherwise but protect what we take to be our own body, when we want to control immigration and asylum (as is said unanimously on the left and the right), let us at least not give ourselves airs and start lecturing on politics with a clear conscience and high-sounding principles. Just as Le Pen will always have the greatest difficulty justifying or regulating the filtration of his "membrane," so there is a permeability between these supposedly opposite concepts and logics that is more difficult to control than one thinks or often says: today there exists a neo-protectionism of the left and a neo-protectionism of the right, both in economics and in matters of demographic flow; there exist proponents of free trade on the right and proponents of free trade on the left; there is a right-wing neo-nationalism and a left-wing neo-nationalism. All these "neo-" logics also pass through the protective membrane of their concepts without any possibility of mastery, and they create an obscure alliance in the discourse and in political or electoral acts. To recognize this permeability, this configuration, and these complicities is not to maintain an apolitical discourse, nor is it to reach the end of the cleavage between right and left, or, the "end of ideology." On the contrary, it is to appeal to a formalization and bold thematization of this terrible configuration, the requisite preliminaries for another politics, another discourse on politics, another definition of the *socius*, especially in its relation to citizenship and state-nationality in general, but more broadly to identity and subjectivity. How are we supposed to discuss all this in an interview and in parentheses? And yet, as you know, these problems are anything but abstract or speculative today. Thus, let me return to France, where the changeover of political power is determined by one or two percent of the vote in presidential elections, by ten to fifteen percent in the rest. So the question, we were saying, is to know how to attract, motivate, and seduce (to worry and reassure at the same time) a fraction of the potential xenophobes who vote for the Front National.

This points to other questions: why is the Front National able to exploit this fear or exacerbate this impatience? Why is it that, instead of doing what should be done (education, the implementation of socio-economic policies, etc.) to defuse this feeling, one tries either to appropriate the positions of the Front National or to exploit the division that the Front National introduces into the so-called "republican right"? All of this, yes, while the level of immigration has, as you noted, remained very stable: indeed, it would seem that it has not changed for decades, though it may not have decreased. So, is this a surprise or not? Analysis always tends to dissolve surprise. It was to be expected, one says in retrospect when one discovers the element that escaped analysis, or when one analyzes differently (the rise of unemployment, the increasing permeability of European borders, the return of religion and claims to identity—religious, linguistic, cultural—among the immigrants themselves, all of which makes the unchanging rate of immigration seem more threatening to the self-identification of the host social body).

But an event that remains an event is an arrival, an arrivance: it surprises and belatedly resists analysis. With the birth of a child—the first figure of the absolute arrivant—one can analyze the causalities, the genealogical, genetic, and symbolic premises, or the wedding preparations. But even if such an analysis could ever be completed, one could never reduce the element of chance [aléa], the place of the taking-place; there will be someone who speaks, someone irreplaceable, an absolute initiative, another origin of the world. Even if this initiative dissolves in analysis or returns to ashes, it remains an absolute bit of grit [escarbille]. The immigration in which the history of France is rooted, its culture, its religions, and its languages, was first the history of all the children, whether or not they were the children of immigrants, who were such absolute arrivants. The task of a philosopher—and therefore of anyone, and of a citizen, for example—is to take the analysis as far as possible to try to make the event intelligible up to the moment when one comes to the arrivant. What is absolutely new is not this, rather than that; it is the fact that it arrives only once. It is what is marked by a date (a unique moment and place), and it is always a birth or a death that a date dates. Even if one could predict the fall of the Berlin Wall, it happened one day, there were still deaths (before and during the collapse), and this is what makes it an indelible event. What resists analysis is birth and death: always the origin and the end of a world . . .

PASSAGES: Can what resists the analysis of the event be called *undeconstructible*? Is there such a thing as the undeconstructible, and in what would it consist?

J.D.: The undeconstructible, if there is such a thing, is justice. Law [le droit] is, fortunately, deconstructible: it is infinitely perfectible. I would be tempted to see *justice* as the best term, today, for what will not let itself be deconstructed, that is, for that which gives deconstruction its movement, for what justifies it. It is the affirmative experience of the coming of the other as other: it is better for this to arrive than the contrary (the experience of the event that will not let itself simply be translated into an ontology: that something should be, that there should be being rather than nothing). The openness of the future is worth more; that is the axiom of deconstruction, that on the basis of which it has always set itself in motion and which links it, as with the future itself, to otherness, to the priceless dignity of otherness, that is to say, to justice. It is also democracy as the democracy-to-come.

One can imagine the objection. Someone might say to you: "sometimes it is better for this or that not to arrive. Justice demands that one prevent certain events (certain 'arrivants') from arriving. The event is not good in itself, and the future is not unconditionally preferable." Certainly, but one can always show that what one is opposing, when one conditionally prefers that this or that not happen, is something one takes, rightly or wrongly, as blocking the horizon or simply forming the *horizon* (the word that means *limit*) for the absolute coming of the altogether other, for the future itself. This involves a messianic structure (if not a messianism—in my little book on Marx, I also distinguish between the messianic as a universal dimension of experience and all specific messianisms) that indissociably joins the promise of the arrivant, the unexpected of the future and justice. I cannot reconstruct this demonstration here, and I realize that the word *justice* may seem equivocal. Justice is not the same as rights; it exceeds and founds the rights of man; nor is it distributive justice. It is not even, in the traditional sense of the word, *respect* for the other as a human subject. It is the experience of the other as other, the fact that I let the other be other, which presupposes a gift without restitution, without reappropriation and without jurisdiction. Here I cut across the legacies of several different traditions, displacing them a little, as I have tried to do elsewhere[1]: the tradition of Levinas, when he simply defines the relation to the other as justice ("the relation with the Other—that is, justice"[2]); and the tradition that emphasizes, by way of a paradoxical thinking whose formulation is first Plotinian, then Heideggerian, and then Lacanian: giving not only what one has but what one doesn't have. This excess overflows the present, property, restitution, and no doubt law, morality, and politics, even though it should draw them in [*aspirer*] or inspire [*inspirer*] them.

PASSAGES: But doesn't philosophy also struggle at the same time with the idea that something, possibly the worst, could always return?

J.D.: Yes, it "struggles," precisely [*justement*] with this return of the worst, and in more ways than one. In the first place, everything that may have heralded a philosophy of Enlightenment or inherited something from it (not only rationalism, which is not necessarily associated with it, but a progressive, teleological, humanistic, and critical rationalism) indeed struggles against a "return of the worst," which both education and an awareness of the past are always supposed to be able to prevent. Although this Enlightenment struggle often takes the form of deterrence and denial, one cannot help but take part in it and reaffirm this philosophy of emancipation. As for myself, I believe in its future, and I have never found myself in agreement with proclamations about the end of the great discourses of emancipation or revolution. But their affirmation itself attests to the possibility of what it is opposed to: the return of the worst, an uneducable repetition-compulsion in the death drive and radical evil, a history without progression, a history without history, etc. And the Enlightenment of our time cannot be reduced to that of the eighteenth century. And then there is another way, more radical still, for philosophy to "struggle" with the return of the worst. It consists in misrecognizing (denying, exorcizing, conjuring away, many modes that require analysis) what this recurrence of evil is made of: a law of the spectral that resists both ontology (the ghost or the revenant is neither present nor absent, it neither is nor is not, nor can it be dialecticized) and a philosophy of the subject, of the object, or of consciousness (of being-present) that, as with ontology or philosophy itself, is meant to "dispel" specters. Thus it also consists in not hearing some of the lessons of psychoanalysis about ghosts or about the repetition of the worst that threatens any historical progress (to which I would add, all too quickly, that it only threatens, on the one hand, a certain concept of progress and that there would be no progress in general without this threat and, on the other hand, that what has dominated psychoanalytic discourse up until now, beginning with Freud's own discourse, is a certain misrecognition of the structure of spectral "logics," a powerful, subtle, unstable misrecognition, but one that psychoanalysis shares with science and philosophy). Yes, a ghost can return as the worst, but without this revenance, and if one challenges its irreducible originality, one is also depriving oneself of memory, legacy, and justice, of everything that matters beyond life, and with which one measures the dignity of life. I have suggested this elsewhere, and it is hard for me to schematize here. But I suppose that when you mentioned the "return of the worst" you were thinking, more closely to us, of what took place in Europe before the war?

PASSAGES: Yes.

J.D.: And not only in Europe, let us not forget. In this context, each country has its own original history and its own economy of memory. My immediate feeling is that what took place in France well before and during World War II—and still more, I would say, during the Algerian War—has reinforced, and therefore overdetermined, the layers of forgetting. This capitalization of silence is especially compact, resistant, and dangerous. In a way that is slow, discontinuous, and contradictory, this pact of secrecy is yielding to a movement of liberation of memory (especially of public memory, if one can say this, and its official legitimation, which never proceeds at the rhythm of either historical knowledge or private memory, if there is such a thing and if it is pure). But if this unsealing is contradictory, in both its effects and its motivations, it is precisely because of the ghost. The moment one remembers the worst (out of respect for memory, the truth, the victims, etc.), the worst threatens to return. One ghost recalls another. And it is often because one sees signs of the resurgence of the one, its quasi-resurrection, that one appeals to the other. One recalls how urgent it is to officially commemorate the roundup of Jews at the Vélodrome d'Hiver or to recognize the responsibility of the French state for some of the "worst" that took place under the occupation, at a moment when (and because) there are signs that point to the return—in a completely different context, sometimes with the same face, sometimes with different features—of nationalism, racism, xenophobia, antisemitism. The two memories relaunch each other [*se renflouent*]; they exacerbate and avert each other; they wage war on each other, necessarily, over and over again. Always on the brink of all possible contaminations. When the abhorrent ghosts return, we recall the ghosts of their victims to preserve their memory but also, inescapably, for the sake of the current struggle, and in the first place for the promise that mobilizes this struggle, for the future without which it would have no meaning—to the future, that is, beyond any present life, beyond every living being who can say, "Now, me." The question of the ghost is also the question of the future as a question of justice. This double return encourages the irrepressible tendency to confuse. One confuses the analogous with the identical: "exactly the same thing is happening again, exactly the same thing." No: a certain iterability (difference within repetition) allows for what returns to be another event entirely. The return of a ghost is another return, every time, on another stage, under new conditions to which one must pay the greatest attention if one does not want to say or do just anything.

Yesterday, a German woman, a journalist, telephoned me (about the "appeal" from European intellectuals to "vigilance" that I felt I had to sign with others and about which there would be so much to say—but we do not have the time to discuss it seriously here). Noting that many German intellectuals welcomed this gesture and judged it opportune, for obvious reasons, especially in the current situation in Germany, she was wondering whether this was a return to the tradition of "J'accuse!" Where is Zola today? she wanted to know. I tried to explain to her why, in spite of my enormous respect for Zola, I was not sure that he was the only, or the best, model for a "J'accuse!" Everything has changed: the public space, the trajectories of information and decision-making, the relation of power to the secret, the figures of the intellectual, the writer, the journalist, etc. It is not "J'accuse!" that is out of date, but the form and space of its inscription. One must of course remember the Dreyfus affair, but one must also know that it cannot be repeated as such. There could be worse, this can never be excluded, but it will certainly not be the same Dreyfus affair.

Thus, to think (but what does "thinking" mean then?) what you were calling the "return of the worst," one would have to inquire—beyond ontology, beyond a philosophy of life or death, beyond a logic of the conscious subject—into the relations between politics, history, and the revenant.

PASSAGES: You discussed this in *Of Spirit: Heidegger and the Question?*

J.D.: From the very first sentence, in fact, that book moved toward a disruptive logic of spirit as specter. The "thing" is treated differently, but I hope somewhat consistently, in the book I am publishing on Marx. This book is no more spiritualist than the one on Heidegger was anti-spiritualist, but it is true that the necessity of a paradoxical strategy pushes me, at least in appearance, to distrust a certain kind of spirit in Heidegger and to plead *for* spirit, a certain spirit, one of the spirits or specters, in Marx.

PASSAGES: You lectured on Marx in a course at the Ecole Normale Supérieure in the 1970s, through allusions.

J.D.: They were more than allusions, forgive me for pointing it out, and it was in more than one seminar. Beyond the references, this little book tries to explain the situation, the relative silence, the difficult but, in my opinion, intimate connections between deconstruction and a certain "spirit" of Marxism.

PASSAGES: What has led you to speak about Marx today?

J.D.: I am going to have trouble saying it in a few improvised words. The little book on Marx began as a lecture delivered in the United States in April, at the opening of a conference entitled "Whither Marxism?" ("where is Marxism going?" but also, through a play on words, whether Marxism was in the process of "withering away"). In it, I indeed sketched out an approach to Marx's text, to everything in it that can be determined by the problematic of the specter (namely exchange value, fetishism, ideology, as well as many other things). But I also tried to mark, in a gesture that was first political, as I think it must be done today, a point of resistance to a dogmatic consensus about the death of Marx, the end of the critique of capitalism, the final triumph of the market and to what would always link democracy to a logic of economic liberalism, etc. I tried to show where, and how, this consensus has become dominant, and often obscene in its euphoria, both troubled and grimacing, triumphant and manic at the same time. I am deliberately using the language of Freud when he describes one of the phases in the work of mourning. My essay on specters is also an essay on mourning and politics. Don't you think it's urgent to rise up against a new anti-Marxist dogma? I find it not only regressive and pre-critical in most of its manifestations but also blind to its own contradictions, deaf to the creaks of ruin, of the ruinous and ruined structure of its own "rationality," this new "colossus with feet of clay." It is, I would say, all the more urgent to fight this dogmatism and this politics that this urgency itself seems to come at an inopportune moment [*à contretemps*]. Another theme of the essay is the contretemps in politics, anachrony, untimeliness, etc. Obviously this is connected with what we were saying earlier about the messianic and the event, about justice and revolution.

The responsibility to rise up belongs to everyone, but especially to those who, without ever having been anti-Marxist or anti-Communist, have nonetheless always resisted a certain kind of Marxist orthodoxy for as long as (and this was a long time for the intellectuals of my generation) it remained hegemonic, at least in certain circles. But apart from this taking-of-sides [*prise de parti*], and also to support it, I set up a discussion of Marx's writings. The discussion is organized around the question of the specter (in connection with those of repetition, mourning, legacy, the event, and the messianic—everything that exceeds the ontological oppositions between absence and presence, visible and invisible, living and dead—and thus, above all, with the prosthesis as "phantom limb," with technology, with the teletechnological simulacrum, with the synthetic image, with virtual space, etc. And here we find the themes that we discussed earlier, *artifactuality* and *virtuactuality*). Remember the opening sentence of the *Communist Manifesto*: "a specter is haunting Europe, the specter of Communism." So I investigate, I look into all the specters that literally obsess Marx. Indeed one finds a persecution *of* Marx. He follows them everywhere; he chases them away, but they also pursue him: in the *18th Brumaire*, in *Capital*, but above all in the *German Ideology*, where, as you know, he sets out an interminable critique—interminable because fascinated, captivated, enthralled—of Stirner's hauntings, a hallucination that is already critical, and that Marx found extremely difficult to shake.

I try to decipher the logic of the specter in Marx's work. I propose to do this in the face, if one can say this, of what is taking place in the world today, in a new public space that has been transformed by what is quickly called the "return of the religious" as well as by teletechnologies. What is the work of mourning in terms of Marxism? What does it want to ward off [*conjurer*]? The word and concept of *conjuration*, highly ambiguous (at least in French, English, and German), play as important a role in this essay as does that of legacy. To inherit is not essentially *to receive* something, a *given* that one could then *have*. It is an active affirmation; it responds to an injunction, but it also presupposes an initiative, the signature, or countersignature of a critical selection. To inherit is to select, to sort, to highlight, to reactivate. I also think, although I cannot argue it here, that every assignation of legacy harbors a contradiction and a secret (like the red thread of the book that binds the genius of Marx to that of Shakespeare—whom Marx loved so much and often cites, especially from *Timon of Athens* and *Much Ado About Nothing*—and to Hamlet's father, who is perhaps the main character in the essay).

Hypothesis: there is always more than one spirit. When one speaks of spirit one immediately evokes spirits, specters; and whoever inherits chooses one spirit rather than another. One makes selections, one filters, one sifts through the ghosts or through the injunctions of each spirit. There is legacy only where assignations are multiple and contradictory, secret enough to defy interpretation, to carry the unlimited risk of active interpretation. It is here that a decision and a responsibility can be taken. Without *double bind*, there is no responsibility. A legacy must retain an undecidable reserve.

If to inherit is to reaffirm an injunction, not only a possession [*avoir*] but also an assignation to be decoded, then we are only what we inherit. Our being is an inheritance, the language we speak is an inheritance. Hölderlin more or less says that language has been given us so that we may testify to what we inherit. Not the inheritance we have or receive, but the one that we are, through and through. What we are, we inherit. And we inherit the language that serves to testify to the fact that we are what we inherit. A paradoxical circle within which one must struggle and decide [*trancher*], by means of decisions that both inherit and invent— necessarily without any set norm or program—one's own norms. Thus, to say that a legacy is not an asset one acquires, to say that we are heirs through and through, is not to imply anything traditionalist or backward. We are, among other things, heirs of Marx and Marxism. I try to explain why this involves an event that no one and nothing can erase, not even— especially not—the totalitarian monstrosity (the totalitarianisms—there was more than one—that were closely linked to Marxism and that one cannot simply interpret as perversions or distortions of an inheritance). Even people who have never read Marx, who do not even know his name, even the anti-Communists or the anti-Marxists, are Marx's heirs. And one cannot inherit from Marx without inheriting from Shakespeare, from the Bible, and from a lot of other things as well.

PASSAGES: To continue on this point: would you be surprised if there were some kind of return—in a different form and with different applications—of Communism, even if it is called something else? And if what brought it back were a need within society for the return of a little hope?

J.D.: This is what we were calling *justice* earlier. I do not believe there will be a return of Communism in the form of the Party (the party form is no doubt disappearing from political life in general, a "survivance" that may of course turn out to have a long life) or in the return of everything that deterred us from a certain kind of Marxism and a certain kind of Communism. I hope it won't come back: it would be very unlikely, but we must remain vigilant. What is bound to return, on the other hand, is an insurrection in the name of justice that will again give rise to critiques that are Marxist in *inspiration*, in *spirit*. There are signs of this. It is like a new International, without party or organization or association; it searches for itself, it suffers, it thinks that something is wrong, it does not accept the new "world order" that one wants to impose, it finds the discourse that this new order inspires sinister. What this insurrectional distress will rediscover in the Marxist inspiration are forces for which we do not have any name. Although in some respects this new International sometimes resembles the elements of a *critique*, I try to explain why it is not, and should not be, only a critique, a method, a theory, a philosophy or an ontology. It would take an entirely different form and perhaps require that Marx be read in a different way entirely. However, it is not a matter of *reading* in the philological or academic sense of the word; it is not a matter of rehabilitating a Marxist canon. There is a certain tendency, a certain tendency that I take issue with in this essay, that might in fact be neutralizing Marx slowly in another way: now that Marxism is dead and its apparatuses disabled, one might say, we can at last settle down to read *Capital* and read Marx calmly, theoretically; we will be able to give him the recognition he deserves as a great philosopher whose writings belong (in their "internal intelligibility," as Michel Henry puts it) to the great ontological tradition. No, I try to explain why we should not be satisfied with such an untroubled rereading.

PASSAGES: You have always claimed that the experience of deconstruction entailed an ethical-political responsibility. How is this different from the old slogan of the "committed intellectual"?

J.D.: I feel neither inclined nor entitled to disparage what you call the "old slogan" of the intellectual engagements of the past. Especially in France. Voltaire, Hugo, Zola, and Sartre remain admirable examples in my eyes. An example inspires us; it often remains inaccessible, and one must certainly not imitate it in a situation that is structurally different, as we were saying a moment ago. Given this precaution, it seems to me, very roughly, that these courageous engagements precisely assumed two identifiable partners and a face-to-face of sorts: on the one hand, a given socio-political field, on the other an intellectual with his discourse, his rhetoric, his literary work, his philosophy, etc., who comes "to intervene" or *to commit himself* to a field in order to take a side or a position. The moment he does this, he is questioning himself and he no longer tries to change either the structure of his public space (press, media, modes of representation, etc.) or the nature of his language, the philosophical or theoretical axioms of his own intervention. In other words, he commits his culture and his authority *as a writer* (the very French examples I cited earlier were popular more for their literary than for their philosophical works); it puts them in the service of a political cause, a legal cause, and often beyond legality, a just cause. I am not saying that Hugo or Sartre never questioned or transformed the form of the engagement that was available to them. I am only saying that it was not a constant theme or a major concern of theirs. They did not think, as Benjamin suggested, they needed to begin by analyzing and transforming the apparatus; they simply began by supplying it with a content, however revolutionary this content might be. The apparatus in question involves not only technical or political powers, procedures of editorial or media appropriation, the structure of a public space (and thus of the supposed addressees one is addressing or whom one should be addressing); it also involves a logic, a rhetoric, an experience of language, and all the sedimentation this presupposes. To ask oneself these questions, even questions about the questions that have been impressed on us or taught to us as being the "right" questions to ask; even to ask oneself about the *question-form* of critique, not only questioning but thinking about the stakes [*le gage*] in which a question is engaged—this is perhaps a responsibility that is prior, as with a condition, to the responsibility that is called *commitment*. It is insufficient by itself, but neither has it ever impeded or delayed commitment, on the contrary.

PASSAGES: We would like, if we may, to ask you a rather more personal question. There is something that is returning in parts of the world today, in Algeria in particular along with its more religious aspects. Politicians, even intellectuals, have a way of talking about Algeria, which consists in saying that it has never really had an identity, unlike Morocco or Tunisia, and that the death and destruction that are taking place there now are due to this lack of identity, to the fact that Algeria is missing something. Beyond the emotional significance of this, how do you see what's happening in Algeria?

J.D.: You said it was a personal question. I wouldn't dare compare my own suffering or my distress to that of so many Algerians, whether in Algeria or France. I do not know how I might have the right to say that Algeria is still my country. What I can say is that for the first nineteen years of my life I never left Algeria, that I returned regularly and that something in me never left at all. It is true that the unity of Algeria seems threatened today. What is happening there closely resembles a civil war. The news media in France are only now beginning to realize what has been going on in Algeria for years: preparations for seizing power, assassinations, guerrilla groups, and in response, repression, torture, concentration camps. As in all tragedies, the crimes are not all on one side, or even on two sides. The FIS [Islamic Salvation Front] and the state would not have been able to confront and revitalize each other according to the classic cycle (terrorism/repression; the social and popular penetration of a movement that has been driven underground by a state that is both too powerful and powerless; the impossibility of pursuing democratization once it has begun, etc.), there would not be this infernal head-to-head, which has already claimed so many innocent victims, were there not an elementary and anonymous third term, by which I mean the country's economic and demographic situation, its unemployment and the development strategy it adopted long ago. All this furthers the duel that I have perhaps mistakenly made symmetrical (some of my Algerian friends contest this symmetrization; they see the violence of the state's response and the suspension of the electoral process as the only possible reply to a well-prepared, long-standing strategy of takeover, which was hostile to democracy itself; one can understand them, but it will be necessary to invent some mode of consultation or exchange that will stop the gunfire and restart the interrupted electoral process). If we consider this nameless third partner, then the responsibility goes back further still and it is not simply Algero-Algerian. I remind you here of what we were saying earlier about the emblematic foreign debt. It weighs heavily on the country. I mention it not to level accusations but to mark our responsibility. While respecting what is primarily a matter for the citizens of Algeria themselves, we are all concerned and accountable, especially those of us who are French, for obvious reasons. We cannot remain indifferent, particularly to the fate and the efforts of all those Algerians who are trying not to yield to fanaticism and intimidation. You know that they risk their lives (the victims of recent assassinations have often been intellectuals, journalists, and writers—which should not make us forget the many other unknown victims; it is in this spirit that some of us have come together, on the initiative of Pierre Bourdieu, to form the International Committee in Support of Algerian Intellectuals (CISIA), some of whose founding members, it must be said, have already received death threats).

You said that, in the eyes of some, the identity of Algeria is not only problematic or threatened but that it has never, in fact, existed in an organic, natural, or political manner. There are several ways of understanding this. One way would be to invoke the fractures and partitions of Arab-Berber Algeria, the divisions between languages, ethnic groups, religious and military powers, and perhaps conclude that basically it was colonization that, in this as in many cases, created the unity of a nation-state and that once independence was formally acquired, it struggled within structures partly inherited from colonization. Without engaging in a long historical analysis here, I would say that this is true and false. It is certainly true that Algeria as such did not exist before colonization, with its present borders and in the form of a nation-state. But that in itself does not render contestable the unity constituted by, against, and through colonization. All nation-states have a laborious, contradictory, complicated history of decolonization-recolonization. They all have violent origins, and because they constitute themselves by founding their right [*droit*], they cannot found these rights on any prior right, whatever they may claim or teach (themselves) on this subject thereafter. One cannot contest a unity under the pretext that it is the effect of a unification. Successful unifications or foundations only ever succeed in making one forget that there never was a natural unity or a prior foundation. The unity of the Italian state, also very recent, is indeed experiencing some turbulence at the moment. But is one therefore justified (as some are certainly tempted to do— from motives that are not only those of the historian) in challenging its unity on the grounds that it was founded recently and remains, as with all nation-states, an artifact? There is no natural unity, only processes of unification that are relatively stable, sometimes firmly stabilized over a long period of time. But all these state stabilities, these statics [*statiques*], are only stabilizations. Israel would be another example of a state that was founded recently and, as with all states, founded on violence, a violence that can only try to justify itself belatedly, provided a national and international stabilization covers it up in an always-precarious oblivion. This is not the situation today. These are seismic times for all nation-states and therefore more auspicious for this kind of reflection. Which is also a reflection on what may (or may not) link the idea of democracy to citizenship and nationality.

The unity of Algeria is certainly in danger of dislocation, but the forces that are tearing it apart do not, as is often said, oppose East and West, or, as with two homogenous blocks, Islam and democracy. They oppose different models of democracy, representation, or citizenship—and, above all, different interpretations of Islam. One of our responsibilities is also to be attentive to this multiplicity and to demand constantly that not everything be confused.

Taking Sides for Algeria

It has been recommended that we be brief: I will be brief. When I ask, as I am going to, in whose name, and in the name of what, we are speaking, it is only because I would like several questions to be heard, without contesting or provoking anyone.

In whose name, and in the name of what, are we assembled here? And whom are we addressing?

These are not abstract questions, I insist on this—and I insist that they engage no one first of all but me.

For several reasons. Out of shyness or modesty *at first*, of course, and out of concern for what an Appeal such as ours may contain both of strength and of weakness. As generous or just as it may be, an Appeal, especially when it sounds forth from here, from this Parisian amphitheater, that is, for certain of us here, not for all of us, precisely, but for many of us, when it is thus launched from afar, such an Appeal, as legitimate and as inspired as it may be, I always fear that it still contains, in its very eloquence, too much authority, and I fear that it also defines a place of arbitration (indeed there is one in our Appeal: I will say a word about this later). In its apparent, arbitral neutrality, such an Appeal risks containing a lesson, an implicit lesson, whether it be a lesson learned or, worse, a lesson given. It is better thus to say it, it is better not to hide it. Modesty is especially *de rigueur* when one risks measuring a few words against a real tragedy, *two features* of which the Appeal of CISIA and La Ligue des Droits de l'Homme rightly underline:

1. The entanglement (the very long history of the premises, the "origins" and the "developments" that led to what looks like an appalling impasse and the untangleable sharing of responsibility in this regard, in and outside Algeria), which also tells us that the time of transformation and the coming of this democracy, the response to this "Algerian democratic exigency" at issue at several points in the Appeal, the time *for* democracy will be long, discontinuous, difficult to collect in the act of a single decision, in a "coup de théâtre" that would come in response to the Appeal. It would be irresponsible to believe or to make believe the contrary. This long time *for* democracy, it cannot even be brought together in Algeria. Things will *also* have to take place *elsewhere*. To recall this seriously is not to deprive the Algerians of their autonomy. Even if we were to doubt this and even if we were to continue dreaming of this "coup de théâtre," the date of our encounter here would be enough to recall it to us. We are in effect in the aftermath of the so-called conference of reconciliation, that is, of a failure or simulacrum, of a disaster in any case so sadly predictable, if not calculated, one that outlines, in the negative, the dream of the impossible that we can neither give up nor believe in.

2. Our Appeal also brings out that in such an entangled situation, the diversity of points of view and analyses is "legitimate." And how true this is! But at this point the Appeal prudently stops and returns to what it defines as a possible "agreement" on "several points of principle." Yet no one is trying to conceal the fact—no one even among the first signatories of the Appeal (of which I am one)—that the "diversity of analyses and points of view," if it is held to be legitimate, may lead some to disagree on the "several points of principle" in question (for example, on what is registered under the three words or major themes of the Appeal, that of *violence* [all violence is condemned: yet what is violence, the armed violence that is the most general concept in the Appeal? Does it cover *every* police operation, even when the latter claims to protect the security of its citizens, and to ensure or claim to ensure the legal and normal functioning of a democratic society, etc.?]; of *civil* peace [What about the civil in general? What is the civil? What does "civil" mean today? etc.]; and especially the idea of *democracy* [which democracy?]).

Finally, these few words engage no one but me, for if I have endorsed and even participated in the preparation of the *Appeal for Civil Peace in Algeria*, if I therefore approve of all its terms (which seem to me both prudent and exigent), I am not certain in advance that, in what concerns the implications or the consequences of this Appeal, my interpretation is at all points the same as that of all its signatories.

I will thus attempt to tell you briefly how I understand certain decisive passages of the Appeal. I will do it in a dry and analytic fashion to save time but also to not yield to a temptation I feel and that some might judge to be sentimental: the temptation to turn the demonstration into a heartfelt or pathos-ridden testimony and to explain how what I am going to say is inspired, above all and after all, by a painful love for Algeria, an Algeria where I was born and that I left only for the first time, literally, at age nineteen before the War of Independence, an Algeria to which I have often returned and that deep down I know I have never really left and that I still carry in what is most profound in me: a love for Algeria which, though it is not the love of a citizen, precisely, and thus the patriotic attachment to a nation-state, is nonetheless what makes indissociable for me heart, thought, and the political taking of sides—and thus dictates everything that I will venture to say in a few words. It is precisely on this basis that I ask in the name of what and whom, if one is not an Algerian citizen, one associates oneself and subscribes to this Appeal.

With this question in mind, I would like to demonstrate telegraphically in four points why our Appeal cannot be held to some commendable *neutrality* in the face of what must, in fact, first of all be the responsibility of the Algerians themselves. "Not to be held to political neutrality," thus, not that one must choose a camp—we exclude this, I believe—from between *two* sides of a front that define, according to the greater part of public opinion, the fundamental given of the actual confrontation. On the contrary, it seems to me, political responsibility consists today in not accepting this given as a natural and immovable fact. It consists in demonstrating, by saying it and by putting it into practice, that such is not the case and that the recourse to democracy has its place and its forces and its life and its people elsewhere.

But to say this is not to be politically neutral, on the contrary. It is to take sides *four times*. It is to take sides
   1. for a new international solidarity
   2. for an electoral contract
   3. for a dissociation of the theological and the political
   4. for what I will call, more or less properly, a *new Third State*

We are for a new international solidarity

The Appeal says that the solutions belong to the Algerians alone, an assertion that is correct in its principle, but the Appeal adds at several points that these solutions cannot arise from "the isolation of the country." This reminds us of what must be made explicit for this consequence to be drawn: political solutions no longer have to do with the citizens of a given nation-state in the last instance. Today, as for what was and remains, up until a certain point, a just imperative, namely the noninterference and respect for self-determination (the future of Algerian men and women belongs, of course, as a last resort, to the Algerian people), a certain manner of saying this, or of understanding this, risks henceforth being at best the rhetorical concession of a bad conscience and at worst an alibi. Not that one must reconstitute a right to intervention or intrusion that would be conferred on other states or on the citizens of other states *as such*. This would in effect be inadmissible. But one must nonetheless reaffirm the internationality of the stakes and of certain solidarities that bind us all the more that they do not merely bind in us the citizens of definite nation-states. This certainly complicates matters, but it marks out for us the true place of our responsibility, a responsibility which is neither simply that of Algerian citizens nor that of French citizens; this is why my question, and the question of the signatory of the Appeal that I am, emerges neither from an Algerian nor from a Frenchman as such, which does not in the least release me, *on the other hand*, from my civil responsibilities—or more than civil—my responsibilities as a French citizen born in Algeria, but forces me to do what must be done according to this logic in my country, in the direction of public opinion and the French authorities (as we are trying to do here; we have talked and will continue to talk about everything that remains to be done in this regard). For example (and this will be my only example, for lack of time), the logic of the Appeal leads us to take a position, indeed this position is indispensable, on Algeria's external debt and what is bound up with it. At issue here is an area that is also, as we know too well (unemployment, distress, catastrophic impoverishment), an essential component of the civil war and all of the sufferings today. Yet we cannot seriously take a position on the economic recovery of Algeria without analyzing the national and international responsibilities in this situation and without being able to indicate levers of politico-economic intervention that are no longer in Algeria and not even only in France. It is a matter here of European and world stakes; those who, as we do, appeal to such international initiatives and to what the Appeal somewhat modestly calls the *international financial institutions,*—those who appeal to these responsibilities and to these solidarities—these people no longer speak, no longer speak *only* as Algerians, or as French citizens, or even as Europeans, even if they do this *as well, and on this very basis*, in all of these capacities.

We are for an electoral contract

One cannot invoke democracy, however abstractly, or what the Appeal calls *the Algerian democratic exigency*, without taking sides in the Algerian political field. A true democracy requires at least the following in its minimal definition: 1. A calendar, that is, an electoral commitment; 2. Discussion, that is, of public discourse that is armed only with reasoned arguments, for example in a free press; 3. Respect for the electoral verdict and thus a change in political power [*alternance*] in the course of a democratic process, the possibility of which is never interrupted.

This is to say that we, the signatories of the Appeal, have already *twice* taken sides on this point, and this had to be done. *On the one hand*, against a state power that would not do everything immediately to create the necessary conditions, in particular those of *appeasement* and discussion, to reengage *as quickly as possible* (and this *rhythm* raises the biggest actual problem today, a problem to be discussed democratically) an interrupted electoral process. The *vote* is certainly not the whole of democracy, but without it and without this form and this calculation of voices there is no democracy. We also take sides, *on the other hand*, by simple reference to the democratic exigency against whoever does not respect electoral arbitration and whoever would tend, directly or indirectly, before, during, or after such elections, to put into question the very principle that will have presided over such a process; that is, democratic life, the state of law, the respect for freedom of speech, the rights of the minority, of political change, of the plurality of languages, customs, and beliefs, etc. We are resolutely opposed—and this is a side we clearly take, with all of its consequences—to whoever would claim to profit from democratic procedures without respecting democracy.

To say that we are logically against these two perversions as soon as we refer to democracy in Algeria is to speak neither as citizens from such and such nation-states, nor as Algerians, nor as French citizens, nor as French citizens from Algeria, whatever the supplementary pressure and intensity of our responsibilities might be in this regard. And here we are in the international logic that presided over the formation of CISIA, a committee that is international, above all. At the same time, beyond the painful example of Algeria in its very singularity, we appeal to it exemplarily, as does, in its own way, the International Parliament of Writers, which shares our exigencies here and joins with us today, with an international solidarity that looks for its safeguards neither in the actual state of international law and in the institutions that represent it today nor in the concepts of nation, state, citizenship, and sovereignty that dominate this international discourse, according to law and fact.

We are for the real dissociation of the theological and the political

Our idea of democracy implies a separation of state and religious power; that is, a radical secularism and a flawless tolerance that not only provide shelter for religious, cultural, and thus also cultural and linguistic communities against all terror—whether it be state terror or not—but also protect the exercise of faith and, in this case, the freedom of discussion and interpretation within every religion. For example, and in the first place here: in Islam, the different readings of which, both exegetical and political, must be allowed to develop freely, and not only in Algeria. This is, moreover, the best response to the anti-Islamism tainted with racism to which a so-called Islamist violence, or a violence that still dares to claim its roots in Islam, can give rise.

We are for what I will venture to call, to go quickly, the "new Third State" in Algeria

This same democratic exigency, like the Appeal to civil peace, can only come, from our side and from those with whom we assert our solidarity, from the living forces of the Algerian people who do not feel themselves represented by either camp or the apparatuses at work on both sides of a nondemocratic front. The hope can only come from these living places, from these places of life; I mean from an Algerian society that recognizes itself fully neither in a certain state (which is also a de facto state) nor in the organizations that fight it by resorting to assassination or to threats of murder, to killing in general. I say *killing in gen-*

eral because, if we do not want to entertain any illusions about the term "violence" and about the fact that violence begins very early and extends very far, sometimes in the least physical, least visible, and most legal forms of language, well then, our Appeal—such as I interpret it at least— nonetheless comes down *unconditionally* on a limit to violence; namely, the death penalty, torture, and murder. The logic of this Appeal thus requires the uncompromising condemnation of the death penalty no less than the condemnation of torture, murder, or the threat of death. What I call by the more or less appropriate [*juste*] term of *the new Third State*, is that which carries [*porte*] our hope everywhere because it is what says *no* to death, to torture, to execution, and to assassination. Our hope, today, is not only the hope we share with all of the friends of Algeria in the world. It is first carried [*portée*], often in heroic, admirable, exemplary fashion, over there by those Algerian men and women who, in their own country, do not have the right to speak, are themselves killed, or expose their lives because they [*ils et elles*] speak freely, they [*ils et elles*] think freely, they [*ils et elles*] publish freely, they [*ils et elles*] assemble freely. I say *these Algerian men and women*—and I insist on this—because I believe more than ever in the enlightened and enlightening role that woman can play; I believe in the clarity of their strength (and I hope to see it breaking out tomorrow, at once peaceful and irresistible); I believe in the place that the women of Algeria can, and will, have to occupy in the future to which we appeal. I believe, I have hope in their movement: irresistible and breaking. In the homes and in the streets, in the places of work and in the institutions. (This civil war is for the most part a man's war. In many ways that are not limited to Algeria, this *civil* war also presents itself as a *virile* war. It is thus also, laterally, by an unavowed repression, a mute war against women. It excludes women from the political field. I believe that today, and not only in Algeria but in Algeria in a way that is more pressing and urgent than ever, reason and life, political reason, the life of reason and the reason for living, are better conveyed [*portées*] by the women; they are within the reach [*portée*] of Algerian women: in the homes and in the streets, at school, at the university, in the places of work, and in all the institutions.)

The anger, the suffering, the upheaval, but also the resolution, of these Algerian men and women: we have a thousand signs of these. One must perceive these signs: they are also aimed at us, and salute this courage—with respect. Our Appeal should first be made *in their name*, and I think that before it is even addressed to them, it comes from them [*d'eux*], it comes from them [*d'elles*], I think that we must also listen.

In any case, this is what I feel resounding in the depths of what still remains Algerian in me, in my ears, my head, and my heart.

For Mumia Abu-Jamal

Nearly twenty-five years ago—this memory causes me anguish and despair still—we came together, alas in vain, in an attempt to pull from an infernal, juridical-prison machination someone who at that time in the United States, in those years, represented an exemplary figure for the young Mumia Abu-Jamal. The latter had already been an activist for several years, since 1968: he was barely fourteen years old at the time when the supporters and the police of the sinister Wallace loosed their fury on Philadelphia; the segregationist governor of Alabama was holding an electoral reunion in the city—Mumia's city—and Mumia, like so many others at the time, was beaten up by the police. The exemplary figure, exemplary for Mumia as well, of the one we could not save in 1971 was George Jackson. Along with Jean Genet and other friends, we decided to write and to speak, for Jackson. Some of us—this was my case—had barely finished writing and shouting our revolt, we had barely finished exposing the imminent crime, when we learned it was already too late: George Jackson had been assassinated in prison under ignoble conditions.

Is there time to stop the foul process that is under way? Will we have the means to do it? Will the huge movement, which has roused so many men and women throughout the world, so many organizations resolved not to let an injustice so barbarous be perpetrated, be powerful enough to stop it?

We must not let ourselves be discouraged, of course, never, even if we know from experience—alas!—that there is little we can expect from one who signed the order of execution by lethal injection, Governor Tom Ridge, or from the voters with whom he has concluded a deal (for he said that he wanted thus to "fulfill a campaign promise"), from this political police brutality; we cannot expect much attention and compassion, much understanding either, for the testimonies, the arguments, the protests in the name of justice and humanity that we may address to them. All of our shouts reach them muffled from a great distance, almost from another world. They hardly disturb those hard of ear and of heart, those about whom we now know, from a thousand testimonies, that they have a good laugh when, among themselves, like a good, crude joke, they utter the expression "presumption of innocence." Under these conditions, the only "calculation" upon which it is perhaps "reasonable" to count still, would be the one that might arouse the memory and fear of the governor—and those who might exercise some pressure on him—of riots that might follow the putting to death of Abu-Jamal, as in in Los Angeles not long ago, but this time in many other cities.

But we must not disarm for all that. We must, on the contrary, accelerate and intensify our action. This duty is dictated to us no doubt and in the first place by the singularity of a history, that of Mumia Abu-Jamal himself. His fate remains unique—let us not forget it—as would his death, as will have been an indescribable suffering. And yet this injustice reveals exemplarily, in its massive generality, a certain state of rights and of penal or prison politics of which so many prisoners are victims in the United States, African Americans in the great majority of cases.

We all know, today the world knows, what for thirteen years will have been the hell of *death row*, the "supermax," high-tech prison in which Mumia Abu-Jamal has been isolated, in truth tortured day and night, after a notoriously shameful trial.

In fact, most of the blacks on the jury were challenged; the means of discovery refused; the lawyer officially appointed by the courts was chosen for his incompetence; a policeman who could have testified in favor of the accused was kept back; all of this without forgetting the countless contradictions of the witnesses to the prosecution. . . .

One could spend hours enumerating all of the irregularities that have marred this judicial farce, all of the elements of which have now been put together and are known by the entire world. Everything proves, on the contrary, that this person is being hounded, he who for a time was a member of the Black Panthers before becoming a courageous and independent journalist, a journalist of the people [*populaire*], and quickly dubbed "the voice of the voiceless." This voice has become intolerable; it is this voice that one wants not only to silence, not even to have heard, not only to prevent from rising up but to prevent from causing other living voices to rise up, other living voices that might protest against the same oppression, the same racist repression.

As Mumia Abu-Jamal reminds us, at the same time that South Africa is relegating the death penalty to the garbage pail of history, Pennsylvania—like other American states that seem more and more inclined to reinstitute the death penalty today or to go back on provisional stays of executions—wants to offer up more "black blood" to its racist intoxication, and this in a state that dares to pride itself on being the state in which the United States Constitution was written, whose very letter and spirit it violates every day, when it destroys evidence of Abu-Jamal's innocence and entrusts the pretrial investigation of his case to a retired member of the lugubrious and now famous Fraternal Order of Police that clamors for death and lynching.

Without ever forgetting the terrible history of Abu-Jamal, without erasing his singularity under the pretext that it also represents exemplarily, in his figure, the condition of so many African Americans, one must nonetheless acknowledge, I am doing it all too briefly, that not only is the prison system developing in the United States at an incomparably greater rate than that in all other countries of the world, that nearly 3,000 people await death by hanging, electrocution, gas chamber, lethal injection, or firing squad, but that—Amnesty International reminds us of this—certain American prisons (for example, in Colorado) are among the most inhumane in the world (automated, roboticized, removed from all human contact, day and night under electronic surveillance, and first of all—let us not forget this in particular—reserved for political prisoners; real death camps that are sometimes run by private companies in the most tranquil good conscience and the best management possible on the market of rights).

In the state of Pennsylvania alone, where almost 150 men and women await their execution, 60 percent of the condemned are African Americans, although they represent between 6 percent and 9 percent of the population (a symptom that obviously translates a general, social, economic, political, and symbolic state that cannot be treated without abstraction in terms of demographic, police, or judicial statistics alone).

These convicts spend between twenty-two and twenty-three hours a day in their cells under cruel and humiliating conditions, deprived of everything to which they should have a right—and more and more harshly since 1992: no more books, no more radios, almost no communication with the outside. What I am recalling here, a little quickly and too dryly, no one certainly could remain insensible to and witness in silence or passively. But beyond the indignation or the revolt to which we all must testify, I would also like to give some of the reasons why the International Parliament of Writers, as such, has immediately judged it necessary to take its part in the initiative of this important movement.

Even if a thousand signs did not convince us that justice had been violated in the case of Abu-Jamal for more than thirteen years and that his trial at least calls for review, the International Parliament of Writers is opposed in principle, in what is its very principle, both to police and prison torture and to the death penalty, which goes without saying from the moment that we rise up against all violations of the freedom to speak and write, all violence and all hindrances to freedom that any force, whether governmental or not, imposes on intellectuals, writers, scholars, journalists.

In this regard, the death threat that weighs on Abu-Jamal is analogous to the one that, everywhere in the world today to some extent, tries to silence (by murder, prison, exile, censorship in all of its forms) so many intellectuals or writers, so many journalists, so many men and women who demand their right to free and public speech.

Without ceasing to be himself, Abu-Jamal, "the voice of the voiceless," is first a political prisoner. Because he risks death, he represents for us today all of those voices, the voice, a voice for all those voices. And we will no longer stop hearing it.

Even before reminding us of it himself [in the moving letter that he has just addressed to us], we knew that what they wanted to make disappear, besides the witness and the lucid activist, is a man of words and a writer.

Abu-Jamal is not only the one who reminded the United States of this first amendment, this freedom of the press and this freedom of speech with which they fill their mouths, all the while gagging to death the freedom of so many others.

Abu-Jamal is not only a people's journalist, he is also someone who has already been punished and subjected to an especially harsh treatment for having been the author of *Live from Death Row*.

This writer will have been the one to describe to the world the conditions of death row. He reminds us with terrible and perfect irony: in Pennsylvania, birthplace of the first amendment of the Constitution, "writing is a crime."

When from death row he exhorts us to "write on," to continue to write, to go forward [*droit*], just where one needs to go, this appeal and this injunction dictate our law to us. This imperative reminds us of our charter and our truth. The stakes of this unconditional perseverance in writing carry far beyond the interests of a company of writers or the protection of a society of people of letters. This was always the case, and today more than ever; we know this too well.

And when the so-called "great Western democracies" profess to give lessons to the world in this field, to all the states, to all the nations that in fact violate imprescriptible rights, and do it more and more a little everywhere, with more and more arrogance, well then, those who give lessons should begin by respecting these principles at home: yes, at home first of all, principles whose rhetoric they are so quick to export. Without which this eloquence of "good conscience" will only be one of those "intimidation tactics" that Mumia Abu-Jamal discusses—to whom I will leave the last word for what will remain, let us hope, an unerasable stroke [*trait*] and the signature of the living that we are greeting [*saluons*]:

That I write at all reveals the utter failure of their intimidation tactics—as does the fact that you read.

Paris, 1 August, 1995

Open Letter to Bill Clinton

Paris, 15 November, 1996

President William Jefferson Clinton
Mrs. Hillary Rodham Clinton
The White House
1600 Pennsylvania Ave., NW
Washington, DC 20500
United States of America

Dear President Clinton, First Lady Hillary Rodham Clinton,

At a time when the whole world is celebrating the reelection of the President of the United States and his confirmation to the highest office, we would like to address you directly and to do so in a personal mode, a mode that is both public and private. For, in speaking to you as much from the heart as from the language of the law, it is first and foremost out of a sense of duty and in the name of justice that we implore you, Mr. President, Madam First Lady, to make your voices heard.

A terrifying tragedy is about to lead an innocent man to death. Imprisoned for fifteen years, tried and sentenced under circumstances that appear more than suspect in the eyes of the entire world, an American risks paying with his life for what may, in fact, be a police machination and a judicial error. It is public knowledge today, in your country and everywhere else, that the trial of Mumia Abu-Jamal was marred from the beginning by many serious procedural irregularities. Indeed, countless rules were broken, and these breaches have been the subject of reliable and detailed publications (dossiers, interviews, books, films). Indisputable testimonies have demonstrated that the trial was side-tracked by pressure groups and by the partiality of a judge (recently appointed and famous for holding the record number of death penalty sentences among American judges), and this to punish at any price, and without sufficient evidence, the past of a political activist (a young "Black Panther" in the 1970s and then a radio journalist, the "voice of the voice-less"). Consequently, Mumia Abu-Jamal is often considered, and rightly so, alas, to be a political prisoner threatened with death in a democracy.

Confining ourselves here only to the latest episode in a long series of police and judicial acts of violence, we will simply recall that on October 1st of last year, one of the principal eyewitnesses for the defense, Veronica Jones, was arrested on the witness stand in the middle of a hearing, for a minor offense totally unrelated to the trial, at the very moment she was giving crucial testimony. This testimony not only contained elements that might have proved Mumia Abu-Jamal's innocence (who, from the begin-ning, has affirmed his innocence); it also gave an account, under oath, of the police threats due to which, fifteen years before, Veronica Jones had been forced to alter her initial deposition the day following the unex-plained death of a police officer in Philadelphia.

At the very moment that we, along with thousands and thousands of citizens from many democracies, appeal to you, Mr. President, Madam First Lady, we would also like to express to you, as should be clear, the greatest respect for the principles of the political and judicial institutions in your country, for the separation of powers and the independence of jus-tice. It is in this spirit, moreover, that many organizations (Amnesty International, International Parliament of Writers, PEN Club, Movement Against Racism and for Friendship Among People) have held demonstra-tions to demand a trial review; it is also in this spirit that certain friendly heads of state have publicly intervened, for example, Chancellor Kohl and President Chirac. On 3 August 1995, Chirac, as you know, authorized the Ambassador of France to "take any step, on a strictly humanitarian basis and with the utmost respect for American law, that might contribute to saving the life of Mr. Mumia Abu-Jamal."

Having closely studied all of the available facts of the trial, we are firmly convinced, as are so many others, that an appalling injustice may lead to an innocent man's death in the worst tradition of the great judicial errors of history. Yet, because we are not in the position of judge, because we accept, hypothetically, that our intimate conviction may not be shared unanimously, because we respect—on principle—any other conviction of good faith, our request is pressing but remains limited: we ask only that the trial be reviewed. We ask that a new trial take place in conditions that are dignified and transparent, that the logic of "reasonable doubt" be rigorously taken into account in favor of an accused presumed innocent and that, however it turns out, any judgment to come be at least founded on indisputable facts. (Allow us to add parenthetically that this review would be not only an act of justice, it would no doubt also avert new outbursts of anger, foreseeable reactions of indignation that might themselves have unforeseeable consequences.)

Once again, Mr. President, Madam First Lady, we would never venture to ask you for an intervention that would be contrary to the democratic principles of your institutions and to the independence of the judiciary, whether it be in the state of Pennsylvania or on a federal level. We are only turning to you today to entreat you, fortified as you are by your legitimate authority and a renewed confidence, to issue aloud words of justice as a reminder of the spirit of the law and of human dignity in a democracy. We believe that the force of your voice will be able to carry these words to where an ultimate awakening of consciousness seems so urgent, which would allow the proper authorities to reopen the trial in complete independence and thus avoid the risks, all of the risks of an unforgivable and irreversible injustice.

Please accept, Mr. President, Madam First Lady, the expression of our confident and most sincere regard.

Mme. Pierre Mendès France
Jacques Derrida

P.S. Of course, if you think it best, we will delay making this letter public—which we plan to do at an appropriate moment and under the title of "Open Letter"—until we have been advised of your answer and your opinion on this matter.

Derelictions of the Right to Justice

(BUT WHAT ARE THE "SANS-PAPIERS" LACKING?)

I remember a bad day last year: It just about took my breath away, it sickened me when I heard the expression for the first time, barely understanding it, the expression *crime of hospitality* [délit d'hospitalité]. In fact, I am not sure that I heard it, because I wonder how anyone could ever have pronounced it, taken it on his palate, this venomous expression; no, I did not hear it, and I can barely repeat it; I read it voicelessly in an official text. It concerned a law permitting the prosecution, and even the imprisonment, of those who take in and help foreigners whose status is held to be illegal. This "crime of hospitality" (I still wonder who dared to put these words together) is punishable by imprisonment. What becomes of a country, one must wonder, what becomes of a culture, what becomes of a language when it admits of a "crime of hospitality," when hospitality can become, in the eyes of the law and its representatives, a criminal offense?

We are here tonight in a theater: we are here to protest and to act by speaking—as one does in the theater, you will say. But today's theaters, certain theaters at least, are indeed more and more *themselves*, fortunately; that is to say, more than theaters (a phenomenon that must be saluted, just as one must salute the courage and the lucidity of the theater directors and the artists who assume thus their responsibilities). Certain theaters today (les Amandiers, la Cartoucherie) are places where one testifies by acting better than anywhere else, exemplarily.

In this way one opens a public space to words that are just [*à la parole juste*] and to the urgency of solidarity, but one also opens an asylum at a time when everything is being closed elsewhere, when every door is being bolted shut, every port, every airport is tightening its nets, where the nation-states of Europe, especially France, are turning their borders into new iron curtains. Borders are no longer places of passage; they are places of interdiction, thresholds one regrets having crossed, boundaries back toward which one urgently escorts, threatening figures of ostracism, of expulsion, of banishment, of persecution. Henceforth we live in shelters that are under high surveillance, in high security neighborhoods—and, without forgetting the legitimacy of this or that instinct of protection or need for security (an enormous problem that we should not take lightly, of course), more and more of us suffocate and feel ashamed to live like this, to become the hostages of phobics who mix everything up, who cynically exploit the confusion toward political ends, who no longer know, or no longer want to distinguish between, the definition of hearth [un chez-soi] and hatred or fear of the foreigner—and who no longer know that the hearth [le chez-soi] of a home, a culture, a society also presupposes a hospitable opening.

As I was coming here I was thinking about the singular word representation. And about the places of representation in a country such as this one. At a time when, in the sacred monument of national representation that a Parliament should be, a majority of representatives—of deputies in this case—has just given us (yesterday, the day before yesterday) the spectacle both dismaying and disturbing of a xenophobic, repressive, electioneering demagoguery that creates scapegoats for itself to exonerate itself from a catastrophic politics and blatant incompetence, desperate to steal imaginary votes from Le Pen. At a time, thus, when this national "representation" gives so disheartening a spectacle, certain theaters, fortunately, in the said localities [lieux dits] of representation that, without representation and without demagoguery, men and women can assemble, whether or not they are citizens, French and foreigners, to pose the problems in their harshest light and to respond to the real exigencies of justice.

We are here for this, we are here to protest and to act first by speaking. This means by raising our voice for the "sans-papiers," of course, on behalf of the "sans-papiers," and as a sign of solidarity with them: for them in this sense, but not for them in the sense of in their place. They have spoken and they speak for themselves, we hear them, along with their representatives or advocates, their poets, and their songsters. To speak here means that the "sans-papiers" have a right to speak: we are here to hear them and to listen to them tell us what they have to tell us, to speak with them, and not only, therefore, to speak about them or in their place.

But because they are being spoken about, and have been so for several months (and what is more, under this strange name of "sans-papiers"), because they are being spoken about, both badly, insufficiently, and too much given what one says about them, the question arises, What is being said, and what does one mean to say, when one says "sans-papiers"? They are "without . . . ," they say. What are they lacking, then, these "sans-papiers"?

What are they lacking, according to the authority of the French state and according to all the forces it represents today? However, and this is something else entirely: What are they lacking today in our eyes, for us who want to mark our solidarity and our support for all the "sans-papiers" who are victims of the laws in force, of the police of yesterday and tomorrow?

I do not know who came up with the locution "sans-papiers," nor do I know how this terrifying expression "sans-papiers" has become established little by little and even has found legitimation in recent days. An entire process has taken place here, a process that was sometimes slow and insidious, at other times explosive, brutal, accelerated like a police raid on a church. This terrifying habituation that has acclimatized this word to our lexicon would deserve long analyses. One assumes that what one calls, in a word, a "sans-papiers," is lacking something. He is "without." She is "without." What is he or she lacking, exactly? Lacking would be what the alleged "paper" represents. The right, the right to a right. One assumes that the "sans-papiers" is in the end "sans droit," "without right" and virtually outside the law. By contesting his normality and civic identity, one is not far from contesting his very identity. One might say that he is lacking more than a determined thing, one thing among others: he is naked and exposed, without right, without recourse, deficient [*en défaut*] in the essential. Without anything. What he is lacking, in truth, the lack he is being imputed and that one wants to sanction, that one wants to punish—let us not deceive ourselves, and I would like to show this, intentionally using this very precise word—is a *dignity*. The "sans-papiers" would be lacking dignity. What dignity? What is a "sans-papiers" unworthy [*indigne*] of? And why is a "sans-papiers" assumed to be unworthy? Why, in the name of what, is he or she refused dignity? For the law and the French police do not content themselves with mistreating the "sans-papiers"; with forcing them to cram themselves into places that are barely livable, before concentrating them into triage camps of sorts, "transition" camps; with hunting them down; with expelling them from churches and from the territory; with treating them often in defiance of the rights of man, I mean precisely of those rights guaranteed by the Geneva convention and by the European convention of the rights of man (Article 3), in defiance of the said rights of man and in defiance of human dignity—which is (I say this weighing my words) literally denied them, explicitly refused them. One refuses this dignity to those one is accusing (I am citing an ancient but topical text here and one to which I will turn for a moment) of being "unworthy of living on our soil."

Before discussing this supposed lack, this failing that one would like to punish as if it were a fault, one would have to speak of the derelictions of justice of which this country is in the process of rendering itself seriously culpable. More and more seriously today, now that a law even more repressive than ever is in the process of being adopted by Parliament. One would have to speak of the derelictions of justice with regard to foreigners, more precisely with regard to those who are strangely called the *sanspapiers*, whom one designates and tries to circumscribe so as to reduce them by accelerated expulsion. Let us not forget that at that moment when, in a debate about these terrible projects of law, the parliamentary left was either absent from the benches of the National Assembly or else discreet and in retreat in its opposition, without any real, coherent, alternative proposal to offer on the subject, well, at that moment one more charter was taking off from Roissy: the thirty-third since the accession or the return to power of Chirac, Juppé, Debré (I prefer to cite these three names: by focusing the accusations on Pasqua or Debré, who certainly deserve it, one risks exonerating the whole majority, even a large part of the opposition—which at times holds forth in the most generous of words but, in fact—yes, *in fact*—remains supportive of the current repressive policy).

There is nothing new about the violence that accompanies this repressive policy, or these derelictions of justice, even if we are at a novel and particularly critical turning point in their history. They date back at least half a century, to the eve of the war, well before the famous ordinance of 1945, to a moment when the grounds for the statutory order of May 1938 claimed, in a language that we find today in all politicking rhetorics, and I quote: "not to undermine the traditional rules of French hospitality." The same text simultaneously argued (like today and in a way—I will come to this—that is just as unconvincing) to reassure or pander to the phantasms of an electorate and declared, I quote (this is in 1938, at the moment of the burdensome arrival of certain refugees, whose features or accent were often judged characteristic and whom Vichy will not delay in sending off to the camps and to the death that you know; like all of the discourses that resemble them, these discourses remind us today, in their very anachrony, of a sort of pre-"Vichyite" night):

The constant rise in the number of foreigners residing in France [this was already a lie, and more than ever today: immigration has not increased in twenty years, and all serious studies show that, even from a strictly economic point of view, even if one were to restrict oneself to the calculation of economic interest specifically, the proportion of foreigners in France does not in the least constitute a threat or a hindrance, on the contrary] has forced the government . . . to enact certain measures that are urgently [*impérieusement*] called for by a concern for national security, the general economy of the country, and the protection of public order.

And in the same text where—once again one brings together and supplies all the weapons used by all French laws in their war against immigrants—the same rhetoric tries to make us believe that the only ones who come under legitimate repression are the ones who do not have a right to the recognition of their *dignity* simply because they have shown themselves *unworthy* of our hospitality.

Again I quote from a text that, in 1938, was preparing, like today, for an increase in legislative action in a pre-war atmosphere. This is what it said in a form of obvious denial, in the insolent, narcissistic and jingoistic boastfulness with which we are very familiar:

We should first indicate . . . that the present project of a statutory order does not at all modify the regular conditions of access to our soil . . . it does not undermine the traditional rules of French hospitality, whose spirit of liberalism and humanity is one of the most noble aspects of our national genius.

These denials show that all is not clear, and, in fact, they call to mind a real breach [*manquement*] of hospitality. Yet the same text, whose resonance has a strange actuality, accuses all those it is preparing to punish of having shown themselves "unworthy"—this is the word, *unworthy* [indigne]—of our genius for hospitality, "unworthy and in bad faith." One might say today that, in the eyes of a law in the process of being made more onerous, the "sans-papiers" are without *dignity* because they are *unworthy* of our hospitality and in *bad faith*. They lie and they steal and they take advantage. They are guilty. I will read from this text of 1938 in which the logic and the rhetoric of today's government are already perfectly recognizable:

This spirit of generosity [ours, of course] toward the one whom we call the foreigner of good faith finds its legitimate counterpart in a formal intention to punish severely, henceforth, any foreigner who will have shown himself unworthy [*indigne*] of our hospitality. . . . Were one to summarize in a brief formula the features of the present project, we would point to the fact that it creates a purified [*épurée*] atmosphere around the foreigner of good faith, and that the project fully maintains our traditional benevolence toward whoever respects the laws and the hospitality of the Republic, but that it shows a just and necessary stringency toward whoever shows himself unworthy [*indigne*] of living on our soil.

In the time since these remarks were made, remarks whose hypocrisy (bad faith, precisely) would be comic were it not terrifying—just before the war—there has been the *Ordonnance* of 1945, which, in chapter III of its "Penalties," already prescribed heavy penalties for foreigners in an irregular situation (one did not yet say "sans-papiers" at the time) or for whoever aided these undesirables; in its chapter entitled "On Expulsion," an entire series of measures prepared the way for those that are now in the process of being reinforced or reactivated; since this time, the conditions of hospitality in France (immigration, asylum, the reception of foreigners in general) have continued to worsen and sully—to the point of making us shameful—the image to which the patriotic discourse on France and the rights of man and the right of asylum feigns to lay claim. Last year, neutral observers went so far as to speak of a "black year" for the right to asylum in France.

When one hears it said that the "sans-papiers" are *lacking* something, one must begin by speaking of the derelictions of the French state, of France and its national state representation, of its *derelictions* [manquements] of justice in the name of a right that, under the name of the "Pasqua law," which, improved, polished, and more offensive still, is getting worse and turning into the "Debré law": derelictions of justice in the name of a right or a legislative apparatus that has equipped itself with a Pasqua-machine, complete with automatic gear change and Debré into the bargain, with a device aimed at discriminating, filtering out, hunting down, expelling more effectively than ever. And this dereliction of justice is generally accompanied by an arrogant good conscience under the pretext that the "sans-papiers" are lacking something that would deprive them of the right to remain in this country, in which most of them have, nonetheless, lived peacefully and worked hard for many years.

Are we beginning to grow accustomed to this expression, then, the "sans-papiers"? Not that someone might not lose his papers, which can happen to everyone, but that someone might become and might be held for *a* "sans-papiers," a being "without papers," a subject "without papers," as if the being "without papers" defined and exhausted the definition of his being in society, in a society that feels itself authorized to hunt him down with impunity from the moment that his being is a being "without papers," in a xenophobic society that feels itself authorized to exclude him, to expel him, and to deprive him in turn of his basic rights.

What are these papers in question? The expression is a strange one, at once disturbing and terribly familiar. One does not know if it is an adjective, an attribute, or a noun, whether it is pronounced in the singular or the plural. One can be a [*un*] "sans-papiers," a [*une*] "sans-papiers," several "sans-papiers," an indistinct multitude, indeed even an international community of "sans-papiers" (for you know that in France the "sans-papiers" are of all nationalities, citizens or no of all countries). And in saying this, the "sans-papiers," one can already hear the rise of a call, the call to which we are perhaps responding tonight: "'sans-papiers' of the world, unite!" or better yet—"to the 'sans-papiers' of the world, let us unite!" Or further, "We are all 'sans-papiers',," or again, "We are all French 'sans-papiers'."

No, alas, we are not all French "sans-papiers" in France. The "sans-papiers" in France form a very distinct category of persons subjected to an inadmissible discrimination, to a blatant injustice, to a repression and a violence to which we, we who are here, know that we must reply at once by analyzing, by protesting, and by fighting.

I therefore repeat my question: are we beginning to grow accustomed to this expression "the being 'without papers'"? To the situation, to the status without status of the "sans-papiers"? The expression is French, purely French; it is an idiom. Someone in a newspaper the day before yesterday rightly noted that we belong, henceforth, to a society of the "sans [without]": the "*sans-abri* [homeless]," the "*sans emploi* [jobless]," the "*sans logis* [without residence]," the "*sans diplôme* [unskilled]," the SDF (*sans domicile fixe* [of no fixed abode]), which one readily abbreviates today as "S." The "sans-papiers" is not the "man without qualities" in the sense of Musil, but one must ask oneself what happens to a society when it ascribes the source of all its ills (for this is pretty much what one would have us believe today) to the "without" of others, of those who are deprived of that with which the society thinks one must be provided.

If the expression *sans-papiers* is in fact a French idiom, we must nonetheless make two things clear about it: on the one hand, the symptom is universal and it is European, first of all; it is the ill of all "rich," "neo-liberal" countries that, according to the needs of their economies, welcome or allow to arrive from countries less economically privileged—and most often from ex-colonies—a work force that they exploit until the day when another set of circumstances, economic, political, ideological, electoral, requires another calculation and stimulates a policy of racist reaction [*allergie*], of protectionist xenophobia, of tracking and expulsion, in defiance of all the principles so highly and loudly proclaimed by the politicians and rhetors of democracy and the rights of man—both on the left and on the right. There is no country or nation-state in the world today, especially in the rich, capitalist countries, where this policy of border closings, this putting-into-hibernation of the principles of asylum, of hospitality to the foreigner—good only when "all is well" and when "it serves us," when it is "very useful" (between efficiency, service, and serfdom)—is not beginning to emerge.

At a moment when, for several decades, a crisis without precedent of the nation-state has thrown millions of what are, in fact, displaced persons into the streets, what remains of the nation-state hardens often into a national-protectionist, identity-bound [*identitaire*] and xenophobic convulsion, a figure both ancient and renewed of racism. There is a word for "sans-papiers" in each national state culture. In the United States, for example, one uses the term *undocumented*, and one organizes hunts for *illegal immigrants*. To speak seriously of the problem of the French "sans-papiers," to fight effectively against what is—let us never forget it—a singular human tragedy, singular every time, which concerns men, women, and children in distress, and simultaneously a general phenomenon, the exemplary symptom of what happens to the geo-political sphere in what one calls the *globalization* of the market under the domination of neo-liberalism, one must therefore take into account the singular situations *and* the particular case of France, and what is more, the European political context (what one does or wants to do with Europe, the Schengen accords, for example, that are still not being applied in France, moreover) *and* a world in so-called globalization. This concept of internationalization or globalization is becoming the last commonplace of the worst confusions and even of calculated mystifications.

Concerning what is taking place here, now, in France today, I will recall several no doubt well-known things, but things that should always be kept in mind.

One must first denounce a project of law that—under the pretext of proposing a more balanced and allegedly more humane body of legislation, under the pretext of resisting the extremism of a far-right one is trying to seduce and compete against at the same time, under the pretext of no longer advocating zero-immigration to focus on clandestine immigration only, under the pretext of granting residence permits that are renewable for a year to certain categories of foreigners (the parents of a French child, the spouse of a French national), under these pretexts of pure appearance—will introduce, once the Senate reconvenes and the law is passed, a large number of measures of exceptional severity and whose violence is without precedent. They concern those foreigners who, even if they have resided in France for more than fifteen years, work and live in France, etc., have not regularized their situation; one will be able to expel these people: after fifteen years of residency! And this owing to the most scandalous and sinister of confusions entertained by a sad, depressed, depressing, desperate, despairing administration.

This administration is looking for alibis at a moment when its unpopularity has reached catastrophic highs, when the failure of its policies, namely in matters of employment, has become spectacular and when it can do nothing but pander to the worst in its voters. This confusion is both sinister in its crudeness and blatant in its hypocrisy: It is the confusion between the "sans-papiers" and the illegal aliens [*les clandestins*].

Is it necessary to recall here that the "sans-papiers" are not clandestine? That most of them work and live, have lived and worked, out in the open for years? As it has often been remarked, it is the iniquity of governmental repression with regard to the "sans-papiers" that often creates clandestinity where it was not. In a debate in the Assembly, a deputy from the most intransigent section of the majority even managed to obtain that this regularization be renounced after fifteen years by taking advantage of this confusion, and he was supported when he declared: "Under no condition should the status of an illegal alien [*un étranger clandestin*] be regularized." Under no condition! he dares to say.

An already cruel government initiative was further burdened by numerous amendments such as the one that extends to two years the duration of a marriage to a French national merely to obtain a temporary resident's permit. You also know that the criminalization of those who show hospitality to the "sans-papiers" has been made more severe, as well. Last year, one even dared to speak officially—I mentioned this when I began—of a "crime of hospitality"; people were even imprisoned for this. Henceforth, then, the "shelterers [*hébergeants*]," as one says now, pointing to these potential criminals, the hosts, those who believe they must offer hospitality, now they will not only be "put on file" but more harshly prosecuted than ever. Any person who invites a foreigner into his home will have to inform the police of the departure of this foreigner within eight days. How can a citizen of this country not be ashamed of such legislation? Ashamed of the majority of representatives who vote for it? And ashamed, above all, of an opposition that does not oppose it with the requisite vigor, that does not commit itself solemnly and clearly to challenging, in very precise fashion, on the given day, such a policy? Testimonies and analyses, others have spoken to you or will speak to you better than I can about this tragedy—global, European, or French. I will simply conclude by recalling certain obvious things—as to what is happening and as to what should to be done, it seems to me. As for what is happening, of course, one must, without forgetting the singularity of the ill, know that the analysis and the fight must be global, European, national, and local at the same time. Serious analyses have shown this: It is futile to think that one will stop certain migratory flows, but it is equally futile to think that these flows can overrun certain limits and above all that they are dangerous; it is stupid and shocking not to know, even from the point of view of the national interest of France and of the cultural French-speaking world, that we have not only duties, duties of recognition with regard to those who choose our country, our culture, and our language (often for having already helped us when they were harshly colonized by France, and for example, during the two world wars), but that their choice is a chance for us. Some of our neighbors have been smart enough to understand this, this chance, and to accept it: for example, very close to us in Europe, the Portuguese, the Spanish, and the Italians have just carried out massive regularizations. On the basis of these analyses and these global struggles, one must never forget that the current policy of repression in France is not only a dereliction of a tradition of honor and a dereliction of rights, it is not only an ignominious betrayal, it is also a lie and a crude mystification, the response to an imaginary danger that only serves as a convenient alibi for what is a complete political failure. This failure, it must also be said, is not only a failure of the actual majority. Whether it is a matter of growing unemployment, of a market economy or a speculation whose deregulation is a misery-producing machine, of marginalization, whether it is a matter of a European horizon ruled by simplistic calculations, by a false science of economics and a crazed monetarist rigidity, etc., by a relinquishment of power into the hands of a central banking system, from all these points of view, it must be known that the politics with regard to the "sans-papiers" and to immigration in general is an electoralist diversion, an operation "scapegoat," a pitiful maneuver to pick up votes, a petty and ignoble bid to beat the Front National on its own ground. And let us never forget that, if the first victims of this bankrupt strategy are our friends, our guests, those who have emigrated and the "sans-papiers," what is instituted by the government is a police system of inquisition, of record-keeping [*fichage*], of control [*quadrillage*] (over French and European territories). This machine threatens all freedoms, the freedoms of all, those "without papers" and those "not–without papers [*non-sans-papiers*]."

To retaliate, I believe that one must analyze the process and fight on several fronts, simultaneously or successively. We must not forget, of course, that there are global and European stakes involved, and we know that this policy against the "sans-papiers" is only a piece in the general mechanism of a politics that must be fought as such.

We must certainly help our friends "sans-papiers" in a way that is individualized, local, day after day, with all the material or symbolic, financial, juridical or legal support they need. Many do this, in the theaters, the churches, the station houses, and the courts; they must be thanked, but there are not enough of them.

We must also—as some of us have done—defy the government by declaring ourselves prepared to determine for ourselves the level of hospitality we choose to show the "sans-papiers," in the cases we judge appropriate, according to our conscience as citizens and, beyond this, our attachment to what they call, without believing in it, the *rights of man*. This is what is called civil disobedience in the United States, by means of which a citizen declares that *in the name of a higher law* he will not obey this or that legislative measure that he judges to be iniquitous and culpable, preferring thus delinquency to shame, and the alleged crime [*délit*] to injustice.

Finally, in the course of every sort of protest and public declaration, it seems to me that we must also fight to one day change the law; this is the only perspective that allows us seriously to hope that we will one day do more than resist empirically, on an ad hoc basis. In view of one day changing the law, let us make this crucial issue, with its full political scope, the focus of the electoral stakes of the next elections. Let us demand in particular that parties of the so-called left be consistent with their principles and with those to which they lay claim in their statements. Let us demand that they do something more than moderately moderate—adopting a discourse that is basically the same as that of the majority—the excesses of the current majority that they claim to oppose. In the time that separates us from the next legislative elections, let us exercise pressure, let us ask questions, let us insist on precise answers: let us demand that commitments be made to another politics, a politics that is truly other, both thoughtful and generous, a politics that will clear the current laws of their shame and infamy—a politics of the foreigner, a right of foreigners that will not be a dereliction of justice.

This will have to be done [*il faut faire*] so we can finally live, speak, and breathe otherwise. We must [*il faut*] be able to rediscover a taste for living in a culture, a language, and a country in which hospitality is no longer a criminal offense, a country whose national representation no longer proposes to punish the welcoming of a foreigner, and in which no one again dares speak of a "crime of hospitality."

PART II

THINKING AT ITS LIMITS

Politics and Friendship

M.S.: You came to the Ecole Normale to teach at the invitation of Jean Hyppolite and Louis Althusser in the early 1960s. I'm sure you knew Althusser, or about him, and perhaps knew some of his early work in the 1950s. But the first formal engagement when there would have been an opportunity to see him on a regular basis and perhaps be close to his projects and so on, would have been when you came back to teach. Perhaps, then, you could talk about that period and your relationship to Althusser, to his students, and the relationship of your own work to Althusser's project.

J.D.: In fact things began much earlier than that—even philosophical matters. I was a student at the Ecole Normale Supérieure from 1952 until 1956. I met Althusser as soon as I got there in fall 1952. Before that I hadn't even heard his name. Our first encounter was in his office. He had already been teaching for several years at the Ecole. In *normalien* slang, he was a *caïman*, that is, a director of study in philosophy. During this first encounter we discovered that we were both born in Algiers, twelve years apart: he in 1918, I in 1930. I remember that we thus began exchanging recollections—trivial matters. It's paradoxical that I never took a single course with Althusser. On the one hand, he devoted what little time he set aside for teaching to third-year students (that is, those preparing the *agrégation*); on the other, he was often ill already (I didn't know what his illness was—some spoke of kidney disorder following his time in captivity). He didn't teach much. Thus, during the time I was at the Ecole, we had a very friendly relation but one that had nothing to do with work. Except this (I am trying to pick out some philosophical signs): when I wrote my first *agrégation* paper for him, I had already, the previous year . . .

M.S.: What was that on? Do you remember?

J.D.: Yes, it was in 1955.

M.S.: No, I meant, what topic? It doesn't matter if you don't recall. I was just curious.

J.D.: I had already worked for a year on the problem of genesis in Husserl. This was for my *Diplôme d'études supérieures*. My paper on time was, I believe, already quite complicated and marked by this problematic. Althusser said to me: "I can't grade this. It's too difficult, too obscure for the *agrégation*. It might be very dangerous. But since I don't feel I can evaluate it, I'll ask Foucault's opinion." Michel Foucault was then an assistant professor at Lille. He came to the Ecole to give courses and I attended some of them. I had a very good rapport with Foucault, also. He had read and liked my work on Husserl. So he read this paper and told me: "Well, it's either an F or an A+." I bring up this episode because it gives a fair idea of my relationship to academic authority—that represented by *agrégation* examination committees in particular (I failed the exam that same year)—and because in the midst of this I wrote that four-hundred-page study on Husserl. It was a period when, in certain circles (even Marxist ones), people began taking a keen interest in Husserl—I mean a different type of interest, different from Sartre and Merleau-Ponty's ways of approaching Husserl. As for the university and the *agrégation* committee, Husserl was still poorly known and poorly received.

M.S.: Yes. In the 1950s?

J.D.: I remember Tran-Duc Thao's book, *Phenomenology and Dialectical Materialism*. This former *normalien*, who, after having graduated the same year as Althusser, returned to Vietnam, had attempted a critical Marxist approach to phenomenology and, following a perfectly acceptable commentary (which Foucault, I believe, had praised in a class or in private conversation), proposed a dialectical materialist reinterpretation of the problems of genetic phenomenology (passive genesis, temporality, etc.). This book probably had a great influence on me: traces of it may be found in my thesis on Husserl.

Tran-Duc Thao was critical of Husserl. But, around the theme of phenomenological genesis, he tried to *translate*, to transcode, one might say, the Marxist problematic by having recourse to genetic psychology, to Piaget, to a science of psychogenetic, ontogenetic, and phylogenetic development. I no longer remember the book precisely, but at that time it pointed to the interest that could arise in certain philosophical milieux for using Husserl's transcendental problematic to pose questions on sci-entificity, on the emergence of theoretical practice, that of the cognitive attitude, questions on the possibility of scientific objectivity, all in a nonformal, nonidealist manner (in the manner of Kant), while at the same time moving beyond empiricism, or at least a certain Marxist em-piricism or positivism, and moving beyond phenomenology as simply "phenomenology of perception." The philosophical and political enemy of Marxists (and first of all Althusser—and this until the end), the ob-sessive enemy was Merleau-Ponty, the author of a *Phenomenology of Perception*. Moreover, he had been a *caïman* at the Ecole before the war, and all of this should be resituated in the strange history of this strange institution and the no less strange "community" that it housed—or, even more precisely, in the genealogy of the Rue d'Ulm philosophers. A work yet to be undertaken: It would clarify a certain number of things about life and about intellectual fashions in this country over several decades.

My personal relationship with Althusser was, at that time, very good, even affectionate (it always remained so, even through some later shockwaves). But philosophical exchanges between us were rare, not to say nonexistent. In any case they were purely implicit (as they undoubtedly al-ways remained). Then (to link up with the starting point that you sug-gested), I left the Ecole. After the *agrégation*, I spent a year in the United States at Harvard (1956–57). Then I did my military service (as a teacher and in civilian clothes). Then I came back to Paris in 1960. As an assistant for four years at the Sorbonne, I saw Althusser a few times. I remember having given him the manuscript of my "Introduction to the Origin of Geometry by Husserl" in 1961. The book appeared in 1962. Althusser wrote me some very generous and encouraging things on that subject. One or two years before that, he had published his first book on Montesquieu. We had corresponded about it. He was ill quite often and often away from the Ecole. I still knew nothing of what was afflicting him. In 1963–64 he invited me to give courses at the Ecole.

I substituted for him occasionally before moving into the Ecole as *caïman* in my turn (upon his invitation, seconded by Hyppolite, who had left the Ecole for the Collège de France, but who had recommended me to his successor). I had an office there and took care of *agrégatifs*. I had been accepted to the CNRS, but I declined in order to be named to the Ecole Normale. So, I moved in October 1964 and stayed for twenty years. Thus, for twenty years I was lucky enough to be Althusser's colleague. I now know that I have never had and never will have colleagues on a permanent basis for as long a time (or at least not in the same French institution—Hillis Miller has been my colleague for twenty-two years, but in three different universities: Johns Hopkins, Yale, U.C. Irvine). Before that, in 1963, I had given courses at the Ecole on Husserl.

M.S.: These would be to some of the same students who collaborated on *Lire 'le Capital'*—Establet, Rancière, Balibar . . .

J.D.: No, no. Not Establet. But Balibar, yes. Macherey had already left the Ecole. Badiou also. They're a bit older than Balibar. But I met Balibar and Rancière when they were *agrégatifs*, as well as some people I would guess you don't know: Jacques-Alain Miller, who is a bit younger, Michel Tort, Patrick Guyomard, Claude Rabant, and Bernard Pautrat— many, many others. But then, very quickly—I'm trying to select things from the perspective you're interested in—very quickly in 1964–65, at the moment I began teaching, there came that juncture: Lacan started teaching at the Ecole Normale upon Althusser's invitation (this invitation was initiated by Althusser, as well as certain students who were following Lacan's seminar), and Althusser began the seminars that gave rise to *For Marx* and *Reading Capital*. This coincided with a period when he was in rather good form, very active, etc.

M.S.: Can I stop you for a second? Were you already, in the 1950s, interested in psychoanalysis and Freudianism? Were you naturally receptive to this conjunction, or did your engagement with psychoanalysis begin at this moment?

J.D.: I had hardly read anything by Lacan at that time. Perhaps "The Insistence of the Letter," but I don't remember when.

M.S.: There was nothing to read then! Or only a very little. The *Ecrits* were published in 1966.

J.D.: Yes, but there were some famous texts that were already published: "The Rome Discourse" and "The Insistence of the Letter."

M.S.: Were these famous and celebrated at the time?

J.D.: Celebrated? . . . Well known, at least in these milieux. I had read only "The Insistence of the Letter," perhaps also "The Rome Discourse," and more or less superficially. But the space, if you will, in which I was situated was a bit strange. I was pursuing my work on Husserl more or less continuously. I was teaching a course on history in Heidegger during that year—a course that some of those same students took. My relations were excellent with Balibar, Rancière, and others whom I had prepared for the *agrégation* the year before. But paradoxically, in that year, just as I began to teach as *caïman*, that seminar by Althusser started and captivated all the attention of those students. I felt quite ill-at-ease, you know, suddenly quite marginalized. I attended one or two sessions of Althusser's seminar: Rancière's exposition, for example. Some of them were later published.

However, from the philosophical point of view, I felt as if I were in an embarrassing situation. That whole problematic seemed to me necessary, no doubt, within the Marxist field, which was also a political field, marked in particular by the relation with the Party, of which I was not a member and which was slowly moving away from Stalinism (and which, while I was a student there, moreover, dominated in a very tyrannical manner). Yet, at the same time, I found that problematic—I wouldn't say naive or lacking culture, far from that—but too insensitive to critical, transcendental, and ontological questions that then seemed to me to be necessary—even necessary against Husserl and Heidegger, but in any case *through* them.

M.S.: We'll talk about this again and again, but perhaps we can begin talking about it now. What were the things that you found most problematic in the theoretical field—shall we call it—in which Althusser and his students were working?

J.D.: To review it very quickly, many questions seemed to me to have been passed over, notably those about the historicity of history or the concept of history. I was right in the midst of debating over these questions (the conditions of possibility for a history of ideal objectivity, thus of a historicity of language and science, the necessity—but also the limits—of idealism and of transcendental teleology of a Husserlian type, the relationship between historicity and objectivity, etc.). Not from, let us say, an a-historical point of view, but by setting into motion, on the subject of history's historicity and of the object's objectivity, another type of questioning (which I believed to be preliminary, thus more radical, more critical, more "deconstructive," that is, "critical" even with respect to criticism and Marxist critique). I had the impression that their concept of history should have passed through the test of this questioning. And I constantly felt not like raising objections but like saying: "You have to slow down. What is an object? What is a scientific object?" Their discourse seemed to me to give way to a theoreticism or a new-fangled scientism that I could have challenged. But, quite naturally, I was paralyzed because at the same time I didn't want my questions to be taken for crude and self-serving criticisms connected with the right or the left—in particular with the Communist Party. Even though I was not a Party member, I understood the situation. I knew that the accusation of theoreticism or of scientism could be formulated from the Party's point of view, for example, and, moreover, it was formulated by them in quite summary fashion—or in terms, at least, to which I would have been the last to subscribe.

I was thus paralyzed, silent before something that resembled a sort of theoreticism, a hypostasis of Theory with a capital "T," before a bit too emphatic or grandiloquent use of capital letters with regard to *the* theory, with regard to *the* science. All of that seemed to me quite worrisome, problematic, precritical, but from a perspective that was not that of some humanism or empiricism. Althusser was conducting a struggle against a certain hegemony, which was at the same time a terrifying dogmatism or philosophical stereotypism within the Party—a struggle that seemed to me (within the limits of that context) quite necessary. Yet, at the same time, I did not wish to, nor could I, formulate questions that would have resembled, from afar, those from the Marxism against which Althusser was fighting. Even though I thought it in another way, I could not say: "Yes, it's theoreticism and therefore leads to a certain political paralysis." I thus found myself walled in by a sort of tormented silence. Furthermore, all that I am describing was coupled, naturally, with what others have called an *intellectual*, if not personal, *terrorism*. I always had very good personal relations with Althusser, Balibar, and others. But there was, let's say, a sort of theoretical intimidation: to formulate questions in a style that appeared, shall we say, phenomenological, transcendental, or ontological was immediately considered suspicious, backward, idealistic, even reactionary. And since I was already formulating things in these manners, this appearance was rendered complicated to the extreme, that is, to the point of making them unreadable for those at whom they were directed. Naturally, I didn't think those formulations were reactionary, but that intimidation was there. I had at least as many virtual questions about what I was beginning to perceive in Lacanianism.

M.S.: You felt intimidated by their manner of handling things you were interested in—Husserl, Heidegger, and so on.

J.D.: Intimidated, but protesting inside!

M.S.: Exactly, but at the same time you thought it was important that the way in which Althusser and his students would talk about history, science, objectivity, and so on needed to engage with this problematic. But at this point you didn't debate these issues with them directly.

J.D.: The social space didn't allow me to.

M.S.: Because you also felt that, from inside the Party, what they were doing was very hopeful and so you observed a certain reticence then.

J.D.: Yes, that's right! I thus felt a bit isolated and had the feeling that the problematic in which I was engaged would be, in the long run, more necessary, more inevitable. Nonetheless, at the same time, I thought I noticed something that's more difficult to formulate: a more or less avowed, more or less surreptitious borrowing—not from me, of course—but from what mattered most to me : Husserl and Heidegger. It was a placed, displaced, replaced borrowing, a contraband borrowing. In spite of everything, in spite of the denials, in spite of the declared rejection of Husserl and Heidegger, there was an incorporation (which I judged to be too hasty and insufficiently refined) of models of reading and types of questions coming from them. Questions like: Under what conditions is the objectivity of the object possible? How can regions of objectivity (of knowledge or of theory) be hierarchized to subject them to general theory, either through a formal or transcendental logic or through a fundamental ontology? In that theoreticism that was also an epistemologism (the price, alas, to be paid for breaking with the dogmatic empiricism reigning in Marxist discourse), it was indeed a matter of regions of objectivity, of regional ontologies as theories of objectivity without any question (of the Heideggerian type, for example) about the determination of the entity as object, about history, and the implications of this determination. The avoidance of making any of this explicit annoyed me in a way, especially since Althusser was always fascinated with Husserl and Heidegger without his having ever given any public sign of this fascination.

M.S.: I don't recall these names ever occurring in any of his published texts.

J.D.: For Althusser, if I may be allowed to say it in such a brutal way, Heidegger is *the great unavoidable thinker of this century*. Both the great adversary and also a sort of essential ally or virtual recourse. (Althusser's entire work should be read following this indication.) As I said to you before, we spoke very little about philosophy together: only in brief, elliptic, ironic, sometimes friendly, sometimes less friendly exchanges. Always against a background of allusions and probably also of enormous misunderstandings. And yet, how many times did he say to me during the last years in the hospital, "Listen, you've got to talk to me about Heidegger. You've got to teach me Heidegger"? He was reading him a bit. He picked things up and then dropped them.

M.S.: Why do you think that Althusser thought Heidegger was the most important thinker of this era? Since he didn't read him very much, what force could he have exerted on Althusser's thinking?

J.D.: We all have an idiosyncratic or idiomatic way of working, reading, not reading, of reading without reading, not reading while reading, to avoid without avoiding, to deny. Althusser had his. And to read and interpret him requires, in turn, that one bear in mind, as in all cases, this singular "economy." But I could certainly confirm that Heidegger was a great (oral) reference for him and that he was never one of those who tried to denigrate or disqualify Heidegger's thought, even for the political reasons of which you are aware. But you are very well aware that a certain configuration, even a reciprocal fascination-repulsion between Marxism and Heideggerianism is one of the most significant phenomena of this century. And we have not finished meditating on it, assuming that we have seriously begun to do so.

M.S.: This is due to the influence of Sartre? Of Hyppolite?

J.D.: The trajectories are no doubt more complicated, more overdetermined, as he would have said. But the shadow of Heidegger is present not only in Althusser's work but in all of the works published at that time, that is, *For Marx* and *Reading Capital.* I suggested in a note somewhere in *Psyché* (in "Désistance") that for a quarter century, Heidegger was never named in any book by those who, in France, were forced to recognize in private or in public much later that he had played a major role in their thought (Althusser, Foucault, Deleuze, for example). Another program for another intellectual history of France.

M.S.: I know without having the texts in front of you and not having read them recently this will be difficult, but can you think of where these traces are visible? Where would you point to in Althusser's texts?

J.D.: Let's take, for example, a big chunk such as the critique of humanism. Just after the war, the "Letter on Humanism" denounces or "deconstructs" a particular humanism as metaphysical. In all his antihumanist discourse, Althusser never cites Heidegger. Yet to state, as he does, that humanism is metaphysical or that metaphysics is humanistic cannot but conserve an echo of the Heideggerian moment. (I tried to formalize some of what was happening at that time with "man" in France in "The Ends of Man.") The text in which Heidegger states that Marx is a great philosopher, a great metaphysician, and that the Marxist concept of work is one of the great interpretations of being is indeed in the "Letter on Humanism." In paying him homage, Heidegger in a way declares that Marx is not essentially a materialist—or that his materialism is not a philosophy of matter but rather of work. He is not essentially a thinker of being as matter. He is a thinker of being *as* work. One must begin to interpret Marx from the perspective of work and production and not from that of material substance. Twenty years later, it's difficult to imagine that all Althusserian (but also Foucaldian) discourse against humanism at the time was without relationship with this text. All the more so for the fact that the "Letter on Humanism" was probably the most read text in France at the time (it's a text meant for France, for the French context, one might say, as that context was represented or described to Heidegger by Jean Beaufret, the letter's addressee), and the allusions to Marx have always been noticed.

Heidegger was very present even at the Ecole Normale, thanks in particular to Hyppolite, who always spoke a lot about him, and to Beaufret, who taught courses there. Thus, there was at least an impregnation. I don't know if that's a good word or what category to use here. I don't believe Althusser ever read Heidegger well. But there was that impregnation, that is, a certain presence, an authority, a legitimacy of the Heideggerian discourse that was in the air, in references: impregnation and avoidance. You know that these motifs weigh upon a philosophical discourse even if one doesn't read the author, even if one doesn't come to terms with the letter of the text as Althusser did with the letter of Marx's text and that of a few others.

At the time, I was sensitive to all this: the traffic of that surreptitious circulation without rigorous reading. Whence a sort of uneasiness. I'll now try to pursue this little narrative. During the next year (1965), I gave a seminar on Rousseau's *Essay on the Origin of Languages*. *Les Cahiers pour l'Analyse* had just been inaugurated. The conjunction between Althusserian discourse and a certain Lacanianism was dominant in its pages. Epistemology was the big word: the thing that was perhaps fetishized more than practiced. In *Les Cahiers pour l'Analyse* I published my first text on Lévi-Strauss. Simultaneously, the *Essay on the Origin of Languages* was published there. There were some curious crossings around the motifs of "text" and "deciphering" at that moment, which was also, for me, the moment of the two "Of Grammatology" articles, where I began to elaborate a certain thinking on writing and reading. My first year as *caïman* at the Ecole Normale was a bit unhappy. I felt a little isolated. Things were not much better the following year. What was called my paralysis a while ago was also a political gesture: I didn't want to raise objections that would have appeared anti-Marxist. One must reflect on that moment in French political history, in which an objection taken as a political sign of anticommunism was, in the milieu that I lived in, very serious. And, right or wrong, giving in both to political conviction and probably also to intimidation, I always abstained from criticizing Marxism head on. And I stress "head on." Where I explain myself the best on that subject is in "Les fins de l'homme" (Actes d'un Colloque de Cerisy-la-Salle. Paris: Galilée, 1981). In a seminar there, I tried to describe the situation that was then mine.

To follow the order of your questions, let's take the example of historicism again. The critique of historicism is, in my own trajectory and my own work, first a determining motif. Althusser was aware of the place that this critique held for me, beginning with my student work and developed in an essential and central way in my *Introduction to the Origins of Geometry*—beginning thus with my reading of Husserl (to my knowledge, the first person to have denounced [against Dilthey] historicism in a systematic and rigorous manner; a denunciation naming historicism; the first to have situated in such a critique of historicism—and not of history or of historicity, of course, to the contrary!—the condition of an access to science and philosophy). I do not wish to reconstitute these steps, which are the very object of my *Introduction to the Origins of Geometry*, but let's just say that for me this is the first axiom of any problematic of scientificity, truth, objectivity in general, etc.

When Althusser criticizes historicism (Gramsci's, Della Volpe's, Coletti's, or that of others, of Sartre also, I think), he cannot ignore (since he uses it) the principal basis of this critique of historicism: he goes back to the first years of this century. This was much discussed at the end of the 1950s and at the beginning of the 1960s in all the works on Husserl (not only mine). This silence or foreclosure seemed strange to me. It irritated me even if I understood, without approving of it, the political strategy involved. Taking into account the context in which Gramsci was writing, I understood the necessity of refounding the concept of history after him, against him. Personally, while taking on the critique of historicism, I was also interested in a certain historicity—the transcendental historicity of which Husserl speaks, a certain history of the meaning of being of which Heidegger speaks, but also a historicity that I was trying to determine beyond, against, and without Husserl or Heidegger. I found that Althusser was subtracting some things from history too quickly: for example, when he said that "ideology has no history." I found his theoreticism problematic: the move to eliminate theory with a capital "T" or theory of ideology as well as ideology itself from history—problematic at least until such time as a concept of history could be produced. It was probably necessary with respect to a certain concept of history, but not with respect to historicity in general. Trained to critique historicism (as relativism, empiricism, skepticism, etc.) to accede to a dimension of transcendental or even ultratranscendental historicity, I did not wish to give up history. The destruction of the metaphysical concept of history did not mean "there is no history" to me. In Althusser I did not see the same movement or sensitivity to the need to think history otherwise, and this bothered me.

I wanted to ask questions. At every step, I would have liked to have had a long discussion with him and his friends and asked them to respond to questions I felt necessary. The fact is—as strange as it might seem—this discussion never took place. And yet we lived in the same "house," where we were colleagues for twenty years and his students and friends were often, in another context, mine. Everything took place underground, in the said of the unsaid. It's part of the French scene and is not simply anecdotal. An intellectual sociology of this dimension of French intellectual or academic life and notably of that *normalien* milieu, in which the practice of avoidance is stupefying, remains to be undertaken. I imagine this appears incredible to a non-French person, especially an American, and perhaps also to a few French. But one has to take into consideration a sort of overtraining in the treatment of problems from an economical, potential, algebraic standpoint—like chess players who don't need for the game to actually advance to anticipate the opponent's moves and to respond virtually in advance, to pre-interpret fictively all possible moves and to guess the other's strategy to the finest detail. All this is related to the theory of philosophical games within a tiny milieu overtrained in decipherment.

M.S.: You said all this was part of the sociology of French intellectual life. I don't know about all of Althusser's students, but certainly Balibar was in the Party at the time. Was it because you were not in the Party that you felt yourself to be outside the domain of their discussion?

J.D.: Yes, probably, to a certain extent. And this fact must not be insignificant or foreign to what I'm describing. Perhaps that was also in part my fault. Perhaps I should have insisted on talking with them. But implicitly, underhandedly, there was such a war, so many maneuvers of intimidation, such a struggle for "hegemony" that one found oneself easily discouraged. Moreover, everyone was inevitably a party to it. There were *camps*, strategic alliances, maneuvers of encirclement and exclusion. Some forces in this merciless *Kampfplatz* grouped around Lacan, others around Foucault, Althusser, Deleuze. When it had any, that period's diplomacy (war by other means) was that of avoidance: silence, one doesn't cite or name, everyone distinguishes himself and everything forms a sort of archipelago of discourse without earthly communication, without visible passageway. Today, the sea between these archipelagos should be reconstituted. In appearance, no one communicated. No one was translated. From time to time, there were, from afar, signals in the night: Althusser hailing Lacan or hailing Foucault, who had hailed Lacan, who hailed Lévi-Strauss. There I was, the new kid—in a certain sense, it wasn't my generation.

M.S.: As we say in English, you were "the new kid on the block."

J.D.: Yet, at the same time, there was no declared hostility. In spite of these differences and differends, I was part of a great "camp": we had common enemies—a lot of them. Never, between Althusser and me, for example, was there any publicly declared hostility. There was publicly declared hostility against me on the part of so many others (Lévi-Strauss, Lacan, later Foucault . . . and the list is far from stopping there). For my part, there were never any objections publicly and frontally formulated. I had questions that I drew back inside myself and that I still keep today for myself. By the same token, on the other side, there was never any attack on what I was doing—rather avoidance.

M.S.: If I am wrong about this, correct me. It seems to me that you have observed a certain reticence about the texts of Marx in your writing. This is not to say that Marx is never cited. I was reading today that one footnote in "La mythologie blanche," which I hope we will be able to come back to—because it is a very important text you cite, a text from Marx on the German ideology; I would like to talk about that. Certainly, unlike Heidegger, unlike Husserl, unlike Plato, Mallarmé, Blanchot— Marx never occupied a central place in your writing. I can understand certain reasons for that reticence, but perhaps, in this context, you could specify them a bit. Let me remind you about the passage I have in mind. It occurs in *Positions*. You say: "I have never found any satisfactory protocols for reading Marx." Two questions I have about that: (1) Why do you think that is the case, that you have never found any satisfactory protocols for reading Marx? (2) Is that still the case? Do you still feel bereft of the protocols for reading that would be required to intervene in the texts of Marx, or are there other reasons for having observed this reticence? We won't call it a silence, because it is not a silence.

J.D.: For this my answer should be a long one. Let's say that I was, at the least, reticent. Indeed, I told myself: Marx's text remains metaphysical, as far as what I had read. For I did read Marx, you know.

M.S.: Most certainly!

J.D.: I did not read him enough. One never reads enough Marx. But I didn't simply pass him by. I had the impression that it was still a largely metaphysical text. The questions that interested me, that is, the history of the essence of being, of the essential interpretation of being, of being as this or that (What is matter? What is labor? What is the being of . . .?, etc.)— those questions were either not posed or still largely depended upon the Hegelian legacy. Not that Marx is, for me, simply an inheritor of Hegel, but he is so to a greater and more essential extent than it was admitted then (through denial, it seems to me, if not through misunderstanding). The questions I had elaborated with respect to Hegel, and that I was formulating at that time (in several places: notably in *Introduction to the Origins of Geometry*, in *La Différance*, "The Ends of Man," or "The Pit and the Pyramid"), seemed to me to concern Marx, as well. From that perspective I was not convinced by what then was referred to as "epistemological break" (after an importation of the Bachelardian concept). I was not convinced that there had been really two Marxes—the still humanistic, anthropological, all-too-Hegelian or all-too-Feuerbachian metaphysician of the Paris manuscripts, and the scientific Marx delivered from all teleo-eschatology. As you know, that distinction played an organizing role in Althusser's entire discourse as well as that of the Althusserians at that time. I couldn't bring myself to believe it upon a simple reading. I told myself, "Okay, Marx's text is heterogeneous like all texts," but the concept of break itself seemed to me incompatible with the meaning I get (and to which I hold) from that heterogeneity, from that nonoppositional difference. Paradoxically, the break homogenizes on both sides of the oppositional border and finally assimilates the two sides, one after the other, between them. This homogenization through opposition is a ruse of dialectics: elsewhere I have tried to demonstrate and formalize it—precisely with regard to Hegel in *Glas*. But that is not the object of our interview.

M.S.: What Althusser intends by the concept of the "epistemological break" is not that at a certain point, Marx ceases to be the humanist Marx. What he means is that the problematic changes in certain determinate ways. I would say that the later texts, as Althusser says, are still contaminated by the early Marx, but what is important is the emergence of different discursive strata. In that case, I have always thought, though Althusser stages it in temporal terms, that is not really what it is about. Isn't it really about extracting from Marx a different set of concerns and problems that had, for a variety of reasons, at that point been submerged in the ordinary discourse on Marx? In that sense, could not one say that you and Althusser would not differ much on this point? Or would you disagree?

J.D.: What you call the *staging* was very strong. Even if the second phase (the second stratum, if you prefer to speak in terms of structure) was contaminated by the first, a new problematic would have sprung forth which should, in principle, not be contaminated. And this second phase was called *scientific*. The order of questions that interested me was not political or scientific "in the last instance." The concept of science was not, for me, the last word. To state that a discourse is scientific does not mean that it is above suspicion or that it is, for that matter, reflective (although I've never subscribed to the Heideggerian assertion according to which "science does not think"—which further complicates the discourse that I am, that I was already trying to make heard).

M.S.: In his texts, Althusser invokes the term *science* in such a way as to make the crucial text for Marx *Capital*. All the labor of these texts is precisely to determine: what is the concept of science—scientificity would be better—that governs Marx's texts? Now, it is possible, I think, for you to say—and I am almost certain you would say—that you are unsatisfied with the criteria of scientificity that Althusser works with or develops in these texts. But I think that for Althusser, what is scientificity, indeed what is an object, is the decisive question. After all, what is the point of the distinction between the object in theory and the object in reality? That very distinction is precisely the problem that one has to work out. How do we relate theory to things? How do we correlate theories with things? How, therefore, can we produce criteria by which we judge this theory better than that theory? It is a question I would like to come back to eventually. For now, I would simply want to insist on this point: that for Althusser, the problem of scientificity is just that, a problem. For him, it is not "the last word." It sounds that way in those texts, but I don't think it is. Would you disagree?

J.D.: It seemed to me that according to his reading of Marx, let's say, the "good" Marx is the one who emerges beyond neo-Hegelian metaphysics, beyond anthropology, etc. to finally reach a theoretico-scientific problematic. But I believed, and I still believe now, that one must pose many historical or "historial" questions about the idea of theory, about the idea of objectivity. Where does it come from? How is objectivity's value constituted? How is theory's order or authority constituted? How did theory become prevalent in the history of European philosophy? etc. And I did not see these genealogical questions, so to speak, on science, objectivity, etc. being posed by the Althusserian discourse, or at least not in a manner that seemed satisfactory to me. From that, it seemed to me that his reading of Marx consisted in dropping a bad text or a pre-Marxist one, let's say, and in constituting the Marxist text—Marx's text of after the break—as a text that had moved beyond metaphysical suspicion, untouchable. My reticence on the order of thought and about genealogical questioning was also, by the same stroke, for the same reasons, at least virtually, a political reticence. Because I think good politics never comes from a limitation on questioning or on the demand of thought. My reservations were not always objections: I didn't want to say, "It's not like that. What you're saying is wrong." I thought that what he was saying was not wrong—not necessarily, not always—but that it was necessary to further question the axiomatic of discourse. Not the scientific but the thinking axiomatic. For me there remains a distinction between the philosophical or the scientific and everything I would call *thought* in a sense where this distinction is not as Heideggerian as it seems. That's why Althusser's and the Althusserians' discourse seemed a bit stifling to me: I sensed a new scientism in it, even the refinement or the disguising of (and this term would have made them scream) a new "positivism" that repressed the possibility of questions like, "What is an object? Where does the value of objectivity or of the theoretical come from?" etc. Since I couldn't formulate such questions without appearing to join the chorus of adversaries, I remained silent.

M.S.: Your reticence, or as you said, your silence was, then, conjunctural.

J.D.: The silence was conjunctural. The fact of not speaking, of not lending, more precisely, *a certain public form* was both a conjunctural and a political gesture. In fact, I think my texts and my behavior "spoke," expressing what was necessary to have understood for those who were interested and knew how to decipher it. For all that, I don't say that silence was *right* or in general *the only possibility*. It was the one that I *believed* right and the only one of which I myself at that place and time was *capable*. On the French scene I didn't wish to attack, in a conventionally coded, utilizable, and manipulable way, a Marxist discourse that seemed, rightly or wrongly, positive inside the Party, more intelligent and refined than what one usually heard. Furthermore, as I've said, I felt intimidated. It wasn't easy. It seemed that maybe silence would be more effective. I believe it was not without effect. Now, you note that the fact that I was not a Party member is not insignificant. Why didn't I join? What history later made more obvious and notorious than ever in France, what was already known and accessible to anyone who was not sleeping or pretending to sleep, what in the end will have caused the degeneration of the Party *and* the covering over of the Althusserian problematic were things that I was sensitive to, like others inside or outside the Party, those who had just left or who were in the process of leaving it. I was anti-Stalinist. I already had an image of the French Communist Party, and especially the Soviet Union, that seemed incompatible with, let's say, the democratic left to which I have always wished to remain loyal.

But, again, I didn't wish to formulate these political objections and risk having them confused with conservative reticence. I didn't want that. I realize that others (few, in truth) found a clear way to take that risk which I didn't take. But I would say also that they did so in a code and according to an axiomatic with which I wanted nothing to do, which were not in tune with the discourse that I was elaborating. That is the deepest reason for my silence, rather than shyness or intimidation. I never let myself be intimidated when I can say what I want with the desired rigor. Basically some of my silences or abstentions still today may be explained thus: the code in which I am asked to express myself seems laden with unacceptable presuppositions. It seems already deconstructed, already deconstructible to me, in any case too inadequate (for there is no adequation possible or that holds here) with respect to the code I seek to elaborate and which I know to be both indispensable and yet impossible, not to be found.

M.S.: At the time, roughly in the middle or late sixties, you saw Althusser as inside the Party; yourself outside. And therefore it was difficult to see Althusser as anything but a kind of Communist militant philosopher, a position about which you had certain doubts.

J.D.: It was the truth!

M.S.: But he was almost thrown out in 1966!

J.D.: What do you mean by "almost"? Lots of intellectuals were leaving the Party at that time! I can think of other Communist friends who did it themselves instead of waiting to be "almost" excluded. You know, when I was a student at the Ecole Normale (we have to speak about this—they aren't anecdotes), the school's communist group was truly hegemonic—Stalinist and hegemonic. And it was extremely difficult for someone on the left (need I remind people that I've always been on the left?) to be thought of only as a crypto-communist or a fellow-traveler. It was very difficult not to join the Party. With the repression in Hungary in 1956, some of those communist intellectuals began to leave the Party. Althusser didn't and, I think, never would have. Gérard Genette, who was a Party member until 1956, told me that he went to see Althusser after the Hungarian revolt to impart his distress, anguish, reasons, and probably to ask his advice. Althusser supposedly told him: "But if what you say were true, then the Party would be in the wrong!" This seemed to Althusser to be precluded and he proceeded to demonstrate *ad absurdum* that what Genette was saying needed to be corrected. Genette laughed when he told me: "I drew my conclusions from that extraordinary formulation and immediately left the Party." Althusser stayed in. I don't know until when—maybe always—in any case, even in the worst moments. For him there was one thing that could not be done and that was leave the Party. Thus, in spite of everything, I considered his struggle to be *inside* the Party. I, on the other hand, was not a Party member and so I couldn't even think of Althusser as someone outside the Party also. He was there; I was not. Do you sense the difference? It cannot be ignored.

M.S.: We have moved away from the philosophical discussion, but we can return. My recollection is that—and this would have been something that would have brought you close together in the late fifties and early sixties—Althusser was very much against the Party's position on Algeria, because the Party, as I recall, supported the Algerian War.

J.D.: At the very beginning, that is, in 1954–55, Party politics were, if I remember correctly, a bit cautious. Then the Party clearly took a position against the Algerian War. Under de Gaulle that position became more and more clear, although it was different from more radical forms of opposition to the Algerian War. And here one should distinguish between the French Party and the Algerian Party, which had "French from Algeria" members whose destiny will have been tragic before and after independence, the new powers persecuting them in their turn.

M.S.: I was obviously mistaken about that. So we will continue with the question. Althusser never broke with the Party. In the middle to late 1960s, it would have been difficult to see what would happen in 1978. He was in the end very critical of the organization of the Party in the *Le Monde* articles on what cannot endure in the PCF.

J.D.: Althusser was someone who, from inside the Party, sought to transform its philosophical and theoretical discourse, believing that through the cause and effect of this discourse he could change the Party's politics. For my little milieu—that of a small group of philosophers of a certain left—this Althusserian discourse was "successful," even if the bureaucratic apparatus of the Party didn't accept it. Among those intellectuals, he was dominant, and the official Party philosophers were considered poor retards—not from the standpoint of the Party apparatus, but from that of the Marxist intelligentsia. Although a minority voice more or less ignored within the Party, the Althusserian discourse, his style and project held much authority in certain circles of the Marxist intelligentsia.

M.S.: In 1968?

J.D.: Absolutely! Until 1968. To me, it was not the discourse of a marginal opposition: It was a dominant discourse. Not from the standpoint of the Party apparatus, but from that of a certain intelligentsia of the Party. Once again, the Party's official philosophers were considered a bunch of mediocrities. I saw the Althusserian discourse as a hegemonic discourse inside the Party, not at all as one persecuted by the Party. It was rejected by the apparatus, if you will, but not by the most visible of the communist intellectuals. It was *the* interesting thing, the novelty, the basic reference. In Paris, when we thought of "Marxism" and "communism," it was always in relationship to that discourse.

M.S.: To come back to where we began, was the word that I imposed upon you, which you hesitated about, what I termed your reticence about Marx, Marxist texts, and so on—you said that part of the reticence vis-à-vis Althusser had to do with a notion of scientificity, of a certain epistemology, being the last word.

J.D.: The concept of production! For me, this concept was very important. But, at the same time, and for the same reason, it was a concept whose philosophical genealogy presented many problems for me. Thus, it was not easy for me to use it, to entrust myself to it, make it a key concept, as was the case for Althusser and his friends. When one is mistrustful of the concept of production, an entire discursive mass becomes problematic. Since I was attempting to elaborate other questions and to advance my discourse toward a level that I considered (rightly or wrongly) to be preliminary and more radical "in the long run," I did not deem it strategically advisable to devote a study to a text (that of Marx and the Marxists) which staked everything upon that semantics, that conceptuality. A preliminary work was indispensable, no matter how long or interminable it might have seemed. What I sought to say would have been amalgamated and massively translated too quickly into a problematic that dissatisfied me. You know, sometimes one prefers to remain alone, not to be read or understood, rather than to be assimilated too fast or misunderstood. However, I meant to read Marx my way when the time came. Later on, I did some seminars on Marx. There was one on ideology in 1976, I think. I wrote some texts on scientism at a time when the scene had changed and the discourse I was proposing was sufficiently articulated and known for confusions not to be so certain (but one is never sure of anything). Meanwhile, before, I felt that it was not advisable to move out onto that terrain that was so busied with the Althusserian problematic. Let's call it a *reservation* rather than a *reticence*. If you wish, to jump a few steps, today, when in France any reference to Marx has become forbidden, impossible, immediately catalogued, I have a real desire to speak about Marx, to teach Marx—and I will if I can. At that time, though, I must have thought I could or should not. It perhaps would have been better if I had been able to devote to Marx a great study to attempt to read him otherwise, following other, more acceptable protocols (to me). But who knows? The fact is I believed I had slower but also more urgent things to do.

M.S.: Let me take another, related question but from a slightly different terrain. Here is your interview with Jean-Luc Nancy, "Le sujet est aussi un principe de calculabilité. Il faut calculer. . . ." The notion of calculation interests me a great deal for a whole variety of reasons. But let me ask the question in this way, because it bears upon what you were saying about the problematic nature of Althusser's work. For example, on the notion of the difference between an ideological and a scientific problematic.

J.D.: To open a parenthesis: I had great reservation about the word and the concept of ideology as well. The word has an enormous history from Plato to the French Ideologues. Yet I didn't see this history being questioned by those who, around Althusser and, to begin with, Althusser himself took the word and the concept precisely as if they themselves had no history either! I believe that ideology has a history, that the concept of ideology has a history, that the word *ideology* has a history—a history that teaches us to mistrust the sharp break between science and ideology. This makes for a lot of differences! Around Althusser people acted as if the word and the concept of ideology were conventionally definable and as if they were going to be able to start all over again to have them accomplish a new task without questioning their genealogy. As if the concept and the word, themselves, were going to begin functioning by *cutting themselves* (scientifically) *off* from their history, from semantics sedimented within it, etc., as if one could obtain a nonideological, uncontaminated, scientific concept of ideology. My worry thus concerned not only the ideology-science break but also the formation of the concept of ideology. The first seminar I did on Marx in the 1970s concerned the word and concept of ideology, the French Ideologues, etc. It's difficult to speak about it here in detail or with rigor.

M.S.: How can one defend Althusser on that point? I don't try. But I would like to come back to the problem of ideology in the relation ideology-science. Perhaps I can put the problem this way, most economically, from the point of view of the empirical sciences. You yourself made the distinction earlier between metaphysical and scientific discourse. There always are grounds for, in a given case, asserting or deciding that some choices are better that others. Calculation is not undetermined in science. The most general question that I would ask of you and of your relationship to your work and your philosophical project is: what are the principles to be observed in this respect—to use a word that you yourself have used—what are the protocols for choice, decision, calculation that Marx's *scientific discourse* has, as opposed to what Althusser calls an *ideological discourse*? It seems to me that one can only proceed on the assumption that some choices are better than others and that there need to be some protocols for deciding. The core of the scientificity of a science is its set of protocols for ruling certain kinds of questions out of court.

J.D.: I'm entirely in agreement. It's simply that in analyzing the field of strategies or "choices" possible, it seemed to me there was room in the long run for other "choices" than Althusser's. I have already stated that I believe in a certain contextual necessity for his "choice." But there was also room for other "choices." (I'm putting the word *choice* in scare quotes.) It was urgent and important that there be other breakthroughs and my calculation, in a context that was precisely not determined in the same way (for all sorts of reasons), was other. It was not *my* place. On this, Althusser would agree: each "subject" (individual subject or subject trapped in a collective field) evaluates the best strategy possible from his place, from the "interpellation" that situates him. For a thousand reasons that should be analyzed, *my* place was other. My personal history, my analytical abilities, etc. made it so that I could not be a Communist Party member. Althusser could be and was. I had been plugged into another type of reading, questioning, and style that seemed to me just as necessary. And I told myself that from the standpoint of my "own" economy and of what I interpreted as being a politico-economic necessity, it was important that I pose the questions that I posed. And that the explanation will have taken place. It takes/took place along more or less identifiable and overdetermined trajectories, even if it has not taken place overtly and directly between Althusser and me. For it to take place, it seemed important to me that the type of problematic I was trying to constitute find its place there. It is an unfinished, insufficient calculation. I wouldn't say that I made it, but that he calculated *me* in a certain sense. In another place, Althusser was the subject, the object of another calculation. The Althusserians, also. Lacan, too. So many others. All the others, don't you agree? Thus a field of differences, of different calculations constituting a *historical formation* (I don't know what else to call it!) may be delimited empirically, crudely, just like what happened in France from 1960 to 1970–75. It was a multiplicity of concurrent strategic calculations in search of hegemony. The formalization of the law with regard to hegemony is itself part of the process, lending it its paradoxical form (I attempted to describe this paradoxical "logic" in *The Post Card* and "Some Statements" in *The States of Theory*). The always incomplete formalization of that law is itself regulated, without any possible metalanguage, by the (mortal) tendency toward hegemony, by that original "instinct for mastery" that Freud discusses in *Beyond the Pleasure Principle*. There were also personal motivations that "represented," as some would say, sociopolitical forces and groups of force. None of these discourses was reactionary, rightist, or conservative in the coded sense of these terms, but each probably "represented" concurrent groups of social forces that would be very difficult to identify. There are no categories for this. Using old categories, I would say that they were subgroups of French capitalist society, which were having it out with each other at that time. (Here, I am pressing on!) I felt, at least indistinctly, that, for example, the category of social class was quite inadequate. Even refined down to overdetermined groups of classes, the idea of social class seemed to me more and more inappropriate for understanding those conflicting structures. I thought much more subtle instruments were needed for defining those things. When he says: "Philosophy is the class struggle in theory . . ."

M.S.: Yes, that is the so-called second definition of philosophy . . .

J.D.: At least in an indistinct way, I felt that the concept of class struggle and even the identification of a social class were ruined by capitalist modernity. As it functioned in the Althusserian discourse, that determining reference to social class, to class struggle, appeared to me to belong to another time. The concept of class struggle and identification of a class are much more problematic than the Althusserians thought at the time. Thus, any sentence in which "social class" appeared was a problematic sentence for me. For the reasons expressed earlier, I could not say it in this form. I believe in the gross existence of social classes, but the modernity of industrial societies (not to mention the third world) cannot be approached, analyzed, taken into account within a political strategy, starting off from a concept whose links are so loose. I had the impression I was still seeing models for sociological and political analysis inherited, if not from the nineteenth, at least from the first half of the twentieth century. From that standpoint, the way in which the discourse of certain Althusserians (Balibar, Macherey, Rancière) later broke open undoubtedly moved us closer together. I feel closer to Balibar's discourse and interests today than to the very blunt discourse of that period. What happened following the big Althusserian moment (that is, after 1966–68) at least virtually moved me closer to all of them because they were themselves obliged to complicate their discourse.

I believe that an interest in what the concept of class struggle aimed at, an interest in analyzing conflicts in social forces, is still absolutely indispensable. But I'm not sure that the concept of class, as it's been inherited, is the best instrument for those activities, unless it is considerably

differentiated. I already felt this then. I cannot construct finished or plau-
sible sentences using the expression *social class*. I don't really know what
social class means. I know some dictionary definitions, but they don't
seem sufficient for understanding particular overdeterminations (as we
say in French) of the field. And if one takes the concept and logic of
overdetermination seriously (and I have less reticence about them), then
this logic can come back and threaten or ruin almost everything to which
it adheres in some way or another. Everything Althusser says about
overdetermination satisfies me more than the rest—alas, this means that
it satisfies me to the detriment of almost all the rest, in particular the "in
the last instance" discourse, which I consider the metaphysical anchoring
of the whole enterprise.

M.S.: I want to question you on that, because everything you say
about "class" can be thrown onto a different level by talking about the
other notion that is linked to overdetermination, namely, what Althusser
calls *la dernière instance*, but, as he says, "the lonely hour of the last instance never comes," "it never sounds," "it never answers the bell." If you
put these two together, it seems to me it is a very problematic moment in
Althusser—one I sort of understand—but let us begin with the first. You
said you would never affirm "determination in the last instance by the
economy." Why?

J.D.: Basically, the concept of last instance would be the general concept of the *deconstructible itself*, if something like that existed. This is why
I saw in it the metaphysical anchoring par excellence. To deconstruct substantiality, principality, originarity, archi-causality, etc. always means to
deconstruct or dismantle recourse to some "last instance." To say "last instance" instead of "infrastructure" doesn't make much difference, and it
destroys or radically relativizes the whole accounting for overdeterminations. Everything interesting and fruitful in the logic of overdetermination
becomes compromised, reduced, crushed by this discourse on the "last instance," which I have always been tempted to interpret as a concession to
the economist dogma of Marxism if not that of the Communist Party.

Nevertheless if, instead of "the economy is the last instance," I now
said "every 'last instance' is 'economic,'" this might just change everything on condition that I define economy otherwise, as I am tempted to
do—otherwise, that is, through the ex-appropriation of any relation of
any proper, or of any last instance to itself. As you know, I use the con-

cept of economy a lot. But I do so without determining it based on production or appropriation. General economy also supposes something
other than productivity and, in the economic process, it even incorpo-
rates (without being capable of integrating it) a certain unproductiveness
or even a nonproductivity—something heterogeneous both to productivity and unproductiveness. My reticence, therefore, toward the economy as last instance is not only aimed at the last instance but also at the
way in which the economy is interpreted by Marxists such as Althusser.
Each time I have discussed economy, I did so by bringing in all sorts of
elements that were not simply forces of production or effects of owner-
ship or appropriation. And nonproductivity, nonappropriation, what I
call *paradoxical ex-appropriation*, that movement of the proper expropri-
ating itself through the very process of appropriation—none of this is a
negativity nor a dialecticizable contradiction nor a dialectical work of the
negative. Simplifying things a bit, one might say that from this standpoint I belong, to a certain extent, to the "antidialectical" configuration
that in France brought together such philosophers as Foucault, Deleuze,
and others. I feel less "antidialectical" than they, but more so than
Althusser (who very occasionally, capriciously, without drawing any in-
ference from it, denigrated the dialectic; this happened only in private, as
far as I know). Moreover, none of this is a question of more or less. But
we cannot approach these things—the meaning of "production" and
"proper"—so quickly, by improvisation. Althusser, in any case, remains a
dialectician. Even if he complicates things, even if he fought to complicate the dialectic by introducing a principle of overdetermination, the dialectical motif remains dominant in his work. What my work aims at also
takes shape around a thinking of the economy—but an economy that is
not, at first glance, that of which Marxist economists speak. The differ-
ance (with an *a*) is in an economy that counts with the aneconomic. But
let's leave that aside . . .

M.S.: I feel silly or embarrassed in a way because I feel in the position
of trying to speak for Marx and Althusser, and I am insufficient to the task.
But what I want to do is simply to formulate what I think are possible objections or points of disagreement that I feel would be raised by them, if
they were speaking here. So pardon me, I am not going to do this very well.

J.D.: Do you think that Althusser, Balibar, or others would today
still say "the economic in the last instance"?

M.S.: Balibar not, I think; I don't know about Althusser. All I know about Althusser is the published writings and my reading of his work. He never gives up on that, as far as I can tell. Perhaps that is a misreading, but it would be my reading. Rancière certainly not! Balibar is complicated, because he comes to make that work in terms of a classical model of class determination. That moves into the difficult notion of the determination in the last instance by the economy. He recently sent me his most recent book (done with Wallerstein), which I have loaned to a friend and therefore have not had the chance to look at. Probably not, I would say, in any simple way would he approve the notion of "determination in the last instance by the economy." The way Althusser formulated it—I put great stress on the notion—as he says, "The lonely hour of the last instance never comes." What he meant by that is that the economy, in the traditional topography of the contradictory unity of the relations and the forces of production, is never accessible or it never operates openly; it is never visible, it is never accessible to analysis in any kind of pure state. You can't simply take the class relations and the productive forces, the factories, and so on. They are always contaminated by what he calls the *other levels and instances*: politics, ideology. Therefore, what society is—and Althusser, at one point, recalls that his only question is, "What is society?"—is the contradictory unity of all those things.

Therefore, I want to reformulate this slogan and say: yes. All the things that you say about all of the "unproductiveness," the waste, if you like, things that are done without any sort of immediate material pay-off or something like that—all of those things are part of the unity of society. There is a footnote in the first volume of *Capital* where Marx says: "In the middle ages, it appears that religion is the dominant instance in feudal society." But as he says, it is very clear that feudal people could not live on religion alone. They had to engage in material production, and in that sense, to use the phrase "in the long run" is just to indicate that the limit of what is possible in a given epoch is set by the economic instance. It puts boundaries around certain things. "Determination in the last instance," I think, simply means setting a boundary.

Let me give you an example to try to illustrate what I am talking about. It would be possible, thinkable at least, for a nation or society today to try to reinstitute feudal relations, agrarian relations, to recapture the feudal mode of production, for instance, to combat industrial pollution. But it would not last, not for very long, because the force of the capi-

talist mode of production globally is so enormous. No society can survive against the tremendous productivity of capitalism. They would do
so inefficiently, they would go broke. It is exactly that kind of "determination in the last instance," I think, that Althusser means. There is a
limit, there is an outer limit of what is possible in a given social formation, and that is set by the relations between the forces and the relations
of production. In that sense, the economy does call the tune. I presume you
are going to disagree with that, and I am interested to see what precisely you
would disagree with.

J.D.: If I follow you, and if one assumes that the last instance never
comes or appears as such, that it remains invisible, nonphenomenal, one's
discourse must then be adjusted to this structure, to the possibility of this
hidden god, this entity, this causality, this thing—the thing itself (with its
effects), a thing that can be named without our ever gaining access to it,
itself, as such. What does its never appearing signify? What does the indeterminability of a last instance mean? This dissimulation, nonphenome-
nality, this truth as dissimulation leads us back toward previously beaten
and familiar paths, toward nearly classical discourses and problematics
with which Althusser and those who worked with him engaged no explanation. If the economy as last instance can never appear as such, then to
what concept of presence, of nonpresence, of phenomenon, or of essence
does one have recourse? Here again, some engagement with Heidegger
or a problematic of the Heideggerian type should have been manda-
tory: it can be done, should have been done, and implied no particular
allegiance to any Heideggerianism. On the contrary, there is much
more allegiance in avoidance than in explicit problematization.

M.S.: You were saying that Althusser never really engaged with what
for you is the fundamental problematic that is raised by this nonappear-
ance of "the last instance."

J.D.: Without speaking of the content of the discourse, the fact that
he never tried to at least articulate a problematic such as the one I am
pointing out (whether referring to Heidegger or others), even if it were
only to criticize that problematic, the fact that he never tried to read or to
take into account a reading of texts of this type already seemed negative,
worrisome, disappointing to me. I would have better understood a formulated and argued disagreement or even an explained refusal to engage

in problems of this type (assuming that one is not always already engaged in them, whether one wants to be or not). I saw in this flight a fault, whether it was a matter of thought or politics. Inseparably.

M.S.: Why in politics?

J.D.: Because I saw these questions as unavoidable. But while they cannot be avoided, they can be repressed, denied. In that case they resurface with their political consequences. They have had the political consequences we know. But the failure—to go quickly and to speak rather generally—the fact that, in spite of everything, the Althusserian discourse of 1968 lacked the necessary duration and vitality, both from the theoretical standpoint and especially from the standpoint of what was anticipated on the field of political combat (that is, an effective transformation of Communist Party practice in France and elsewhere)—these facts bear witness to its limitations.

M.S.: Wait a minute! You think that the Althusserians didn't have a more important effect on the theoretical apparatus of the Party because they didn't confront Heidegger?

J.D.: Expressed in this form, I would agree it sounds ridiculous! But in his not having posed "fundamental" questions or questions on foundations, questions on his own premises, even on his axiomatic (on "What does present mean?" "What does phenomenon or truth mean?" "What does the dissimulation of the last instance mean?" "What is the meaning of 'being' or 'event'?"—I'm going too fast, of course; surely I'm being unjust; the interview genre elicits that; I'd refine this if we had the time and the texts in hand), I then saw a lack of radicality and a yet-too-dogmatic relation to his own discourse. And this could not be without political consequences in the long and the short run. Even more generally, this meant perhaps that it has always (or at least then) been vain to hope to stay in the French Communist Party to transform its discourse and thought without giving up posing questions that threaten all dogmatism. You'll urge me to say that the fault lies in still hoping for something from the Communist Party, but I won't state it in that form.

M.S.: Even if we say that—I'm sorry if it was a crude way of putting it—still, the actual reason they didn't have a greater effect is because the apparatus simply chopped them down, and not for philosophical reasons.

J.D.: If the Party chopped them down and the Party chopped itself down, it's because the failure was not limited to Althusserianism: It was the failure of the French Communist Party and Communist parties in general. It's the sign that Marxist discourse of the time, including its Althusserian breach, was incapable of analyzing the socio-politico-economic reality of that time and of regulating its practice based on that analysis. I don't claim that, if the Communists had read Heidegger, it would have been otherwise: that would be stupid! Well, maybe not as stupid as all that! But I do claim that their concepts were not refined or differentiated enough, and that cost them. It cost them politically. It was already visible from various perspectives. For example, from the perspective of political thinkers on the left, even revolutionaries who, in France, had already then broken with the Communist Party, with Marxist discourse, or at least that of "dominant" and dogmatic Marxism. By *dogmatic* I mean when, at a given moment, one ceases or prohibits oneself from posing a question. This is a practical and political limitation. That's what I meant. "Heidegger" alone cannot save someone from that dogmatism. But asking more genealogical questions (in a "deconstructive," Nietzschean-Heideggerian style—and you know very well that things are very complicated for me on this point—but we're not here to speak of me . . .), asking more questions on the origins of one's concepts, on the weight of tradition, on the notion of ideology, of phenomenon, of presence, of truth, makes all the difference, demonstrating one's readiness to change, that transformation is taking place, or at least possible. But what I meant was that the limitations were not simply discursive or theoretical: they were also political. In that sense, I feel more Marxist than they. I'm not saying the Communist Party was stronger than they: it was weaker than they. The proof? It was at once a theoretical, philosophical, and political debacle not only in Europe but throughout the industrialized world. Somewhat indistinctly, this debacle was predictable in the 1960s. Personally, I saw the Party as being closed up in suicidal politics already then. It was losing. It had two alternatives: either it hardened its Stalinism and would lose through losing its electorate (and therefore become isolated in Europe) or else it would transform into reformism, a moderate socialism of the social democratic type and would lose also, since the Socialist Party already occupied that space. That was the dilemma, the fatal aporia.

Althusserianism's paradox was that it claimed hardening and transformation simultaneously. Philosophically and theoretically, it was harder than the political party at the time—harder and more of an advocate of transformation. But in both traits, and for the reasons I've just evoked, it was playing to lose—more and faster.

That's an interesting indicator for following the competition, shall we say, between the apparatus and Althusserianism. The apparatus renounced its axioms (class struggle, dictatorship of the proletariat, etc.) faster than Althusserianism did. They all ended up renouncing them. In relation to the apparatus, Althusserian discourse was, at various levels, both more innovative and more radically, more rigidly conservative, both more and less adapted in its analyses to current history.

M.S.: Under French conditions.

J.D.: Yes, under French conditions. Althusserianism was a model for many theoreticians abroad, notably in Latin America, but it was also a very Parisian, very French product, which one cannot fully understand without knowing something about the history of the French Communist Party and the Parisian theoretical scene. In a certain sense, it represented a tough current in the French Communist Party. And from this standpoint, it was even more suicidal than the Party. Although in another sense it was less so because it sought to regenerate a true theoretical thinking to which I sincerely believe it is correct to pay homage.

Even before 1968 it was visible to me in any case, and probably for many others, that the French Communist Party (I wouldn't say *Marxism in general*) was being drawn toward an irreversible decline. It was beginning to lose out before 1968. And in 1968 it was the big loser. At the time of the Programme Commun in 1972, the logic of this condemnation of the Communist Party was obvious. The two alternatives were: either it hardened and lost out or else it softened and blended with the Socialist Party and there would be no more need for it—no more than as a slight electoral edge. The Socialist Party carried out the "common" function very well, while perversely marginalizing its Communist ally. This was proved true in 1983–84. Dogmatism is not a contradiction in Marchais or someone else's head or in the thinking of a political apparatus: this contradiction is in things themselves, as one might have said only a short time ago—in things and in the course of history well beyond France. Where European industrial society was heading, what the new resources of capitalism are: these are the questions that needed to be analyzed. From that point of view, what's happening right now in the Soviet Union provides food for thought. I cannot say that I was ready

to formulate this theoretically in the 1960s, but it's certain that I was thinking that way. And this determined my political choices: that's why I wasn't
a Party member. For someone like me, it would have been easy to be in the
Party at that time. There was no question of being anywhere but on the left.
Most of my friends were Party members. And the fact that I wasn't didn't signify anything like a class reaction (which would be a stupid supposition) nor
anything reactionary. It simply signified what I've been talking about.

M.S.: I have two questions, one of which I posed in the initial set
that I sent you, and then another one that occurred to me as I was taking
notes in your seminar yesterday. They are related, so why don't I give them
both to you, and we can talk about them alternately or together. The first
question we have already talked around a bit, and you were just talking
about it now: It concerns the Althusserian slogan that "philosophy is the
class struggle at the level of theory." What I want to ask about is not so
much your view on that particular way of putting the matter, but again to
come back to this problem of specific relations between philosophy and
political activity. Philosophy as a discipline—what political effect does
philosophizing have? How does one intervene in the political arena from,
in general, the point of view of a philosophical project that you yourself
have pursued? This is one set of questions.

The second set is as follows. Listening to you yesterday, I kept asking myself, since the topic was the politics of friendship: what exactly are
the politics licensed or authorized (perhaps these are not the best words,
but I'll use them anyway) by the manner of proceeding that you pursued
in these particular seminars? Or, one could say, if you like, what kind of
political actions are authorized by, or are necessitated by, deconstruction?

So, those are the two sets of questions. Yesterday, when we were
walking to the car, I gave you a hint of what politics I think are authorized by your work, mainly by referring to Saint-Just. But you don't have
to pick up on that.

J.D.: That's very difficult.

M.S.: All the important questions are difficult.

J.D.: For an articulation between deconstruction and politics to be
possible must imply a radical re-elaboration of the concept of politics in
its general circulation. Politics is a concept heavily marked by a great number of traditional and deconstructible philosophemes. The "political" itself

is a philosopheme—quite an obscure one. Obviously no deconstruction is, for all that, apolitical. But to say that deconstruction is political through and through is too easy an answer. In any case, a deconstruction cannot first be something other than a genealogy, a series of genealogical questions on the whole of discourse that has lent justification to politics, that has constructed political philosophy. For example, since you alluded to it, that seminar on friendship is at least an attempt, by following that guiding thought, to reconstitute the matrix of a great number of political philosophemes and to place them in a network. In this domain nothing is clear or given any more than in any other. However, this does not stop one from calculating strategies and taking decisions or responsibilities. I would even say that it is to the extent that knowledge does not program everything in advance, to the extent that knowledge remains suspended and undecided as to action, to the extent that a responsible decision as such will never be measured by any form of knowledge, by a clear and distinct certainty or by a theoretical judgment, that there can and must be responsibility or decision, be they ethical or political. I am a citizen, too. It happens that I take politico-institutional initiatives, that I "intervene," so to speak. I vote and do other such activities in a context determined by old political discourses. For the time being, I vote Socialist in France. But this does not mean that the political philosophy of the Socialist Party satisfies me, nor that it is one and homogeneous. I have great stocks of questions about all the words, sentences, and concepts used to define the Socialist Party platform. One must distinguish between levels of analysis, critique, deconstruction, action . . .

M.S.: I can understand that. But I think there is a theory of political action that is emerging out of your discussion of friendship, and the key to it is the notion of violence, struggle. I think that is the word you used—its ineluctability—and it's that I'd like to get at. Perhaps it's too difficult because you are in the middle of thinking about this question.

J.D.: Yes, and also I've spoken about it only at a single session, during a reading of Heidegger. Very briefly, the seminar is oriented toward a thinking of democracy. But a democracy for which the current concepts that serve to define democracy are insufficient. One might say that it's a deconstruction of what is called the *given concept of democracy*. This is always very dangerous. It's always dangerous to try to come to terms with Heidegger. This is the danger that the Althusserians ignored. But in thought, that is, anywhere, one must run risks. Otherwise there is no responsibility. One must investigate in places where thought is exposed to what is the worst, in political terms. If not, things get even worse—the worst along with good conscience.

In that seminar, what interests me is to understand how the idea of democracy arose in the West and what can and should be conserved out of it. That's why I have kept the word *democracy* and why, for me, democracy is not just a mode of government, social organization, or regime among others. Let's say that there is an idea of democracy with respect to which all of the determinations that there have been of it since the Enlightenment, the American and French Revolutions, different types of democracy have all been inadequate. But they all refer to this idea through a unique mode of memory that I am trying to analyze and that justifies, to a certain extent, why I keep this old word. The old word *friendship* as well, despite all the phallogocentric determinations (especially in the figure of the brother in the "fraternalist" schema) that have dominated it. I'm trying to think democracy after deconstruction starting with Aristotle (but we are also discussing Montaigne, Kant, Nietzsche, Schmitt—who himself discusses Hegel, Marx, and Lenin, among others—Blanchot, and a few others, to limit ourselves to proper names), all the philosophemes, politico-philosophemes if you wish, that have structured this thinking of democracy. The guiding thought of friendship is very useful for this: it relates to everything. I'm trying, for example, to think out an equality that would not be homogeneous, that would take heterogeneity, infinite singularity, infinite alterity into account. In my opinion, neither the motif of equality nor even that of responsibility is reconcilable with the concept of subjectivity or subjective identity (which I believe to be de-responsibilizing or bound, in any case, to limit ethico-political responsibility in the order of calculable law). On the contrary, equality calls for a consideration of a certain infinite heterogeneity, an infinite distance. This is very difficult to reconcile with the current discourse on democracy. It's not at all Heideggerian, either. But I think one must approach, cross through, and go beyond Heideggerian questions. This is what I attempt to do elsewhere, in any case, in particular in that seminar that I cannot reconstitute here. What I call *democracy to come*, which is not the future of democracy, is what this work is striving toward.

So what political action is possible? For me the place of the political is the place of *negotiation* between, let's say, the open set of present or presentable data such that I can attempt to analyze them (always a finite analysis), and this "democracy to come," which always remains inaccessible, not just as a regulating ideal but also because it is structured like a promise and like a relation to alterity, because it never possesses the identifiable form of the presence or of the presence to self. But the event of that promise takes place *here*, *now* in the singularity of a here-now that, as paradoxical as it might seem, I believe I must dissociate from the value of presence. Everything is at play in this paradox that I cannot develop here: Singularity is never *present*. It *presents itself* only in losing or un-doubling itself in iterability, thus in the mark and the generality or ideality that, moreover (threat or luck), will allow later for a calculated negotiation between the presentable and the nonpresentable, the subject and a-subjective singularity, rights and a justice beyond rights and ethics, and perhaps even beyond politics (we can come back to this). The here-now indicates that this is not simply a question of utopia. There is constant and concrete renewal of the democratic promise as there is of the relation to the other as such, of the relation to infinite distance, incalculable heterogeneity, etc. It is a matter, then, of a negotiation between that thinking that resembles something messianic (but I wouldn't say *messianic* in the current sense of the term) and the present givens of democracy, which are unsatisfactory, but which remain (by using the same word, the same paleonym) "mindful" of the promise of a democracy to come. They are the guardrails against the worst—what I would call the worst. Today, I prefer democracy as it is—the present democratic model—to monarchy, oligarchy, etc. Yet this doesn't seem enough. There is violence, repression, and even the concept of the calculable subject, as I said before, appears insufficient—insufficiently democratic. There is no lack of concrete signs of nondemocracies in "our" societies. They are even becoming more and more generalized.

For the present, to me, democracy is the place of a negotiation or compromise between the field of forces as it exists or presents itself currently (insufficient democracy, European democracy, democracy American-style or French-style, for example) and this "democracy to come." This negotiation must readjust itself each day in relation to differing places. The responsibility one must take for it is always unique. Political action for me today cannot, must not be the same as that for anyone else in another place, another class, another country. From this standpoint, political action is not empirical but constantly strategic. For me, the rule of this strategy would be this "democracy to come." But this rule is not that of a calculating or calculable knowledge through and through. In this respect, it is not altogether a rule like other rules. Rather it is a law without rule, even without obligation—in the sense of obligation to be, obligation to be present. A leap is necessary that would liberate one from the rule as knowledge, as a knowledge forever ordered around the objectivity of a presence, around a theory, a logic or an ontology—perhaps even around an ethical, juridical, or political system. Voting Socialist, which I said a while ago that I do, is a political gesture that I can only try to justify as a compromise between the state of forces as I can analyze them from my position in France and this incalculable idea of democracy. *Today in France*, I think it's better that the Socialist Party be in power than the UDF or the RPR. Not that I'm satisfied with it, but I believe that this hegemony in itself is rather plural and that it leaves open more opportunity for discussion, protest, and, in the end, that "democracy to come" than any other party. This is where the place of political action lies. But if on occasion not only have I voted Socialist, subscribed to a discourse, or even publicly written "One must vote Mitterrand," perhaps the next day I might say, "No, we must not, we must no longer do so." It's to be evaluated at each moment from standpoints that are finite.

I would not say that the concept of "democracy to come" is a *political* concept alone, through and through. At this point it's perhaps no longer a question of politics and that the "best" or the least-lousy politics orders itself with something that exceeds politics. Here the term *politics* itself is subject to negotiation. Perhaps the term *democracy* is not a good term. For now it's the best term I've found. But, for example, one day I gave a lecture at Johns Hopkins on these things and a student said to me, "What you call democracy is what Hannah Arendt calls republic in order to place it in opposition to democracy." Why not? I am only employing the term *democracy* in a sentence or a discourse that determines certain things. I think that in the discursive context that dominates politics today, the choice of the term that appears in the majority of sentences in this discourse is a good choice—it's the least lousy possible. As a term, however, it's not sacred. I can, some day or another, say, "No, it's not the right term. The situation allows or demands that we use another term in other sentences." For now, it's the best term for me. And choosing this term is obviously a political choice. It's a political action. There is nothing relativistic in what I'm saying. On the contrary. An action that did not take all singularities into consideration would be a dogmatic and irresponsible mechanics that would drown decision in the environment of a dogmatic generality.

M.S.: Would you object to calling what you have been referring to as *democracy to come* what in the Marxist lexicon would be called *the classless society*?

J.D.: Why not, if the concept of class is totally reconstructed, noting the reservations I formulated a while ago with regard to the concept of class? What's important in "democracy to come" is not "democracy," but "to come." That is, a thinking of the event, of what comes. It's the space opened for there to be an event, the to-come, so that the coming be that of the other. There is no coming or event that is not, that does not imply the coming of the heterogeneous, the coming of the other. "To come" means "future," not the present future, which would be present and presentable tomorrow. It means the space opened for the other and others to come. Nondemocratic systems are above all systems that *close* and *close themselves off* from this coming of the other. They are systems of homogenization and of integral calculability. In the end and beyond all the classical critique of fascist, Nazi, and totalitarian violence in general, one can say that these are systems that close the "to come" and that close themselves into the presentation of the presentable. What I have said elsewhere about the coming, the event, the "come here" [*viens*]—of *différance* and the deconstruction of presence, is where I would begin to try to articulate a thinking of the political.

M.S.: Let me ask you a specific question along that line. When I think about politics, I think about this and that, very much in the way you have said. You are strategically in a different situation. You have been very honest and forthright about particular choices you made yourself. But, to take an example, what about the Sandinistas? Because one reading of them, one that you might support, would see in the Sandinista dictatorship—and that's what it is, after all—a closing, as you just said, of the possibility of any kind of "democracy to come." I would not read it that way, but you might, I guess. What do you think about the Sandinistas?

J.D.: Following a rather spontaneous movement of sympathy, it's clear that I'm against the way the American administration treats them. But I don't have absolute confidence in them. I demand to be shown, and perhaps my position could change from one day to the next. Perhaps for a while I would say, "Up to a certain point, they must be helped"; then, perhaps one day, in another context, I might say "They've got to be fought." I demand to be shown. No more here than anywhere else does my reservation signify a de-politicization that suspends. As such, every political question implies an extremely complicated, constantly readjusted strategic analysis, and I have no fixed response to the question you are asking me. I believe that, if I were American, I would fight what I understand about the American administration's policies, but not to applaud a priori everything the Sandinistas do—the Sandinistas who might tomorrow turn out to be the enemy to be fought. If you had asked me, "What do you think of Fidel Castro?" I would have been disturbed. None of what I can observe appears very reassuring or acceptable. This doesn't mean that I approve, from beginning to end, of the American policy with regard to Castro. To many questions, I have complicated, disturbed answers. When I have to vote, that is, when the response is a binary yes or no, it's rare that I'm sure. Since the situation in France is basically relatively stable, clear enough, and not very "revolutionary," domestic choices are, for the time being, rather easy. But when it comes to burning questions, when analysis must be micrological and attuned to both geopolitical and local stakes, I have the greatest difficulty orienting myself. In these cases, the current codes of traditional political problematics appear insufficient to me. But on the "Sandinista" question that you asked me, and to give a response that is immediately decipherable in the current code, the moderate and cautious standpoint of the French government and of the Socialist Party seems to me, within the limits of my information and thought on the subject, acceptable.

I, too, want to ask you some questions. What do you think of the Sandinista situation? Do you have a clear and simple position?

M.S.: My position is very straightforward, I think, and not especially complicated. Obviously you stop the contra aid, and you resist the policy of the United States. But my own feeling—whatever reservations I might have about this or that, which the Sandinistas have done—I feel that the only possibility for any kind of social amelioration in Central America is some kind of regionalization of the Sandinista revolution. They can't go it alone. There have to be revolutions in Guatemala, in El Salvador.

J.D.: Okay. You're generally like me, like so many others, against North American imperialism. And first of all in Central and South America. Okay. But now does this mean that you support, at all cost, Sandinista policies from A to Z? That's the question you asked me. To that question, I don't have a firm and fixed answer, so I'm sending it back to you.

M.S.: I understand and I respect people who say, "Look, this is an extremely complicated process." There are a lot of reservations one has. But my feeling, perhaps too simple, is that the Sandinistas at this moment, given the balance of forces on the other side, have to be defended at all costs. Whatever they do to defend their revolution is justified. You said earlier that you observed a certain silence about Althusser because of certain critics. I would observe a certain silence about some things in Sandinista Nicaragua, because the discourse of anticommunism is so powerful in the United States, much more powerful than it ever is in France, I think, because it has a longer tradition and because the political position of the Communist Party in the United States has not been what it was in France, for fifty years at least.

J.D.: A while ago I said: if I were American, if I spoke in a discourse determined by the American situation, perhaps it would be more "Marxist," but a Marxist discourse with other connotations. Even if something can be exported from it, my discourse is formed from a situation in which something such as Western Europe exists and constitutes some sort of continent. If I were American, without contradicting what I said on the subject of principles, I would accentuate things differently. Certainly as an American citizen! Of course, I never speak as an American citizen.

M.S.: That will take us down another path, but let's pursue it anyway. I mean, it's not my interview, but I feel very much the obligation— and I'm sure I'd feel differently if I grew up in France or if I grew up anywhere in Western Europe—I feel the absolute obligation to, for example, teach the texts of Marx, because they are not well-known here, are not part of "general discourse."

J.D.: I agree. But what allows you to say that a discourse such as mine teaches Marx less than some other discourse that cites Marx at each page, while neutralizing, paralyzing, doing nothing with him? I ask this without trying to justify myself.

The manner in which the discourse I find myself engaged in constituted itself historically—a discourse whose stability remains relative—
signifies for someone who knows how to read it that Marx is always there.
People who decipher my discourse on the French scene of the 1960s know
that I speak with Marxism, that I explain myself, for example, with regard
to the Marxist concept of production. Marx is always immediately or virtually taken into account. There are traditional or stereotyped discourses
that cite Marx at every page, but do not elicit a reading of Marx or that
would tend to make one forget about him. Some might even disgust people with Marx: look at what's happening in the Eastern European countries where the least allusion to the name of Marx today produces an ex-
plosion of anger and rejection among intellectuals—people don't even
want to hear about him any more! My ambition (which is perhaps excessive) is to call for a new reading of Marx—a greater ambition than many
Marxists. And the fact that, for example, on a regular basis, people come
and say to me, "So, what about Marx?" or "Yes, but, in Marx there's
something. . . , One must . . . ," means that because the blank on Marx
is situated in my text in a certain way, that blank is not just any blank.
That blank corresponds neither to a distraction nor to a repressive denial that it *brings about*, but rather to an *active* calling into account of
the Marxian legacy. I feel as you do the obligation to have Marx (and a
few others) read, but there is more than one way to respond to this obligation, not one! The best way is not necessarily to always give lessons
on Marx or to cite *Capital*.

M.S.: Agreed, having said one needs to read and teach Marx, the
question remains: What does it mean to teach Marx? I accept that. We are
not in disagreement on that.

J.D.: Let's take another path to respond briefly to the same question.
We are both in academic or intellectual institutions. You know very well
that to a large extent traditional Marxist discourse is accepted or judged to
be sufficiently reassuring that, in spite of everything, teaching Marx is allowed. There is no war or prohibition on Marxist professors or those who
teach Marx—at least neither in the United States nor in France.
Whereas deconstructive questions and practices, while they enjoy a certain success, encounter a greater and increasingly bitter resistance from
the institution and thus from dominant intellectual normativity. I

could give you a thousand concrete and current indications of this, no-tably in this country—indications both inside and outside academia. This perhaps means that, even politically, deconstruction affects and disturbs the academic institution's dominant discourse much more than the tranquil inscription of Marxist teachings or Marxist readings. I don't want to over-simplify: there is also a tranquilizing legitimation of deconstruction that interests me very little. But what is alive and at work in deconstruction seems much less tolerable, by which I mean that it incites more intolerance than traditional Marxist discourse, which I believe to be largely academized. The political implications of these two phenomena should be analyzed.

M.S.: In the United States?

J.D.: In the United States and France, as well.

M.S.: No, not in the United States; there I disagree. If the teaching of Marx was not officially forbidden, it was virtually killed in the 1950s. You know about McCarthyism, but I think it would be impossible for you to register the total ideological effect of the first decade of the Cold War on the American academy. Marxism was purged from intellectual life in America in a very, very systematic way, in a way that it really was not in France. That is my impression. It makes an enormous difference.

J.D.: I think that either in its tough or softer form, left Marxist dis-course is very marginal. It's much easier to digest, accept, institutionalize than a certain Marxist practice.

M.S.: You are absolutely right about that, but this is really the legacy of the last twenty years, only since the 1960s. And what it has not led to, I think, with only very, very few exceptions, is a serious reading on any level of the texts of Marx himself. I think you are right. A certain *gauchisant*—which is really the word for it—discourse is, if not hege-monic, very widespread in the United States. What is not widespread is the knowledge of, and the sophisticated command of, *Capital*, of, I don't know, even of the *Eighteenth Brumaire*. These are not texts that have been widely read and talked about.

J.D.: This state you describe can perhaps partially be explained by a widely held conviction that reading Marx, as it has been practiced until now, is no longer useful in order to understand modern economics or geopolitics, literature or science (social or not) today. Either to understand them or to transform them. If today it were possible to produce a new reading of Marx that would be necessary to "understand and transform," I would subscribe to it with open arms. If I could participate in such a project, I would do so with no reservations. Is it, moreover, certain that I am doing none of that now? In any case, if someone did it well, I would follow. Up till now, this has not taken place and, in my opinion, this is not just coincidental. But if you can do it, I'll follow you!

Let me say parenthetically that I am shocked to see that, after the extraordinary success of Marxist discourse (until the beginning of the 1970s, notably in France, Marxist discourse had quite an authority), the page has been turned to the point that it's almost forbidden, condemned, or ridiculed, old-fashioned to cite Marx. I'm not saying this to please you, but it appears quite shocking and politically dangerous. I say so publicly any time the opportunity arises. The same goes for Freud, and Lacan a bit, too.

M.S.: You said a moment ago that you thought the branding of Marx and Marxism as old-fashioned in America was not simply by chance. Nor is it by chance in France. In France, it could be the decline of the authority of the Communist Party. I would understand that.

J.D.: Which is certainly not a coincidence!

M.S.: But in America, it can't be that. We don't have that cause. Among even so-called left intellectuals, the sense that the classical texts of Marx are *dépassés* is very strong. I think that is politically and intellectually dangerous. I don't think we have gone beyond the problematic of Marx in any serious sense. It's not that all the answers are there in Marx's texts, but we still must learn to read Marx.

J.D.: In rereading the pages you photocopied in preparation for this interview, I state that I consider myself Marxist to the extent that I think that Marx's text is not an immobile given, and that we must continue to work, etc.

If the discourse of an economist in the Marxist tradition withstood the test, let's say, of the economic realities of our time, do you believe that discourse would remain repressed, unknown, marginalized? I think the result would stand on its own. If a Marxist theoretician of literature produced a discourse effectively formalizing or mightily transforming a given situation, would we remain ignorant of it because of political censure? I don't think so. If a discourse of that type—for example, yours—can effectively convince, it's because it has integrated theoretical or conceptual motifs that are not exclusively Marxist. It's not certain that the necessity or pertinence of your discourse corresponds to its Marxist project. The references to Marx are not enough to prove the contrary. Now, if a new theoretical configuration integrated certain motifs with Marxist ones, I would not have the least objection in principle. "Mine" (if one can say "mine"), well, what I try to do, integrates to a certain extent motifs that could be considered Marxist, which in any case owe something essential to that heritage, to a passing *from* Marxism, *through* Marxism. Inasmuch, for example, as my discourse is freed from certain idealistic naivetés. But that's not enough to call it a *Marxist* discourse, don't you think? It's not a discourse dominated by the Marxist reference. It's not a discourse foreign to Marxism or anti-Marxist, either. Moreover, I will always wonder if the idea of Marxism—the self-identity of a Marxist discourse or system or even a science or philosophy—is not in principle incompatible with the event-Marx.

M.S.: Maybe by following some itinerary through Marx, to the degree that I'm capable of producing anything new about Proust, for example, I will necessarily go beyond classical Marxist categories. Is that the force of what you are saying?

J.D.: Going beyond classical Marxist categories is perhaps an injunction of Marxism. An injunction in itself contradictory, because there should not be any Marxist injunction. Such an injunction would produce dogmatism and must therefore remain foreign to Marxist discourse.

M.S.: With that I agree. That is probably right. If you continue to do and practice the forms of intellectual inquiry that Marx would license in the United States—that, I think, remains important for a variety of reasons.

J.D.: I would quite agree. I believe in the political necessity of taking Marxist argumentation or critique into account, to listen to it, and to never close off access to it, provided that this Marxist critique itself remain alive, open, that it not become sclerotically dogmatic. I have on occasion attacked caricatures of Marxism that didn't interest me because I found them to lack pertinence. But I have never attacked the radicality of Marxist critique as such. I stress the term *critique* as a motif from the Enlightenment: I hold it to be essential in Marx's language and project as well as absolutely indispensable today—insufficient, but vitally necessary.

M.S.: Let's look at a specific text in which you cite Marx's critique of etymologism. Maybe it's a hostile question, I don't know, but I'll put it in a way that will perhaps sound a bit less hostile. In what sense are the procedures that you yourself adopt when you read a text allowed to escape that critique of etymologism that Marx levels at Stirner, et al.? Someone such as Marx—or perhaps Althusser would say, "There is a sliding between levels," when you move from the linguistic description of a phenomenon to what that description designates. We have talked in and around this, and you said, quite conspicuously, that this is one of the central questions for you. How do you escape Marx's ironic denunciation of Stirner?

J.D.: I cannot say that I escape that criticism altogether. Who can say he does? In fact, *in fact and apparently*, I am more concerned with language than with "economic reality" itself when I speak of the *proper* [*oikos*]— which is nonetheless economical through and through. To the extent that there is this appearance, my text cannot absolutely guard against the risk that you are justifiably denouncing: I am not directly concerned with what one may call *economic reality* in the strict and scientific sense (if that exists, independently and objectively). No one escapes this risk, not even Marx.

Now, furthermore, since in the passage you quoted and in many others: (1) I expressly critique etymology and etymologism; (2) I critique, or rather deconstruct, logocentrism, that is, the hypostasis of language through the reduction of reality to language, etc.; (3) it should not be forgotten that deconstruction starts with the deconstruction of logocentrism, continues with the elaboration of a concept of the text that does not leave "reality" outside, and avoids reduction to simple writing [*graphie*] on a page or in a book; (4) thematically, clearly, and insistently, I have formulated a critique of linguisticism, rhetoricism, etymologism, etc., which means that when I speak of the proper, I have already taken the precaution of saying that it is not simply the semantics of the proper or the word *proper* that interests me—that would be what others would call *reality*. I am trying to show precisely the impossibility and the recurrent failure of the reappropriation of the proper within the limits of language or even semantics. Naturally, for me the problem of reality is more complicated than it is on the side of those who think they can throw it up to me as an objection. Precisely for the reason that through *différance*, the necessary reference to the other, the impossibility for a presence to gather itself in a self-identity or in a substantiality, compels one to inscribe the reality effect in a general textuality or a differential process that, again, is not limited to language or writing as they are understood pre-scientifically and pre-grammatologically. I have explained quite thoroughly elsewhere the necessity (also strategic) of elaborating this new concept of the text.

That is why if one thinks that words are on one side and things or reality on the other, one is just as naive. Furthermore, I believe that when Marx rightly criticizes Stirner, his discourse implies at least the possibility and the aim of a reappropriation (class struggle, expropriation, final reappropriation, etc.). He thinks that the proper makes sense and that appropriation, reappropriation is not only possible, but that it is the motif itself of history as class struggle. In this, I am tempted to deconstruct the use Marx himself makes of property value. And that critique is not linguistic. It is quite the contrary! In believing reappropriation possible, one remains, knowingly, willingly or not, within the logocentric legacy.

Such would be my "critique" of Marx, or in any case my discrepancy with respect to a certain Marxism or a certain Marxist-inspired onto-theo-teleology. Benjamin himself perhaps does not escape it, despite his heterodoxy. Unlike Althusser, I believe that onto-theo-teleology is ineradicable in Marx. Althusser and the Althusserians say, "Marx is, or must be, Marx, *minus* the onto-theo-teleology, Marx *minus* the eschatology" through an operation that is no longer Marxist, through the *coup de force* of an artificial strategy (and I have nothing against this strategy as such, because why should one be strictly loyal to Marx, even in interpreting his texts?), through an interpretative violence (but it would be better to announce it, to thematize and reflect within its possibility). Now *that* is interesting! I will always be ready to subscribe to that gesture. But when they do this, there's no point in citing Marx any more or in pretending that Marx *meant–to–say–this—* there's no point, in any case, in lending privilege to that reference and excluding all others. They could perform that gesture without Marx or else with so many others. And then one would say that at least *they* don't teach Marx. One could say to them: "Okay! Go ahead and unfurl this anti-onto-theo-teleological discourse if it's possible, as well as the deconstruction of onto-theo-teleology, of property, of the value of the proper (what I myself try to do), of eschatology. But if you do, appealing to Marx is a more than problematical operation, which you would do well to problematize critically as such." Perhaps at a certain moment, given the state of political forces, the "history-of-the-workers'-movement," "class struggle," etc., it will have been important to refer or to pretend to refer to Marx or to Marx-Lenin in a dominant or exclusive way, all the while saying things that neither Marx nor Lenin ever said or could have said. Perhaps this was necessary: I don't know! Perhaps at a certain moment it was necessary to say yes to Marx, to soften, harden, or violently transform the reading of his writings to serve a "cause." But those who would deconstruct the motif of the proper or the idea of a final reappropriation of the means of production by the proletariat, for example, would have a discourse that is no longer Marxist, or called Marxist only by metonymy and for reasons of strategic convention. Besides, a significant deconstruction of property should no longer make any reference to a discourse, a work, or a proper name the dominant, hegemonic, or exclusive reference. Nondogmatic Marxists know this very well. They know very well the political consequences of the sacralizing capitalization upon a proper name.

M.S.: I understand. Actually, what you said at the beginning was, "No one can escape it entirely, not even Marx." I think that's probably right. It leads to one of the questions that I gave you, to which I'd like to turn now. Again, it's a sort of methodological question, dealing with one of the passages that I xeroxed for you from *De la grammatologie* on reading. As you know, it's a frequently cited passage, and, if it is not the establishment of a set of protocols or methods for reading, it is very close to being so. It moves in that direction, you know. Okay, this is how you go about reading a text. Also, I believe the section is entitled in French "Question de méthode"—an obvious reference to Sartre.

Now, once one reads Althusser, once one reads you, it is difficult to separate what he calls *symptomatic reading* from the kind of procedures of reading that you adopt or recommend. I think Althusser's "symptomatic reading" is something like a method, provided we take "method" in a slightly loose sense to include what one might call a *heuristic*, in the sense that Aristotle thought rhetoric was methodizable. It is not a science. That doesn't mean it is just anything at all. There are protocols.

Perhaps I can get you to talk about that in relationship to your own practice. When you go to read a text, you do proceed, I think, systematically, in a way that is, if not the same, does have what Wittgenstein calls a *family resemblance* to readings of previous texts. You may hesitate to talk about this, but I'd like to hear what you'd say. To put it in the sharpest possible formula and the simplest (which will probably be the most erroneous): is deconstruction as you do it (to the degree that it can be done)

192 THINKING AT ITS LIMITS

a method of reading in the loose sense I've suggested? Is it a method for interpreting, remobilizing, reconfiguring the text?

J.D.: This is a question to which one cannot furnish an adequate response without rethinking from top to bottom the concept of method, thus of path [*voie*], of way [*chemin*], of becoming-method of the way (from Parmenides to Hegel and beyond). I have tried to suggest as much elsewhere, with and without Heidegger . . .

M.S.: Would you accept the reformulation that I gave?

J.D.: If instead of method, you say *heuristic* and *family resemblance*, the concept of family resemblance is already absolutely devastating. It recalls that there are nothing but differences. The manner in which resemblances are constituted and stabilized is relative, temporary, precarious: One must take all singular occurrences into account. I realize that some things *overlap*. But the "rules" for these overlappings are not general rules, applicable from the outside. A relative generality strives each time to adjust itself to a text, a case, a problem, a singularity. You say, "if the procedures of deconstruction are possible, 'successful.'" I'm not sure deconstruction is possible, that it is of the order of the possible. On this question of possibility, on deconstruction as the experience of the impossible, I have explained myself abundantly in *Mémoires* and in *Psyché*.

Deconstruction is not "possible" if "possible" means to work as a technical instrument functions or obeys a program. Deconstruction is an explanation *with*, an experience *of* the impossible. Moreover, it is to the extent that one does more and something other than developing the necessity and the possibilities of a program that something happens and a form of responsibility, a decision, an action *takes place* precisely where one begins to make out the limits of the possible. Deconstructing is not possible in someone's, a group's, a discourse's, an institution's mastering a methodology or technique applied to making something happen. This deconstructs. From this standpoint, what is called *deconstruction* in the sense of a relatively coherent set of discursive rules at a given moment in Western discourse is only a symptom—an effect of deconstruction at work in what one might call *history* (all of the geopolitical earthquakes: the 1917 revolution, the two world wars, psychoanalysis, the third world, the techno-economico-scientific and military mutations, etc., etc., etc.).

All this, this open and non-self-identical totality of the world is decon-struction. It's a deconstruction in act or at work. And this must be brought back into play without recourse to either a theory of reflection or of ideology (be it refined to the extreme) to analyze this relation be-tween these "real" deconstructions and the apparently academic discourse to which we grant this name and which, moreover, is no longer or never was as academic as some people sometimes thought or allowed it to be thought.

Deconstruction happens [*ça arrive*] and it already happened in Plato's discourse in another form, with other words perhaps, but there was already an inadequation, a certain inability to close itself off, to form, to formalize itself, which was of a deconstructive order. If it has always been at work everywhere—in particular in the grand philosophical discourses—why does it attempt today to formalize and thematize itself, to name itself, as well, but without being able to do so? I don't believe that deconstruction can be formalized. "This" attempts to formalize, thema-tize, name itself in this name. An excellent question would be: Why does it take *this* form and *this* name today? Well, what I would like to call *de-construction* would be above all an effort to respond to that question or, rather, to elaborate it as question, to perhaps go beyond the elaboration of a question toward the presuppositions of such a problematic, even toward the problematic and the questionable in general. What is happening today that causes "deconstruction" to become a theme under this name? What is "today"? Really, when I think about it, this is what interests me and seems to me not to have any fixed limit. What *interests* me, that is, what engages me before and beyond the question itself is not the success of a method, a search or a powerful discourse. Rather, what interests me is to try to think about what happens there, what happens to thought as thought, which here is everything except a subjective, speculative, theoretical representa-tion or a philosophico-academic discourse. Why is it not only that we speak this way today, but why also are we not able to rid ourselves of these questions and motifs? Why is it that for decades now we can merely de-cree that we are finished with them, that they are outdated, as if to exor-cise, in a kind of animist denial, the persistent necessity of these decon-structive questions? Powerlessness interests me also: impossibility at least as much as possibility. Isn't politics or the political also this engagement with powerlessness?

When I spoke a while ago about opening to the event, the coming of the other, etc., that also is the experience of the impossible. It's the sole true provocation to be reflected upon. Thinking takes place not on what we can do, but beginning with what we cannot do. And a democracy in which one thinks everything possible and that democracy exists is already gone. If I may be allowed an aphorism, democracy, for me, is the political experience of the impossible, the political experience of opening to the other as possibility of impossibility. The event only happens under the aegis of the impossible. When an event, efficiency, or anything is deemed possible, it means that we have already mastered, anticipated, pre-understood, and reduced the eventhood of the event. Our relation to the event as our relation to the other, that is, as nonvoid (thus possible) experience of impossibility—this perhaps is a (barely figurable, nonrepresentable) figure of deconstruction. It can take many other discursive forms, but, for me, the "liveliest" aspect of deconstruction, its very resource, is this singular experience.

However, I mistrust the formulas I've just used. Taken in themselves, alone, without any other contextualization, without supplementary discourse and precautions, they can become politically quite dangerous and compromised with that which should have been avoided: "opening to the other" has already become a moralizing and unpalatable stereotype; "possibility of the impossible" or "impossible possibility" is not far from the formulas with which Heidegger defines being-for-death. Without wishing to set myself in opposition either to the ethics of opening to the other or to the existential analytic of *Dasein* as being-for-death (here associated in a very significant way with *the other and death*), I would not want what I've just said about the subject of the impossible and of the other to be simply assimilated to the discourses I have evoked. I will thus, for lack of time, space, and appropriate situation, keep in reserve a great number of precautions necessary for avoiding these confusions—precautions that would also be, to a certain extent, political. I believe that those interested in this can find the principle and the development in several of my texts, for example, those on Heidegger and on Levinas. I would add other protocols. The themes of the impossible and the incalculable can allow for the worst abuses if they are not articulated carefully, I dare say if one does not *calculate* their articulation with calculation, the possible, the measurable, the homogeneous, etc. One must master and calculate democratically also; there must be votes, thus identifiable subjects, subjects by right, majorities, determinable legalities, etc.—a perpetually indispensable negotiation between the singular opening to the impossible, which must be safeguarded, and the method, the right, the technique, the democratic calculation; between democracy to come and the limited present of democratic reality. The law of *iterability*, which I recalled earlier, but which I cannot explain here (cf. "Signature Event Context" and *Limited Inc*) is decisive here for defining the possibility, chance, risks involved in such a negotiation between singularity and concept. This negotiation is indispensable: it is included with the rules, but "in the last instance" (yes!) it is without rule and guaranteed rigor.

M.S.: Precisely.

J.D.: This is perhaps what politics is!

M.S.: What I was going to say in response to what you said earlier—this is Lenin's point and this is also what Althusser picks up from Lenin—to realize this sort of slightly unrealizable revolutionary "democracy to come," for that to happen, there has to be science.

J.D.: Absolutely.

M.S.: That which will bring the incalculable into play will be rational calculation about the possibility at any given moment.

J.D.: Each day, one must change, find a way, attempt to calculate without rules a way between the incalculable and the calculable. What I call *negotiation* does not simply negotiate the negotiable, it negotiates between the negotiable and the nonnegotiable, it negotiates *tragically* because it is terrible and fatal (but would be at least as much so otherwise), it negotiates the nonnegotiable. This negotiation is everything but a position or an assurance, it advances without assurance after having exhausted all the possibilities of calculation and, thus, of science.

M.S.: One more question very quickly, and probably then we should stop. I know that you think philosophical discourse and the reading of philosophical texts and the activity we are in general engaged in are important interventions in contemporary life. The question I would want to ask is: How do you think theoretical discourse intervenes in political life? A while ago, you said that to some extent the stopping short of the Althusserians was in part responsible for the demise of Marxism in

France. You didn't quite say that. But the implication is that if they had thought further, had they not simply drawn a line, things might have been different.

J.D.: I'm still too Marxist to think that. At that time, *in the place* they were, and thus who they were, *interpellated* and *situated* as they were, they (those "subjects") could not think or act otherwise, since the general situation—the place in which they were inscribed—did not allow it. Bad luck.

M.S.: That is what I would say, but still, if we are in the business of producing theoretical discourse, we want to say that theoretical discourse matters. The question is, precisely, how? What is the weight of theoretical discourse in contemporary political life in places such as France and the United States?

J.D.: Minimal. I've never thought or hoped (especially not hoped!) that a deconstructive practice (as such) would invade the entire field and occupy a dominant position fit for transforming the existence of a party, not to speak of all the rest. It is absolutely indispensable that other types of practices—scientific or otherwise—be pursued. But the idea that a de-constructive discourse might come to command and replace other prac-tices, discursive or not, is a kind of madness or comedy that doesn't inter-est me in the least. Deconstruction's motif, impulse, or stimulus is doubtlessly necessary and at work in places one least expects (today in nu-merous nonliterary and nonphilosophical fields), but without its replacing or substituting for anything else. As to the effects of theoretical discourse in general upon political reality, they cannot be analyzed as they were in the nineteenth century, or even before World War II. Everything is to be revamped in this respect. A developed capitalist society is characterized by the fact that the worlds of education, research, and information (universi-ties and research institutes) directly or indirectly irrigate the entire social fabric. The circulation of languages and ideas is following altogether dif-ferent trajectories. And, paradoxically, what is called *theoretical discourse* has, I would say, no more "influence," but is more directly in contact with the decision-making instances—it is both more permeable and more pen-etrating. It communicates along new, more diversified, more overdeter-mined trajectories with the "general" discourse of society, with "public opinion," with the discourse of politicians, with the military discourse, with the juridical discourse. We should not, therefore, underestimate what is happening in places where this discourse appears too complicated or sophisticated. It is indeed less decipherable, more confined, more "private" than before on account of the mass-mediatization that homogenizes, and thus simplifies and censors, more and more. But the inverse is also true: it benefits from a growing capillary action that undoubtedly carries along with it great waste, but that, all told, causes more communication than before. Our analyses must be adjusted to these paradoxes. We must return to the "infrastructure/superstructure" model(s), the figure of the intellectual, the relations between the university, the nonacademic research institutes, and the sociopolitical space—and thereby so many other things.

M.S.: Well, two things I would say at this point. What you said, I think that's true. It's wrong to underestimate the effects of theoretical discourse.

J.D.: Not the effects in the sense of effects of a cause or in a sense where theoretical discourse would be the cause of effects it would produce all by itself, as a cause or as *causa sui*. The relation of causality is too overdetermined to enable us to say, "This, which is this, identical to itself, has many or few effects (i.e., this or that, which is identical to itself) upon this or that, etc."

A small example in closing. I burst out laughing when I read twice in the press (notably in the *Wall Street Journal*) that Allan Bloom, the author of *The Closing of the American Mind*, accused Foucault and me by name of a whole bunch of negative things in the United States, such as, for example, Judge Bork's failure and the destabilization of discussions about original intent in the Constitution. Then, after laughing—and judging—I said to myself, "Of course!" Neither Foucault nor I nor any individual nor "deconstruction" is responsible for the fact that at the time of the hearings all those questions about original intent took on the proportions they did and led to those conclusions. We didn't produce those questions: they were produced by a general deconstruction where everyone asks himself, "What *is* original intent? What axiomatic ensures its authority? What interests serve this axiomatic? What is the meaning of the Constitution?" These questions are not the effects of a theoretical discourse, but, rather, they are theoretical or theoretico-political events that happen and that cannot be without relation to the work Foucault and I, among others, took an interest in, the work whose interest commanded the attention (and not fortuitously) of so many people—work on intentionality, will to say [*vouloir-dire*], meaning and signification, the text, the concept of the author, the theory and limits to the theorization of speech acts, etc. None of these projects is a cause, but they are not accidents or isolatable epiphenomena, either. Between the constitutional debates over original intent (with their enormous direct or indirect stakes) and a certain state of genealogico-deconstructive research, there is a certain configurativity. To say that it's Foucault's or "deconstruction's" fault is stupid; but to claim that there is no relationship and to be insensitive to this configuration would not be serious, either.

Translated by Robert Harvey

The Aforementioned So-Called Human Genome

The Norm and Its Suspension

No one in this workshop has asked for the abolition of any norm. We know that there are norms and that these norms are necessary. The question that was raised was essentially the following: The concept of norm is a very equivocal concept because it encompasses both the concept of moral, ethical, political law as well as the concept of factuality. The norm is also sometimes imposed as a fact, in the name of which one normalizes precisely, and normativity may be distressing under certain conditions. Consequently, in view of the equivocation and obscurity of the concept of norm, we have proposed to stop and to reflect, and not to leap up as soon as the question of norm is raised. In the face of this polymorphism, in the face of the multiplicity of norms, of normalities, the question was raised of knowing if a monomorphism did not risk, in the name of the norm and under various figures, leading us to what some might consider to be ethical-political acts of violence. We must also remember that, if the norm and the reference to normality are necessary for morality (for law, for therapy, etc.), it is also in the name of a certain reference to the norm, to norms, real or alleged, that some of the most disturbing practices and politics have been developed; thus, prudence as far as the reference to the norm is concerned.

The second aspect on which I personally insisted: there is a troubling and painful paradox when we have to acknowledge the fact that the concepts of responsibility and freedom do of course call for the establishment, the institution of norms, or the reference to norms, but that they also, at the same time, call for a suspensive attitude with regard to the norm and normality. A responsibility or an ethical decision, intent on modeling itself after, or ordering itself according to, a scientific or allegedly scientific knowledge that establishes the norm or normality—that is, a responsibility or an ethical decision that would be satisfied with unfolding a theoretical program or the content of a knowledge regarding a norm—obviously would not be, in the rigorous sense of the term, an act of responsibility or freedom. What this means, abstractly—I will say it abstractly first, then I will say it concretely—however paradoxical it may seem, is that freedom and responsibility are incompatible with the mere reporting of the existence of a norm, a normative reality. Freedom is free with regard to such a normative reality, as is responsibility. If there is responsibility, if there is an ethical and free decision, responsibility and decision must, at a given moment, be discontinuous with the normative or the "normal," not in their misrecognition of norms, not in their ignorance of a knowledge about norms—rather they must take a leap and welcome a sort of discontinuity, a heterogeneity in relation to the normative as such. This may seem shocking, but it follows from the very concept of freedom and responsibility. The statement thus appeared a little speculative. But concretely, what this means is that the decisions we need to discuss here, the recommendations we need to make, if they are ethical, political, juridical, etc., if they involve *freedom* and *responsibility*, must naturally take into account the scientific knowledge about the aforementioned norms, mononorms, polynorms, but must not leave to knowledge or expect from the knowledge that science has at its disposal, any of the political, ethical, etc. decisions that we are discussing here. This means that, at a certain moment, questions of norm must escape scientificity, they must escape a techno-scientific programming.

Freedom and responsibility demand that one know what is known [*savoir le savoir*], that one take knowledge into account as rigorously and in as unlimited a way as possible, but the moment of the decision, of responsibility as such, is not a moment of knowing, and neither, consequently, is it a moment that depends on what this knowledge of norms might have to teach us. If one does not want to abandon the concept of norm absolutely (which I can understand), we must distinguish between norms and norms. There are norms that have to do with factual normality, which knowledge can describe, record, observe, formalize as normality or as normative fact: there are normative facts. And then there are, if one absolutely wants to keep this word, norms that are heterogeneous to these, heterogeneous to normality and to the normative fact. If, that is, one wants to keep these words and these values or these concepts of *freedom* and *responsibility*—and this is a question. If one thinks that there are, or that there should be, a free and responsible decision on this matter, one must either suspend the normative or else establish, take into account a radical heterogeneity between different kinds or structures or concepts of norm. This is what was sketched out, in a problematic mode.

The Norm Must Be Lacking

A word about the link between patentability and the norm, and, in short, about the action of man that we have been discussing from the beginning. What makes the question of the patentability so difficult is, as Charles Auffray has reminded us, not only the difficulty but even the impossibility of distinguishing rigorously between invention and discovery. And I fear that this distinction may never (and less than ever, I would say, in the future) be maintained rigorously. On the one hand, there is the problem of mathematics and of the difficult or impossible distinction between invention and discovery, a difficulty that thus renders precarious the statements of right concerning the patent. On the other hand, there is actually something that is more concrete still: the question of the creation of genetic, robotic, computer, etc. databases; and even if one generously declares, as the French have done, that there should be no patentability in this respect, the massive, geopolitical, economic reality of the appropriation of data banks by a certain number of world powers makes it such that, legal patent or no, there is appropriation. There will be appropriation of knowledge and technical ability with the constitution of these databases. Even if one generously protects knowledge against patentability, there is no denying that modes of appropriation of all kinds will continue to be practiced, to be developed, with various social consequences. The passage from therapeutic medicine to predictive medicine, which is on the agenda of all these discoveries, will privilege the rich to the detriment of the poor in our societies—to speak schematically—and

202 THINKING AT ITS LIMITS

will hugely benefit the industrial societies that have these databases, to the detriment of other societies. And here the question of human universality arises, as does the question of ethics, beyond or independently of norms. There are two ways of raising the question of man, the essence of man, and the unity of man, of the human species: is man the being that possesses a knowledge about itself? With the possibilities of self-fashioning [*auto-façonnement*] (this is an expression that I heard a lot this morning and that intrigues me greatly . . . self-fashioning with the knowledge it would have of its own norms), is this what man is, essentially? Or is man an *I* that, given the radical experience of a certain lack of norm, will raise the question of ethics, of freedom, and responsibility? These are two competing definitions of man, are they not? They concern the same being, if you like, but on the one side this being is defined as one that knows its own norm, that knows itself, that knows its normativity, its normality, and that draws the consequences from this knowledge, as scientist, techno-scientist, etc.; whereas in another way, this being is one that at least asks itself the question of ethics, of freedom, of responsibility, where not only a norm and a knowledge of this kind are lacking, but further, *must be lacking*. I am not saying that they are lacking because of some deficiency, but rather *must be lacking* for a responsible decision to be made. Finally, is the disposition of techno-knowledge about the norm not itself conditioned by, does it not arise from a lack, from a deficiency—which one can describe in a negative way or not—in any case, from what we have been calling, for convenience sake, a *lack of norm*? Thus, this *lack of norm* would be the condition, not only of a possible ethics of responsibility but of knowledge itself, and even the developments of techno-science. What is man? What might the so-called *genome* of the said *man* be?

Toward a Reconstruction of the Legal Concept of the "Human"?

The example of virtual machines challenges not only the content of a legal conceptuality and the concepts that the law has been relying on until now to legislate and organize the field of patentability but the mode of production of the law itself. What is patentability, for example, when it is a matter of legal statements themselves? In other words, if one takes the legal body not simply as the place in which these problems are addressed but as an example, an "object" of the problem to be studied, then the acceptability, the receivability, the legitimacy of legal statements will, in turn, be subjected to questions, which, as you will remember, were indeed asked. What this means is that the problems preoccupying us are not simply scientific or philosophical examples to which one could simply adjust what is called the *law;* rather, they are examples that call for a deconstruction and a reconstruction of the legal and of the legal concept of the "human." It is obvious that what we think we hear in the word law, in the auto-interpretation of law, if you will, as complex as it may be, cannot measure up to what is taking place today. This does not mean that it ever measured up to it; perhaps, in retrospect, what was calmly called *technology, industry, activity*, the *sacred right of patents* etc., *copyrights* etc., was already problematic; one might have pointed to difficulties of the same kind. What is required, then, is a reconstruction of the axiomatic, not only the axiomatic of such and such a law but the axiomatic of the legal in general. This is obviously enormous. The limits of the fields under consideration are not even certain. And it is not the scientist or the philosopher who is going to ask the jurist to change his axiomatic; the limits of these very competencies are being made fragile by what is taking place, by the event in question, and one does not really know where this event is taking place. Yet another question about the secret. Obviously, the example of Coca-Cola, as complex as it may be, is only one example. There are choices, the position of disclosure and the position of the secret. But the position of the secret assumes that the secret is protected *publicly*, so to speak. For there to be a patent, one must be assured of a certain phenomenality, a certain visibility, publicity even, of the secret. Where is a secret, in a sense, registered? With whom, to be protected as secret? In other words, what is the secret *as secret* in the context of the patent?

Even the Other

In spite of the very spontaneous sympathy that I have for these positions, and even though I most often raise questions from a non-"scientistic" place, as you have done, I would have liked to ask for further clarification on several formulations. For example, this one: you said that "not knowing the hour and the day" is sometimes the condition of freedom, something like this; I think I know what you meant to say; nonetheless, taken to its extreme consequence, I find this formulation somewhat worrisome, even contestable. I can perfectly well see someone who, without "scientism," could tell you that knowing the hour and the day is also the condition of a certain freedom . . . I had a question of the same kind concerning another formulation, about the engendering of the similar, and of the identifiable: one must be able to recognize the being one engenders, etc., while making room for what you regularly assigned to uncertainty and chance; nonetheless, there was a tension, which I would insist on, between the law of humanity and the similar (the engendering of the similar, the recognizable, which is the law, and that you mentioned in your conclusion), and then, in the name of freedom, the place recognized and reserved for the random, that is to say, in short, for the unpredictable that can be, if it is truly unpredictable, not what is similar, but other, and even totally other. At one moment, in commenting on chance, randomness, the unpredictable, you said that the dissimilarity that must also be acknowledged in reproduction should not be "too pronounced." Here I would have liked for you to give me, if possible, a more precise answer on what you meant by *too pronounced* or *not too pronounced*. I find this formulation rather troubling. You know, concerning the recognizable, the similar, and the identifiable, I wonder—this is a speculative question, and not at all an objection—whether the men that we call *prehistoric*, and without even going back so far, if the men of the sixteenth and seventeenth century would have easily recognized the men that we are as Men. They would have recognized all sorts of things, of course, and very quickly, but if we had drawn their attention to a certain number of technological transformations that, without affecting our physical appearance and certain features of our social relations, have radically changed our relation to space, to time, to Earth, etc.; if we had gathered them for a colloquium and had asked them: do you think that people who could do this or that, go to the Moon, freeze their sperm, open a virtual space, etc., would still be Men? I am not retrospectively prejudging their answers. In other words, in the forms that I have given it, forms of the similar and the dissimilar, my question amounts to wondering whether the ethics to which you so firmly hold does not also bind us to the other and to what is dissimilar, radically other. Who, then, is not unquestionably human according to the way *we* define the human, today?

Decidedly Keeping Watch

In the fascinating and impassioned discussions that have brought us together, I have been constantly split between two contradictory feelings. And thus, between two forms or two regimes of questions. There are those questions that affect us with pathos or with tragedy in a way that is unique and unheard-of in the history of humanity and in history: an acceleration of the progress of knowledge that is incommensurable with its earlier rhythms, an unprecedented power, a power both scientific and technical but also inescapably techno-economic and techno-political, which is sometimes controlled by private enterprises, sometimes by state agencies, sometimes by agencies whose unprecedented forms largely exceed the calmly received opposition between public and private, or even collective and individual. They exceed even the old concepts of state and nation-state, or the concept of international law that presupposes them. And let us never forget that whatever the universalism and humanism of its declared aims and whatever its necessity, and even if it is in fact preferable to an absence of law, this international law is still largely dominated in its concepts and in its implementation by certain nation-states. It remains under the conceptual, constitutional, and techno-economic-military hegemony of a few rich and powerful countries that find themselves, not by chance, to be the only ones in a position to have this knowledge and this power at their disposal, as well as the knowledge-power [*savoir-pouvoir*] that we have been discussing here.

The progress of knowledge thus, a virtual extension of a power without precedent might, in fact, push us in a way that is inescapable and fatal—whence the pathos of these discussions—toward stakes and decisions that engage our freedom and our responsibility. For it would be a matter, this time, of a knowledge and a power, a power of knowing [*pouvoir-savoir*] turned toward us, that is, toward what we might be tempted, rightly or wrongly, to understand as what is proper to man, what is originally most proper to man. But the freedom and responsibility of whom, before whom? Who is claiming freedom and responsibility here, and before whom? The form of this question seems all the more disturbing that this "who before whom"—appearing and answering for one's freedom is what is at issue here—might perfectly well define the *who* that we are, so to speak. It is a little as if the judge and the tribunal, for example the human tribunal, were defining, constituting, or inscribing in the constitution of its law, the essence of what appears before it; namely, man, who would not know who he is before appearing before these alleged or self-constituted judges—judges who would basically be the only possible witnesses or the only ones able to call witnesses to and challenge them on the stand.

In other words, from this trial and these judgments we would learn who we are, something, therefore, that we did not know before: an unheard-of dilemma, a dramatic or tragic dilemma, in fact, and one that appears to be without precedent. Whence the pathos that sometimes affects our debates . . . Freedom of whom and before whom? we were asking: who is claiming or assuming a free responsibility here? before whom? I say "free responsibility," on the one hand, to join the two concepts that make up the new subtitle of this colloquium and mark its differences with regard to the preceding one on genetic patrimony and the rights of humanity, but also, on the other hand, in order not to challenge, as we may have to do, what, in a classical philosophical tradition, forms an indissociable link between responsibility and freedom, that is, autonomy. For a classical philosopher, there is no responsibility without autonomy and without freedom, and this leads to several essential and paradoxical consequences as far as the concept of decision that follows from it is concerned, and which, in fact, requires that any free decision not be commanded as such, not only not by any knowledge but not even by any preestablished norm, any preexisting and pre-given rule that might simply be applied with consequence. This is a difficult *topos* of the classical philosophy of freedom in which I do not want to engage here, but it continues to provoke us in concrete and urgent ways in our debates, whether or not we pay attention to it, and whether or not it is made explicit. For a classical philosopher, and not only Kantian, it would be an untenable contradiction to speak of a responsibility without autonomy, that is, without a law that one gives oneself. And yet, one could perhaps think a responsibility before the other that would be *heteronomic* in its essence and would begin by giving up a certain kind of autonomous freedom, that is, by renouncing the self-fashioning of man that has been under discussion here for several days. But I will leave this problem aside, noting only that the said self-fashioning might just as well be understood as reproductive programming of the same or the similar, as the unpredictable production and invention of the totally other. And one of the many paradoxes is that one can, in the name of the similar, authorize both the eugenic reproduction of the same and that which opposes all eugenics, both the eugenics that one strangely calls *negative* and the eugenics in which, conversely, one finds some justification. In the same way, in the name of difference and the dissimilar, one can just as well justify the respect for alterity or singularity as a discriminating hierarchy or selective programming. The logic of the similar/dissimilar is a terrible logic; it demands, in any case, that we not hold ourselves to any simple opposition here between the similar and the dissimilar. Therefore, let us repeat the question: *freedom or responsibility of whom, and before whom?* Of "us, humans," we say, and if we were prudent enough, philosophically and scientifically, not to rush to say: "we, humans," for as long as we do not clearly know what this essence or this identity of the human is that serves as the horizon for our reflections, supposing even that it could be an object of knowledge—which is another question, precisely—if then we were so prudent as to guard against the problematic expression of the *human genome*, as I did in a workshop when I spoke of the *aforementioned so-called human genome*, taking into account thus several reservations here and there . . . , then we would speak not of the freedom and responsibility of "the humans –that –we are," but of *our* freedom and *our* responsibility, in order not to say what this "we" refers to or what the *what* is of this *who*, of this *we*: our responsibility, therefore, a responsibility that is ours, we who would appear before an alleged essence of man, we who would have to answer, therefore, both for ourselves before It [*Elle*] and for It in *us*, in us as its heirs or its guardians, thus to answer for them, and before this *human species*, whose concept will then for the first time have become a legal concept, inscribed as such in the text of law. But let us not forget that this concept was already inscribed in it in a certain way when the International War Tribunal tried the crimes against humanity, or today when courts of national justice in France find themselves in a situation in which they again refer, in a way that is so problematic and so dramatic, to this same concept. This is not a simple parenthesis nor is it a fortuitous association. One has the impression (and I am describing my first impression, that of a tragic, apocalyptic pathos), at certain moments, which I am trying to describe, that the risk that is run at this unique moment in the history of humanity is the risk of new crimes being committed against humanity and not only, if I can say this, against millions of real human beings as was the case, but a crime such that a sorcerer's apprentice who was very cunning, the author of potential genetic manipulations, might in the future commit or supply the means for committing—in the name of science, of techno-science—against man, against the very humanity of man, no longer against millions of representatives of real humanity but against the essence-itself of humanity, against an idea, an essence, a figure of the human race, represented this time by a countless number of beings and generations to come, a human race (on the subject of which some will say that we know and should already know what it is, and about which others will maintain a questioning reserve, at the risk of being taken for antihumanists). If I evoked the crimes against humanity . . . and not only against men as such—hence, precisely, the unprecedented jurisdiction of the International War Tribunal—but crimes against a heritage, a future, or a potential of humanity of which we are supposed to be the responsible guardians—it is not only because both the question and the concept of the *crime against humanity* have recently come across a sinister actuality in this country, nor is it only because the concept of *crime against humanity* already assumed, before its recent mutation, the inscription in law, in international law, of a certain concept of the humanity of man, of what makes man man, a critical concept for this dogmatic stance (I will leave this question aside for the moment), critical or dogmatic in its formulation but also in its legal implementation, either the one or the other . . . I also evoke the ghost and the reality of the crimes against humanity because basically it is this ghost that will have haunted all of these debates, whether we spoke of it or not—that will have haunted them as the possible underside of everything that, in the given or promised knowledge of the genome, might also herald the good-doer [*bienfaisant*] (good [*bienfaisance*] for health or for the salvation of man), and especially because the crimes against humanity that were tried after the war, under certain conditions, were committed by men, by a regime, by nation-states, which, in a way that was not accidental, found themselves acting, selecting, or eliminating in the name of a certain human norm (or normality or normativity) and which, with the help of bio-powers and scientific or pseudo-scientific references, practiced a kind of eugenics. Are we not, on the one hand, at this unheard-of moment in the history of science or techno-science and of humanity, in a situation where a terrible suspicion sets the stage for a grand dramatic judgment whose apocalyptic proportions begin to resemble a last judgment? Chief accusation: *crimes against humanity*, potential or premeditated crimes. A judgment that would accuse or keep guard over we-know-not-whom: scientists in their research, research that is termed *basic* and whose technical use is perhaps even at the origin of the said *research*, as well as the decision-makers, the users of this knowledge, politicians, citizens, but also philosophers and ideologues, or the improvised pseudo-scientists who auto-legitimate themselves as *philosophers* or *moralists*, psychoanalysts, and all of those who challenge—at the risk of dissolving them— the classical concepts of *consciousness, freedom, responsibility*; but also exigent philosophers who demand precisely that more questions be asked about the essence of man, about history, about the philosophical, theological, metaphysical, scientific history of the concept of man, about its interpretation, about norms, and even the concept of norm that it brings into play. I was thus (as I was saying) split between two feelings. On the one hand, there was this feeling of dramatic and tragic seriousness concerning a unique moment in the history of humanity where the question, *What is man?* could no longer wait as it seems to have done formerly, considering the time and patience of theological or metaphysical speculations, but was today taking on, here, now, a terribly concrete and urgent form at an infinitely accelerated rate in the very place where decisions about the processing of the aforementioned so-called *human genome* could no longer wait.

Along with this feeling of fatal precipitation of the question, "What is man?," I had the opposite feeling, a feeling that had a calming effect, relativizing or demystifying in some sense . . . Indeed, one might just as well say—and it is equally true that these questions and their staging have a whole history and that this history is not so new—this archive was often recalled in the course of our workshops . . . And what is more, the genome, even the *human genome*, is not man; an ability to map the genome is not the manipulation of the genome . . . And what is more, biologists, geneticists, even the decision-makers who make the necessary investments for the so-called *basic* research (money, training, institutions) are on the whole pretty vigilant. They have enough historical memory to set up security measures against what, henceforth, is identifiable as the temptation of *negative* eugenics, normative and negative, that would seek to eliminate the alleged subhumans or to produce superhumans . . . And what is more, a vast political and legal consciousness is indisputably in the process of rising to meet this incredible progress of knowledge, and sometimes, it was recalled, by inscribing itself in commitments and texts of law . . . And what is more, one can and one must resist—we must arm ourselves for this—the phantasm and the pathos of ignorance, which ignorance and disinformation may produce or propagate . . . And what is more, between occultist obscurantism and positivistic scientism (which is rarely, moreover, the doing of men and women of science), there is another way to which I think, I hope, this colloquium in fact testifies. In fact, even if we do not really know what the human is, and even if it is not the object of a knowledge but of another type of performative engagement, even if we do not know who we are, for lack of a knowledge about the norms of humanity, the human is no more in danger today, at least insofar as the lack of knowledge is concerned, than it was yesterday or the day before . . . Finally, let us not forget that, practically speaking, today this progress promises us extraordinary but predictable feats of predictive or therapeutic medicine. These are my two feelings. And it seems to me, upon reflection, that the two feelings I am describing here somewhat summarily, at too great a length but summarily (the most disturbing, most apocalyptic feeling as well as the more reassuring feeling, a relativistic and confident optimism) are both equally legitimate and thus also equally unfounded and equally inappropriate. However, as inadequate and inappropriate as they may be, they warn us; they give us contradictory signals to which we must neither renounce nor remain blind.

This is why it seemed good and desirable to me, I also said this yesterday, that the two contradictory logics remain; that this contradiction itself be inscribed in the "recommendations"—I use this word for convenience's sake—or in the messages that we will have to formulate at the end on this great encounter and that instead of positing [*poser*] theses or registering [*déposer*] conclusions, we issued a call to vigilance, that is to say, to the necessity of keeping the debate wide open by multiplying the signs of critical tension, of contradictions, of dilemmas, even aporias. Before recalling or formalizing, to conclude, several of these signs, as examples, I repeat that a responsibility can only be taken—and a decision, and an act of freedom—where one does not know, whatever one's knowledge (and one must know, it is always better to know), the decision is made where knowledge as such does not dictate rules or norms from which we would need, in short, but to unfold the program of action or draw the consequences. Thus, it is always in a dilemma and a certain non-knowledge [*non-savoir*] as to what it would be best to do, it is at the moment when two contradictory imperatives are in competition, that a responsible freedom can be exercised as such. Here, to be brief, are several examples of these contradictory imperatives.

Under the concept of property or appropriation, I will inscribe two themes. The first involves the appropriation of knowledge power [*savoir-pouvoir*] regarding the genome: on the one hand, of course, one can, one must certainly see to it, in the name of universal, universalist, or humanist values, that one opposes the patentability of certain contents of pure knowledge, what we call *discoveries*—as French researchers have done in an exemplary fashion. On the other hand, on the opposing side, one must neither forget nor cease to take actual account of what still radically limits the scope of such a decision; namely, the fact that we do not have at our disposal criteria rigorous enough to distinguish by right an *invention* from a *discovery* (the distinction between what the law holds to be patentable and non-patentable is not rigorous), and the fact that this inadequacy is not provisional but essential. It touches on problems of a philosophical nature that neither jurists nor scientific researchers, at least as such, are equipped to address. In this regard, the appeal to a critical and genealogical reflection of a philosophical kind in its traditional forms or less traditional forms cannot be considered an embellishment or an incidental—sometimes synonymous with rhetorical—supplement, as I have heard it suggested here and there. One cannot know what one is talking about when one speaks of the possession of a patent without treating the philosophical problem of the criteria of the *invention* and the *discovery*, for example of the mathematical objects that form an essential part in the integration of software and data banks. Second, one must also remember that the legal theory of patenting dates back in its concept and its texts to a period in industry that can no longer be translated into the state of techno-science we are talking about. Theorists and producers of law are thus faced with an enormous task: there must be law immediately [*sans attendre*], but we should not hide the fact that this law is inadequate, and that the task is immense and difficult. Third, if, on the one hand, it is a good thing to exclude patentability in certain cases, or to limit it, we must nonetheless remember, the issue being the possession of knowledge, that access both to the content of knowledge and to discoveries though it may be good to make access universal in principle and public by right must go through what defines and controls the public space today in a way that is dominant; namely, the state. In fact (and this is not a temporary accident), data banks, the actual body of knowledge are and will remain at the disposal of the countries that produce them, that is to say, the rich and so-called *developed* countries that will, in fact, be the first, if not the only, beneficiaries of this knowledge, which limits significantly the universality to which one lays claim. The public space today, as state space, is not universal. It is also national.

This is also true of the beneficial effects of *predictive medicine.* If we want to keep this thing and this concept, we must know that these effects will not only shatter the concepts of health insurance that govern our societies, and which are based on a therapeutic, nonpredictive, goal of medicine, but that they will also necessarily and for a long time benefit and even increase the privileges of certain social groups in our countries as well as the inequality between the so-called developed countries and the developing countries.

All of these serious questions about appropriation lead to dilemmas more fundamental still when one refers them to the paradoxical concept of the possession of what is proper (what is that which is proper?) that organizes them. When we speak of the property of the living or of the body, of an inalienable character, noncommercializable, etc., or of what is properly human—if we do not recognize in that which is *proper,* and proper to the human in particular, a certain indeterminability and a certain capacity to dispropriate itself or to expropriate itself—we will also be able to justify, in the name of what is "properly human," thinking we know what this is, the programmable reproduction of the identical to infinity, excluding mutability, progress as well as history . . . Without being able to engage here in the nonetheless necessary analysis of this disconcerting logic of the proper, I wanted to underline that if, here again, one only remains on the level of philosophical pseudo-proofs, or if one dismisses philosophy as a simple rhetorical gesture on this subject, about what *proper* and properly human and *human* mean, then none of the problems that we are posing here can be treated with any rigor.

Another related dilemma should be neither hidden nor mitigated. Certainly it must be recalled that purely scientific research and its breathless desire to know must not, in principle, be opposed by any limit: this is the unconditional intra-scientific ethics that Gérard Huber discussed. And because there is something here that is *properly human* insofar as humans have opened the question of what is proper to them, and because there is an ethics of the Enlightenment here that must remain unconditional, and because science is a part of culture—even if, exceeding the multiplicity of cultures, it may seem removed from every religious, national, linguistic culture—*it is always better to know than not to know*. These axioms or norms, let it be said in parentheses, *have nothing to do with knowledge*. To say that one *must know*, that there *must be knowledge*, this does not have to do with knowledge. Even to say that there *must be knowledge unconditionally* is not a statement of knowledge. Certainly, but at the same time, in the same way that we know that a *discovery* that is supposed to be of pure knowledge is difficult to dissociate and is less and less dissociable from an *invention*, that is, from its *technical application*, of the technical application of knowledge (one cannot therefore separate knowledge from technics here); we know that so-called *basic* research, which could not in fact be curtailed by laws, censors, interdictions, finds itself, given the *technical* character of basic research and the means it employs, irreducibly governed by econo-political decisions that are set by priorities. These decisions have nothing to do with science itself, and, as decisions, they never will. One could multiply the examples of dilemmas that one would do well to leave open or to maintain in a critical state to avoid shutting down the debate on dogmatic theses or assurances . . . This is what must be avoided—dogmatic theses—this is a categorical imperative; dogmatism, this is to my mind what must be avoided at any price . . . One could, if we had the time, find the same form of the dilemma with the concept of *norm*, the concept of *model*, concept *or* reality, concept *and* reality, no sooner concept than reality, we can now say, even of the concepts *freedom* and *responsibility* that give our meeting its title.

The discussion must remain open on the meaning of these two words and these two concepts, open regarding their history and even their genealogy, their complex genealogy, the displacements that might be introduced into this genealogy by traditions of "religious" thought: I do not, in fact, think that these concepts are the same from one religion to another; for example, from one of the so-called religions of the Book to another, not to speak of other religions, not to speak of what might be introduced into this genealogy by events such as psychoanalysis or other types of modern knowledge. The discussion must remain open on these two words; and because we cannot wait on their account, or on account of the many kinds of oppositions that structure our debates, or on account of the many levels that

214 THINKING AT ITS LIMITS

Gérard Huber has distinguished between . . . (a decision does not wait, the decision cannot wait for levels to be distinguished). Well then, since we cannot wait for these oppositions to be analyzed, for these levels be distinguished, for the discussion to be over and for satisfactory conditions to be found to act and make decisions, given that urgency and precipitation are part of the very essence of the decision, our duty here is to *discover* and to *invent*, each and every time, in singular situations, that is to say, without a given rule. Our duty is to invent, to give the rule. And the example. Thus, not to wait and to know how to wait at the same time. It is vertiginous, but only in this situation can decisions be made. Not to wait, while holding oneself back nonetheless to continue to reconsider things; a responsible decision, if there is one, always comes at this price, as does vigilance, as does everything that might tear us from our dogmatic slumber, if this is possible.

Nietzsche and the Machine

R.B.: It has been an insistent point on your part, informing the reading strategy of each of your engagements with Nietzsche's philosophy, that there is no one truth to Nietzsche or to Nietzsche's text. Your relations to Nietzsche distinguish themselves explicitly from those of Heidegger, which are marked by a persistent, if not anguished, desire to contain Nietzsche within the history of Being. As you observe in *Otiobiographies,* "The future of the Nietzsche text is not closed."[1] I hope that my questions keep to the spirit of this remark, not only by remaining as open as possible but also because they concern the future(s) of Nietzsche (what Nietzsche had to say of the future as well as the future of Nietzsche's thought today). I want, nevertheless, to engage you with the Nietzsche text in relation to a specific historical context: that of a world emerging—politically, economically, and culturally—from the Cold War. The general orientation of my questions is thus not related too intently to questions of interpretation (whether of Nietzsche's text, your texts, or your texts on Nietzsche); it is guided, rather, by the consideration of the name *Nietzsche* as an "index" of a series of problems that are ever-more pressing at the end of the Cold War—namely, the relations between government, technology, justice, and the future. Let the name of Nietzsche in this context be a way of *opening up* possibilities of approach to these problems. I should like to entitle the interview "Nietzsche and the Machine."

QUESTION ONE: I will start with a very general question. When one considers all the writings that you have published to date, one is struck by a paradox. Since "Force and Signification" in *Writing and Difference,* various voices of Nietzsche have intimately inhabited your work, and yet, compared to the long analyses of Husserl, Plato, Hegel, Freud, Blanchot, etc., you have written, or at least published, few pieces explicitly on Nietzsche. Is there a particular reason for this?

J.D.: In response to question one—this apparent lack of sustained reflection on Nietzsche can perhaps be explained by following one of the threads of your introduction. I have indeed found it difficult to bring together or stabilize, within a particular configuration, a "thought" of Nietzsche. By the term *configuration* I mean not only a systematic coherence or consistency (no one has seriously tried to identify a philosophical or speculative "system" in what is called—a proper name more problematic and enigmatic than ever—*Nietzsche*) but also the organization of an ensemble, of a work or corpus, around a guiding meaning, a fundamental project or even a formal feature (of writing or speech). It is this irreducible and singular multiplicity, this resistance to any form of *Versammlung,* including that of the end of metaphysics (in the sense that Heidegger's interpretation constitutes an attempt to "arrest"— *comprehendere* rather than *verstehen*—the essential elements of Nietzsche's unique thought within such an end): it is this irreducibility that it has always seemed to me more just to respect. The diversity of gestures of thought and writing, the contradictory mobility (without possible synthesis or sublation) of the analytical incursions, the diagnoses, excesses, intuitions, the theater and music of the poetic-philosophical forms, the more-than-tragic play with masks and proper names—these "aspects" of Nietzsche's work have always appeared to me to defy, from the very beginning to the point of making them look somewhat derisory, all the "surveys" and accounts of Nietzsche (philosophical, metaphilosophical, psychoanalytic, or political). As you say, several voices can be heard; they return with an insistence that, I believe, will never cease, and that demands these voices never be reduced to a "monology." In this sense, such voices already resound in their future, in the reserve with which, to use a very Nietzschean figure, they are "pregnant." What will Nietzsche's future be? This question has always left me *on the verge* of a "general repetition" of Nietzsche.

That said, I have, *mutatis mutandis,* a similar feeling for those thinkers to whom I have apparently devoted more lengthy analyses. What

I have just said about Nietzsche, I would also say about Plato, Hegel, Husserl, Freud, Blanchot, and so on. My writing on them remains fragmentary, oblique, elliptical, open—I hope—to surprise and to the return of other voices. And so your question cannot be answered. Now, what is the privilege of Nietzsche in this respect? I don't know: he is perhaps, of them all, the most mad! Two consequences are to be drawn from this: first, through this madness thought is perhaps unleashed all the more violently and with all the more freedom; second, it is unleashed with all the more suffering. As a result, one must forbid oneself—with Nietzsche above all—to force his name into the straight jacket of an interpretation that is too strong to be able to account for him, in that it is claiming to recognize the identity of a meaning, of a message, of the unity of a word, or of a particular work.

QUESTION TWO: Your work has often been criticized for being too "Nietzschean." Informing such criticisms is a very determined reading of Nietzsche and of yourself that argues (whatever the differences of each critique) that your work, by following Nietzsche too closely, falls into an uncritical and irresponsible irrationalism and replaces rational norms of philosophical thinking with the creative playfulness of art. I would like to ask you two related questions in this context. First, has the predominantly "literary" reception of your work in the anglophonic world (and particularly the United States) detracted from a certain philosophical necessity to your consideration of the literary text? In this context it would appear that this necessity has been partially covered over by the accusation, leveled against deconstruction, of "Nietzscheanism." Second, and more particularly, following this reception of deconstruction ("Derrida's work is ultimately irrational and relativist"), how do you consider your relation to Nietzsche in "White Mythology"? In this often misunderstood essay (as you yourself point out to Paul Ricœur in "Le *retrait* de la métaphore"), you deconstruct any attempt—and here the early Nietzsche's reduction of truth to metaphor is paradigmatic of this empiricist, if not modern, attempt—to reduce the founding concepts of philosophy to the sensible word. I will come back to the moves of this essay in a moment. Can I ask you here, how the deconstruction of Western philosophy, of which "White Mythology" is one sustained example, differs from Nietzsche's overriding belief that the Western tradition needs to be *destroyed?* What are the differences between deconstruction and destruction?

J.D.: First, the accusation of "Nietzscheanism" makes no sense in its own terms. As the last answer made clear, the more faithful one may claim to be to Nietzsche, the less one can make a claim on the identity of a particular "feature" of Nietzsche's thought. The closer one is to "Nietzsche," the more one is aware that there is no such thing as the Nietzsche-text. This text demands interpretation in the same way that it argues that there is no such thing as an entity, only interpretations—active and reactive—of that entity. "To be Nietzschean" is a journalistic slogan that cannot cope with the names and pseudonyms of Nietzsche; its *raison d'être* is, ultimately, to conjure away anxiety.

Second, it is wrong to argue that Nietzsche is irrational and wrong, therefore, to say that deconstruction is also irrational following its passage through Nietzsche. This is hopelessly simplistic. There are many more names in this historical configuration of which deconstruction forms a part than that of Nietzsche. Nietzsche, yes, but also Heidegger and Benjamin, and so forth. The term *irrational* fails totally to come to terms with the "method" of genealogy. The point will come up again when we discuss question four. Genealogy is an attempt, in Nietzsche's eyes, to give an account of the history of reason. There may be problems with this account, it may at times go too quickly, but as such, genealogy inscribes itself *in the back of* reason; it cannot be, accordingly, an irrational procedure of thinking. The method and purpose of genealogy preceded and exceed such distinctions, re-organizing the tradition's identifications of what is rational and what is irrational. To accuse either Nietzsche, or those thinkers partly inspired by this account of reason, of irrationalism, is to fall back into a discursive position that genealogy exceeds.

The third point concerns the question of the literary reception of deconstruction in the Anglo-American world. Just one remark, here, since the issue is extremely complex. If it has been the case that deconstruction passed initially through literature rather than philosophy departments, there is a clear reason for this. Literary theory, especially in America, was more ready to listen to arguments and strategies of attempts to get behind reason's back than institutional inscriptions of philosophy. The politics of these departments (or at least some of them; those which were receptive, precisely, to deconstruction) were, in this sense, more philosophical.

Fourth, you ask in your question what the differences are between deconstruction and destruction. You have said the essential in questions two and three, so let me add something else: the question of originary affirmation. To take up again the three thinkers Nietzsche, Heidegger, and Benjamin, it is quite clear that something is happening at the end of the nineteenth century and the beginning of the twentieth for thinking to want to affirm the future. However negative, however destructive one's account of the history of the West may have become at this time, something is calling thought from the future; it is this call that makes both the passage via destruction, and an affirmation within this destruction, absolutely necessary. What do I mean by this? Before setting up tribunals or criticizing particular discourses, schools, movements, or academic tendencies, one must first admit that something is perhaps happening to humanity in the crossover from the nineteenth to the twentieth century for affirmation, for an affirmation of the future or of an opening onto the future, to be marked within a discourse of apparent destruction or mourning. Think of the problem of messianicity in Benjamin, the question of the future in Nietzsche, the privilege of the futural *ecstasis* in Heidegger. These thinkers are all thinkers of the future. . . . Now, why is it that any opening onto the future, both yesterday and today, passes through what looks like a destruction, a negative destructuration? Nor is it simply these three thinkers, either. However important their thought may be, they are symptoms of, spokesmen for something that is taking place in the world—at least in the West—that causes affirmation to be carried through by a devastating upheaval, a sort of revolution that cannot proceed without destruction, without separation or interruption, or without fidelity. For these thinkers are also thinkers of fidelity, of repetition—eternal return in Nietzsche, the question of Being in Heidegger, which, conveyed through an initial destruction, is presented by Heidegger as repetition, and so forth. These thinkers of the future are at the same time thinkers of eternal return, of repetition. So, my question is the following: why is it that this reaffirmation can have a future only through the seism of a destruction? But this is hardly a question; rather, it is the experience of *what is taking place,* of the revolution that bears us along. One can describe this movement as a seism, an earthquake, a maelstrom, or even a chaos, and there is a certain truth to this description. For the above are thinkers of the abyss (*Abgrund*), of chaos, of *khaein*—that is, where there is an opening, where the mouth gapes, and one does not know what to say, here there is an experience of chaos.

QUESTION THREE: It could be argued (I think here of Geoffrey Bennington's recent appraisal of the essay in "Derridabase") that "White Mythology" enacts an adventure of thinking typical of deconstruction's strategies toward, on the one hand, the discipline of philosophy, and, on the other hand, those of the human sciences. Your relation to the position of metaphor in the philosophical text is, consequently, one forceful enactment of deconstruction's displacement and re-organization of the metaphysical opposition between the transcendental and the empirical. To recall the major gesture of "White Mythology": on the one hand, you show that it is impossible to dominate philosophical metaphorics from *outside* philosophy, since the attempt meets with an essential limit in the fact that the very concept of metaphor is a philosopheme based on the metaphysical difference between the visible and the invisible, etc. On the other hand, and for the same reason, you argue that philosophy is incapable of dominating its metaphorical productions, since in its very attempt it would deprive itself of that which sustains it. "White Mythology" traces this double impossibility leaving itself and the reader in an aporetic and uncontrollable "position," neither inside philosophy nor outside it, in another science that would wish to dominate philosophy (linguistics, psychoanalysis, history—the list would include, precisely, all modern endeavors to make thought finite).

This said, I have two questions. In what way is this ambivalent "saving" of philosophy, its re-inscription, different from Heidegger's wish in his *Nietzsche* lectures of the 1930s to save Nietzsche's thought from his Nazi contemporaries' consideration of it as "a philosophy of life"? Heidegger opposes the anti-conceptualism of these readings by placing Nietzsche within metaphysics. You have yourself suggested on various occasions (*Of Grammatology,* "The End of the Book and the Beginning of Writing," *Spurs/Eperons: Les styles de Nietzsche,* "Interpreting Signatures, Nietzsche/Heidegger: Two Questions") that Heidegger thereby "loses" Nietzsche. In what ways does your double move toward the place of metaphor in the philosophical text save and lose Nietzsche differently?

J.D.: There are two questions in your question three. I will respond to both of them through the problematic of life. First, yes, I do not have the same approach to Nietzsche as Heidegger does for reasons of history, of generations, and of context. I am not writing between the two world wars. My major concern is not to prize Nietzsche from Nazi reappropriation. My approach is different as well, because I am deeply suspicious of this kind of maneuver. As I make clear in *Otobiographies,* it is not by chance that Nietzsche could be reappropriated by Nazism. Heidegger's history of Being, his metaphysics, cannot cope with this contamination. My first concern, then, is not to "save" Nietzsche, although I understand why Heidegger wanted to save Nietzsche by showing that his thought was not simply a philosophy of life. At the same time, I am aware that the question of *life* is much more obscure and difficult than Heidegger claims. Indeed, if there is one theme in Heidegger's work that makes me very uneasy, it is the theme of life. I, like everyone, want to be a vigilant reader of the political risks of biologism following its particular use of the concept of life, and yet the question of life is much trickier than Heidegger makes out. Heidegger's gesture is, in fact, extremely equivocal: he cannot save Nietzsche from the biologism and racism in which the Nazis want to enclose him except by making him a metaphysician; the last of the metaphysicians; that is, by reducing him in turn. I have tried to formalize this scene in several texts: Heidegger saves Nietzsche by losing him and loses him by saving him. I try to read Nietzsche—the thinker of the "perhaps" (*Vielleicht*), as he says in *Beyond Good and Evil*—in a much more suspensive manner to avoid these reductive gestures *and* affirm something else.

Regarding your second question, I cannot bring together anything whatsoever in Nietzsche, whether it concern life or anything else. On the contrary, I am neither able to, nor want to, save Nietzsche. My relation in general to thinkers just does not follow this kind of logic. Deconstruction cannot pose the problem of the proper name in terms of levels of allegiance or nonallegiance. There is no trial in this sense. There are, for example, discursive elements in Nietzsche that lend themselves to Nazi reappropriation; one can discern a lineage from Nietzsche to Nazism, and this cannot be ignored. At the same time, there are many other elements, sometimes the very same elements, many other strands of thought, sometimes the same strands, which are far from reducible to *either* the enterprise of Nazism *or* that of Heidegger. As I have said in *Of Spirit,* Heidegger's gesture actually capitalizes on the worst—the sanctioning of Nazism and the metaphysical counterappropriation. It is important in this context to take Heidegger's Nietzsche and show that there are *other* possibilities in Nietzsche that are not programmed by a history of metaphysics, that there are moves that are stronger, that go further than what Heidegger calls the *history of the completion of metaphysics*; moves that actually put in question Heidegger himself: his reading of Nietzsche in particular and his philosophical orientation in general. Briefly, there exists a reserve in Nietzsche that allows one to read Heidegger's own thought genealogically.

Perhaps it is a little clearer now what I meant earlier when I spoke of my preference for texts that are open, multiple, fragmented. As for Nietzsche, there are parts that the Nazis could take, there are parts that Heidegger could take, and parts that resisted Heidegger, which are "stronger" than Heidegger's thought. The openness of the Nietzsche-text does not prevent me at the same time—far from it—from knowing, feeling, and recalling that this multiplicity has a singularity to it; that, despite everything, it carries the name and pseudonyms of Nietzsche, that there has been an event called, among many other names, *Nietzsche*. I am concerned to reflect on the historical-theoretical possibility of this singularity, however open and chaotic (in the positive sense) it has proved to be.

QUESTION FOUR: I will now turn more explicitly to the ethical implications of Nietzsche's "destruction" of the Western tradition. This "destruction" always already implies a re-evaluation of values given that, for Nietzsche, science is a reactive evaluation of life. In *The Will to Power* he notes,

My insight: all the forces and drives by virtue of which life and growth exist lie under the ban of morality; morality as the instinct to deny life. One must destroy morality if one is to liberate life.[2]

In a gesture that is in part the same as his reduction of truth to metaphor, Nietzsche's *Genealogy of Morals* performs this destruction of morality by ascribing all ethical ideals to a reactive force hostile to life: what has always been understood as morality is either immoral or uses immoral means to attain its own end. In this sense morality has never been, never taken place, and it is ultimately derived as a set of reactive affects from the will to power. At the end of your readings of Lévi-Strauss (in "Violence of the letter: From Lévi-Strauss to Rousseau" in *Of Grammatology*), having deconstructed Lévi-Strauss's opposition between writing and speech, you remark: "There is no difference without the presence *of the other* but also, and consequently, without absence, dissimulation, detour, difference, writing. Arche-writing is the origin of morality as of immorality. The nonethical opening of ethics. A violent opening. As in the case of the vulgar concept of writing, the ethical instance of violence must be rigorously suspended in order to repeat the genealogy of morals."³ First, to what extent does Nietzsche's reduction of morality to life prevent him from thinking the necessity of *law* of which you have spoken about at length (for example, "Before the Law") and, therefore, from thinking the "prescriptive" modality of his own text? Second, in what ways does your final call to a repetition of the *genealogy* of morals (although the essay is already engaged in this repetition) differ from Nietzsche's enterprise, explicitly concerning the question of violence?

J.D.: So as not to repeat several of your arguments, let me tackle question four head-on. I am very unsure that, when Nietzsche speaks of a destruction of morality, he is speaking against any law whatsoever. I believe there to be a relation in Nietzsche to the law—not, obviously, what one calls "the moral law"—that takes the form of a step back behind the ethical to explain it. I would call this gesture of thought *arche-ethical.* The move can be found in Heidegger, in his analyses, for example, of *Gewissen, Bezeugung,* and *Schuldigsein* in *Being and Time,* which concern a pre-ethical, pre-moral, pre-juridical conscience. Just as Heidegger attempts to return to an instance or space of originarity that precedes the ethical and thereby gives an account of it, so Nietzsche's genealogy of morals can be seen as the effort to get behind the moral and the political. *Qua* "genealogy," Nietzsche's gesture cannot fail to reaffirm or promise something that can be called *arche-ethical* or *ultra-ethical.* This "something" is of the order of the law or the call [*appel*]; without it, genealogy would be impossible. The critique of the ruse of life is, in fact, carried out in its name. I am not just referring, then, to a possible reading of Nietzsche in terms of law: The law of which I speak is *constitutive* of Nietzsche's destruction of morality in the first place.

When, for example, Nietzsche speaks of the prejudices of philosophers, when he espies the ruse of life behind each philosopher, he must set up his analysis under the sign of truth, no longer in the sense of *adequatio* or *aletheia,* but in the sense of an opening to the law of truth or to the truth of law. This law—another name for which is eternal return—is the same thing as reaffirmation. Nietzsche's so-called destruction of morality is, consequently, far from being a destruction of law. On the contrary, Nietzsche's genealogy of morality implies an affirmation of law, with all the attendant paradoxes that being-before-the-law implies. Whatever these paradoxes, there is always law [*il y a de la loi*]. The law, or this "must," can, indeed, be read in all the prescriptive modalities of Nietzsche's discourse. When he speaks of the different hierarchies of force and of difference of force, there must also be law. The reversal of values or their hierarchical ordering presupposes law—hence the foolish simplicity of aligning Nietzsche's thought with relativism. To respond to your question fully, we would need to turn to the problematic of "value," to Heidegger's critique of value in the thought of Nietzsche and of others—but an interview is not the place to do that.

R.B.: I would like to insist on the relationship you are making between the law, affirmation, and promise, to chart some important distinctions within what is often called *contemporary French thought*. For many readers of Nietzsche—with or without Heidegger—Nietzsche reduces the question of ethics to that of life. To do so, he has to return the *question* of ethics to a *history* of morality, although this history of morality is ultimately underpinned nonhistorically by a hierarchy of forces or *puissances*. Foucault follows the "Nietzschean" path of historicization, actively forgetting the problem of law which, as a happy positivist, he cannot consider methodologically. You showed very early on in "Cogito and the History of Madness" the aporias to which such a path leads. Although the essay does not concern Nietzsche's philosophy explicitly, your reading of Foucault's inability to reduce the *logos* to history anticipates what you have just said on the "method" of genealogy. As for Deleuze and early Lyotard—I am comparing those of you who have represented, for many, a "corpus" of thought—the name of Nietzsche is obviously not neutral since it has often served as one important thread that gathers you into this corpus; they follow the "Nietzschean" path of force. By doing so, they certainly prove to be more philosophical than Foucault, but they seem equally to avoid, even denegate the problematic of law. Hence their respective readings of force in terms of energy and intensity. For you, it always seemed to be more complicated: like Deleuze, you argue (in your early essay "Force and Signification") that force in Nietzsche is always a difference between forces, you show that this difference cannot be historicized; but you also argued at the end of that essay—and what you have just said I believe to be a radicalization of your earlier argument—that force and law are inextricable. Could you speak more of this complexity in terms of what you are calling today *the promise?*

J.D.: Take, as an example, the passage in *On the Genealogy of Morals* where Nietzsche says, to gloss:

"Up to now philosophers have always believed—and this prejudice constitutes them—in the logic of opposition or contradiction, that two contradictory things cannot get along with each other—hence the contradiction or dialectic, which will try to reconcile these contraries. Now, however, philosophers must not only learn to welcome contradiction as such, learn to understand that contradiction is not really contradictory; we must also come to accept a logic of 'perhaps' in which the so-called contradiction is neither this nor that, but perhaps something else. This logic concerns chance and the future. The future can only be of the nature of 'perhaps,' so philosophy has never been able to accept the future. . . ."

At this point Nietzsche announces a philosopher of the future, a philosopher of "perhaps," saying that philosophers have been like this or that up to now, but that soon there will come a new philosopher—and this is what he means by "new"—who will think the "perhaps" *dangerously* ("this dangerous perhaps," he calls it). This example—there are many others—shows that Nietzsche's demolition, his reversal of all values, his critique and genealogy are *always* made *in the name of a future* that is *promised*. The promise does not come over and above the critique, as a post-face at the end. The promise inspires the critique in the first place. This new philosopher is *already* there, *already* announced through the way in which Nietzsche presents himself, even in his most hubristic and hyperbolic moments. The presentation shows that he partakes of the promise himself, that the promise is not something that one hears from elsewhere; like all promises, it must be assumed. For a promise to be assumed, someone must be there who is sensitive to the promise, who is able to say, "I am the promise, I am the one to promise, I am the one who is promising, and I am promising the coming of a new philosopher." This means that the one who is promising is *already* the promise or is *almost* already the promise, that the promise is imminent. This reflection upon imminence—the category of imminence together with that of "perhaps"—is what bears this promise. I am not using the term *promise* in the sense that Heidegger would use it, that of a god who would come to save us, but in the sense of the promise that *here* I am, that what I am doing, I am doing *here,* in this text here, saying *performatively* what I am saying.

There is a promise, then, in the very move of genealogy, in its most destructive, "negative" moments, and this promise has to be attended to, has to be theorized as far as possible. Only in this way can its effects be negotiated in an interesting manner. These effects are everywhere. Take, since you referred to it, Nietzsche's analysis of force as the difference between forces. The analysis, notably in *On the Genealogy of Morals*, is always commanded by an attention to a possible reversal in the logic engaged with. Nietzsche is fascinated (intrigued and alarmed) by the way in which reactivity causes the weakest to become the strongest, by the fact that the greatest weakness becomes stronger than the greatest strength. This is the case with Platonism, Judaism, and Christianity. This law of inversion is, of course, what makes the promise just as easily very strong as very weak, very strong *in* its weakness. As soon as there is reversibility, this principle of inversion, Nietzsche himself cannot prevent the most puny weakness from being at the same time the most vigorous strength. Hence, this logic of force bows to a law stronger than that of force. The logic of force reveals within its logic a law that is stronger than this very logic. We are witnessing here a virtuality that escapes what is normally attributed to the authority of Nietzsche's name or Nietzsche's discourse. In other words, this discourse is *also* the most disarmed and disarming. When Nietzsche says that the strong have been made slaves by the weak, this means that the strong are weak, that Nietzsche comes to the rescue of the strong because they are weaker than the weak. In a certain sense, by coming to the aid of strength, Nietzsche is coming to the aid of weakness, of an essential weakness. It is in this essential weakness that one can locate the place of the "arche-ethics," of the "law" that I mentioned earlier. One must defend the weakest who are pregnant with the future, because it is they who are the strongest. Here the oscillating play—one which is as much political and moral as it is philosophical—is difficult to stop: to speak in the name of the strongest in Nietzsche is also to speak in the name of the weakest. One can always argue, just as with Heidegger, that a particular discourse of Nietzsche is anti-Judaic, anti-Platonic, anti-Christian *and* hyper-Judaic, hyper-Platonic, hyper-Christian. There will always be someone to say, "Yes, your deconstruction of the Judaic and Christian aspects to St. Paul is made in the name of a message that is hidden in Judaism, in Christianity, in Islam, even in twentieth-century thought. You are 'hyper,' you speak 'hyper' at the very moment that you are speaking 'against.' You are in the process of developing a discourse that is hyper-Jewish, hyper-Christian against these very instances." And, in a sense, this person is right.

There are many indices in Nietzsche that show the above machine of hyperbolization to be constantly at work; it is this process of hyperbolization that restarts the machine. And the point does not just apply, of course, to Nietzsche.

R.B.: To take up the wording of question four, you once said in *Of Grammatology* that one had to suspend the ethical instance of violence to repeat the genealogy of morals. We will come to the problematic of violence in a moment. In the context of your response to this question and of your more recent strategies of reading, could one say that this repetition of genealogy consists in showing that there is the "messianic" in Nietzsche?

J.D.: Yes, so long as one follows through my re-inscription of the term. In, for example, *Specters of Marx,* I distinguish the messianic from any form of messianism. The messianic concerns a notion of the future that precedes—is the very condition of—the future constituting messianism. The messianic is heterogeneous to messianism in the precise sense that the horizon of the messianic is indeterminable. Messianism will saturate this absence of horizon by turning it into a horizon. Not only would I want to show this through a fairly abstract analysis, on the basis of all the predicates that seem to me to make up the concept of messianicity—annunciation of an unpredictable future, relation to the other, affirmation, promise, revolution, justice, and so on—but less abstractly, more immediately, I would want to show the difference in, for example, the *tone* of Nietzsche, which is prophetic and messianic. *Also sprach Zarathustra* is a countermessianic book, but, of course, any countermessianic text is at the same time messianic. Even when Nietzsche laughs at prophetic and messianic preaching, he nevertheless assumes the same tone *to* laugh at it. He presents himself as the countermessiah; the Antichrist is messianic, *Ecce Homo* is a messianic text.

R.B.: Yes, but isn't this where one could say that Nietzsche remains "Platonic"? After all, his prophetic tone could be considered metaphysical, revealing Nietzsche's inability to mourn the tradition *in* his very move against it.

J.D.: Yes, it is that *also*.

R.B.: Perhaps we can resituate this complication—the difference between two kinds of future, one an absolute futurity that allows for the future, the other a temporal horizon called *the future* that actually closes off the future—when we come to questions seven and eight. Can we turn in the meantime to question five?

QUESTION FIVE: My last two questions take me to the relations between violence and *justice*. For Nietzsche, the founding of any law is necessarily violent. It is only *once* the law is instituted that normative criteria of justice and injustice come into play. It is, however, an illusion, a reversal of cause and effect to claim that these criteria precede and guide the institution of the law. The imperative declaration of law is rooted in force. For Nietzsche, moreover, legal conditions can never be other than *exceptional* conditions since they constitute a partial restriction of the will to life, which is bent on power, and are subordinate to its "goal" as a means of creating greater units of power. A legal order is thus doubly violent; both in its institution and in its constant struggle, once instituted, with the powers of life. Heidegger's understanding of justice in *Introduction to Metaphysics* (his reading of *dike* in the second major speech of the chorus in *Antigone*) is marked by this account of the juridical and political. To go quickly: in this reading there is a singular stress on the Nietzschean "moment [*Augenblick*]" of decision in and through which the "statesman" sets the worlding of the world (its original *polemos*) into political form without covering this world over. Although this setting is, as for Nietzsche, contingent, Heidegger gives it a certain ontological priority, one that accords with his prior stress in *Being and Time* on the *futural* ecstasis of temporality and with his later attempts to ground national socialism philosophically. Now, given that this moment of decision in both Nietzsche and Heidegger is inscribed within a philosophy of the will (one that you have always placed in suspicion), given also that your account of originary violence and of the subsequent violence of all laws is, however, not entirely dissimilar in "Violence of the Letter," how does your thinking of the relation between violence and justice "avoid" a prioritization of the moment of political decision? I realize that this question is enormous, perhaps engaging with all your thinking, and I will be coming back to it constantly (if almost inversely) in the following question.

J.D.: Going straight to the end of your question, I would hesitate to say that I am not proposing a philosophy of decision. I believe that if there is such a thing as justice or responsibility, there must be decision. However, it is only the *implication* of the decision that is irreducible. Hence I always say: "The decision, *if there is one,* must interrupt causality, be revolutionary, and so on." I say, "if there is one," not because I doubt that there is one, but because, simply, I don't know if there is one. A decision, if there is such a thing, is never determinable in terms of knowledge. One cannot determine a decision. Whenever someone says, "A decision was made there and then. I know this to be so, and I also know what the decision was," that person is mistaken. A decision is an event that is not subsumable under a concept, a theoretical judgment or a determinant form of knowledge. If it could ever be subsumed, there would no longer be the need for a decision. A decision, if there is one, disappears in its appearance. Thus, the implication or presupposition of the decision is a particular type of presupposition. The same thing applies to all concerns closely related to the problematic of a decision. For example, responsibility, freedom, and justice can never form the object of a determinant form of knowledge. This is not to say that they are obscure or occult; they are simply not homogeneous with theoretical knowledge of determinant judgment, with what makes something present as an object or theme.

That a decision cannot become an object or a theme for knowledge is the very site of violence. You recall at the beginning of question four the violence accompanying the institution of any law—this institution can be nothing but violent not because it is a violence accompanying the transgression of the law, but because there is as yet no law. What precedes the law cannot not be violent for the law. The violent movement that imposes the law is a violence that is both asymmetrical and heterogeneous to every transgression that could then be identified in the name of the law. Once this institution has taken place, one can of course always contest—and this is the history of all revolutions—the imposition of the law, argue that it was violent and unjust, seek reparation, revolt against it, and so forth. Such dispute is necessarily endless. If, however, the laws in question, whether they be general or particular, are violent for the reason adduced above and are deconstructible—that is, they can be considered to be a historical artifact that is suitable for analysis and deconstruction—that in the name of which one deconstructs is not in the last instance deconstructible. I call this irreducibility *justice*. In *Specters of Marx* I oppose this concept of justice—as disjunction, as "being out of joint," as what is always already "out of joint"—to what Heidegger says of *dike* that he opposes (and, in a certain sense, rightly so) to what one commonly calls *justice*. This justice he prizes from a whole history of the juridical and of juridical representation. The concept of justice that I am elaborating is opposed to the Heideggerian one of *dike* as joining, as *Fug*, as bringing-together; it suggests that justice is, and must be, a discordance. As soon as justice implies a relation to another, it supposes an interruption, a dis-joining, a disjunction or being-out-of-joint, which is not negative; an out-of-jointness that is not deconstructible, that is justice as deconstruction, as the possible deconstruction of any determined law [*droit*].

R.B.: You began your response to this question by stating firmly that it would be wrong not to see your philosophy as a philosophy of decision, and all you have just said points to the way in which your thinking could be seen as an endless and varied reflection—philosophical, ethical, political—on the irreducibility of the moment of decision. I am aware that both on the continent and in the Anglo-American world this aspect of your work causes confusion, so I would like us to stay with my question for a moment. There seem to be at least two criticisms leveled against deconstruction concerning the problematic of decision; a problematic, which, as you say, implies that of freedom, of responsibility, and of justice—the stakes are consequently high. First, your work on *différance* is seen to be concerned with a restless movement of deferral, with the remainder that any work on paradox implies, and that, as a result, you are little interested in the moment of arrest, the moment of decision. Following this sort of argument, your philosophy cannot, given its very merits, constitute a philosophy of decision. This second criticism, which one hears a lot in the Anglo-American world, runs something like this: "when it comes to the question of violence, to the crucial role violence plays in Derrida's thought, one sees that Derrida is following Heidegger's fidelity to thinking closely, that his 'originary violence' is in fact a mystification of something that needs to be either developed, or accounted for, in historical and social terms, that this violence of the law before the law is a violence that is blind. Derrida's understanding of originary violence thus leaves us blind in turn as to the specificity of each and every judgment." In the worst cases, both criticisms end up saying the same thing; namely, that deconstruction leaves the notion of justice undetermined, and therefore prey to the most evil reappropriations. How would you respond?

J.D.: First, I do not accept the term *blind.* The accusation derives ultimately from my argument that a decision, if there is one, cannot take place without the undecidable, it cannot be resolved through knowledge. Given the nature of the misunderstanding, let me sum up this point simply and in a pedagogical manner. As to a decision that is guided by a form of knowledge—if I know, for example, what the causes and effects of what I am doing are, what the program is for what I am doing, then there is no decision; it is a question, at the moment of judgment, of applying a particular causality. When I make the machine work, there is no decision; the machine works, the relation is one of cause and effect. If I know what is to be done, if my theoretical analysis of the situation shows me what is to be done—do this to cause that, etc.—then there is no moment of decision, simply the application of a body of knowledge, of, at the very least, a rule or norm. For there to be a decision, the decision must be heterogeneous to knowledge as such. Even if I spend years letting a decision mature, even if I amass all possible knowledge concerning the scientific, political, and historical field in which the decision is to be taken, the *moment* of the decision must be heterogeneous to this field, if the decision is not to be the application of a rule. If there is such a thing as a decision—the point must always be recalled—then a decision must first be expounded. Of course, I am not advocating that a decision end up deciding *anything* at *any* moment. One must know as much as possible, one must deliberate, reflect, let things mature. But, however long this process lasts, however careful one is in the theoretical preparation of the decision, the instant of the decision, if there is to be a decision, must be heterogeneous to this accumulation of knowledge. Otherwise, there is no responsibility. In this sense only must the person taking the decision not know everything. Even if one knows everything, the decision, if there is one, must advance toward a future that is not known, that cannot be anticipated. If one anticipates the future by predetermining the instant of decision, then one closes it off, just as one closes it off if there is no anticipation, no knowledge "prior" to the decision. At a given moment, there must be an excess or heterogeneity regarding what one knows for a decision to *take place*, to constitute an *event*.

R.B.: This excess is the experience of death?

J.D.: Yes, indirectly, but the point cannot be followed up here, it would take too much time! Let me stick to answering your previous question. The preceding does not imply that the decision is blind. On the contrary, a decision must be as lucid as possible. And yet, however lucid it is, as a decision, it must advance where it cannot see. This blindness is *not* a lack of knowledge—I repeat, it has nothing to do with what could in principle come to know—it is the *very structure* of *any* decision, what relates all decisions, immediately, to the undecidable. If there is no "experience" of the undecidable at the moment of decision, then the decision will be nothing but the mechanical application of a rule. At a given moment, I must not know whether it is better to do this or that, I must in this sense be radically "ignorant" for there to be a decision. All that I am saying here is nothing but the modest analysis of the concept of decision; in other words, it is implied by the concept of decision itself. Now, as I mentioned earlier, as for knowing whether a decision has ever taken place, given the very concept of decision, I can never know, in the sense that it is structurally impossible for me to have an objective knowledge of it. It is the same thing for the concept of responsibility. Whoever says that he is responsible, that he has assumed "his" responsibilities has mistaken the meaning of responsibility. One can never know if one has been responsible or not, one cannot have a good conscience: "I made the right decision," "I fulfilled my responsibilities," "My debts are paid," "This is where my (or your) responsibility lies," and so on—all such statements are contrary to the essence of responsibility as well as to the essence of a decision. This is why responsibility is infinite. It is infinite because of the finitude of the one who "decides" or who "takes responsibility."

To answer your question head-on, I would quite simply say that not only is the language I am using neither antiethical nor antipolitical, not only is it a language that assumes the moment of decision, it is literally the most ethical and political way of taking seriously what is implied by the very concepts of decision and responsibility. In this sense, what I am proposing could not be more ethical or political! Let me conclude this point by saying that those who accuse deconstruction of irresponsibility, of blindness, of arbitrary violence, or of indecision or hesitation are—according to the radical structure of the decision that I have developed—enacting the very thing of which they are blaming the accused. To show this in detail—and following all that I have said about the essence of a decision, this detail is crucial—would again demand more time and care than an interview can allow.

R.B.: You have nevertheless made it very clear that an experience of the undecidable or aporetic (I am also thinking here of your essay on aporia in the very recent *Le passage des frontières*) is the passage through which a decision must pass if it is—

J.D.: If it is to come close to being a decision, if there is such a thing as a decision. Not only will one never know whether a decision is good or bad, one will never know whether there was a decision, whether a decision took place as such. And this is the only condition for there to have been a decision.

R.B.: To anticipate my last question here, since it is appropriate. This experience of the aporia, which can appear to many people to be a refusal of the necessary relation between a decision and a particular "moment" in time, this experience allows, in your eyes, for the future, it allows the future to arrive *as* a future (and not a future present) and so allows for the future of the decision (a future in which decisions can "take place" and decisions in which the future is not anticipated). I would want to stress here that you are speaking of undecidability at a moment in time when more and more "decisions" are closing off the future.

J.D.: To allow the future to arrive as the future—if, in other words, the future is precisely that . . . the *future*—is not to be understood in a passive sense. This relation to the future is active, it is affirmative; and yet, however active it is, the relation is also a passive one. Otherwise the future will not be the future. As for decisions that close the future off, are they indeed "decisions"?

R.B.: Perhaps we can come back to this when we again discuss your understanding of the "promise." Shall we turn now to question six?

QUESTION SIX: Nietzsche's genealogy of morals is a forceful critique of progress and of modern democracy: not simply because of his nonnormative exposition of justice, but also because democracy is considered as a reactive organization of human beings that increasingly makes humanity undifferentiated and calculable. Democracy is the political realm in which man is delivered over to the reactive power of reason. Before engaging more explicitly with the question of technology, could I ask you how your analysis of originary violence situates you again in the broadest possible terms, in relation to Nietzsche's critique of democracy? Is it because Nietzsche fails to situate the question of law in the effraction of originary violence that he wraps up so quickly the problem of democracy? Or, is there *another* thinking of democracy in Nietzsche that simultaneously goes against the overriding tone of his critique?

    J.D.: My response will be rapid and minimal. I do not believe that Nietzsche's critique of democracy concerns democracy in general, certainly not what I call *the democracy to come.* It seems to me that Nietzsche isolates several traits particular to democracy as it existed in his time, in other words, he focuses on a highly determined form of democracy. What he says about this particular democracy is sometimes apposite and just; he can touch the very springs—necessarily hypocritical and undemocratic—of what moves forward under the banner of democracy. But—and this takes us immediately back to the "hyper-ethical" procedure of genealogy—this critique is made in the name of what I would call *a democracy to come,* which is a quite different concept of democracy from the one critiqued by Nietzsche. What we were saying earlier about the call and the promise opens up a notion of democracy that, while having something in common with what we understand by democracy today, notably in the West, is reducible neither to the contemporary reality of "democracy" nor to the ideal of democracy informing this reality or fact. I have highlighted this difference at length in *Specters of Marx.* Since, in my eyes, Nietzsche critiques a particular form of democracy in the name of "a democracy to come," I do not consider Nietzsche to be an *enemy of democracy in general.* Those who say so are going far too fast; it is they who have little understanding of responsibility, of the complexity of the ethical and the political; it is they who are flattening out the future. Nietzsche will always get the better of them. No, although one cannot subscribe to all that Nietzsche says when he lambastes the democracy of his day—far from it—I believe Nietzsche to have espied particular risks in what he foregrounded under the name of "democracy," in the various traits of society that rallied round the principle of "democracy." There are at the same time critical and genealogical motifs in Nietzsche that *appeal* to *a democracy to come*. Since all of this has to be shown through the text, it is difficult to improvise further. Let this be the protocol of an answer to your question.

R.B.: Question seven, then.

QUESTION SEVEN: I would like at this juncture to focus very particularly on what you say of Heidegger's *Rektoratsrede* in *Of Spirit: Heidegger and the Question*. I recall that in *Of Spirit*, in what is an extremely dense and complex passage, you criticize virulently the effects of Heidegger's founding "spiritualization" of biological racism. Whereas, elsewhere (*Spurs*) you have recognized a certain necessity to Heidegger's *philosophizing* gesture—*at least* concerning Nietzsche's empiricism—here the problems of this gesture—as one that *spiritualizes* biologism—is explicitly analyzed within the political context of Heidegger's engagements with Nazism. Let me quote the passage in full:

Because one cannot demarcate oneself from biologism, from naturalism, from racism in its genetic form, one cannot be *opposed* to them except by re-inscribing spirit in an oppositional determination, by once again making it a unilaterality of subjectivity, even if in its voluntarist form. The constraint of this program remains very strong, it reigns over the majority of discourses which, today and for a long time to come, state their opposition to racism, to totalitarianism, to nazism, to fascism, etc., and do this in the name of spirit, and even of the freedom of the spirit [Note: This liberty of Spirit always runs the risk rigorously determined by Hegel: that of a merely formal liberty and of an abstract universality] in the name of an axiomatic, for example, that of democracy or "human rights"—which, directly or not, comes back to this metaphysics of *subjectivity*. And the pitfalls of the strategy of establishing demarcations belong to this program, whatever place one occupies in it. The only choice is the choice between the terrifying contaminations it assigns. Even if all the forms of complicity are not equivalent, they are *irreducible*. The question of knowing which is the least grave of these forms of complicity is always there— its urgency and its seriousness could not be over-stressed—but it will never dissolve the irreducibility of this fact. This fact [*fait*], of course, is not simply a fact. First, and at least, because it is not yet done [*fait*], not altogether [*pas tout à fait*]: it calls more than ever, as for what in it remains to come after the disasters that have happened, for absolutely unprecedented responsibilities of "thought" and "action." . . . In the *Rectorship Address*, this risk is not just a risk run. If the program seems diabolical, it is because, *without there being anything fortuitous in this*, it capitalizes on the worst, that is, on both evils at once: the sanctioning of Nazism, and the gesture that is still metaphysical.[4]

As Dominique Janicaud has noted in *L'Ombre de cette pensée: Heidegger et la question politique,* it would be difficult to find a greater accusation of Heidegger. My question concerns, however, the so-called program of logics that you allude to in this passage. I note that you make a similar, if more local, intellectual gesture in *Otobiographies* concerning the necessary contamination of Nietzsche's texts by Nazi ideology. There it is a question of "a powerful programming machine" that relates, before any human intention or *will,* the two contrary forces of regeneration and degeneracy in Nietzsche's early *On the Future of Our Educational Establishments,* determining in advance, before any historical eventuality, that each force reflects, and passes into, its other. We are here, perhaps, at something like the "heart" of deconstruction given its concern with what you call *the lesser violence* in "Violence and metaphysics" (*Writing and Difference*).[5]

My question, after this necessary preamble, is short: *in what sense* have, for you, *all* thought and *all* action up to today been inscribed within this machine? And, how do you understand those enigmatic words "absolutely unprecedented responsibilities" of thought and action? In what sense, "absolutely"?

J.D.: First, I certainly believe that the contaminations discussed in this passage are absolutely undeniable. I defy anyone to show a political discourse or posture today that escapes this law of contamination. The only way to do so is in the form of (de)negation (*Verneinung*), the law of contamination can only be (de)negated. If it is true that these contaminations are inevitable, that one cannot side-step its law whatever one attempts to do, then responsibility cannot consist in denying or (de)negating contamination, in trying to "save" a line of thought or action from it. On the contrary, it must consist in assuming this law, in recognizing its necessity, in working from *within* the machine, by formalizing how contamination works and by attempting to act accordingly. Our very first responsibility is to recognize that this terrifying program is at work everywhere and to confront the problem head-on; not to flee it by denying its complexity but to think it as such.

Second, this means that the political gestures that one will make will, like all political gestures, be accompanied by discourse. Discursivity takes time, it implies several sentences, it cannot be reduced to a single moment or point. On each occasion one will have to make complex gestures to explain that one is acting, despite contamination, in this particular way, because one believes that it is better to do this rather than that, that a particular act chosen is in such-and-such a situation more likely to do such-and-such than another possible act. These gestures are anything but pragmatic, they are strategic evaluations that attempt to measure up to the formalization of the machine. To make such evaluations, one has to pass through thought—there is no distinction here between thought and action, these evaluations are *actions of thought.* Whoever attempts to justify his political choice or pursue a political line without thought—in the sense of a thinking that exceeds science, philosophy, and technics—without thinking what calls for thinking in this machine, this person is not being, in my eyes, politically responsible. Hence, one needs thought, one needs to think more than ever. Thinking's task today is to tackle, to measure itself against, everything making up this program of contamination. This program forms the history of metaphysics, it informs the whole history of political determination, of politics as it was constituted in ancient Greece, disseminated throughout the West and finally exported to the East and South. If the political is not thought in this radical sense, political responsibility will disappear. I would not go so far as to say that this thought has become necessary only today; rather, today more than ever, one must think this machine to prepare for a political decision, if there is such a thing, *within* this space of contamination. Very simply, then, what I am trying to do is to prepare for such a decision by tackling the machine or law of contamination. For reasons that should now be clear, what I say is *always* going to run the risk of being taken in an unfavorable light, it cannot fail to lead to misunderstandings, according to the very same law of contamination. There is no way out. As to the criticisms of deconstruction brought up earlier, one has indeed to assume the risk of being misunderstood, continuing to think in modest terms what is after all exceedingly ambitious, in order to prepare for these responsibilities—if they exist.

In the passage you quote, I call these responsibilities *unprecedented* [inédites]. What does this term mean? In your terms, what is their *time?* Rather than implying a heroic pathos of originality, the term testifies to the fact that we find ourselves in an unprecedented situation. After recent events—whether one gives them the name of Nietzsche, of Heidegger, of the Second World War, of the Holocaust, of the destructibility of humanity by its own technical resources—it is clear that we find ourselves in an absolutely unprecedented space. For this space one needs equally unprecedented reflections on responsibility, on the problematics of decision and action. To say this is not a piece of speculative *hubris*. It simply acknowledges where we are. We need the *unprecedented;* otherwise there will be nothing, pure repetition. . . . The unprecedented is, of course, highly dangerous. Once on these paths of thought, one is liable to get shot at by people who are in a hurry to interpret texts, who call you a neo-Nazi, a nihilist, a relativist, a mysticist, or whatever. But if one does not take such risks, then one does nothing, and nothing happens. What I am saying is very modest: without risk, there is nothing.

R.B.: Why did you write "absolutely unprecedented"?

J.D.: It was just a form of emphasis. Of course, the unprecedented is never possible without repetition, there is never something absolutely unprecedented, totally original or new; or rather, the new can only be new, radically new, to the extent that something new is *produced,* that is, where there is memory and repetition. The new cannot be invented without memory or repetition. So, two things: first, there can be no break, no experience of the break that does not presuppose a non-break, that does not presuppose memory. Second, contamination follows from this iterability that is constitutive of the unprecedented. Contamination happens because iterability inhabits from the very first what is not yet thought. One has to confront this paradoxical logic to be able to think the unthought.

R.B.: Let me take an example related to what you have just been saying about repetition. You have mentioned *Specters of Marx* several times in what you have been saying, so an example taken from this work is more than appropriate. In this combative, ironically "timely" text, you speak about our responsibility before the unprecedented. One particularly interesting aspect of the book concerns what you call a *new International.* I will not gather together all the threads that determine the conceptual strategy of this term in the book. Suffice it to say that *Specters of Marx* remains faithful to a notion of internationality in Marx that, you argue, Marx himself betrayed by ontologizing, among other things, the temporally indefinite structure of revolution and the "supplementary" relationship between humanity and its productions. This new International is a configuration of bonds [*liens*] that are in the process of being formed, which go beyond citizenship, the nation-state, and national sovereignty, but which are neither working towards nor anticipating a cosmopolitan superstate. This notion of a new International forms part of the book's strategy to prepare the ground for a new socio-political critique of contemporary political discourses. . . . With *Specters of Marx* in mind, how would you respond to the following?

Before the inadequate structures of international law, we are at present witnessing two repetitions. The first is that of the nation-states of Europe, which find themselves confronted once more by regional and ethnic determinations of a people's identity. Like all repetitions, however, there is a difference: today's nationalisms and fascisms are produced in, and constitute themselves within, a world that is technologically different from that of the 1920s and 1930s, a world that is much smaller and more "international" due to the accelerated processes of technicization. The difference has ambivalent implications for any form of nationalism: the repetition of nationalisms is certainly dated, and yet it is all the more dangerous and singular for being dated. The other repetition is that of the nation-states that, *as* nation-states, are constitutively unable to think, and practice, a notion of international law. For international law remains determined by the concept of national sovereignty, a principle that is stopping, for example, the United Nations from acting effectively beyond the wishes of one or other of its permanent members. These two repetitions, although of a different nature, are tending to paralyze inventive moves. How, then, do you conceive the relation between this emerging new International and the present sluggishness of institutions of international law?

J.D.: The "International" I am interested in would indeed exceed the concepts of nation, of state, and of nation-state that determine the concept of international. I believe that we are at present involved in a process that demands an accelerated transformation of international law. Every event in the contemporary world shows international institutions to be powerless, dependent, as they are, for their means of enforcement on the decisions of particular, powerful nation-states that curtail the general will of such institutions. The reason for this is clear: the very concepts upon which the missions of international institutions are built—I especially have in mind the United Nations—need to be rethought, deconstructed. All these concepts belong to a Western tradition of the political that implies the police, the sovereignty of the state, the modern concept of the nation-state. The notion of the political is being completely undermined—technically, economically, and politically. International law, international institutions need to be rethought and thereby improved. The process is infinite and interminable, but it is absolutely necessary.

In this respect I have nothing against international institutions. I believe one must accept their history, agree to their perfectibility, and so on. That said, we are at the same time witnessing something like an aspiration toward—I do not dare to use the word *solidarity* or *community* because these words have too much of a particular resonance—a *bond* [lien] (the term is only suitable given its high level of abstraction), a bond between—here, again, I do not want to use a term like *citizens of the world* since it is a concept excessively marked by a tradition of the cosmopolitan, not *political subjects,* nor even *human beings*—let us say, then, *singularities,* a bond between singularities. There is today an aspiration toward a bond between singularities all over the world. This bond not only extends beyond nations and states, such as they are composed today or such as they are in the process of decomposition, but extends beyond the very concepts of nation or state. For example, if I feel in solidarity today with this particular Algerian who is caught between the F.I.S. and the Algerian state, or this particular Croat, Serbian, or Bosnian, or this particular South African, this particular Russian or Ukrainian, or whoever—it is not a feeling of one citizen toward another, it is not a feeling peculiar to a citizen of the world, as if we are all potential or imaginary citizens of a great state. No, what binds me to these people is something different than membership in a world nation-state or in an international community extending indefinitely the limits of what one still calls today the *nation-state.* What binds me to them—and this is the point; there is a bond, but this bond cannot be contained within the traditional concepts of community, obligation, or responsibility—is a protest against citizenship, a protest against membership in a political configuration as such. The bond is, for example, a form of political solidarity opposed to the political *qua* a politics tied to the nation-state. "The democracy to come" is a democracy whose bonds are no longer those that can be deduced from the concept of democracy, such as this concept has emerged and developed in the history of the West. The concept of democracy has always been tied to the city, to the state, to the *polis* as *topos,* and in modern times to the nation-state; democracies have always been conceived and conceptualized as a phenomenon of the "nation-state," and this is where the problem lies. Where democracy is necessarily related to the old concept of *politeia,* to the *topos* of the *polis,* it is challenged by the de-localizing resources of present and future technics and media.

What I am calling a new *International* both signals the need to radicalize the critique of law, of the state and the nation, and bears witness to an international which carries the promise of itself, which is hearing the promise of a "democracy to come," linking singularities beyond the structures of the nation-state. This democracy is *not* an abstract utopia. I believe this solidarity, this bond to be what is provoking the gradual and necessary transformation of international law; it renders account of the sense of dissatisfaction we all have toward present events in the world. If no one is happy with the present state of the world, it is because nothing is satisfactory: neither the state, nor the nation-state, nor international law, nor the world "order"; and because this dissatisfaction derives in the last instance from a "bond" that demands thought and negotiation. Since this bond between singularities, as well as the promise it carries, is what I call *spectral,* it cannot be made into a community; the promise of the bond forms neither a national, linguistic, or cultural community, nor does it anticipate a cosmopolitan constitution. It exceeds all cultures, all languages, it even exceeds the concept of humanity. A final point: our dissatisfaction requires, at the same time, in the same gesture of thought, rethinking the limits between the human and the animal, the human and the natural, the human and the technical. For the question of animality, that of the earth, of what we may mean by "life" in general also makes up the promise of this bond.

R.B.: What you are saying is extremely dense and complicated. I wonder whether we could not progressively untangle some of these thoughts through the last questions. Let us start by the temporal modality of this "democracy to come." It is not an Idea in the Kantian sense— a temporal horizon that guides ethical or political thinking in principle. We know that the idea of this Idea is very vulnerable to the Hegelian critique of Kant's distinction between reason and understanding. What

Hegel basically says to Kant is: "Your Idea of freedom is a 'bad infinity' and ends up destroying the very possibility of freedom that it promises." Now, your notion of *différance* has often been equated with this bad infinity, and presumably your notion of the promise of democracy awaits similar misunderstandings. However, you are, in fact, saying something *beyond* this opposition between Kant and Hegel, since this democracy, while *neither* a norm *nor* a fact, is taking place *now,* is it not?

J.D.: Yes, it is now, it is not an Idea in the Kantian sense. I am always a little worried, however, when I argue against the Idea in the Kantian sense, for this idea should also be retained. For example, one must retain the idea of an unending development of international institutions toward universal peace. This horizon must not be destroyed. Nevertheless, there is as it were a horizon to this horizon that has no horizon. Where the Idea in the Kantian sense leaves me dissatisfied is precisely around its principle of infinity: first, it refers to an infinite in the very place where what I call *différance* implies the here and now, implies urgency and imminence—we return in a sense to our earlier discussion on decision; second, the Kantian Idea refers to an infinity that constitutes a horizon. This horizon is, as the Greek word says, a limit forming a backdrop against which one can know, against which one can see what is coming. The idea has already anticipated the future before it arrives. So, the Idea is both too futural, in the sense that it is unable to think the deferral of difference in terms of "now," and it is not "futural" enough, in the sense that it already knows what tomorrow should be.

The relation to the other—which in turn guides everything that I am saying regarding the democracy to come—is without horizon. It is what I call the *messianic*; the messianic can arrive at any moment, no one can see it coming, can see how it should come, or have forewarning of it. The relation to the other is the absence of horizon, of anticipation, it is the relation to the future that is paradoxically without anticipation, there where the alterity of the other is an absolute surprise. If one can be prepared for an absolute surprise, then one must be prepared for the coming of the other *as* an absolute surprise—that is what I understand by the messianic. If the relation to the other is that anything can happen at any moment, if being prepared for this absolute surprise is being ready for the "anything can happen," then the very structure of horizon informing, among other horizons, the Idea in the Kantian sense has been punctured.

In saying this, I am more than aware that the stakes here are very high. The structure of horizon commands all modern thought: phenomenology, ontology, hermeneutics, Husserl, Heidegger, Gadamer, etc. The notion of horizon is indispensable to the movement of phenomenology, to that of interpretation of the meaning of Being, indeed it is indispensable to *any* critical enterprise (in the sense of *Kritik*). But let me be clear—the experience of an *absence* of horizon is not one that has no horizon at all; it is where the horizon is, in a sense, "punctured" by the other. With the coming of the other there is a non-horizon.

R.B.: It could indeed be argued that your deconstruction of the Idea in the Kantian sense constitutes at the same time a deconstruction of the whole of what one calls in political philosophy *modernity*. You have rarely put it in these terms, preferring to speak more widely of the *closure* of metaphysics. But I think your criticism of the Idea in the Kantian sense—in terms of the relation to the other—is just that: a deconstruction of modernity that calls for a reinvention of the modern. This is a good point to go back to Nietzsche and Heidegger. Question eight?

QUESTION EIGHT: This takes me to my next two questions. From the later *Nietzsche* lectures onward, Heidegger argues that will to power not only forms the end of metaphysics but constitutes its accomplishment as the technicist calculation of Being *as* value. Will to power is the realization of reason in the form of a willful, technological "schematization" of the word, which forgets Being. Following this interpretation, Heidegger begins to conceive of the relation between Being and man in terms of a non-willful encounter between thinking and the withdrawal of Being. The supreme danger becomes that of the destiny of the essence of technology, a destiny through which man's essence in its openness to Being risks falling from memory. Resistance to this danger and to calculative thinking in particular is thought more and more in terms of a composed "releasement [*Gelassenheit*]" toward beings and of the listening to the "call" of Being. The earlier "Nietzschean" moment of decision in resoluteness is thus reappraised as particular to a metaphysics of the will. At this point Heidegger has theorized a certain renunciation of political agency. There are, of course, many questions here. I will remain initially with Heidegger's above interpretation of Nietzsche. Is not Heidegger's interpretation of will to power in the early 1940s as consummate subjectivity even more violent than his earlier spiritualization of Nietzsche's physiology? For could one not argue that the problematic of will to power exceeds the axiomatic of subjectivity and that "life," in the differences of its forces, precedes both Being and humanity? If this interpretation is to a point legitimate, does it not suggest that Nietzsche's text allows one to think the "inhumanity" of technology more interestingly than the text of Heidegger, who, despite everything, remains himself metaphysical given his belief that "the essence of technology is nothing technological" ("The Question of Technology")?

J.D.: In response to your two questions, I would first focus on what Heidegger says about the concept of life, since any living being, in fact, undoes the opposition between *physis* and *technè*. As a self-relation, as activity and reactivity, as differential force, and repetition, life is always already inhabited by technicization. The relation between *physis* and technics is not an opposition; from the very first there is instrumentalization [*dès l'origine il y a de l'instrumentalisation*]. The term *instrument* is inappropriate in the context of originary technicity. Whatever, a prosthetic strategy of repetition inhabits the very moment of life: life is a process of self-replacement, the handing-down of life is a *mechanike,* a form of technics. Not only, then, is technics not in opposition to life, it also haunts it from the very beginning. Now, in Nietzsche there is indeed no opposition between technics and life, and this undoubtedly means that one can reconsider technics *through* Nietzsche. He leaves the field open for one to do so.

R.B.: Heidegger's reflections on technics are ambivalent. As you have yourself shown, he is one of the first philosophers to confront technics in philosophical terms, and yet he wishes to purify thinking of originary technicity. Technics remains a *question,* and *as* a question asked by thinking, thinking is not "technical." In other words, thinking for Heidegger, while no longer philosophy in his sense, is still metaphysical, given its difference from technics. Thinking is indeed constituted through this very difference. A classic philosophical move, despite everything else in Heidegger that works against this move. Where would you situate Nietzsche here, given what you have said about the resistance of Nietzsche's philosophy to Heideggerian "thinking"?

J.D.: Heidegger's move is not a Nietzschean gesture, that's true. I would want to reinforce the point, however, that there is no simple evaluation of technics in Heidegger. Nor is there any simple evaluation of technics in Nietzsche. One could argue that in Nietzsche's work there is something like a process of technicization that corresponds to an affirmative moment of life, a sign of strength, just as one could argue that there is a reactive instance of technics as well. There are statements in Nietzsche where he denounces technics and technicization; for example, his trial of democracy is also a trial of urban technicization. And so, there is not the good and the bad in Nietzsche, either: technics is both good and bad. This is, of course, the case for everything in Nietzsche; it is the reason why, as a protocol to all discourses on Nietzsche, all interrogations of him—Heidegger's, for example—one must remember that each philosopheme, each concept in Nietzsche's does not harbor any identity, each time it must be evaluated for both its active and its reactive sides. Nietzsche never writes that x is exclusively good or bad. Each entity is submitted to interpretation, this interpretation is an evaluation of what is active or reactive. As a result, there is, for Nietzsche, no entity that is not interpretable as both an active and a reactive form of life. It is this that distinguishes Nietzsche from Heidegger: everything is, for Nietzsche, interpretation.

I have always admired this aspect of Nietzsche's thinking. In specific relation to your question, it implies that technics is an interpretation, an interpretation submitted in turn to other interpretations. Technics is both active and reactive. So, if one can think technics through Nietzsche, this does not mean that Nietzsche is going to give us a particular determination of the technical that is more interesting than the reflection of, for example, Heidegger. No—indeed, this is precisely the lesson that can be drawn for today. Rather than being either fought against or defended, technics is to be *interpreted each time*. Each time one must interpret what one is doing and what one wants to do with technics, which is sometimes affirmative and sometimes reactive. Technics lends itself to interpretation, there are also technics of interpretation that *also* lend themselves to interpretation, and so on. It is in this sense, then, that Nietzsche allows us to think technics technically.

R.B.: We are going to have to accelerate to get through the last questions within the allotted time. Perhaps this is an occasion to move from question eight to nine, since what you have just said cuts right across Heidegger's later reading of will to power as the technicist calculation of

Being. From this reading onward, Heidegger elaborates a notion of radical passivity, *Gelassenheit*, which you compare in *Of Spirit: Heidegger and the Question* to his work on the originary promise of language in *On the Way to Language*. These are complicated waters; much is at stake. Despite the complexity of what is going on, can I ask you in what sense your notions of the promise and of double affirmation distinguish your thought here from those of *both* Heidegger *and* Nietzsche?

QUESTION NINE: Although you have voiced clear disagreements with Heidegger's thinking of technology, there is a side to your work, more insistent since the 1980s, which is partly in accord with Heidegger's rejection of a philosophy of the will. This is your analysis of the radical structure of the promise. As you argue in *Of Spirit* and *Mémoires for Paul de Man,* the promise prohibits the (metaphysical) gathering of Being in presence, which Heidegger's thinking on language also troubles. The promise is the remainder of the necessary undecidability of thinking and action upon which any *act* of thought (or) language (philosophical, political, juridical, literary) will fall upon and fail to untie. We are back here in the contaminating machine of *Of Spirit.* This remainder is an absolute past (it cannot be recalled in any act) that *gives the chance* of the future. In what sense is this promise, which, as you say, is always already the memory of this promise, nevertheless an *affirmation* of the future? What is the relation between this "double" affirmation and the single Yes-saying of Zarathustra, who affirms an innocent *creating* of the future? Does this double affirmation trouble, in turn, Nietzsche's *willful* of forgetting in *Ecce Homo*; namely, the affirmation that he is "the anti-ass par excellence" ("Why I write such excellent books")? My questions are partly provoked by what you say of affirmation in "Nombre de oui" in *Psyché: Inventions de l'autre.*

QUESTION TEN: I will now link the question of temporality alluded to earlier concerning your phrase *absolutely unprecedented responsibilities* with the previous two questions on technology, affirmation, and the future. In your essay "Psyche: Inventions of the Other," deconstruction's future is intimately related to the promoting of chance. Deconstructive inventions serve this furthering of chance not by opposing the techno-rational programmation of the aleatory but by letting the radical other of calculation "arrive." As you remark in that essay: "[D]econstructive inventiveness consists in opening up, unclosing and destabilizing fore-closed structures, in order to leave a passage for the other."[6] This radical alterity is the "promise" of invention and is, again, a reformulation of your deconstructive argument that there is no beyond the undecidable, the aporetic event; for example, there is no politics of invention to *op-pose* to modern politics of invention. Such an invention would, follow-ing your undecidable logic of the "machine," fall back into the tendency of modern politics to integrate the aleatory within their programmatic calculations. Hence your stress in this essay on the impossible experience of the other as the invention of the impossible. Could you elaborate in this context the *temporal* relation between the responsibilities of which you spoke in the passage I quoted from *Of Spirit* and the absolute futu-rity of this absolute other of invention?

J.D.: I believe all the problems we have been discussing in this in-terview are to be found in the very reduced and highly schematized form of what I call *double affirmation*. To consider the problem in a slightly simple, pedagogical way: the "yes" is neither a descriptive ob-servation nor a theoretical judgment; it is precisely an affirmation, with the performative characteristics that any affirmation entails. The "yes" must also be a reply, a reply in the form of a promise. From the mo-ment that the "yes" is a reply, it must be addressed to the other, from the moment that it is a promise, it pledges to confirm what has been said. If I say "yes" to you, I have already repeated it the first time, since the first "yes" is also a promise of this "yes" being repeated. To say "yes" is to acquiesce, to pledge, and therefore to repeat. To say "yes" is an ob-ligation to repeat. This pledge to repeat is implied in the structure of the most simple "yes." There is a time and a spacing of the "yes" as "yes-yes": it takes time to say "yes." A single "yes" is, therefore, immediately double, it immediately announces a "yes" to come and already recalls that the "yes" implies another "yes." So, the "yes" is immediately dou-ble, immediately "yes-yes."

This immediate duplication is the source of all possible contamination—that of the movement of freedom, of decision, of declaration, of inauguration—by its technical or technical double. Repetition is never pure. Hence the second "yes" can eventually be one of laughter or derision at the first "yes," it can be the forgetting of the first "yes," it can equally be a recording of it. Fidelity, parody, forgetting, or recording—whatever, it is always a form of repetition. Each time it is originary *iterability* that is at play. Iterability is the very condition of a pledge, of responsibility, of promising. Iterability can only open the door to these forms of affirmation at the same time as opening the door to the threat of this affirmation failing. One cannot distinguish the opening from the threat. This is precisely why technics is present from the beginning. What duplicity means is this: at the origin there is technics.

All this is true before we even get to the word *yes*. As I argue in "Ulysses Gramophone: Hear Say Yes in Joyce," the "yes" does not necessarily take on the form of the word *yes* in a particular language; the affirmation can be pre-verbal or pre-discursive. For example, the affirmation of life in the movement toward self-repetition, toward assistance, may well be pre-verbal. Both movements can also be ones of degeneration, they can be an act of mockery, a copy, an archive, and so forth. With this duplicity we are at the heart of the "logic" of contamination. One should not simply consider contamination as a threat, however. To do so continues to ignore this very logic. Possible contamination must be assumed, because it is also opening or chance, our chance. Without contamination we would have no opening or chance. Contamination is not only to be assumed or affirmed: it is the very possibility of affirmation in the first place. For affirmation to be possible, there must always be at least two "yes's." If the contamination of the first "yes" by the second is refused— for whatever reasons—one is denying the very possibility of the first "yes." Hence all the contradictions and confusion that this denial can fall into. Threat is chance, chance is threat—this law is absolutely undeniable and irreducible. If one does not accept it, there is no risk, and, if there is no risk, there is only death. If one refuses to take a risk, one is left with nothing but death.

R.B.: You have already answered question ten by maintaining that *différance* is a movement of deferral and difference that allows for the temporality of now and is immediately concerned with this moment now. As you have just made clear as well, your understanding of invention is to be located in this structure of temporality as well as in the logic of contamination that works through it. There can be no invention that is absolutely new and no invention either unless the promise of invention is subject to possible contamination. It is this law that thinking has to confront to be inventive. Shall we turn, then, to question eleven?

QUESTION ELEVEN: How does a certain affirmation of technology relate to what you have called in *The Other Heading: Reflections on Today's Europe* the *promise of democracy*? I recall that, for Nietzsche, democracy is the modern reactive fate of calculative reason and that, for Heidegger (both "early" and "late" Heidegger), democracy is "inadequate to confront the challenges of our technological age" (*Spiegel* interview of 1966). In distinction and differently to both Nietzsche and Heidegger, your work can be seen to affirm both *technology* and *democracy*. Although the promise of democracy is not the same as either the *fact* of democracy or the regulative *Idea* (in the Kantian sense) of democracy, deconstruction does "hear" *différance* more in a democratic organization of government than in any other political model; and there are no new models to be invented. If I understand you correctly, your affirmation of democracy is, in this respect, a demand for the sophistication of democracy, such a refinement taking advantage, in turn, of the increasingly sophisticated effects of technology. I pose the above question, then, with the following points in mind. First of all, democratic institutions are becoming more and more unrepresentative in our increasingly technicized world—hence, in part, recent rejections of "*la classe politique*," not only in France and the United States; the anxieties that the question of a centralized European government raise form part of the same rejection. Then, in the second place, the media are swallowing up the constitutional machinery of democratic institutions, furthering thereby the de-politicization of society and the possibility of populist demagogy. Third, resistance to this process of technicization is at the same time leading to virulent forms of nationalism and demagogy in the former Soviet empire, forms that are exploiting technology in the domains of the media, telecommunications, and arms, while denying the de-localizing effects of technology, culturally, in the domain of ideology. And, finally, the rights of man would seem an increasingly ineffective set of criteria to resist this process of technicization (together with its possible fascistic effects) given this process's gradual effacement of the normative and metaphysical limit between the human and the inorganic.

J.D.: Your question concerns the contemporary acceleration of technicization, the relation between technical acceleration (acceleration through, and of, technics) and political-economic processes. It concerns,

in fact, the very concept of acceleration. First, it is more than clear that
the idea of the acceleration of history is no longer a *topos* today. If it
is often said that history is going quicker than in the past, that it is
now going too quickly, at the same time it is well-known today that
acceleration—a question of rhythm and of changes of rhythm—does not
simply affect an objective speed that is continuous and that gets progressively faster. On the contrary, acceleration is made up of *differences* of
rhythm, heterogeneous accelerations that are closely related to the technical and technological developments to which you are alluding. So, it
makes no sense to "fetishize" the concept of acceleration: there is not a
single acceleration. There are, in fact two laws of acceleration: one derives
from the technosciences, it concerns speed, the prodigious increase in
speed, the unprecedented rhythms that speed is assuming and of which
we are daily feeling the effect. The political issues that you evoke bear the
stamp of this form of acceleration. The second kind is of a quite different order and belongs to the structure of decision. Everything that I was
saying earlier can now be said in these terms: a decision is taken in the
process of infinite acceleration.

Second, taking into account these two laws of acceleration that
are heterogeneous and that capitalize on each other, what is the situation of democracy today? "Progress" in arms-technologies and in
media-technologies is incontestably causing the disappearance of the
site on which the democratic used to be situated. The site of representation and the stability of the location that make up parliament or assembly, the territorialization of power, the rooting of power to a particular place, if not to the ground as such—all this is over. The notion
of politics dependent on *this* relation between power and space is over
as well, although its end *must* be negotiated with. I am not just thinking here of the present forms of nationalism and fundamentalism.
Technoscientific acceleration poses an absolute threat to Western-style
democracy as well, following its radical undermining of locality. Since
there can be no question of interrupting science or the technosciences,
it is a matter of knowing *how* a democratic response can be made to
what is happening. This response must not, for obvious reasons, try to
maintain at all costs the life of a democratic model of government,
which is rapidly being made redundant. If technics now exceed democratic forms of government, it is not only because assembly or parlia-

ment is being swallowed up by the media. This was already the case after the First World War. It was already being argued then that the media (then the radio) was forming public opinion so much that public deliberation and parliamentary discussion no longer determined the life of democracy. And so, we need a historical perspective. Today, the acceleration of technicization concerns the borders of the nation-state, the traffic of arms and drugs, everything that has to do with internationality. It is these issues that need to be completely reconsidered, not in order to sound the death-knell of democracy, but to rethink democracy *from within these conditions.* This rethinking, as you rightly suggested earlier, must not be postponed, it is immediate and urgent. For what is specific to these threats, what constitutes the specificity of their time or temporality, is that they are not going to *wait.* Let us take one example from a thousand.

It is quite possible that what is happening at present in the former Yugoslavia is going to take place in the Ukraine: a part of the Ukrainian Russians is going to be re-attached to Russia, the other part refusing. As a consequence, everything decided up to now as to the site and control of the former Soviet Empire's nuclear arms will be cast in doubt. The relative peace of the world could be severely endangered. As to a response, one that is so urgently needed, that is obviously what we have been talking about all along. And yet, it is hardly in an interview that one can say what needs to be done. Despite what I have just said—even if it is true that the former polarity of power is over with the end of the Cold War, and that its end has made the world a much more endangered place—the powers of decision in today's world are still highly structured; there are still important nations and superpowers, there are still powerful economies, and so forth.

Given this and given the fact that, as I have said, a statement specific to an interview cannot measure up to the complexity of the situation, I would venture somewhat abstractly the following points.

Note first that I was referring with the example of the Ukraine to *world* peace, I was not talking in local terms. Since no locality remains, democracy must be thought *globally* today, if it is to have a future. In the past, one could always say that democracy was to be saved in this or that country. Today, however, if one claims to be a democrat, one cannot be a democrat "at home" and wait to see what happens "abroad."

Everything that is happening today—whether it be about Europe, the GATT, the Mafia, drugs, arms—engages the future of democracy in the world in general. If this seems an obvious thing to say, one must nevertheless say it.

Second, in the determination or behavior of each citizen or singularity, there should be present, in some form or other, the call to a world democracy to come, each singularity should determine itself with a sense of the stakes of a democracy that can no longer be contained within frontiers, that can no longer be localized, that can no longer depend on the decisions of a specific group of citizens, a nation, or even of a continent. This determination means that one must both think, and think democracy, globally. This may be something completely new, something that has never been done, for we are talking here of something much more complex, much more modest, and yet much more ambitious than any notion of the universal, cosmopolitan, or human. I realize that there is so much rhetoric today—obvious, conventional, reassuring, determined in the sense of without risk—that resembles what I am saying. When, for example, one speaks in the name of the United Nations, when one speaks in the name of a politics that transcends national borders, one always does so in the name of democracy. One has to make the difference clear, then, between democracy in this rhetorical sense and what I am calling a *democracy to come.* The difference shows, for example, that all the decisions made in the name of the rights of man are at the same time alibis for the continued inequality between singularities, and that we need to invent other concepts than state, superstate, citizen, and so forth for this new International. The democracy to come obliges one to challenge instituted law in the name of an indefinitely unsatisfied justice, thereby revealing the injustice of calculating justice whether this be in the name of a particular form of democracy or of the concept of humanity. This democracy to come is marked in the movement that always carried a present beyond itself, makes it inadequate to itself, "out of joint" (*Hamlet*); as I argue in *Specters of Marx,* it obliges us to work with the spectrality in any moment of apparent presence. This spectrality is very *weak;* it is the weakness of the powerless, who, being powerless, resist the greatest strength.

R.B.: What you have just said concerning time and spectral weakness takes us to question twelve, if not also to question thirteen.

QUESTION TWELVE: Penultimate question: how would you react to the following proposition? The time of technology and the time of philosophy (in particular that of deconstruction, which can only go *slowly*) are becoming more and more disarticulated, disjointed, out of joint. The *law* of our time to read is at the risk of being "overpowered" by the *law* of the time of technology, a law whose end appears to be the "overcoming" of time. Here, the worst side of Nietzsche's prognostications for the future could come true, although it would not be the reign of democracy that would have brought about this monstrous future of indifferentiation. Either there will be another suicidal attempt to harness technology to the ends of man (fascism in alliance with biogenetics is perhaps our worst future) and/or technology, an inhuman will to power, will overpower humanity. Is this proposition too oppositional, too human, too pious? Too *apocalyptic?* Or, conversely, is today another "noontide" for decision? This decision would not, however, be in the "grand style" of politics. It would undoubtedly do violence to the memory of the promise of the other; but the violence would be committed so that the future does not risk forgetting this promise in the greatest violence.

QUESTION THIRTEEN: Finally. In the preamble to this interview I suggested that the name of Nietzsche could serve as an "index" to a series of questions that have become all the more pressing since the end of the Cold War. My final questions, following from those to do with justice, pushed relentlessly the question of the relations between his name and the futures of this end. I am aware that you are publishing a text on Marx.[7] Is another text with which these futures are to be thought and acted upon those of Marx—a new Marx (with Hegel, perhaps), one "after" Nietzsche and Heidegger, and at the end of Marxism?

R.B.: Given the time left, let us end with question twelve. I am situating the problem of acceleration in Nietzschean terms of the will. Just as we need to invent new concepts to deal with today's political complexity, so, I am suggesting, we need to develop a notion of the will to respond to the imminent dangers facing the post–Cold War world. This would be a will that would learn how to put the brakes on the accelerating processes of technicization *so that* there would be *time* to face this acceleration in the spirit not of the greatest simplicity (that is the threat), but of the greatest complexity. Is this recourse to the notion of will too apocalyptic for you, despite its taking into account of the non-horizonal promise?

J.D.: As I said in response to question seven, I have always thought that thinking is acting provided that one considers thought otherwise than as theoretical speculation. So, your question, if I understand it rightly, is slightly misplaced for me. Thought is tied to language, tied to statements, and statements are acts, they are primarily performative; thinking always concerns the will, even if it enacts an experience of "radical passivity." There is no thought of the future that is not at the same time an *engagement* with the question, "What should I do?" In a sense, Heidegger is saying the same thing when he argues that there is no difference between *denken* and *handeln*. To think is to do. This can be said differently by recalling that there is no thinking without speaking, that there is no speaking without performative utterances, without events, without promises, and that such promises are not promises if they are not inscribed in conditions that are real. As is clear to all today, the most conventional theoretical logic of *speech acts* tells us that a performative works only if it is inscribed in a specific context, if it takes account of particular conventions, and so forth. A true thought cannot fail to be a performative language that produces events, that is inscribed therefore in what ordinary language calls the *practical* or *historical* reality of things. Thought is that which has an impact [*fait événement*] in the world. This conception of what constitutes thought is extremely ambitious today. Contemporary thought can think nothing but the present process of globalization to which we have constantly referred, whether the question be that of technics, the nation-state, democracy, the media, and so on. This kind of thinking is hyperbolically ambitious, although it must be extremely modest as well. Under the pretext that our discussion of the actual state of affairs in the world is taking place within the confines of an interview, recorded by a tape-recorder, in an office, and that it is to appear in an academic journal that will be read by a handful of people, under the pretext, then, that this is all too modest, one must not renounce giving a very modest form to these hyperbolically ambitious thoughts. To do the contrary would be to give up the responsibility of thought. And so, one must accept that the hyperbolic could well end up as a grain of sand. This is, of course, the fate of all actions. Since thought is also an action, since it is not in opposition to action, it must undergo the same fate.

R.B.: You are allying here action, the law of contamination, and incalculability?

J.D.: In a sense, yes. I have no right to abandon my responsibility under the pretext that this responsibility is modest, under the pretext that its effects are incalculable; one cannot calculate one's responsibility, so its effects may well be nothing, almost nothing. In response to an emergency, I do what I can. I may well be able to do a lot, I may well be able to do very little, even nothing—whatever, I have no right to withdraw from doing something, under the pretext that it will be done in vain. This is irresponsibility itself. Imagine a fire emergency and a fireman who under the pretext that he is unlikely to douse the fire with ten buckets of water, may think of giving up. Does he? No, of course not. Responsibility implies a question of measure *within* the measureless [*la démesure*] and a question of the measureless *within* measure. We are dealing always with measurelessness [*la démesure*].

R.B.: Do you consider that the threat (of simplification) could be so great that one could run the risk of forgetting the promise or the messianic?

J.D.: No, it is a priori impossible because the threat is not something that comes from the outside to place itself next to the promise. The threat *is* the promise, in the sense that the threat threatens the promise. There would be no experience of threat, of danger, unless there was the promise. One could not feel the waiting for justice as a threat, unless there was the promise. The threat is the promise itself, or better, threat and promise always come together *as* the promise. This does not mean just that the promise is always already threatened; it also means that the promise is *threatening*. The messianic is threatening: there are people who are very frightened of the messianic, as we are going to see in the years to come. People are not just frightened of messianism, they are also frightened of the messianic, quite simply because it is frightening. One must accept that the promise is both threatened and threatening.

R.B.: You are saying here what you said earlier regarding duplicity and iterability of affirmation. The promise affirms the threat in this sense.

J.D.: Yes. To put it much more simply—when I promise or when I give something to someone, it is both good and bad. Bad, because the promise or gift is felt as a threat. Even when I say "yes" to somebody, the "yes" can be felt naively as gratifying, but the "yes" is also worrying. Any gift, any promise is worrying at the same time as being desired. And it is a good thing that it is both good and bad. So you see, in fact, nothing can be simple, and contamination is a good thing!

R.B.: It's time.

Translated by Richard Beardsworth

"Dead Man Running": Salut, Salut

NOTES FOR A LETTER TO 'LES TEMPS MODERNES'

22 March 1996

Dear Claude Lanzmann,

The deadline arrives, I am not ready. Will I ever have been?

On the telephone, when you generously invited me, I nonetheless promised to "try." Tempted, I wanted to try to write something that would not be too unworthy of an anniversary—my God, already fifty years!—yes, of an anniversary that you have good reason to celebrate and that I would be happy to attend among the crowd. To myself as well, if I can say this, at least to what I confess to liking of my memory, I had promised to give some sign that would testify to my grateful, admiring, and faithful attachment to this enigmatic thing that is still called *Les Temps Modernes*. The thing carries and deserves its name so well, what a fine name, finally, today more than ever—I would like to return to this.

Giving in to an intractable necessity, but which for that very reason often ends up dictating the cliché, I first wrote: "This enigmatic thing that *will have* been called *Les Temps Modernes*." And then, no; no future anterior is called for here, the adventure continues, and it is your future that must be hailed [*saluer*]: Long live *Les Temps Modernes*! Greetings [*salut*] to you! Yes, I would like to salute [*saluer*] your future. But your future as *our future*.

Our future, he says: this appropriation will perhaps be judged indecent to those who know, supposing of course they should ever have been interested in this, that in a thousand ways I have never been, as they say, one of *Les Temps Modernes*. This may seem very clear indeed: I have never been *one of you*. Hasty people might foolishly conclude that I am, therefore, against *Les Temps Modernes*—or a stranger to *Les Temps Modernes*. But here, once again, it is so much more complicated! I feel, and I know, that I have always been *for* and *with Les Temps Modernes*. This is precisely what I would have liked to explain—to explain to myself first of all—but this history remains so labyrinthine and unfathomable that here I am, at the appointed date, and for a long time still, no doubt forever, stuck [*en panne*].

A greeting [*salut*], then: I have just said that I wanted to address a *greeting* [un salut] to *Les Temps Modernes*. But as so often happens to me before a deadline, I stumble across the equivocal chance, close to the formidable ambiguity of this word, salut, especially when one throws out the performative apostrophe ("salut!") at a moment of encounter or separation, at the moment of parting or meeting again, and each time it is both the moving away and moving toward but each time, even at the instant of departure or of death, it is a "salut" at the coming of what comes, I would even be tempted to say, already quoting from a text of Sartre to which I will return, and whose words are otherwise alive today, more alive than ever, "a pure event."[1]

At this moment comes another temptation: to escape, as in the course of a race [*le cours d'une course*] (the racing cyclist escapes by moving away from the pack, as one says in the trade), and to liberate myself, to absolve myself thus or to deliver myself, if you prefer, in a word to save myself (salvation, salvation [*salut, salut*]) by means of a short treatise on *salut*, or more precisely to save myself to interpret, in a way that is patient, analytic, micrological—taking my time to gain time or to ramble [*battre la campagne*]—what the vocabulary of a soteriology of modern times (deliverance, "saving," salvation and "saving oneself") has inscribed in the history of Sartre and his journal, of your journal.

What exactly did Sartre mean, for example, in 1948, when he claimed to have chosen this "salvation" against that other one? "We affirm [*he declared at the time*] against certain critics and against certain authors that *salvation* [salut] is achieved on this earth, that it is of the whole man and by the whole man and that art is a meditation on life, not death."[2] Why do I still like what he had to say about salvation thus one day, almost fifty years ago, when I am still not ready to subscribe to it? For I will never consent to it without voicing an objection, at such and such a moment,

one of those intimate objections that one would turn against one's own beliefs, an argued contestation that I would then oppose to the firm authority of this "affirmation," of this *incipit* that takes the form of an attack
("We affirm . . ."), as I would to each word of this verdict.

And Sartre, furthermore, did Sartre *himself* subscribe to it? And
Roquentin? When I say Sartre himself, I mean all of Sartre, if this is possible. Which is another way of asking: and Roquentin himself, would he
have subscribed to it? This same Roquentin who had already torn to pieces
the preaching of this lesson of salvation (if I can say this) before giving in
to it himself in the last pages of *Nausea*? But in the process, his critique of
the "humanist" had left traces of a devastating passage, as if in advance, on
many of the discourses to be held with great confidence several years later
by Sartre in "Existentialism is a Humanism" as well as in, precisely,
"Writing for One's Age." I will quote several lines from the latter. They
touch on what the "humanist philosopher" (following the "radical humanist," the "left humanist," "the Communist writer," "the Catholic humanist") or the humanist in general declares himself prepared to spend, to
give in order to *save*. "To save": here is the word for the first time, one
must "save one's brothers":

[T]he humanist philosopher who bends over his brothers like a wise elder brother
who has a sense of his responsibilities; the humanist who loves men as they are,
the humanist who loves them as they ought to be, the one who wants to save
them with their consent and the one who will *save* them in spite of themselves
. . . the one who loves death in man, the one who loves life in man.[3]

Basically, the Sartre that I have always taken the unjustifiable liberty
of choosing, among others, himself among his-selves, is perhaps the one
who regularly let himself be *stamped* [frapper], imprinted [*imprimer*] by
this stamp [*frappe*], who thus let himself write, while exposing himself in
his writing (another answer to the three questions of "What Is
Literature?": "What Is Writing?" "Why Write?" "For Whom Does One
Write?"), stamped, write or fight with the contradiction, both assumed
and rejected, the one who also let himself be torn apart by the tension between, for example, this "anti-humanist" moment of Roquentin's discourse (nearly ten years before *Les Temps Modernes*!) and the one who exposed himself in it in advance and imprudently—and this is also of course
the director-founder of *Les Temps Modernes*. Sartre is at times *the former*
Roquentin and at times his most identifiable target. And even after 1945,

one still sees him at times on the side of the one who denounces the discourse on fraternity, the "myth of fraternity" and of the notion that "all men are brothers"[4] that is sustained by "bourgeois charity"; and at other times, in the same "Introducing *Les Temps Modernes*," the one who still wants to *save,* to redeem, or more precisely to "deliver."

What difference would there be between saving and delivering? Delivering whom? But the "free man," of course, yes, "the whole man." As paradoxical as this may seem, it nonetheless follows that one can only "free" a freedom, a freedom that is already possible, it is all or nothing: one cannot speak of "delivering," in terms of atonement, salvation, or redemption, except by referring to a being who is free and capable of freedom. A living being. One does not deliver a stone; common sense at least would tell us this. One does not free an "in itself," as Sartre might have said, on the side of common sense here (for my part, I will always wonder if there is no sense in delivering something else, an animal, for example, or a god).

"Introducing *Les Temps Modernes*" even emphasizes, we should emphasize it in turn, the word *delivering.* After having shown the "antinomy" of "contemporary consciousness" and refused to let himself be "torn between thesis and antithesis," after having attempted to derive a new concept of "freedom" from metaphysics, Sartre still speaks of *deliverance;* he has also just reminded us that we have a tendency, over time, to forget that commitment consists less in committing oneself by means of a derisory heroism of will than in recognizing that, in any case (and even if one did not recognize it) one *is committed,* that is, passively thrown before any decision, into a situation in which the action decided upon remains—one still has a tendency to forget this—a *bet* [pari] that has the *undecidable* as background and in a space that remains heterogeneous to knowledge. Commitment is both the being-committed to a situation that is not chosen and, in this situation, the gage [*gage*] of a singular wager [*gageure*]:

He is not at all free to choose: he is committed [*engagé*], forced to wager. But he is free to choose at the same time his destiny, the destiny of all men, and the value to be attributed to humanity. Thus does he choose himself simultaneously as a worker and as a man, while at the same time conferring a meaning upon the proletariat. Such is man as we conceive him: the whole man. Totally committed and totally free. And yet it is the free man who must be *delivered* by enlarging his possibilities of choice. In certain situations there is room for only two alternatives, one of which is death. It is necessary to proceed in such a way that man, in every circumstance, can choose life.[5]

Several pages earlier, the vocabulary of deliverance had already asserted itself. It always serves as a translation between a thinking of liberation (the liberation of a freedom) and a thinking of salvation. In this secularization of salvation, in this soteriology of total liberation as deliverance, how does one sort out (but is it a question of this?) what may stand out [*faire date*] and is thus dated [*daté*] on this anniversary, and what still seems irrecusable, lucid and in truth to come, especially when Sartre, in the passage I will quote, states the conditions under which man "must" "free himself totally—that is, make himself *other* . . ."? What remains of this living promise, to which we must hold ourselves, to which we cannot not hold? And where does one situate this promise, once one has let the idea of a "synthetic anthropology," the discourse on "totality" and the secular translation of a sermon on salvation that appeals to redemption, "expire"? One would need pages and pages of exegesis to *discern* what remains, I would not dare say "alive [*vif*]" (so as not to give in all too quickly to this axiomatic of life that, as I reread, I notice remains at the heart of the Sartrian discourse), but open to what comes, and what opens itself at least, in sentences such as:

We would like our journal to contribute in a modest way to the elaboration of a synthetic anthropology. But it is not, we repeat, simply a question of effecting an advance in the domain of pure knowledge: the most distant goal we are aiming at is a *liberation*. Since man is a totality, it is indeed not enough to grant him the right to vote without dealing with the other factors that constitute him. He must free himself totally—that is, make himself other by acting on his biological, constitutional as well as on his economic condition, on his sexual complexes as well as on the political terms of his situation.[6]

It is especially imperative and difficult, to *discern* here, and Sartre himself is vigilant enough to warn us, immediately following, of the "grave dangers" that "this synthetic view" presents. Indeed this view risks clearing the way to totalitarianism, to a totalitarianism that will again be—it too—a soteriology of deliverance ("The spirit of synthesis cannot be apportioned its mere share: no sooner is he glimpsed than man as a totality would disappear, submerged by his class; only class exists, and it alone must be delivered"); and Sartre will then denounce the totalitarianism of the left as well as the Nazi totalitarianism and will be led, on the very subject of the value of "totality" (without totalitarianism) to assume and to sharpen what he rightly and more than once calls the *antinomy* that I mentioned above (and on this point as well, I like to feel myself his heir!). But here, too, an antinomy within the antinomy, an antinomy without antinomy: he not only refuses the antinomy as such but he writes the following, in the name of a "we" that would require another long letter, for himself and for his heirs, consenting or no: "So far as we are concerned, we refuse to let ourselves be torn between thesis and antithesis" ("Introducing *Les Temps Modernes*," 261–264). One must therefore seek salvation and deliverance without letting oneself be torn, and this is Sartre's "passion," which, I will confess, I still share—*at moments*. And if I confess to this "at moments," it is very simply in order to confess. Everything that I might try to say remains thus inflected; one would have to add "at moments" to each of my sentences. Nothing is more unstable, divided, split, antinomic than my friendship for whatever it is that is called *Sartre* and *Les Temps Modernes*, and this instability will have been one of the traces of the *T.M.*, of the "epoch" of the *T.M.* in my life, almost all my life, most of the time. No doubt with other "intellectuals of my generation" (as one says) I am, I will have been this, that which will not have been what it was without the *T.M.*: I + *T.M.*, in two words.

So, I would have to, I would then have to tell you a little bit about all of this, about everything that I would have liked to go into my "greeting [*salut*]" here to *Les Temps Modernes*: not to put forth something that would count in itself or for itself but to recall to memory what—using a vertiginous metonymy—one would call *the voice of Sartre*. I would like so much to bring back its taste, and the taste for the word *taste* in his mouth, I will come to this, its taste and its timbre. I can dream of imitating it almost—but I can never succeed, in testifying *for him*—to hear again the living voice itself, or more precisely the specter of this living voice, by letting thus resound, but only for a time, a phantom or phantasmatic voice of Sartre, thus by *saving* it a little, for example in reproducing it or playing a certain record for myself, like *Some of these days* at the unforgettable forgettable ending of *Nausea*, to listen once again to what a certain Sartre, for example, said one day in his editorial of sorts entitled, "Writing for One's Age." He wanted us to hear and to understand what "writing" and "age [*époque*]" and above all what "saving" or "not saving" meant for him. Yes, I think that *saving* is a word with which one must contend [*s'entendre*] if one wants to follow Sartre in his wake.

Furthermore, since I have just evoked the oblivion at the end of *Nausea*, and reproduction and record

(*The voice sings:*

> Some of these days
>
> You'll miss me honey

Someone must have scratched the record at that spot because it makes an odd noise. And there is something that clutches the heart.)

remember that the end of *Nausea* is already a spectral scene. It speaks of this "taste" that I want to talk to you about (". . . a taste of smoke in his mouth and, vaguely, a ghost of a tune in his head. "Some of these days."). Let us call this a scene of *salvation unto death* [salut à mort]. Who will be saved? This is the question. Saved, thus chosen—for one does not save oneself any more than one commits oneself, *one is saved* just as one is committed. I am still the one underlining here: "She sings. So two of them are *saved*: the Jew and the Negress. *Saved*."

This scene of *salvation unto death* warns against resurrection ("My error, I wanted to resuscitate the Marquis de Rollebon"), and it preserves, of course, the taste of the "last time" for someone who dreams of "accepting" himself but "in the past, only in the past." The appeal to salvation, its calling also resounds for the "last time," the ultimate "pure event" that becomes in this way a last judgment. A calling that is eschatological in essence:

> I get up, but I hesitate an instant, I'd like to hear the Negress sing. *For the last time*.
>
> She sings. So two of them are *saved*: the Jew and the Negress. *Saved*.

And above, again the emphasis is mine:

> "Your record, monsieur Antoine, the one you like, do you want to hear it *for the last time?*"
>
> "Please" . . . Still, I'm going to pay attention because, as Madeleine says, I'm hearing it for *the last time*: it is very old, even too old for the provinces . . . into the center of disc, it will be finished and the hoarse voice singing "Some of these days" will be silent *forever*.

Yes, you will say, but *Nausea* remains a fiction, it is literature, and the one who says "I" is not Sartre who—he—analyzes the eschatology of salvation *in* the other, in Roquentin. Of course, but one could cite so many words of Sartre "himself," words that say the same thing as Roquentin's words and that were also the watchwords of *Les Temps Modernes* ("Introducing *Les Temps Modernes*" or "Writing for One's Age"); in any case, the same words as those of Roquentin at such and such a moment (everything is valid for him "at moments" as well, as was the case for me above), for Roquentin also holds an unstable and contradictory discourse; he welcomes in himself contradictory desires. Moreover, even within this great fiction (that I still admire and that I remember having read in a certain ecstatic bedazzlement at seventeen, in Algiers, in philosophy class, sitting on a bench in Laferrière square, sometimes raising my eyes toward the roots, the bushes of flowers or the luxuriant plants, as if to verify the too-much of existence, but also with intense movements of "literary" identification: how to write like that and, above all, not like that?), within this true fiction I also like how the supplementary simulacrum of a certain "as if" and of a certain "perhaps" comes insistently to spectralize death. But this fiction *en abyme* spectralizes or virtualizes life as well as death, complicating thus—unless it is to ruin it in advance—the scope of the statements that stand as "watchwords," which, I will also come to this later, bring everything together around the "age [*époque*]" as "the living absolute" that "is always right when it is living" ("Writing for One's Age," 242).

"Perhaps" and "as if," thus, and "a little like," again my emphasis:

[T]he disc is scratched and is wearing out, perhaps the singer is *dead*; I'm going to leave. . . . I don't want to know anything about him—besides, he *may be dead*. . . . So two of them are *saved*: the Jew and the Negress. *Saved*. *Maybe they thought they were lost* irrevocably, drowned in existence. Yet no one could think of me as I think of them, with such gentleness. . . . They are *a little like dead people for me*, a little like the heroes in a novel; *they have washed themselves of the sin of existing*. (*Nausea*, 176–177)

Dear Claude Lanzmann, because one should not multiply the footnotes in a letter, allow me to open a long parenthesis to give, as "references," the sentences of Sartre that, had I the time, the place, and the strength, I would have liked to analyze closely. They all zero in on a certain concept of "epoch" that was also a concept *of the time* [de l'époque] and which seems to me, today at least, to bring together the direction, the destiny, and the "taste" of *Les Temps Modernes* from the beginning and for always, through the many displacements, mutations, reconfigurations, in short, through all the "epochs" that have marked the journal and no doubt continue to do so. What is this "epochality" (*for* which and *from* which one would have to "write"—"to write for one's age," thus—that does not so much presuppose a *knowledge* of what is specific to one's own age as the *commitment* to appropriate one's age for oneself, to appropriate oneself more originarily in the specificity of "one's age")? Such a movement engages everything except the suspense of a *skepsis* or the phenomenological suspension of an *epochē* that Sartre was able to understand or expose; on the contrary, it is the release from this putting into parentheses that is presupposed by the *gage* [gage] that is given, as much as by the wager [gageure] of *commitment*. Although it has so often been discussed, at times to satiation, as a past modality of the responsibility of "intellectuals," I find that *commitment* remains a very fine word, a word that is accurate and still quite new, if only one chooses to hear it as the summons *to which* what we still call writers or intellectuals respond and *for which* they are answerable.

In one of the passages on the age that I will quote in a moment, Sartre strongly links the two values of the word: (1) to give a *guarantee* [gage] (affirmation, promise, vow, covenant, sworn oath, symbolic pact, sharing of the *symbolon*); and (2) to *enter* into something without hope of return, heart and soul, indeed headlong, to work one's way into, or even sink into a space or time in which one already finds oneself: to find *oneself* where one *finds-oneself*, in short, and this is never easy, never a given, nothing perhaps is more inaccessible. This definition and especially this implementation of the two values of the reflexive verb *to commit oneself* [s'engager] and therefore of the word *age* that is indissociable from it, I believe that they require a thesis on salvation [*le salut*], a thesis that is both historicist and antihistoricist at the same time: on *history, truth, the absolute* (*the word* absolute *occurs ten times per page*), *on life and death—on passion and testimony, on evil, and thus on salvation*—nothing less.

Here, I am the one underlining all these words whose chain cannot be undone; Sartre underlines only *lived*:

At the time, man *committed himself* to them *completely*, and, in manifesting them at the peril of his life, he brought truth into being through them, for truth *never yields itself directly, it merely appears through errors*. . . . *[I]n testifying* for it [evolution] against the clerics, the American teachers lived the truth, they lived it *passionately and absolutely*, at their own risk. Tomorrow they will be wrong, today they are absolutely right; the age is always wrong when it is dead, always right when it is alive. Condemn it later on, if you like; but first it had its *passionate* way of loving itself and lacerating itself, against which future judgments are of no avail. It had its *taste* which it *tasted* alone and which is as incomparable, as irremediable, as the *taste* of wine in our mouths.

A book has its *absolute truth* within the age. ("Writing for One's Age," 242)

I do not think that this is true, absolutely true—but no matter— and that one could just as well say the contrary. Precisely on an anniversary, both for the books and for the strange events that we are celebrating [*saluons*]. And what is more, Sartre himself had done so in advance, in his "Introducing *Les Temps Modernes*," several years earlier, when he said that "an era [*une époque*], like a man, is first of all a future" (253). That I should therefore object to this, even if I am right, this proves that Sartre is not wrong, especially at a moment when he is recognizing his mistake by speaking: I find this magnificent, it has an "irremediable" taste. How, one will ask, can the taste of wine be "irremediable" and what is this language of fault or sin? What is the logic of confession doing here? The essential, precisely. As with the "sin of existing" of which only the "heroes of novels" that I discussed earlier "have washed themselves." Sartre had reminded us of this feature earlier, a feature, which, today, one would say was an originarily performative one of language, and this is what makes the epoch before being epoch-making. Moreover, he says this in a text that is a response, a retort, an altercation: "We affirm against certain critics. . . . Within the age, every utterance, before being a historical byword or the recognized origin of a social process, is first an insult or an appeal or a confession" ("Writing for One's Age," 241).

I will content myself now with quoting sentences and underlining several words in them, sentences whose quasi systematic concatenation I would have liked to analyze, the chain that runs between *history, truth, the absolute, life and death, passion and testimony, salvation* (*rescue* [sauvetage] or *safeguard* [sauvegarde], *that which keeps safe* [sauf]). I have chosen all of these sentences from "Writing for One's Age," and—as if to justify the fact that I am calling this letter addressed to you, "Notes for a letter to *Les Temps Modernes* "—they are contained between *two sequences* (1 and 2) on the *course of history*: *between the race* [course] *or the mail* [courier]. I am addressing these lines to you from the place where they touch me, copying them from Sartre, on this anniversary, even when I find fault with them, drawing them from Sartre who first says the following, first sequence, shortly after the *incipit* that I quoted earlier:

1. The *course* of history, thus, as a *race* [course]:

But I haven't entered into history and I don't know how I shall enter it; perhaps alone, perhaps in an anonymous crowd, perhaps as one of those names they put into footnotes in literary handbooks. At any rate, I do not have to bother myself with the judgments that the future will bring to bear upon my work since there's nothing I can do about them. Art cannot be reduced to a dialogue with the dead and with men not yet born;[7] *that would be both too difficult and too easy; and I see in this a last remnant of Christian belief in immortality.* . . . But at least, among Christians, it is this stay upon earth that decides everything and the final beatitude is only a sanction. Whereas it is commonly believed that the course run by our books [*here is the race*], when we no longer exist, refers back [*revient*] to our life to justify it [*this re-venir from a race after death, is it not the revenance of a specter?*]. This is true from the viewpoint of the objective mind. In the objective mind one classifies according to talent [*this cannot suffice in exhausting the objective mind, an obviously Hegelian concept about which I will only say that it presupposes, in an essential way, this destinal spectrality that I have in view here*]. But our descendants' view of us is not a privileged one, since others will come after them and will judge them in turn. It is obvious that we write out of a need for the *absolute*, and a work of the mind is indeed an *absolute*. . . . First of all, it is not true that a writer transmits his sufferings and his faults to the absolute when he writes about them; it is not true that he *saves* them. (239)

2. Second sequence, the *course* [cours] of history as the *race* [course] *of a courier,* the dead courier, the dead runner who no longer has his head and who continues to run, close to the end, indeed right at the end, given over to the end, at what is the end of "Writing for One's Age" (I can also remember the chickens sacrificed in the garden of my childhood, several days before the Great Pardon, and who set about running still, after they had been decapitated, headless in short, as if to save themselves covered with blood from the misfortune that had already befallen them; and it is perhaps thus that I see myself, the time of writing, but I only see myself *running after my death in this way, after it truly*; and there where I already *see myself* thus, I try to understand, without ever having gotten there, for what and for whom, after whom and after what I am running, in the experience of an anticipation that is without head [*cap*] and without capitulation; I try in vain to know who and what returns to me from this strange time of the dead courier, *returning to me* meaning *at the same time, at once*, identifying with me, constituting my ipseity there where *I find myself*—or else the ipseity of my time—for this ipseity does not find itself before this

strange possibility, and *returning to me* as the ghost [*revenant*] of me *after* which I run out of breath: the specter goes so much faster than I do!). Here comes the end, then, of "Writing for One's Age":

It was said that the courier of Marathon had died an hour before reaching Athens. He was dead and he was still running; he was running dead, announced the Greek victory dead. This is a fine myth; it shows that the dead still act for a little while as if they were living. For a while, a year, ten years, perhaps fifty years; at any rate, a *finite* period; and then they are buried a second time. This is the measure we propose to the writer: as long as his books arouse anger, discomfort, shame, hatred, love, even if he is no more than a shadow, he will live. Afterwards, the deluge. We stand for an ethics and art of the *finite*.

These are the last words of the text. Sartre underlines *finite*. This logic of the "second time" and of the "even if he is no more than a shadow, he will live," is this not what en-gages itself [*se gage*] as an anniversary? (I am running, I am hastening toward the end).

Here now is the chain of quotations and underlined words. They still come from "Writing for One's Age," I am quoting them a little arbitrarily (this remains but one essay among so many others, an occasional article that was not at first intended for *Les Temps Modernes* and which was only published that same year as a fragment of "What is Literature?"[8]). But I am only focusing on this contingency to raise, in passing, on this anniversary, the question of the age: what do the rings of age do? Do we still belong to the same age as "Writing for One's Age"? And why and how is this text still intelligible and necessary to us? These words, thus (*history, truth, the absolute, life, death, the passion of testimony, salvation: rescue or safeguard, what keeps all of what precedes safe as greeting* [salut] *to the other*), they seem to be distributed according to a serial multiplicity of sentences that could be largely extended throughout Sartre's corpus (and perhaps throughout that of *Les Temps Modernes*). In truth, I think that they secretly form one single, long *absolute* sentence whose subject, which is also its own attribute (like the *absolute*, precisely, in the sentence of the speculative dialectic in Hegel), could be any of them. The signature of my testimony could be reduced to the choice of several terms and to the virtual sentence that is magnetized by them. It is I who, to testify here, in the sacrificial and acephalous precipitation that I described a moment ago, to what seems to me to be the history, the passion, the truth, or absolute of that of which I am speaking or of those to whom I am addressing myself, it is I, thus, who will have chosen to privilege, in a greeting [*salut*] to the other, a certain vocabulary of salvation [*salut*]: the safe, the unharmed, or the immune [*immun*],[9] rescue, safeguard, atonement, or redemption. I would like to bring this vocabulary to bear on the age—to relate it to *that* age, certainly, to *that* thinking of the age in which someone wrote "Writing for One's Age," but also to the thinking of epoch in general, to epochality itself. Dear Claude Lanzmann, in a letter written while traveling, in so little time and space, with these few works within reach, I will never manage to deploy a fine enough, convincing enough argument that would make clear what I would like to try to think. What then? Well, a discreet—but according to me—irrecusable alliance: the alliance which, beyond *that age* (beyond the age that Sartre and *Les Temps Modernes* represent, speak, or condense par excellence) but also for that age, of course, in it, would hold together *both* the age *and* salvation, *both* the thinking of epochality *and* the thinking of the salutary, safe and sound, the immune, the holy and the sacred. To speak of movement, of motivation, and of tendency rather than of being and essence, I would have liked to think and better describe the irrecusable or rather incontestable alliance (incontestable because it belongs as an attestation to the order of performative testimony and to the act of faith rather than to the order of evidence) that, in the same experience, links the process of epochalization and the process of sanctification, indeed redemption. To say it in a word, the scheme I would have needed to carry off this demonstration of an alliance between the concept of *epoch* and the concept of *salvation*, or, if you prefer, between a certain historicity, eschatology, and soteriology, would have been the concept of *reserve* [retenue], of pause [*halte*] or of suspense (*Verhaltenheit*, Heidegger would have said) that conditions the *epochē* of the epoch, the *epochē* of skepticism or of phenomenology for example, as well as the modesty, the respect, the distance, the abstention or the retention, the attention, too, before that which of the other must remain safe, holy, immune (the condition of the ethical, juridical, political or religious law). This *epoch*-making thinking of the *pause*, this is what I would have liked to show at work, in particular in Sartre and in his discourse on salvation. (I would have maintained, as I do elsewhere, that the two meanings or the two uses of the word *salut* are incompatible or irreconcilable and must remain so: the *salut à* presupposes a renunciation of the *salut de*. To address a greeting *to* [salut à] the other, a greeting from one's self as other to the other as other, for this greeting to be what it must be it, it must break off all hope of salvation or redemption, of all return and restitution of the "safe," etc.). What I am sending you are only notes, quotations or preparatory documents in view of such a demonstration.

1. *The absolute, evil, and salvation.* It is scarcely useful to recall it: existentialism (according to one tradition or to a French translation of Kierkegaard and of Heidegger) immediately put itself forward as a new thinking of evil, perdition, shame or originary culpability-responsibility-imputability (*Schuldigsein*), of the "sin of existing" of which only "the heroes of a novel" could wash themselves ("the dirt" or the "I am ashamed," the "I am ashamed of myself" in the experience of nausea, the examples of which could be multiplied almost endlessly in the literary and philosophical texts of Sartre). Yet in a passage already cited, Sartre in fact noted that "we all write out of *absolute* need" and that "a work of mind is indeed an *absolute*." Denouncing thus two errors, he immediately links them to the question of the salvation that saves as well as to the salvation that does not save. The reference to salvation asserts itself, in effect, since it is a matter of evil every time, of "literature and evil":

But here one commits a double error. First of all, it is not true that a writer transmits his sufferings and his faults to the *absolute* when he writes about them; it is not true that he *saves* them. It is said that the unhappily married man who writes about marriage with talent has made a good book *with* his conjugal woes. That would be too easy: the bee makes honey *with* the flower because it operates on the vegetal substance of *real* transformations; the sculptor makes a statue *with* marble. But it is with words and not with his troubles that the writer makes his book. If he wants to keep his wife from being disagreeable, it is a mistake to write about her; he would do better to beat her.

Following this discussion that is a little too slick and not very convincing (especially on the word *with*, which is underlined by Sartre, as is the word *real*) about what writing "with words" is, following a series of examples that would deserve a vigilant reading, Sartre concludes this soteriological argument with the appeal to an absolute salvation that brings together and reconciles in itself, that *saves* both man and artist *together—as a single man*:

The most beautiful book in the world will not *save* a child from pain; one does not *save* evil, one fights it; the most beautiful book in the world *saves itself*; it also *saves* the artist. But not the man. We want the man and the artist to work their *salvation together*, we want the work to be at the same time an act; we want it to be explicitly conceived as a weapon in the struggle that men wage *against evil*.

Such an absolute, absolutely absolute, if it must save "man and artist" "together," whole man, one must know that it is never given, never given as the fact of a given, only as what remains *to be done* ("we want the man and the artist *to work* their salvation together") in a history en-gaged [*gagée*], in the acting, the process, and the experience of what must indeed be called an *absolution*.

2. *The absolute of the "epoch": truth, testimony and presence, touch as taste.* Allow me to pass very quickly over the inexhaustible recurrence of the word *absolute* to point to what must be saved, namely the age, the "living absolute" of the age in which "man has committed himself wholly" and this "truth" that one lives only by "testifying" to it. I will pull together several quotations very quickly to come to this *singular* taste for the word *taste*, which, as I said earlier, I would also like to save or resuscitate in Sartre, in his way, in "Sartre's way"—which seems impossible where these absolutely *singular* things remain, as he himself says so well, "inimitable" "absolutes."

Naturally, to introduce "taste," it would be better to begin with hunger—or thirst. The absolute is to be drunk and eaten, always a matter of taste, thus also of distaste. Of the palate. Like speech, it always passes by way of the mouth, the lips, and the tongue. Even the pipe.

Here, then, is *hunger*:

The other error is just as grave. There is such a hunger for the absolute in every heart that eternity, which is a non-temporal absolute, is frequently confused with immortality, which is only a perpetual reprieve and a long succession of vicissitudes. I understand this desire for the *absolute*; I desire it too. . . . We produce the *absolute* as M. Jourdain produced prose. *You light your pipe* and that's an *absolute*; you *detest oysters* and that's an *absolute*; you join the Communist Party and that's an *absolute*.

Following which we find *thirst* and the taste of wine on the palate; this is several lines down, to introduce the "pure event" as the absolute of the age and to introduce its truth attested to as "taste," the inalienable property of presence:

Our grandfathers were right in saying, as they drank their glass of wine, "another one that the Prussians won't get." Neither the Prussians nor anyone else.

They can kill you, they can deprive you of wine to the end of your days, but no God, no man, can take away that final trickling of the Bordeaux along your tongue. No relativism. Nor the "eternal course of history" either. Nor the dialectic of the sensible. Nor the dissociations of psychoanalysis. [*Here he accelerates, he gets carried away and moves too quickly, with psychoanalysis, this could be shown, but this is not the issue. We must let him continue his race.*] It is a *pure event*, and we too, in the uttermost depths of historical relativity and our own insignificance, we too are inimitable, incomparable absolutes, and our choice of ourselves is an *absolute*.

This figure of taste is insistent. Why? A phenomenon that is first tactile, as they say, taste brings together sensible, sensual, immediate presence without distance, and unobjectifiable and thus inalienable singularity: it is also *absolute* in this sense. But above all, insofar as it touches and touches the mouth, taste resembles live speech, it works likes words (S.'s taste for "words"), it recalls one to pure affection as auto-affection—or to the phantasm, the trap, the simulacrum of auto-affection; and it does this at the very instant that I find myself passively affected in it by the singularity of what is not me but altogether other. An intersubjective auto-hetero-affection: the speculative and specular absolute. Hence, there is nothing surprising about finding this scene of taste asserting itself again three pages later, immediately after a series of definitional approaches to the absolute as "age," and of the latter, indissociably, as "living absolute," "truth," "commitment," and "testimony": ". . . in producing a new absolute which I shall call the *age*. [It is Sartre who is underlining the word age here.] The age is the intersubjectivity, the living absolute."

The value of life (of life that is full and without livable lack) predetermines or overdetermines that of epochality, as it does that of *testimony*, even if life must be risked and gambled in what might be called *martyrdom*. And we will see this again, the present life of the "living absolute" cannot let itself be dissociated from itself, nor thus from the value of property, totality, wholeness, integrity, or integrality. Yet what is integral to integrity or integrality is also the safe, the unharmed, the immune, the being safe and sound of salvation:

Within the *age* [époque], every utterance, before being a historical byword or the recognized origin of a social process, is first an insult or an appeal or a confession. . . . History is made with *dead ages* [époques], for each *age* [époque], *when it dies*, enters into relativity . . . its limits are suddenly apparent, and its ignorance too. But that is *because* it *is dead* [*Sartre underlines these last two words*]; the limits and the ignorance did not exist "at the time [*à l'époque*]"; no deficiency was seen. . . . At the time [*à l'époque*], man *committed himself* to them [the errors] *completely*, and, in manifesting them *at the peril of his life*, he brought *truth* into being through them, for *truth* never yields itself directly, it merely appears through errors . . . [T]he fate of Reason . . . is at stake in *every age* [époque], *totally*, in regard to doctrines which the *following age* [époque] will reject as false. Evolution may someday appear to be the biggest folly of our century; in *testifying* for it against the clerics, the American teachers *lived* [Sartre underlines this word] the truth, they *lived* it *passionately* and *absolutely*, at their own risk. Tomorrow they will be wrong, today they are *absolutely* right; the age [*époque*] is always wrong when it is dead, always right when it is *alive*.

Immediately afterward, no surprise, taste returns, and the taste for taste, and auto-affection ("loving itself" or "lacerating itself"), and the solitude of irreplaceable, "incomparable," "irremediable" singularity ("its taste which it tasted alone"):

[T]hey are *absolutely* right; the *age* is always wrong when it is dead, always right when it is *alive*. Condemn it later on, if you like; but first it had its passionate way of loving itself and lacerating itself, against which future judgments are of no avail. It had its taste which it *tasted* alone and which is as *incomparable*, as *irremediable*, as the *taste* of wine in our mouths.

A book has its absolute truth within the age.

The analogy will be extended between the book (literature and philosophy) *and* what one brings to the mouth, between writing or reading— "for one's epoch"—*and* what leaves a taste, so to speak, on the tongue. One understands how the singularity of this taste can be said to be "incomparable." I have made this the theme of this letter a little bit. But the other theme may have been imposed by this other adjective, so much more strange for a taste: "irremediable." How could a taste be "irremediable," were it not that a certain evil already characterized it and inscribed in it, along with the flavor, some desire for salvation, some desperate nostalgia that was *running after* the loss or the perdition of that which waits in vain to rediscover its living present? Taste is lost—irremediably. Because there is no remedy for saving from this perdition, no remedy for restitution, the resurrection or the redemption of this taste, and thus of the age, a soteriological language asserts and inscribes itself precisely in the place of the impossible, as the inverted relief of "there is no salvation for the taste of the age": it is finite, remember: "We stand for an ethics and art of the finite." This declaration in the form of a manifesto came in conclusion, you will remember, it brought together in the end, as in a final watchword or as an injunction, the meaning of what "writing for one's age" should be. And it closely follows the passage where "he was dead and he was still running; he was running dead, dead he announced the victory of Greece." What is most striking in this passage, which I have just reread, its most miraculous—and thus least apparent—secret is perhaps not so much the race [*course*] or the message [*courrier*] of a dead man, and the fact that he is running, he runs, the dead man, as the fact that he remains capable of *announcing*: "he announced . . ." No doubt he announced a past event, the victory of Greece, but one never announces anything of the present or of the past without promising and committing, with one's own mouth, that which remains to come. Where otherwise would he had found the strength to run dead if not from the sur-vival [*sur-vie*] already of a future [*à-venir*]? The strength to run dead but also to announce, to speak, dead, with his own mouth? To speak dead, that is, to write for one's age, *for it*, addressing one's age but also to testify to it, *for it*, in its place and in its favor, and thus to save it one day from a last judgment? By announcing the *tidings*, the good tidings?

Because it is finite, yes, but the anniversary remains whose possibility must be taken into account, as must the memory and the date, that is, the living legacy of what still remains of what did not remain—and the "bounds [*cap*] of non-infidelity" that one commits oneself to observing even if it means losing one's head—that one should not lose out entirely by orienting oneself in this way. Bounds without bounds [*cap sans cap*]. Holding one's course and keeping one's given word—with one's own mouth.

From the head I return therefore to the mouth, which always reemerges here even when one has lost sight of it. For I am not simply asking myself how a taste might seem "irremediable" but also what words such as *taste*, a *real live taste* might have meant to Jean-Paul Sartre himself and then today to "us," when they sound like the watchwords of a manifesto, the agenda of an ethics and a politics. And here again is the analogy between written and oral things, literature and orality, books and those things of the mouth, which are fruit here. There are living fruit and there are dead fruit:

[B]ut the judgments of posterity will not invalidate those that were passed on it in its lifetime. I have often been told about dates and bananas: "You don't know anything about them. In order to know what they are, you have to eat them on the spot, when they've just been picked." And I have always considered bananas as dead fruit whose real, live taste escapes me. Books that are handed down from age to age are dead fruit. They had, in another time, another taste, tart and tangy. *Emile* or *The Persian Letters* should have been read when they were freshly picked.

Thus, one must write for one's age, as the great writers have done.

As I read this, and almost as always, I share and I understand (I think) his feeling, just as I do the truth of his desire. But I do not subscribe to a single word of what he is writing here. All the more so that he will raise an objection and contradict himself, he will pass over to the other side of what he has just said, and, as I suggested earlier, it is to this Sartre in disaccord with himself that I feel the most in tune. It is when he disputes himself and does not agree with himself that I feel myself ready to agree with him, from both sides at once. How can one speak of him (without speaking of me) under these conditions?

Because a "But . . ." will follow this paragraph on the age that one would have to "eat on the spot." Indeed, Sartre adds the following, which will complicate, even contradict, what precedes: "But that does not mean that one has to lock oneself up in it. To write for one's age is not to reflect it passively; it is to want to maintain it or change it, thus to go beyond it towards the future, and it is this effort to change it that places us most deeply in it . . . it is constantly surpassing itself; the concrete present and the living future of all the men who compose it coincide rigorously within it," even if, he adds further regarding an example, "it is true that this future never became a present."

Here is a contradiction or a noncoincidence (for when Sartre says "coincide rigorously," he is pointing, strangely, to a rigor of a noncoincidence of the "present" and the "future," and a noncoincidence of what is present to itself insofar as it must "return to itself *from* this future"): here is a dehiscence or a discordance with which I feel myself in even greater "accord" today, precisely because it is a matter of a disjunction in the self-identity of the age or the present. The taste for taste, it seems to me, is always due to this disjunction, to this abyss that the future opens [*creuse*], in both its anticipated and unanticipatable return, in the present of the age. One must then either break off the analogy with the bananas and the dates or else take into account (which I would be more inclined to do) this non–self-identity of the age *even* in the case of the bananas and the dates, of the *taste*, in any case, of the bananas and the dates in our mouths, the taste with which we are affected and the "irremediable" taste that we preserve of them. In any case, without this noncoincidence in the present coincidence, without this anachrony, there would be no memory of taste or of the age, no anamnesis, no date, or anniversary. A certain "synchrony" of the age seems to us otherwise "anachronistic" today.

Not that he convinced me then, even when I read this for the first time, and I was an adolescent, but this is not the question: the important thing is to hear him, Sartre, and to rediscover, as he says himself, a certain "taste" of the age, and the taste that his discourse on taste had at the time. Here is a taste, and a taste for the love of taste to which I am attached. I enjoy my attachment to it. "What we have here is mourning, the work of mourning, and narcissism," the hasty doctors will say, "this is you and your taste, the taste for a youthfulness and a past that you would like to find again by pretending to celebrate Sartre and those who followed him to *Les Temps Modernes*." Well, yes and no. The verdict seems incontestable, and yet I hold in reserve, on mourning and narcissism, enough that would disarm the assurance of this diagnosis in which, in addition, one would have to integrate the fact that I have never been one of the *T.M.* nor close to the *T.M.*, and it has so happened that I have thought on more than one occasion (and even said so publicly) that they had passed over just about everything that, from a certain moment on, mattered for me in the literature and philosophical thought of this century; I would then have to explain my sentimental attachment to this person with multiple faces that is called *Les Temps Modernes* with which I have sustained a kind of permanent altercation that must have been animated or nourished by some profound agreement, but let us leave this; one cannot make of this a letter to one's friends, especially on an anniversary. In any case, it is indeed Sartre and *Les Temps Modernes themselves* that I mean to salute [*saluer*] here.

Thus, dear Claude Lanzmann, I promised you to try . . . Failure. I have not yet been able to write what I dreamed of writing. There are reasons for this that might be called external or contingent, certainly, emergencies, overload, fatigue, displacements (I am writing to you as I travel, from far away, and I have with me only the texts that I have cited, plus a book to which I would have liked to devote a long and attentive note, if I had the time). Nonetheless, I think that other reasons have been still more determining, reasons that stem first of all from the impossibility of limiting my "subject," the space and the time (the "field [*champ*]"!) of what I would have liked to talk about. Limits get lost, as does the horizon. I wonder how others do it. For this, which is no doubt true for so many others, is also true for me (and hence how to divide the idiom?): I can say this without risk of making a mistake, namely, that everything I have lived, read, tried to think and write, to teach, too, for nearly fifty years (from the time I was an adolescent in Algiers before ever coming to the Metropolis, I was reading Sartre and *Les Temps Modernes* or I admired *No Exit* that was being performed in a theater in the city that was also a great Algerian hotel), everything, indeed everything, will have been "oriented" by *Les Temps Modernes*, configured in relation to *Les Temps Modernes*, a title under which one must point to the journal and what is inseparable from it, the "environment," the "scene," the quasi institution so named, the borders that were in constant movement, and especially the ruptures (internal and external), yes, especially the ruptures, which marked its history and sculpted its landscape. I especially remember the ruptures, having intimately felt myself to be a convinced ally of both (Merleau, Camus, to cite just the most spectacular, but the others that followed were also important for me. Such a genealogy! Such lineages! Such a family without a father and without a leader and without a head [*cap*]!). But as I was saying earlier, I remained no doubt on Sartre's side not because I was on his side (on the contrary, many times) but because I believed I could discern from this sign or that (I would now have to reread all of these texts) that he himself crossed over to the other side, here and there, and with more or less "bad faith" always integrated the position of the opponent, going so far as to make him in the end a sort of declaration of "irremediable" love. Oriented, I said, I was oriented in any case and in every way by what was taking place there and in which I nonetheless never participated directly, personally, immediately. "Oriented in thought," as someone said, by the very "line" from which I nevertheless thought I had to distance myself [*m'écarter*] or hold myself at a distance [*me tenir écarté*], or from which I felt myself "sidelined [*écarté*]" in a way that was more or less manifest. To try to explain these divergences [*écarts*], this is perhaps what occupied me constantly, even if it was not always made explicit or thematic at the time—and whole books would have to be written about the reasons, good or bad, about the multiple modalities of these divergences [*écarts*]. How could I get them to fit, if such is the case, in an article or, even less, in a letter?[10] (Furthermore, these books have already been written, in part, by others—and perhaps a little by me, it is enough to want to-know-how [*vouloir-savoir*] to read.) Everything seems secondary to me today with regard to this massive fact without limit: in spite of everything I might recall or analyze endlessly, the distances, the movements of agreement or disagreement, the murmur of an interminable conversation, the untangleable web of solidarities and troubling questions, the differences of gesture, style, place, etc., and whether I felt myself in accord, "agreed" or not, for or against, often neither the one nor the other, I have always been "with" *Les Temps Modernes*, belonging to them in a way that is all the more essential in my eyes, and indubitable, that I have never belonged to them in any determinable or statutory way (as sponsor, collaborator, or even as subscriber). To speak seriously of this silent association of an entire lifetime would have required such expenditures of writing, analysis, anamnesis, and I would even dare say, the honing of concepts so new that I must finally, today at least, concede defeat, and add it to the open file, fortunately, of the thing itself, *Les Temps Modernes*, that I want to salute [*saluer*] here. In addressing you these notes and a first draft, barely the outline of what I would have liked to attempt, I am thus appealing to your indulgence and I am trying to convince you at least of my good will, of the sincerity or the good faith of my promise and the friendly wishes that I send for the long life of a journal that we need, I am sure, more than ever. Here, then, are some scattered notes. You can do with them what you please, as you can with the impulsive letter that precedes them and which, at this date, is neither private nor yet public (the modern times and what follows from them, here is perhaps the most profound seism that has ever affected what will one day be instituted in the West under the fragile distinction of the public and the private). I will stop here, the deadline has already passed, I will fax you this letter that is too long and too short and I will attach to it some notes that I brought along with me and which are like the formless remains of a small shanty that has fallen into disuse.

My best to you, dear Claude Lanzmann, and to *Les Temps Modernes*.

Jacques Derrida

Note 1. (For the title, heading, and *incipit*): "Dead Man Running": Salut, Salut. Notes for a Letter to *Les Temps Modernes*.

It was said that the courier of Marathon had died an hour before reaching Athens. He was dead and he was still running; he was running dead, announced the Greek victory dead. This is a fine myth; it shows that the dead still act for a little while as if they were living. For a while, a year, ten years, perhaps fifty years; at any rate, a *finite* period; and then they are buried a second time. This is the measure we

propose to the writer: as long as his books arouse anger, discomfort, shame, hatred, love, even if he is no more than a shadow, he will live. Afterwards, the deluge. We stand for an ethics and art of the *finite*. ("Writing for One's Age," *T.M.*,
June 1948)

". . . and then one buries them for the second time." The essential is
that "the second time" should not be the last time. . . . Logic of the date
and the anniversary.

Bring together this "dead courier" with that other passage in "What
is Literature?" between these two moments:

1. "God knows whether cemeteries are peaceful; none are more
cheerful than a library. The dead are there; the only thing they have done
is write. They have long since been washed clean of the sin of living."[11]
[Why always the "sin of living" in J.-P. S. and this obsession with a re-
demptive salvation that seems inseparable from it? In what does this exis-
tentialism-humanism remain Jewish and Christian, "secularized" in spite
of so many de-negations, such as Heidegger's originary *Schuldigsein*?
Unless it is useless to think a freedom and a responsibility without this
possible imputability, without this liability as infinite bad conscience,
without this debt before all debt, etc.]

And 2. "From one point of view, it [the book] is a possession; he
lends his body to the dead in order that they may come back to life. And
from another point of view it is a contact with the beyond. Indeed, the
book is by no means an object; neither is it an act, or even a thought.
Written by a dead person about dead things, it no longer has any place on
this earth; it speaks of nothing which interests us directly." (*"What Is
Literature?" and Other Essays*, 41–42).

To speak of this mimetic possession-resurrection-identification during anniversary orations . . . of what begins-again [*du re-commencement*].

Note 2. To begin again (*bis*): Beginning-again? . . . Anniversary? But
whose? Of what, precisely? Of a living being, a dead person or a specter?
Who is *Les Temps Modernes*? What a title! A title that had to be made
brand new and irreplaceable but also durable, a title that had to be invented and that couldn't be worn out with words that were already hackneyed at the time, worn to threads, contestable, tolerable only as the title
of a great Chaplin film that said all there was to say! As we might say, "And
liberty for all!" What strength it took, has it ever been said, to make these

words, "modern times," snap like a flag, and who else could have held out against half a century of global and Parisian storms, who else could reduce to oblivion, exhausting and exceeding them in advance, all the analyses, pseudo-analyses, ruptures, diagnoses, prognoses (without speaking of the other journals . . .). What wind or what spirit will have blown in this flag that still snaps [*claque*] without snapping [*claquer*]: "the wind of history" and of "modern times," certainly, but what can be said about them that has not already been said and thought in some way or another by the *T.M.* at the *T.M.*? (To think of a journal that would have dared to call itself "The Enlightenment" in eighteenth-century France. There will never be a journal of the "Post-Modern Times.")

Note 3. "But yes . . ." and basically I would like to know whom I am addressing by writing to *Les Temps Modernes*, to *T.M.*, to tell them, to these generations who have made the *T.M.*, to tell him or her, to tell this "person" who is not only anonymous henceforth but split (we will have to speak further of this split, a split that was more important to me than any supposed unity or identity) not "yes, but . . .", but "but yes," playing the *but* and the *yes* in the "three card trick" in such a way that, finally, the only thing remaining exposed at the end is the "yes," the "yes" of gratitude, of approbation, of affirmation, of justice rendered *without the least trace of resentment.* I love the *T.M.*, I love them with narcissistic fondness (why deny it and how to love otherwise? And here one must take the most serious account of age, of the moment, and thus of the "situation" in the trajectories of all of these "lives": I would not have dared nor even thought several decades ago that I might declare all of these things in the disarming way of a young child), a narcissistic affection that leads me to love all of my past, and even that which in this past refers me to what apparently has nothing to do with me [*ne me revient en rien*] and what does not belong to me in the least: in truth, it does have to do with me [*cela me revient*], by way of phantasm, from the moment that I was or believed myself to be a contemporary. I am therefore happy to be able to say so freely, having never belonged either to its editorial staff or to its "family," and for a thousand reasons that would justify an entire book, a true analysis (for I have still not read anything that has satisfied me on the *T.M.*), I am happy to be able to say so freely that I am happy to have belonged to the "age" of *Les Temps Modernes*, very simply, as a reader more or less faithful but who has always known that he was being addressed to be told, to be taught, to be interrogated, to be taken to task on just about everything that mattered to the age, that made the age or was epoch-making. (In France and, better than in any other journal, throughout the world. This journal that was so Parisian in many regards will have been the only non-Parisian and non-Gallocentric journal, at least, let us say not-too-Gallocentric, at least I mean less Gallocentric than most of the others).

Of course, I would like to declare this, as I already said, *without the least trace of resentment,* for it is not enough to speak against resentment to be without it; we are too familiar with the ruse of denegation, one could cite so many examples. I will thus speak right away of resentment and denegation. One might indeed think that, having never publicly given any proof [*gage*] of friendship to the *T.M.*, no signs of proximity, affinity, or alliance, even less of membership, I am in a position of hostility or reticence. But this is not the case. Well yes, of course, I could formulate well-argued reservations on so many things that were done or said (they and their opposite), almost all of them, at the *T.M.*, but all the same, it does not matter. Then I would say to *T.M.*: "yes, I have almost never published anything with you, I have always felt 'close' to you but have never been one 'of you' or one of your 'family'; and yet, yes, I am happy that you are here and more than ever I hold your longevity, which does more than survive, for a good thing in life, in the life of the culture and of the country and of the world in which I live": of the "age" as the author of "Writing for One's Age" says. A strange and naive declaration, but I hold to it even when I do not know to whom (as inconsequential as it may seem) I am addressing it. It will perhaps be published by *Les Temps Modernes* and read by its readers if those who have inherited the responsibility from this great institution decide in favor of it; for they are also the heirs who, I assume perhaps naively, perhaps know no better than I do, at bottom, what it is and from whom they are inheriting; and they feel perhaps, as much as I do but otherwise, overwhelmed by the identity of this history that has preceded them and will continue, one must hope, after us.

Note 4. Who is speaking to whom, here? . . . Who is "*Les Temps Modernes*"? If I knew this clearly, it is not only a long sequence of my life that I could begin to understand, identify, appropriate (I discovered and began to read this journal before any other, in 1947, in Algeria and yes, at the E.N.S. that—this is too-well-known—was indissociably linked with the history of the *T.M.*: Compare in this regard the two "conflicts" (between Sartre and M.-P., and between Sartre and Camus) that mattered all the more to me, played an all-the-more-"structuring" role that I felt myself each time to be (but like Sartre himself, no doubt, I think this can be read from more than one sign) in the contradiction and on both sides at the same time, mine and the other that was also mine . . . Basically, the history of the ruptures was more significant for me and more marking than any continuity (Sartre/Aron, Sartre/Merleau, Sartre/Camus, Sartre (68)/Pingaud, Pontalis, etc.).

Note 5. Urgent necessity of keeping the word *commitment,* a fine word that is still brand new (gage, wager and language, "situation," infinite responsibility, critical freedom with regard to all apparatuses, etc.) perhaps drawing it a little elsewhere: turned in the direction in which we find ourselves looking to find ourselves, "us," today. To keep or reactivate the forms of this "commitment" by changing its content and its strategies. Indeed this is what is taking place, or is looking to take place, no doubt at present at the *T.M.,* to a certain extent, although in a "style" that often remains very foreign to me (but why? it would take books to explain it— unless, that is, these books are already readable, in fact, as a grounds of possible citations: one doesn't do this on an anniversary, any more than one explains to one's hosts, on an anniversary, what the social code is of an anniversary, or what reserves of aporia are harbored by a discourse of invitation or an experience of hospitality).

It is good form today for many intellectuals to make a face before the concept and the word *commitment.* Idiotic and suspect. For in rereading certain definitions of commitment after the war, I have the feeling that one could often *literally* make of these definitions the most accurate watchwords for "intellectuals" today. On several conditions, however. Multiply the citations (beginning with "Introducing *Les Temps Modernes*". . .) and analyze or dissociate certain "blocks" in it. I would be prepared (like so many others no doubt today) to subscribe—such that I might inherit from it—to the reaffirmation of infinite responsibility in singularity ("absolute and singular project," "singularity of our age," etc.), but I would also be prepared to suspect or to "date" the reference to the "metaphysical choice," the eternalist cliché or the humanist peace of rhetoric that were perhaps the price to be paid for the strategy of a "journal" of the "age" "at the time [*à l'époque*]," after the war in Spain, the occupation and the resistance. Thus I want to retain the right (precisely in the name of another age, my own, that nurtured other questions and does work of a different kind) to understand and approve of, certainly, sentences such as these (but one could multiply the examples to infinity), I enjoy retaining the right to enjoy the taste of these sentences, while at the same time making a severe and uneasy selection from them:

> . . . when adversaries clash on the subject of disarming the FFI or the help to be given the Spanish Republicans, it is that metaphysical choice, that singular and absolute project which is at stake. Thus, by taking part in the singularity of our era [*époque*], we ultimately make contact with the eternal, and it is our task as writers to allow the eternal values implicit in such social or political debates to be perceived. ("Introducing *Les Temps Modernes*," 254)

Develop if there is room *two remarks*.

1. If the word *eternity* bothers me and seems to me "dated,"[12] precisely, it is not because I want to put a historicist logic of the ephemeral in its place, but I try elsewhere to develop a discourse on "sur-vivre," "survivance," spectrality, a messianicity that no longer complies with these oppositions. As for the "metaphysical choice," too much would need to be said to explain, here too, or to justify a hesitation.

2. Here then, perhaps, is one of the questions and thus one of the tasks that remain before us: did the history of *Les Temps Modernes* allow itself to be dictated to by the letter of this "Introduction . . . ," for example, that of the sentences I have just quoted? Did it, too, not make a "selection" during half a century, a selection that will have been its history and its life and its "age"? The answer is no doubt "yes and no," "yes and no" to a certain point, and the answer could not be homogenous. One would have to reread everything!

In the same way, another example, how can one not subscribe to such a statement today, a statement concerning the refusal of the journal to become an organic instrument of organic intellectuals (the journal wants only to be an "organ of inquiry" and "we have no political or social program" ["Introducing *Les Temps Modernes*," 265])? How is one not to espouse such a statement on the political independence of the committed intellectual and even on his independence with regard to the politics of the journal, indeed to politics in general ("concerning the political and social events to come, our journal will take a position in each case. It will not do so *politically*—that is, in the service of a particular party")? "Politically" is emphasized by Sartre. But how can one not want to change several words in what immediately follows ("but it will attempt to sort out the conception of man that inspires each one of the conflicting theses, and will give its opinion in conformity with the conception it maintains" ["Introducing *Les Temps Modernes*," 255]).

In the same way, I certainly think I understand and approve up to a certain point what Sartre "means to say" in this context (refer to it) when he speaks of "speaking so as to say nothing [*parler pour ne rien dire*]" and against "speaking so as to say nothing":

We do not want to be ashamed of writing and we don't feel like speaking so as to say nothing. Moreover, even if we wanted to we would not be able to: no one can. Every text possesses a meaning, even if that meaning is far removed from the one the author dreamed of inserting into it. ("Introducing *Les Temps Modernes*," 251)

But I would be tempted to add so many conditions on what "speaking so as to say nothing" can mean to say! On the necessity of respecting, in a certain way, this *possibility* ("speaking to speak," "to say nothing," "just to speak to the other," to testify to the possibility of speaking), as on the responsibility of a certain speech that speaks in order to speak, to put speech, writing, or language to the test of itself, that is, of the other, and in the name of what is still called *thought*, *poetry*, or *literature* (without speaking of the enormous problem of "meaning" and its limits . . .)! What philosophy of language and what practice of literature, what concepts of language, of poetry and of literature, what philosophy and what concepts, in short, are being put to work in this way in the banishing of a "speaking so as to say nothing"? And how does one reconcile the latter with the following conclusion in which my agreement stops short, in fact, right in the middle of the sentence, at customs, on the border of a little "and" from which point I can no longer follow. I am underlining the "and": "I recall, in fact, that in "committed literature," *commitment* must in no way lead to a forgetting of literature *and* that our concern must be to serve literature by infusing it with new blood even as we serve the collectivity by attempting to give it the literature it deserves."

Note 6. Short, imaginary interview, in response to one of those surveys. . . :
"—It would seem, Sir, in reading what precedes, that in spite of your admiration that is so eloquently declared, and the friendly gratitude whose signs you multiply, that you are no more ready to follow Sartre and what at least is inherited from him *through a direct line* at the *T.M.* What would the motives

be? Could you, in fact, put a name to that about which you seem to have some reservations, whereas, with such insistence and a tone of conviction, you say that you are nonetheless so close and in such solidarity?

—Well . . . the literature . . . but I have explained myself elsewhere on this. . .
—Indeed? Only this? The literature of Sartre?
—Almost all of it (except perhaps *Nausea*) but in particular literature and the experience of language *for* Sartre . . . His scholastic models and his rhetoric. As if he had passed by [*à côté*] everything that is important for me. But it is he who, beyond what he has to say about them, led me to discover, almost fifty years ago, Bataille and Blanchot and Ponge, and other things . . . Hence my endless gratitude . . . And I can't forget that the *T.M. also* published excellent literary or poetic texts that had nothing Sartrian about them . . .
—And what else? Psychoanalysis?
—Well . . . yes and philosophy . . . his scholastic models and his rhetoric, I have explained myself elsewhere on this. But it is Sartre . . . philosophy . . . his scholastic models and his rhetoric, I have explained myself elsewhere on this. But is it Sartre who, well beyond anything he has to say about them, and more and more against what he has to say about them, led me to discover, almost fifty years ago, Hegel, Husserl, and Heidegger, and consequently so many others . . . I would like to reread him, to reread everything otherwise. Hence an enormous debt . . . And I can't forget that the *T.M. also* published philosophical texts that had nothing Sartrian about them . . ."

Note 7. The question of *salvation*, such as I would like to discuss it in a letter to C.L., would have led me to broach directly the enormous problem of *prophesy* and the messianic, as well as the question of the holy, the sacred, evil, "shame," as well as the unavowed, unavowable secularization of a religious thematic, etc. Did I not do this elsewhere? Begin with this fact (attested to by a thousand quotations that I would have to specify, analyze, etc.): obsessed by the paradoxical soteriology of "saving oneself [*se sauver*]" without salvation [*sans salut*] (safe safe safe), Sartre thought he had to reject all prophetic discourse. He said this in any case, expressly, although, one remains doubtful, it is not enough to say it, or to say what one will not do to do what one says. But whoever denounces prophetism will, in fact, do something "like it." For example, he no longer wants to resemble the poet-prophet of former times ("In former times, the poet took himself to be a prophet . . .").[13]

How does one reconcile this *explicit* declaration with the central thesis, in truth unique, if I have read it properly, of the remarkable work of

Anna Boschetti that I have brought along on my trip to prepare this short text?[14] Her thesis is thus that the dominant feature of this whole adventure, what she calls the *prophetic discourse* (p. 150), the *religious prophetism* (pp. 149, 151), the *prophetic position* (p. 179), the *prophetism of the T.M.*, (p. 214), the *prophetic essays* (p. 235, Sartre's essays, of course, for all of these features of "prophetism" are attributed to Sartre), the *high prophesy* (p. 239), *literary prophetism* (p. 246), *existentialist prophetism* and the *prophetic temptation* (p. 252), the *prophetic model* (p. 254), the *prophetic intervention* (p. 262), the *prophetic meaning* (p. 289), the *prophet of freedom* (p. 314), *political prophetism* (p. 31), this entire proliferation of effects of prophesy, all the *functions of Sartrian prophetism* (p. 146) would be *field effects* [effets de champ] or *the state of the field* [l'état du champ] in which one would nonetheless have to distinguish, and how difficult this is, this "field within the field" which is the Journal (p. 258). I will raise several questions on this subject in a moment but I first want to pay hommage— and do justice—to a book that is so smart, lucid, informed, more interesting in any case than so many others of the same genre. And yet, what a deception. Apart from a few details (I am exaggerating, a good number of details) I learned nothing new, with regard to "facts" or "explanation"; and I presume that no "intellectual" of my generation and of my environment will discover anything new in it (except here and there, a fact, a date, a name, with the emotion that comes over us when we rewatch a black and white film that has been much beloved—Paris and the left bank shortly before and shortly after the war—or when, close to tears, one glances at the pages of a too-familiar album of family photos, turning the pages, and one says to each other, among relatives: "I don't think I've ever seen this photo, and that one, look, I didn't know that he was there that day, he has really changed, and there behind *X*, you recognize *Y*, she hasn't written to me for a long time, I haven't either, it's my fault).

But I am sure that this fine book will be an indispensable synoptic archive and a useful introductory documentary in one volume for future generations. What is unfortunate is that this was not, apparently, its primary goal. Yet in addition to not teaching me anything essential, it explains nothing and adds nothing to this well-known content. Known "empirically," one might say, if a pure empiricity were not more than ever excluded in this case and for a symbolic corpus as complex as this one, known in any case or apprehended, and already overinterpreted in a thousand ways of which we are told nothing. One would at least like to credit this book insofar as it "objectivizes," as the author often and calmly says. But we would at least have to know what "to objectivize" means, we would have to know what it means in general (what is an objectivation? a determination as "object"? what is the genealogy of this model, and from where does it draw its authority—in a given field, if one likes, but which one, etc.? for this "field" is never rigorously identifiable within its limits; here is, then, roughly, a source of abyssal and preliminary questions). We would also have to know what it means "to objectivize" in this particular case, to objectivize things that are familiar and well known *both* by attentive readers— who were already agents actively participating in the "field" of this adventure which is still open (the proof!) of the *T.M.*—*and* by those, so numerous, so diverse and divergent, and not only by generation, who participated in it under the statutory title of sponsor or author. Above all, the alleged objectivation would have to be done from a place *external* to the supposed field, a place in which one disposed of a criteriology and conceptuality that were independent of the field (one could show, I am convinced of this, I will perhaps do this a little later, that this is not the case of *any of the criteria and the concepts that play an organizing role in this book*). This would have required that a clearly designated and conceptualized exteriority ensure an "objective" and rigorous division of the field and of the "field within the field" in question. At no moment, in no sentence of the book was I convinced that such an objectivation was possible and practiced. This book belongs almost entirely to the field it claims to "objectivize"; it draws most of its axioms from it (the "Marx" evoked at one point, and who speaks of the "dominant dominated by his domination" is not only, more than anywhere else, the legacy of a particular Hegel but it irrigates the entire "field" of the *T.M.*; one could say the same of the constant reference to the "social layer" or of the axiom according to which "objectivation" makes us freer and conditions or accompanies a liberation of the gaze). Implicit or explicit, the protestation against "prophetism," especially (since this is what matters most to me here), this protestation that does not go without a certain "objectivation," is already an (inherited) theme of the Sartrian rhetoric; I just recalled it when I said that it was certainly not enough to escape from what one denounces; but can this structure of denegation be as legible in a discourse that announces the science of field effects and the absence of all "resentment" in the analysis of an "overarching ambition" (back cover)? Moreover, the denunciation of prophetism as false prophetism is as old as the prophets; indeed, this is how one recognizes the prophet even before one is able to distinguish the true from the false prophet: both begin by taking issue with prophetism.

I would have been more surely convinced by the analysis of the alleged prophetism had it been explained to me: a) *on the one hand,* what a prophet is (a great enigma that at no moment seems to disturb the sociology of prophetism that moves forward as if it had at its disposal a knowledge of this kind); b) *on the other hand,* not only what the relation is between prophesy and the social act called *prophetism* (outside the field of the so-called religious, properly speaking, if it ever exists in a pure state, in philosophy, in literature, in politics, all of these things being a little different) but what the analogy consists of—thus the difference as well as the identity—between religious prophetism and that other one (that of "Sartre and *Les Temps Modernes*"). I have been taught to be wary of analogies, especially in the "field" of analyses that move forward under the banner of scientific objectivity. And everything here seems to rest on an analogy whose status is never justified or even problematized. One notes only "a series of important analogies ['important'? What does this mean? Decisive, essential, determining? Or only *somewhat* important? Or *very* important?] with the conditions and the functioning of religious prophetism." This "series of important analogies . . ." with the phenomena of religious prophetism does not teach us anything about the difference in the analogy (which is always more interesting, more incisive and more determining than the identity) or about the relations between prophesy and prophetism; and yet, as gravely indeterminate as it remains, it "can," we are told, "confirm the ideological nature—as a discourse that claims to be universal but expresses and privileges a particular social layer—of the position that Sartre inaugurates in this way . . ." "Inaugurates in this way"? But how, then, under these conditions, can he inaugurate anything? And if he inaugurates, then what is he inaugurating that is not only analogous but also different? I do not think that one must necessarily be born Jewish, that one must live in ardent faith or revelation, in fear or trembling to be surprised, as I am here, to see the first or paradigmatic term of the analogy, namely "Hebraic prophetism," thus evoked as the most well known, the most familiar, and the most objectivable thing there is, to the point of writing with imperturbable calm, "*As in* Hebraic prophetism . . .": "As in Hebraic prophetism, one has a relatively autonomous field of production . . ." I would refer the reader to the paragraph and to the pages that follow,[15] but as long as the differences as well as the resemblances between the two series of the "analogy" have not been demonstrated to us, one has said nothing to us and above all nothing has been explained to us. For example, in the following description of the "field of production that is relatively autonomous" and rich in effects of prophetism: ". . . the appearance of a new clientele (intellectuals produced by education); a situation of acute social crisis, which the doctrine of the institution seems incapable of understanding; prophets, renegades from the institution, endowed with the faculties demanded by the role." But who does the endowing and who is endowed with these "faculties demanded by the role," namely, if I understand correctly, faculties for "understanding"? And is this not the surest and basically the most satisfying thing one could say to describe the situation of the author of such a statement, or of this entire book, its objective inscription in the ("prophetic") field that is to be objectivized but that is impossible for this very reason to objectivize in a determining way?

If it were not already too late for the deadline of this anniversary issue, if I were not afraid of being indecently, excessively "too long," I would have liked to focus the question on the words that I will emphasize in the following passage. They situate, it seems to me, the limit, not to say the abdication, of the analysis before a sort of mysterious and circular "preestablished harmony," a rather "prophetic" scene, in its logical range ("here is what happens, what will happen because, I am telling you, it is already foretold, has thus already arrived"), and secretly mystical, which is also to say, empiricist. I am emphasizing thus the site of a thousand questions, the place where, to hold myself to the code of "taste" as far as the epoch is concerned, I remain particularly unsatisfied [*sur ma faim et sur ma soif*]:

After having described what she calls "the affinity of ideas," something all the more obscure and vague that we are invited to recognize in it "an indispensable condition but not the fundamental principle of identification," Anna Boschetti writes the following:

Similar conditions explain why the analysis of Sartre's position, at the moment that it becomes dominant, appears to be inseparable from the analysis of the *T.M.* The journal alone would certainly not have sufficed to explain the duration of Sartre's domination were it not for *the fortuitous agreement that persisted between the situation and Sartrian practices*: the difficulties of reconstruction, the Cold War, the dramatic events of decolonization first in Indochina and then in Algeria *contributed to maintaining the social demand for prophetism.* But the journal was necessary to explain the force and the form assumed by this hegemony. (*Sartre et "Les Temps Modernes,"* 181)

What this "situation" is, is already precisely what needs to be explained, beyond a mere report. But what does one say, then, of a "fortuitous agreement" between a "situation" and "practices," especially when one must recognize that it "persists" for such a long time, this "fortuitous agreement"? That it persists at the moment of diagnosis (which thus constitutes a part of the situation, in the same country, the same language, the same "field") and that it "persists," my word, well enough into the moment at which I am writing this, on this anniversary. This is above all what I wanted to salute [*saluer*]. And if these or those events "contributed to maintaining the social demand for prophetism" ("contributed"? how, to what extent, with what, what else is there?), it is because this demand is both larger and certainly much earlier. Indeed, where does it come from? And understood historically, does not the notion of "field" raise the same problems as the notion of "epoch," in the Sartrian sense, the problems with which we are struggling here? What follow are some of the questions I would have liked to outline, if only to do justice to "Sartre and *Les Temps Modernes.*"

Note 8. Gift and gift, to give without countergift. To give without saving, without saving oneself and without hope of salvation, is this possible? And a greeting [*salut*] to the other without soteriological horizon? A greeting [*salut*] to the other that would even have as its condition that one give up saving and even saving oneself?[16] A last telegram in two words, where I would have liked to carefully analyze the subtle economy of this sort of *essay on the gift* that "What Is Literature?" also is. In it two logics seem to enter into competition, indeed into contradiction.

On the one hand, the work is *pure gift,* an *exigency of justice* that commands one to give without economy, without circular restitution, without the safety [*salut*] of reappropriation, a pure disinterestedness that does not return [*revient à*] to itself and does not return [*en revient*]. It is to obey this unconditional imperative that there is an *oath,* a performative event, a *naming;* and this is why, written or read, the work not only *unveils,* it *creates* what it unveils. This creation is my *responsibility:*

The error of realism has been to believe that the real reveals itself to contemplation, and that consequently one could draw an impartial picture of it. How could that be possible, since the very perception is partial, since by itself the naming is already a modification of the object? . . . As for me who reads, if I create and keep alive an unjust world, I cannot help making myself responsible for it. And the author's whole art is bent on obliging me to *create* what he *unveils*, therefore to compromise myself. So both of us bear the responsibility for the universe. . . . Not, of course, that this generosity is to be expressed by means of edifying discourses and virtuous characters . . . remind us that the work is never a natural datum, but an *exigency* and a *gift*. And if I am given this world with its injustices, it is not so much that I may contemplate them coldly, but that I may animate them with my indignation, that I unveil them and create them with their nature as injustices, that is, as abuses-to-be-suppressed. Thus, the writer's universe will only unveil itself in all its depth to the examination, the admiration, and the indignation of the reader; and the generous love is a promise to maintain, and the generous indignation is a promise to change, and the admiration a promise to imitate; although literature is one thing and morality another, at the heart of the esthetic imperative we discern the moral imperative. (*"What Is Literature?" and Other Essays*, 66–67)

But on the other hand, and elsewhere, an economy still has the upper hand since for the writer this pure gift amounts to *saving himself*, to clearing himself of the very gratuitousness that seemed implicated, in his social status, by the disinterestedness and even by the generosity that were in question above. Before a discussion on "the present" that would deserve a long discussion, Sartre in fact asks himself some fifty pages later, in relation to the writer who "testifies," how it is that one can *save oneself*, escape, remove oneself:

And as the writer thinks that he had broken the bonds which united him to his class of origin, as he speaks to his readers from the height of universal human nature, it seems to him that the appeal he makes and the part he takes in their misfortunes are dictated by pure generosity. *To write is to give*. In this way he *assumes* and *saves* what is unacceptable in his situation as a parasite in an industrious society; this is also how he becomes conscious of that absolute freedom, that absolute gratuity which characterize literary creation. (*"What Is Literature?" and Other Essays*, 101, my emphasis)

No doubt Sartre is right in the two sentences of this very strong argument, even if they seem to contradict each other a little, turning the pure moral imperative, the meaning of justice and generosity into a kind of economy of self-justification or a strategy of personal salvation, of expiation. My hypothesis is that this discourse was headed for this from the moment that it linked the gift to generosity (this *natural* gift that makes one apt to give and which thus cancels out the gift) and justice to the imperative, to duty and to debt, thus to economics, to savings that save, to the salvation that expiates (itself), to redemption. Thus one would have to "think" justice and the gift otherwise. And therefore literature, among other things, since it is a matter of literature here. But these are the premises of another discourse on salvation [*salut*], for another salvation [*salut*], another time. Salut!

Jacques Derrida

PART III

ETHICS AND POLITICS TODAY

Ethics and Politics Today

Good, I think that everything has been well situated. I am going to speak briefly and as if in retreat to say things that are both weak and—how shall I say it—decelerated. I will propose an abrupt deceleration, but in order to speak to you about urgency.

There was a first decision, an impossible decision: how does one lead a discussion on ethics and politics in fifteen or twenty minutes? There isn't time. An emergency situation. So what does it mean to say, there isn't time? Is it only a matter of the fifteen or twenty minutes' time allocated to an intervention on this important issue that is both very old and, as it has just been suggested, modern in certain of its dimensions? Is it then simply a matter of this lack of time? Not at all. If I had been given an hour or two hours, for example, or even more, the problem would have remained substantially the same. Thus faced with this huge question, the question of ethics and politics, responsibility—and I am not only speaking here of philosophical responsibility, and even less of the responsibility of professional philosophers—responsibility of course requires that any answer be preceded *in principle* by a slow, patient, rigorous elucidation of the concepts that are used in discussion, of their structure in extension and comprehension, of their provenance, of their genealogy, of the discursive contexts that may affect them, etc. For each of the words *ethics* and *politics*, but also for all of the words that one immediately associates with them—mention has been made of the human and the universal, etc.—the task, needless to say, is immense. However, as a rule, we know how to do this, even if it is very difficult. Yet this task, if it is possible in principle, also seems endless and seems infinitely suspended. And not simply beyond a quarter hour. Any resolution, any decision, any act of responsibility in the face of this problem seems infinitely postponed. For, if we refer to the most common experience, if there is one, and to the horizon that compels us all here today to talk about, or to debate, ethics and politics, and to the fact that they are connected or disconnected, well then, the most common determination, I think the least disputable of the minimal determinations that are suited to producing consensus, as they say, about the concepts of ethics and politics, is that . . . I will name three things. It is that: (1) Ethics and politics command an action—to use this old word—an *act* and an answer to the question, "What should I do?" "Ethics" and "politics" have this in common. (2) They demand that the answer to this question be as thoughtful and responsible as possible, thus preceded by a questioning that constitutes an essential part to any ethical and political act. *A questioning without limit* and to the depths of the axioms that appear to be the most incontestable, such as, for example, the "human" in the rights of man, morality and politics . . . (3) The responsible decision must also and above all—and this is what I wanted to insist on—be made *with the utmost urgency*. And by *urgency* I mean the necessity of not waiting, or rather, the *impossibility of waiting* for the end of the reflection, of the inquiry, whether it be cognitive, philosophical, metaphysical, or metametaphysical. This structure of urgency is not a contingent determination. On the one hand, there is urgency, even if the time given to reflection is very long, because it must always be *interrupted*, which creates a situation, let us say, of essential *contretemps* between the decision, the responsible action in politics and ethics. On the other hand, and more radically, because the inaction with which one would choose to prolong and complicate the aforesaid reflection on the principles, axioms, origin of concepts, etc., this inaction is *already* an action, a decision, an engagement, a responsibility that has been taken. Already, in saying this, I modify the concept of responsibility. If responsibility is taken even before I am conscious of it (practically speaking, that is), one must already put a stop to the concept of responsibility. If I am responsible even before I want to be, this does not mean that responsibility dissolves, but that one must think it differently, according, precisely, to the dimension of dissymmetry that was alluded to earlier. It seems that what I am saying here is perfectly obvious. I am describing the essence of the relation to the ethical and the political, and I do so not merely to give nontreatment an alibi. I am speaking about nontreatment. There is no question of treating the question today. This is not only to supply an alibi for my not-treating this important issue in philosophical depth. That is, the fact that I will keep in reserve an elaboration that would begin with a long genealogy, in the deconstructive style, for example, of the meaning of *ethos*, of *polis*, from Plato to Heidegger, via Hobbes, Rousseau, Kant, Hegel and a few others, and not merely within the Western tradition—and here I echo what Miguel Abensour said earlier about Levinas. Levinas is undoubtedly, is he not, someone who thinks or places the ethical above the political, a thinker of the ethical and not the political. But perhaps there is at the source of his thought something that cannot rightly be determined by this pair of—let us say—Platonic-Western oppositions. If I may be permitted to open a parenthesis and to quote a remark of Levinas made in private, I remember that one day, rather recently, he said to me: "They say that I, that it's ethics I'm interested in. No. What interests me is the "holy [*le saint*]," saintliness. And the difficulty here of translating what he meant by "le saint" in an idiom of Jewish thought, of translating it into the realm of ethics or politics, determined by the Greeks, as it were, this difficulty reflects something of the issue at hand. It is possible that the conjunction, the disjunction, and all of the aporias about which we have spoken here tonight between ethics and politics already belong, or are determined by us, in a space—let us say, a philosophical-ontological space of Western metaphysics—and that this issue is not an issue at all, does not let itself be translated outside of such a space. I only note this in passing.

In a culture or in social situations in which politics is absent, inside these communities of writing, the very concept of politics, like that of ethics that serves as its corrective, and that is either connected or disconnected but in some relation to it, the very concept of politics is completely irrelevant. What happens is that one encounters limits. I am thinking of a text of Rashi, without being able to quote it precisely, a philosophical study in which he demonstrated—and I was very tempted to follow him in this demonstration—that, for Jewish thought, the political, the concept of the political, not only in political philosophy but in philosophy in general and everything that follows from it, from Plato to our philosophy today, cannot, does not correspond to anything in Jewish thought close to that political idiom, and that, consequently, to introduce, to speak of the political inside Jewish thought makes no sense. I cannot repeat this demonstration, but I quote it as an example of the displacements about which one needs to think. I close the parentheses.

The structure of urgency that I mentioned is both paradoxical and aporetic. But in ethics and politics, the two domains that, for the moment, I do not dissociate, this structure is simultaneously the condition of possibility and the condition of impossibility of all responsibility. No responsibility is taken if at a given moment one could not decide *without knowing*, without knowledge, theoretical reflection, the *determinate* inquiry having encountered its limit or its suspension, its interruption. Without this interruption—and this interruption is what defines the structure of urgency that I am talking about—there would never be a decision or responsibility, but only the deployment consequent to a *determinate* knowledge, the imperturbable application of rules, of rules known or knowable, the deployment of a program with full knowledge of the facts. For there to be decision and responsibility, I am not saying that one needs ignorance or some form of not-knowing; not at all, on the contrary, one needs to know and one needs to know as much as possible and as well as possible, but between one's knowledge and the decision, the chain of consequence must be interrupted. One must, in some way, arrive at a point at which one does not know what to decide for the decision to be made. Thus a certain undecidability, contrary to what one says and often pretends to think, the undecidability—this one, in any case—is the condition or the opening of a space for an ethical or political decision, and not the opposite. And the undecidability makes the urgency something other than, let us say, the empirical briefness of a lapse of time. Even if one had at one's disposal a virtually unlimited amount of time, the structure of urgency, that is, the *interruption* of reflection, of reflection according to a determinate mode, would be irreducible. There can be urgency—the urgency I am talking about—at the end of a thousand years of reflection. And one might ask whether the interruption of deliberation and the deliberation itself have different modes, depending on whether it is a matter of ethics or a matter of politics. No doubt. We will come back to this. But for the moment there is a structure common to both of these relations, and I will restrict myself to this common ground for the moment. Conversely, the paradoxical condition of possibility of the decision, the urgency of the interruption is, in its very principle, an impossible condition, a condition of impossibility: there can be no ethical or political responsibility without time for reflection, without the possibility of reducing the urgency, however little, thus without a differing, which here is the urgency—as can be understood if one stops for a moment: *différance* and urgency are the same thing, they have always been the same thing. Thus there can be no responsibility without a structure of deliberation being regulated by a double rule, theoretical and practical: (1) Knowing what it's about, in what way and how to act accordingly. (2) Which practical laws—and the word *practical* here should cover the two domains—which practical laws, which principles, the principles to which, the rules to which, the maxims to which one must address one's respect in one's action, to use this old word, whether it be ethical or political.

To this point I will add two remarks or two questions: does one not have the right to consider it a duty, and thus an essential responsibility in the face of these questions and the great question entitled "ethics and politics," to begin by (or in any case never to dispense with) never to stand clear of the most uncompromising, radical deconstructive critique, genealogical or not, of the axiomatics that are the most untouchable: the rights of man, the *human* quality in the other to be respected, the being-with, etc., etc.?

For example, should one not consider—I would like to say in parentheses—that the human determination, anthropological, of the other, of the singularity of the other that I must respect beyond the formal rule, beyond the universal and formal rule of this respect, that this singularity, from the moment that it has been determined human, would risk precisely no longer being what it is or what it should be (this is the question, for example, of the living in general, of the animal, etc.)?— should one not consider the untiring vigilance regarding this subject, whether it be in its critical or deconstructive style, to be already the exercise, the first exercise of a responsibility of which one must only ask oneself if it can still, and until what point, be called *ethical* or *political*? Does the responsibility of these questions, of having to bring these questions as far as possible without any kind of limit, answer to a dictate that one could call *ethical* or *political*? I don't know. It all depends on the way in which these words will be determined. It is evident that if it is a matter of the determination of these words, in this questioning, the prescription to question is not necessarily determinable, definable, as ethical and political. This does not suspend its prescriptive quality, on the contrary. This questioning, this pre-ethical-political deconstruction, in that it does indeed have a *pre-* as a request or as a *prel*iminary *pre*scription, is, perhaps, ethical-political. This prescription—and here one rediscovers the *double bind* of the condition of possibility as condition of impossibility—is both an imperative of the greatest urgency and something that, nonetheless, one would always be tempted to be put off or to have to put off until later, faced with the urgency, faced with the *no* of the urgency: it is what can always wait, these questions can always wait, and yet they are the most urgent.

But where and how does one interrupt the exercise of *this* responsibility? Urgency against urgency. The aporia here (or the *double bind*, if you prefer) is not the knowledge of whether one must choose the urgency over the nonurgency, rather it is always urgency against urgency. And this type of aporia can be found elsewhere, and I am going to try to rediscover it quickly in other instances. This was the first remark I wanted to add.

The second was the following: faced with urgency, or in urgency, in the double bind might one say that the rule of rules is a kind of hybrid *economy* that attempts to tie the most successful knot between two irreconcilable tensions or to cut the knot of the aporia that blocks the passage, to cut the knot in the best place? This presupposes a strategy, this presupposes a good use of practical and discursive rhythm, good formalization, the best (or in any case the least bad) that would answer to contradictory imperatives in a single gesture. I suppose, then, that this is what we are trying to do at this moment, as I see the end of my half hour approaching. I cannot exceed it if I want to respect the rules. I must say the most, the least poorly possible, formalizing in the most economic manner possible without transgressing too much, if I transgress, and hoping that you will give me another few minutes.

For good formalization, as we know, one must sacrifice examples, but not sacrifice too many of them. An ethical and political rule: not to sacrifice too many of the examples. One must choose them well. Therefore, I leave to improvisation the casuistic analysis of two or three examples. My thesis, if you like, to say it bluntly here, is that it is on the basis of examples and on the terrifying casuistry of these examples that these philosophemes or these meta-philosophemes must be put to the test. And an aporetic casuistry, naturally. I thus leave to improvisation two or three examples taken from the immediate context in which the organization of this forum indeed urgently imposed itself on us. Yet with urgency, that is, three months after the time that motivated the decision. The two examples to which I will return in a moment are, first, that of a certain moment in the said student movement of November-December, and secondly, that of Abdallah's trial.

I will turn presently to the most sensitive point in the title of this debate: the small *and* of conjunction and disjunction between ethics *and* politics. According to the main theme that I have chosen, that of urgency, the most apparent difference between ethics and politics would be a difference of rhythm in their relation to urgency—I emphasize the *apparent* difference in their relation to interruption. *Perhaps*, though, this rhythmic difference reflects a structural difference. One does, in fact, have the impression that the ethical response or the ethical responsibility, being unconditional—this is generally how one presents the ethical, at least since a certain Kantian caesura that we will not re-interpret in this debate—there isn't time . . . Because ethical responsibility appeals to an unconditional that is ruled by pure and universal principles already formalized, this ethical responsibility, this ethical response can and should be immediate, in short, rather simple, it should make straight for the goal all at once, straight to its end, without getting caught up in an analysis of hypothetical imperatives, in calculations, in evaluations of interests and powers. Because its urgency is infinite, immediately infinite, it is either absolute or null. It is no longer even an urgency insofar as a waiting time should not exist. Whereas, on the contrary, still according to the same appearance, political responsibility, because it takes into account a large number of relations, of relations of power, of actual laws, of possible causes and effects, of hypothetical imperatives, requires a time for analysis, requires a gamble, that is, a calculation that is never sure and that requires strategy. So many things that have no place, theoretically, in a pure ethical responsibility. There is neither gamble nor strategy in an ethics thus determined.

However, all of this is but an appearance, perhaps an inevitable appearance produced by this obscure concept of urgency, which one should then dismiss or problematize as a bad lead, a lead, in short—one could say with Kant—that is impure, sensual, empirical, in the analysis of the relations between ethics and politics. And one should dismiss it, because it is too empirical precisely where things must be analyzed in terms of structure and not temporal experience. It would thus only be an appearance, because, if one were to follow common sense, one should say on the contrary that the political is the sphere of urgency, where no action can be deferred, is the moment at which the gamble cannot be deferred, even when the givens of the problem are ethical. I will return to these examples later on. At this moment one is in politics. Ethical problems are already taken up in the so-called space of the political, of calculation, of negotiation, of deliberation. That is, of the hypothetical regimentation of the categorical imperatives. Pure right, the instance of pure right is itself never pure, and there is neither the time nor the space necessary to purify the givens of an ethical problem.

Now I will accelerate. I think that if this discussion, if discussion and concentration of a discussion there must be, perhaps it is not a bad thing to let it cross, or maybe only be introduced by questions that cut across fields, questions that: (1) Have a certain relation to some *here and now*, the *here and now* being the common requisite [*requête*] of ethics *and* politics, that is to say, the inescapable. There can be ethics and politics only where a decision or an action is inescapable. (2) Refer as quickly as possible to this point of *and* where the disjunction appears both indispensable and impossible, impracticable. And (3) engage examples that manifest the uncompromising character, aporetic so to speak, of these apparently irreconcilable requisites [*requêtes*].

Here to conclude are several questions that might answer to the three rules that I have just posited. Following which I will improvise the beginning of an analysis of the two examples that I invoked earlier: that of Abdallah's trial and that of a particular moment in the events of the so-called student movement.

So the questions—quickly: (1) Is there an original responsibility of the philosopher in the face of this issue? I say this referring not only to what I said earlier of the necessity of thinking a genealogy of concepts, etc., but I am also thinking of the intervention, of what the intervention of a philosopher might be in political discourse today. What type of intervention could a philosopher have in the ethical and political debates as they are elaborated today, under conditions that are both very old and very modern? (2) Is there a difference, in this respect, between philosophical responsibility (I am not necessarily thinking of professional philosophers, I am speaking of a philosophical type of discourse and intervention) and intellectual responsibility in general? Is there a difference here between the philosophical type and the intellectual type? (3) But here I would only be repeating what Miguel Abensour said earlier: in the context of the situation in France or in the West, what has taken place, let us say, over the last twenty or twenty five years that all of the sudden a reference to the ethical should dominate as a protest against an "everything is political," against a politicism that we experienced at a certain time? Why, what does it mean, this reference to the ethical? What does it show? What does it hide? Why is it insistent? What is the motivation, what are the motivations for this reference? I do not have a simple answer. Like Miguel Abensour, I simply appeal to vigilance in the face of what, sometimes, the arrogant modalities of this reminder may mark, may give to understand concerning certain motivations. The analysis of it is very complicated, and I cannot attempt it here.

Now let me move very quickly—I have already been too slow—to my two examples. Naturally, I do not have the time to analyze them as subtly as would be necessary. Nevertheless, let us remember the moment at which discussions took place at the Collège and where the decision about this forum was made. The moment where, in the rise of the said student movement, the murder of a student seemed intolerable, unbearable, and as if, all of a sudden, a mutation was at work in the ethical or political conscience of a large number of those who belonged to the French right and the French left. What was often said at that time was: "political oppositions do not count any more. This is unbearable. It is therefore in the name of principles which are no longer essentially political that we must say 'never again'." Moreover, the student movement was often presented as a movement that at last was . . . (this interpretation was then also exploited) no longer political, politicizable, that no longer wanted to be politicized and that thus acted in the name of principles, of principles that were often qualified as ethical, or nonpolitical. This analysis always seemed insufficient to me. I think that when indignation reached its peak, the interpretation that underlay it, that obviously motivated it, was no longer political according to a certain code, in reference to a certain code, but was, nevertheless, political through and through as ethical protest. Why was it political? Well, because it is evident that the interpretation of this unacceptable murder only achieved such force insofar as, implicitly at least, the context of the whole political action was held accountable: murders of this type—alas! alas!—occurred every month, and all of a sudden one had forgotten that under this government, but undoubtedly under other governments as well (and the question was so quickly posed for those who indeed meant to organize themselves so that "never again will this happen"), murders of this type were very often committed. I could give numerous examples. If this one appeared particularly unacceptable and caused a "this is ethically intolerable, this is no longer a question of politics" to arise, it is because the whole context as I see it—the problem of the nationality code, the fact that the student in question was not entirely French, etc.—I no longer remember all the factors of the political context that caused the indignation—all of this clearly showed that the political was constantly present in a so-called ethical evaluation. As for the student movement, I think that a quick analysis would show that if it was not political according to certain criteria, it was political in other ways. The principles that were advanced to justify the student movement, or to justify the indignation before this horrible murder referred back to the principles of democracy, the rights of man, etc., but also at the same time, to a very determined political model and not to some sort of metapolitical morality. What happens at this moment—and it is simply this law of structure that I wanted to point out—is that every time the ethical and the political are caught in a knot, in an irreducible intrication, this does not mean that they are simply tangled, but that what seems not to have to be negotiated politically, not to have to be reinscribed in a relation of powers, thus the nonnegotiable, the unconditional is, as unconditional, subject to political transaction: and this political transaction of the unconditional is not an accident, a degeneration, or a last resort; it is prescribed by ethical duty itself. One should not have to negotiate between two negotiables. One must negotiate the nonnegotiable. And if at this moment, the ethical is on the side—thus determination: a certain type of Kantian determination—on the side of the unconditional, thus of the nonnegotiable, etc., well then, negotiation here is always, and this is its aporetic fatality, negotiation is always negotiation of the nonnegotiable. There are examples of this every day with the problem of terrorism.

This is the second example, and I will stop here. The trial of Abdallah. It is very difficult to talk about it today, things evolve all the time. Nevertheless, what is happening here at first glance? Political questions, the said reasons of state, appear to enter into the arena. Some suspect the government of having wanted to negotiate the imminent liberation of Abdallah, for reasons that one will interpret as political. But the said government could very well and will not miss the opportunity of accounting for these reasons as ethical. One can negotiate the liberation of Abdallah. Why? To save hostages' lives, of course, or to liberate hostages, and potentially to save human lives because it is, so one thinks, the way to stop terrorism. Thus, it is in the name of human lives, of human life above all, in any case, and of singular lives that politics attempts to justify itself. The political discourse here refers to ethical principles while at the same time having to negotiate life against life. Because the calculation, of which I spoke earlier, is the terrifying responsibility of the judge or of anyone at all. At a given moment, when everyone agrees in condemning terrorism and saving human lives, there is a choice to be made between singular human lives, all infinitely precious; that is, in some cases, one says "no"—this is still a type of negotiation—"you do not negotiate with terrorism, because if you give in once then you will always give in. It is better to give up." Whom then does one give up? One gives up those who are actually hostages, who are in the hands of the said terrorists, or else a certain number of victims, all equally respectable, to save more. And one negotiates the nonnegotiable. And no one can raise an argument against this imperative: calculating with the incalculable. On the other hand, with the same principles, the reverse strategy: one negotiates. One negotiates, that is, one liberates, one makes transactions, one tries to win time. In both cases, the political imperative and the ethical imperative are indissociable.

The trial takes place. One has the impression that a public prosecutor, in the name of the reason of state or the political advice that he has been given, or that he has given himself, asks for a weak sentence, while in the name of the purity of right and ethics, etc.—right here being indissociable from ethics—the unconditional condemnation of terrorism cannot be negotiated. Honest judges give Abdallah the maximum sentence. But these judges know—and everyone knows, and Mitterand announced it three or four months ago—that the thing done, the political power in its highest form could grant a pardon, always in the same market of negotiations, but once the hostages had been returned. This is what Mitterand said at a certain point during an interview: "Yes, I am prepared to commit myself to the procedure of granting a pardon. The government still has to present me with the file, but only if all the hostages are returned." Etc. . . . Thus the ball is passed back to the side of the political, however, the head of state, responsible for the reason of state, maintains that he, too, acts in the name of ethics, that is, to save human lives, etc. . . . And here, in all of these cases, the dissociation between ethical and political is not only impracticable, but it is not by accident that it is not; yet on the other hand, this does not mean that the one is dissolved in the other. To the extent that one increases the specificity of both dimensions, their inextricability will become increasingly knotted. The practice of disjunction not only does not achieve the disjunction but binds in the same aporia elements that are thus rigorously disconnected. This is urgency.

BUCI-GLUCKSMANN: Well. There is perhaps some urgency in opening up discussion, either here, if someone would like to intervene, or in the room.

QUESTION (IN THE ROOM): Simply a question that takes off from the end of Jacques Derrida's talk. I did not hear Buci-Glucksmann's talk, and, therefore, I do not have an overall sense of what was said. How true is it that everyone has agreed to condemn terrorism? And to what degree have our discussions here forgotten, in the wake of the revalorization of ethics, what we knew a few years ago about the constant reality of political violence?

J.D.: Yes, this is a point that, in haste and urgency, I neglected to situate, although I did have the intention of doing so. It goes without saying that for those who, on the side of those whom we call *terrorists*, speak most strongly in justification of what we call *terrorism*, also put forward ethical arguments. They project on to all of the Western governments, unanimous in condemning terrorism, an image of violence to which the said terrorism responds. They argue the fact that the ethics that makes all of these Western political discourses unanimous, this front, this ethical surface hides a violence both ethical and political. This is Abdallah's discourse and that of many others; it is the discourse that we have known for a long time and that naturally declaims against ethical good conscience as the alibi for ethical-political violence, that of oppression, for example, the crushing of Arab countries, the oppression of the Palestinians, etc. But it is evident that the condemnation of terrorism in the form that it takes everywhere, raises a certain number of ethical and political questions. The answer of those whom we call *terrorists* consists in saying: "You put forward the rights of man, a formal ethics, a universal ethics, the protection of life, etc. . . . , to conceal a much greater violence to which we are responding." Thus, ethics here is a well-concealed political violence. The ethical discourse, the ethical negation is a well-concealed political violence. I do not know if this is what you were thinking of.

THE SAME QUESTIONER: More to the point, should the ethical, public consensus be taken seriously? [Reference to Chirac and to the uncompromising condemnation of terrorism that no political activist can truly take seriously.]

J.D.: This is the process of ethical cynicism, of a cynicism regarding ethical discourse, and we know where it leads.

THE SAME QUESTIONER.: But without even entering into the argumentation. [Reference to the conditions that made the emergence of the student revolt possible.]

J.D.: But the denunciation of ethical cynicism, of cynicism in the name of ethics, also belongs, I did not want to repeat these things here, to grand philosophical programs. It is already there in Hegel. The critique of Kant's morality as hypocrisy, as effective hypocrisy, one can find it, by modifying and adjusting things, the effects and examples of it are to be found everywhere today.

QUESTION: Following up on this question, the question that I wanted to ask you . . . Do you see an ethical dimension in the discourse of those whom we call *terrorists*?

J.D.: I will not answer that question without a long protocol.

QUESTION: First, I would distinguish . . .

J.D.: I think that the discourse of Action-Directe, for example, is, in its axiomatic, very different from the discourses that come from certain Middle Eastern countries, where the ethical and political question is posed in altogether different terms. Could you repeat your question?

THE SAME QUESTIONER: In the action of those whom we call *terrorists*, I was thinking less of Action-Directe than I was of Abdallah's case, because it is the one you were talking about. Whether, indeed, some links or connections . . . should not be made between ethics and politics in the discourse of people such as Abdallah . . . ?

J.D.: When they say "the fight against oppression," for which the United States, France, and the West in general are the agents and those responsible, is their motive only political? I don't think so. I am speaking of their discourse. What would be interesting to analyze closely—but we cannot do it in the present situation—is the strategy of Vergès, the discourse of Vergès, what he calls his *strategy*. The way he litigates. Its strategy of rupture. He negotiates, nonetheless, he presents himself as a lawyer, he does his job as a lawyer, he uses all of the resources of the law, while *radically* contesting the legitimacy of this law and all of its consequences: the politics and the cynicism and the political hypocrisy that demand the exercise of this law, within which, however, he places himself. Does he do this in the name of ethics, politics, or of some other law? This is a very difficult question that, in my opinion, we cannot treat without bringing everything back to the beginning again. But it would be interesting to analyze the quite fascinating—I find, very strong, very coherent—discourse of Vergès, however shocking it may appear, on the other hand, in this country.

MIGUEL ABENSOUR: I think that we cannot clearly pose the problem that we have just posed, perhaps, because of a misunderstanding that may be implicit in what you said before. That is to say, the misunderstanding is the following: in effect, the "nue vie" can never be an evil bearer of ethics. Let me remind you of what Benjamin said in this regard: the "nue vie" can never, as such, be an ethical value and it is a falsification of ethics when one holds a discourse that identifies ethics with the values of the "nue vie." Perhaps this was what was made difficult, for in the examples you gave, it might have seemed that, on the part of the state and the others, an ethical position was the one that defended life as such. Yet this is already something about which we could have much discussion . . .

J.D.: I am not the one . . .

M.A.: Precisely, precisely. I am thinking of the questions that were raised. Perhaps it is because of this that . . . Never were ethics made compatible with a position of the "nue vie" as such. This is never an ethics.

J.D.: Which is why one generally says *human, a human person*, letting it be understood that it is the personality, the nonbiological character of life that must be saved, and that is at issue in this discourse. It is not life itself, but human life par excellence, the human being, the sin-gularity of the human being. There will never be a moral or political dis-course on animal life, or rarely, even for the singularity of animal life. This is a very serious question.

M.A.: Now I would like to express a doubt. I mean, is there really . . . urgency is an inescapable dimension of ethics and politics, but in privileging urgency does one not risk being brought, in the end, to think the political in a decisionist schema, where the dominant factor is deci-sion, and neglecting a whole aspect, it seems to me, fundamental in mod-ern politics, that is one of form, the idea of creation, of the institution of form, and that indeed introduces here the idea of space, and not merely a space of communication—I do not know what you think—which is very weak or very soothing, but which is also a space of conflict, and thus one no longer risks privileging, complicating the strategic, the gamble, etc. The decisionist schema is part of the political, but I think that it is also counterbalanced by another dimension. This is a question that I would like to ask you. Another, more interrogative question: is this return to ethics in the end, if return to ethics there is, could it be attributable to an excess of politicism . . . of the last twenty-five years? Because, in the end, if we have truly lived an excess of politicism, have we not confused the political and are we not, in fact, actually in the process of rediscover-ing the political under the name of the ethical? That is to say, are we not in the process of dismissing certain ideas that we had, let us say, two decades ago? For example, we thought that . . . I am thinking of Foucault's text, the text of his course given at the Collège de France on power that was greeted at the time as the first theory of power since Marx and Freud, in which Foucault tells us in the end: "one must think power as military model." That is to say that, in a manner of speaking, we will go beyond economic logic, we will go beyond the logic of property . . . but we are incapable of thinking power . . . sudden appearance of the eth-ical that is a way of saving a possible politics.

J.D. On this last point, of course, I give, wrongly or rightly, a very large extension to the concept of negotiation, thus making for example . . . I would be tempted to answer that, when Blanchot says: "Let us not negotiate"—to preserve the chances of another future politics—he nego-tiates. He calculates. He says: "this is what we have to do in order . . . ," and not to negotiate is a way of negotiating, it is a way of handling the problem so as to calculate the coming of a new politics, of another politics, of a future chance. Here I think there is, therefore, negotiation. And I return insistently to what I said earlier, that negotiation does not negotiate between negotiable things, by exchanging negotiable things, negotiation—and this is what makes it terrible—must negotiate the nonnegotiable, to save its being nonnegotiable. This is what is terrifying. The word *negotiation* is perhaps not the best suited to describe such a thing. As for the decision, I did not take upon myself the concept of decision. Moreover, in insisting on the fact that urgency was contradictory, that it was urgent to wait as well as not to wait, and that when I said urgency and différance were the same thing, that is what I wanted to say. Also, when I placed decision on the side of nonexperience of the undecidable, the experience of the undecidable, it is not simply the impossibility of deciding between A and B, or black and white: the zone is one of experience in which the decision still does not emerge, in which the relation is, in fact, not of the decision type. What you have just evoked is a zone of experience; it is on the basis of nondecision, not of indecision but of nondecision, that the decision emerges. I would completely agree with you in making me attentive to this experience that is not commanded by a decision. I would simply have some reservation when you call this space a *political* or *ethical* space. I think that, in our tradition and in our society, when we speak of ethics and politics, a decision is irreducible. The moment of the decision one cannot do without it. And this community, this dimension of being together that would not be ruled by the necessity of decision, I am very attentive to it, indeed, but I will not define it as ethical or political. There are, perhaps, dimensions of the community, of being together—the word *community* has always bothered me a little—of being together in the interruption, as one says today, in a relation without relation, which are, perhaps, neither ethical nor political. But when there are ethics and politics—at that moment, one must decide. And one cannot, whatever the legitimate reservation may be (and that I share with you in relation to this decisionist tension) there are moments at which one has to decide. And what one calls *ethics* or *politics* in our culture, is the moment at which one cannot not decide. There are decisions to be made, which are inevitable, and not to decide is still to decide. The space of the decision here is irreducible. This does not prevent us from thinking of something that is before or after or further . . . This does not prevent us from being-with-the-other or from opening, from knowing that a space is open with the other in which this decisionism does not take place. Nevertheless, there are places where it takes place. And this taking place is what one calls, I think, the *ethical* and the *political* in our society.

QUESTION: [Agrees with the vigilance—nevertheless supplement to vigilance: uncircumventable question of the rights of man. Who is the man of the rights of man? Procedure of Heidegger and reference to "Les fins de l'homme."]

J.D.: As you can well imagine, I have nothing against the rights of man in general. However, to think, to answer the question that you ask, one should not give oneself, suppose that one has acquired a definition of the humanity of man. If only out of *respect* for the rights of man. Suppose today that one wanted to refound the rights of man, with the knowledge that the theory of man's right has a very long evolution, that the concept of the rights of man has very different profiles, so that to *re*-think the rights of man, to refound them, one should begin with nothing that had been previously acquired. The place from which one poses this question of the refounding of the rights of man cannot be man, it cannot guarantee any kind of knowing what man is. It is from this point of view, in effect, that Heidegger represented, I think, a movement that we cannot not take into consideration. But I think that, and I will come back to this in my conference on Heidegger next week, I think that for Heidegger, too, there is—I will not say it as he himself says it, an unthought, because the way in which he characterizes the unthought is already too determined for me—but that there is something there that one cannot regard as a stable [*assurée*] axiomatic, either. Thus, we not only need to keep these questions open, but to keep open, to remain vigilant, even with regard to the form of the Heideggerian question and the necessity of the question. Even the question of the question is an axiom that one should not prevent oneself from displacing. If there must be prescription, if there must be duty in the face of something such as the rights of man, then it demands that all of this be rethought constantly: and to rethink, to question this, one must begin from a place where man is not, where there is not man, where one does not know what it is. This absolutely does not mean, naturally, opposition to man. But rather vigilance, because this is not only a fundamental and superfundamental question. It is also a matter of providing oneself with the means of detecting what in certain discourses on the rights of man may hide something else. There is much discourse on the rights of man, and many strategies to this discourse. And to remain vigilant about the questions that I have just invoked, is also to provide oneself with the political means of analyzing the strategy of those who, in a given situation, make use of the reference to the rights of man. Thus, it is also a political gesture and responsibility to remain vigilant.

QUESTION: [Returns to the decision—regicide and the rights of man—Claude Lefort on the rights of man.]

J.D.: I agree with you. But then, from this point of view, what have *you* done? From this experience of being together that is not yet called for by decision, what would you have done, or what would you have said, faced with the discourse of Saint-Just? But if you had said nothing, and if you say nothing now, you are saying something. That is decision. Rather, it decides. The decision that I discussed is not a decision that you make. It is a decision that is made even if you do not make it. It ends matters.

QUESTION: [Reference to Condorcet.]

J.D.: That is to say that he put an end to it. He opposed the death penalty.

QUESTION: [On the negotiation of the nonnegotiable and the out-of-the-world. What does it mean to negotiate a limit?]

J.D.: I think I agree. I would simply say that the negotiation that takes place at that moment, the strange negotiation that takes place with a limit, is a negotiation that I do not negotiate, that I do not calculate. It is a negotiation in which I am taken, or, let us say, the subject said to be deciding is taken, and the negotiation takes place regardless of what one does, regardless of what the particular deciding subject does or does not do. The decision takes place. At that moment perhaps one should attribute the value of the decision to something other than a free and calculating subject.

QUESTION: [On the human-animal division; the first political act of the Shining Path: to hang 100 dogs . . .]

J.F. LYOTARD: [Question of a third party, of the distinction between ethics and politics, and of the regard for the law.]

J.D.: Just two words, because it is getting late. I find it a little ironic that what I have said concerning decision has been interpreted, not only by Miguel Abensour, as decisionist. It is exactly, let me say, the opposite. On the other hand, this is perhaps a historical point or a philosophical reading, or concerns a detail, but I think that it entails a certain number of things. It is about what you said, Jean-François, about Kant. Although I agree with what, I think, you mean, I am still a little perplexed as to the necessity, the need that you feel to have it said through Kant, as you read him. For example, you say: "Law for Kant does not tell me anything," there. . . . When you say: "there is no third party in this situation of obligation," I would be tempted to say that, if there is a discourse that is an *immediate* appeal to a third party, that is to the universal, then it is, in fact, the discourse of Kant. The rupture of the singular empirical relation, indeed, passes through a pure third party and the universality of the law: the condition of its being universal, is that there should be a third. It is not the third party, not a third, but what breaks the empirical dual. Here indeed, from this point of view, Levinas is and is not, as always, Kantian. He is very Kantian and at the same time he is not Kantian. He is Kantian insofar as he wants what he describes in terms of responsibility, hostages, obligation, to be universal. He needs the law. He does not want simply to lose himself in Kierkegaardianism, or, like Buber, in the I-You relation. He says "Thou." In the relation, he prefers the "Thou" to the "You," and says so. Even in a face-to-face dual, there must be, for the obligation to be an obligation, an element of universality or of law which implies that a third instance, not a third person, be there between us. Without which it is an empirical singularity. Thus it seems to me—I have no time to justify or to elaborate it—that the practical discourse of Kant is, on the one hand, an immediate appeal to a third party, while, at the same time, it leads the way to a democratic politics that is articulated with pure practical reason, because there is indeed a third. And here, I no longer agree with the system you have invoked. And furthermore, that the "I," the ego should be constituted with respect, from the obligation of interpellation undoubtedly, I agree completely; but this does not mean that there is no "I" and no deciding "I." I think that there is, for Kant there is. Here I do not speak for myself. For me, the decision is much more complicated, as

I tried to suggest earlier. But to suggest that for Kant decision is something inessential or secondary, etc. . . . , this is very risky. My reading of Kant is much more conventional than yours, but I would firmly defend it with texts to support it. There is still something that is very paradoxical. There is also a decision that is not a voluntary decision; look at Kierkegaard. It is the decisionist interpretation with which everyone [opposes] me, yet when it is a question of decision, no, the decision that I was speaking of is not decisionist. That is all.

On the "Priceless," or the "Going Rate"
of the Transaction

(The last time I had the honor of speaking at Le Mans was thirty-one years ago, in June 1960; I had just finished my first year of teaching *terminale* and *hypokhâgne* at the Lycée Montesquieu. I say this to convey the value [*prix*] and the emotion that I attach to this reunion. In 1960, the speech I gave at the time was not without relation to price [*prix*], already, since the speech in question was the one given on "prize day [*distribution des prix*]"—which traditionally falls to the youngest teacher or the teacher most newly arrived at the Lycée. Which was my case that year.)

One must sacrifice, one must save—time, first of all.

I will begin by keeping literally to the title that was proposed for the session in which I was initially supposed to participate—a title that, incidentally, I find quite felicitous: *the spirit of the market*. Is it possible to take this expression literally [*à la lettre*]? And does one not often oppose the spirit, precisely, to the letter?

Would the "spirit" of the market not be, among other things, precisely, what one must oppose, under the term "money [*argent*]," *to the letter*, to the literality of the market, indeed, both to the body and to the coded, inscribable, countable, that is to say, calculable body of monetary objectivity? "The spirit of the market": among other things, this expression would thus apply to everything under the term *money* that is not simply reducible to economics. Money as *spirit* of the market would be what, in the market and even in exchange in general, is *either* no longer a matter of economics in a strict sense of a *restricted economy* and no longer reducible to the circumscribable field of a theory, as objective, material, technically masterable calculability, *or else* what, without exceeding economics in general, would overflow the strict and cold monetary accounting of material interests, of exchanges, or of the production of useful goods. In both cases, the spirit of the market would designate, at least as a problem, a set of laws, motivations, or finalities that, while putting in motion the system or the cycle of exchanges, would not be contained within it; determinant or overdeterminant, this motor excess would at times be money as noneconomic value, at other times money as value, and certainly therefore as economic value, but as metamonetary value in some sense, as a value irreducible to some monetary equivalent. Money [*l'argent*] would be more or less than currency [*monnaie*].

In both cases, the element of calculability would be overwhelmed by this obscure thing, disconcerting and perhaps immaterial, that is called *money* [argent], in opposition to *currency* [monnaie], at least if one still wants to rely on this distinction. Such a distinction can be substantiated or disqualified according to the context and the convention. In certain cases, like the one here tonight, we have decided to remain more attentive to what is no longer strictly monetary in the money-value [*valeur d'argent*] or in the value of money [*valeur de l'argent*], as if, in some sense, the origin or the history of currency occurred later than that of money and were relatively autonomous, as if the monetary were the object of a science or a more narrow project of objective science than the science of money, and even, in short, of all economic value.

I have just said that it is by convention and according to context that one distinguishes money from currency. I will return to this in a moment, but this seems to me immediately to demand two remarks or two reminders.

1. In any case, the two concepts or the two words, *money* [argent] and *currency* [monnaie], whether or not one distinguishes them, have this in common: one must never forget it, that they designate things that are not natural. The money we are talking about in this context cannot, any more than the currency can, be found in nature. Money and currency depend on the *credit* one gives to conventions, to technical artifices, to laws. Even before giving rise to credit procedures, to the fiduciary dimension, they are both (money as much as currency) phenomena of credit and convention;

they no longer belong to what we commonly call *nature* but to the symbolic experience of "public faith [*foi public*]" (*fides publica*) that was in question earlier, of confidence and the "sworn oath [*foi jurée*]." They force us to turn back toward the enigma of this experience that is so strange and so familiar that is called *believing*: inexhaustible for philosophy. And what I am underlining in this way has value and is legitimated in turn only on the basis of an old and fundamental distinction between nature and convention, nature and law, nature and art or artifice (*physis/thesis, physis/nomos, physis/technè*), a fundamental but historical opposition whose genealogy in turn one may question: an enormous task and one that it is out of the question of undertaking here, be it even to the smallest degree. I will only note in passing that the notions of exchange or economic production, of value, or of commodity, of money, or of monetary sign are not only one of its examples. There is no history, no convention, no art or technics without production, without division of labor, without the emergence of exchange value and monetary sign. If, even when one keeps in reserve more radical questions on the opposition "nature/convention," one must insist on the conventionality of money (silver) or of gold, it is in order to resist a *naturalizing* tendency in the interpretation of the history of currency or value. One of the examples of this tendency consists, for example, in considering as a de-naturing history, the passage from gold currency or silver currency to paper currency (whose convertibility is ensured by the state), then to fiduciary paper currency (the bank note) whose guarantee is not ensured, then finally to the conventional, inconvertible paper currency or legal tender (after the First World War). Indeed, one often represents this history as the movement of a simple degeneration—far from the golden age of a currency that is truly natural and truly reliable, originary, true, authentic, as if the gold currency or the silver currency, as if the decision to consider the natural metal (gold or silver) as value or natural wealth were not already a nonnatural effect of convention, of credit, of quasi fiction. The condemnation of this degeneration into inauthenticity or this denaturation belongs to the whole register of the morality of money (silver) or gold, an intra-economic code of ethics of sorts that would have to be questioned for itself—and in relation to all phenomena of fetishism (of money or of the commodity) about which we will no doubt speak further tonight. The classical analysis, even the denunciation of fetishism, and in particular commodity fetishism, by Marx or Freud, rests on philosophical axioms that also raise many questions (we do not have the time to address this problem here; I have tried to do it elsewhere).

2. If, in certain contexts, a secondary or supplementary convention at times establishes a distinction between the words *money* and *currency* (opening up thus the problem concerning the "spirit of the market") it is on the basis of a more general conventionality and a more essential co-implication. There is nothing fortuitous, in fact, about our having so often used the model of tender [*du numéraire*] and of monetary sign to analyze the functioning of language—or of a system of signs in general. Well before Mallarmé and Saussure, and no doubt since Plato, one could cite numerous examples of discussions that have had recourse to this analogy. Valéry, for example, makes extensive use of the analogy between capital and the linguistic sign, and even between capital and spirit, capital and *logos*. One could show that this is more than an analogy, or, in any case, more than one analogy among others or one analogy that is like other analogies. Here perhaps is where what we propose to call *the spirit of the market* arises in its most proper dimension. For two reasons, here again.

—To the extent that language is the medium of economic transactions, of information and stock exchange, to the extent that the market is completely caught up in systems of communication—which are themselves committed to an unceasing technical transformation and whose growing acceleration gains speed to the extent that language can be considered an accelerator, we will return to this—well then, this essential implication of language in monetary geopolitics introduces into geopolitics everything that language and speech import in their folds: rhetoric, connotations, theatricalization, fiction, one would almost say literature, in short, the overdeterminations for which we have obscure terms that I am using here for the sake of convenience: qualitative, affective, imaginary, phantasmatic, ideological overdeterminations, the irrational movements of opinion, for example, the humors and rumors that determine the movements of a machine that is nonetheless hypermetronomized, by which I mean capable of measure, of quantification and clockwork calculation. I am alluding thus to the microphenomena that the geopolitics of our time depend on, namely, the obscure folds of a feeling or a passion, an anxiety or an exaltation, which are always difficult to locate in an individual or collective subject; we know the effects of such folds, of these ephemeral wrinkles of affect. They are never totally objectivable. At maximum speed, thanks to satellites and computer technology, and by playing with the networks and the time differences over the entire surface of the earth, they can provoke historical quakes that will affect humanity for long sequences of its history, in its experience of war and peace, in its labors and its sufferings, in its modes of life, and this to furthest reaches of villages that seemed the most removed from Wall Street, from the London, the Paris, the Tokyo Stock Exchanges. Like economic speculation in general, the stock market scene remains a scene of coding [*chiffrage*], of information, of communication and computerization, but also a writing and a language whose medium cannot be totally formalized. It is a "human" scene, obviously, but it cannot be reduced to calculability. There is a *spirit* of the market because the market is a language, and a language that can never be totally quantified or formalized. This "spirit of the market" does not discredit economic science, but it forbids its closure, its autonomy, its absolute specificity; it limits its ambition and even its quantifying mastery.

—What precedes concerned the spirit of the market as a language in general. I will propose a second remark, this time on money and language [*langue*]. The distinction between money and currency certainly implies language in general, in the broad sense that I have just indicated, but it is not marked in the same way from one language to the other. The German series (*Silber, Geld, Münze, Geldstück*) or the English series (silver, money, currency, change) cannot be immediately translated, without long and laborious mediations in the French idiom that has, for example, only one word to designate *l'argent* as natural metal (*silver, Silber*), *l'argent* as money or monetary sign and *l'argent* as currency invested, and invested precisely because of its homonymy with natural wealth, with all sorts of values projected according to complex and overdetermined figures of desire or hatred, of covetousness or disgust, of retention in anal avarice or rejection of the excrement, etc. What we call *l'argent* in French (and which is not simply the monetary sign nor simply the *monnaie* that one gives back in the course of a sales operation—"change" in English—nor simply the metal one finds in mines or in jewelry) cannot be translated in one word by *silver* or *Silber*, no more than it can be translated strictly speaking by *Geld* or *money*.

But it is only in French that the word *argent* immediately communicates, at least in what ties the phantasm or the imaginary to the linguistic signifier, that which associates *argent* as monetary sign of value with the precious metal, with the sensual and brilliant substance out of which coins or jewelry have been made. To have a bank note, a bank account, private property is to have *argent*. In English or in German, one does not say that it is to have something that might be called *silver*[1] or *Silber*. And all the idiomatic locutions, such as *le temps, c'est de l'argent* [time is money], *l'argent ne fait pas le bonheur* [money can't buy happiness], "*prendre pour argent comptant* [to take at face value] are not translatable without remainder. In some sense, the spirit of the market also finds its space in an investment that is irrational, or in any case very difficult to analyze, formalize, calculate. This investment accrues; it complicates its own overdetermination, and it enriches its own surplus value in the course of a sedimented [*sédimentée*] history. Such a history deposits itself [*se sédimente*] and deposits [*sédimente*] the investment not only in the supposed value of a metal but in the values of the semantic exchange of a word or in the discrepancies between the use value and the exchange value of the word. There is too much to say in the time we have about this investment of value and meaning: it commits itself to an idiom whose translatability is limited, and yet it does so by means of one of those terms that, we believe, signify the most universal, the most transcultural, the most translatable thing there is: indeed money is considered to be the neutral, indifferent, impersonal medium, the general equivalent of all exchange and all transaction, the universal substitute, in fact, the best shared thing (when its quantity is the least well-shared thing in the world). And what is more, the same universality is presupposed when one considers money to be the pole of contradictory or ambivalent drives (desire or rejection of a noble or vile thing that, on the one hand, calls for appropriation and can signify by metonymy everything that is appropriable in general but can just as well signify everything that one can, with natural generosity or not, sacrifice, offer, give). In any case, money's belonging to the illimitable order of language or inscription—of the mark—is precisely that which overflows monetary calculation or economic objectivity. Money drags this calculation toward infinity or toward the incalculable, toward the abyss of a speculation that is no longer strictly that of the stock exchange or contained within the institutions of economic transactions.

Here we rediscover an old distinction proposed by Aristotle. It is interesting, and it still makes us think even if it seems untenable, precisely for the reasons I have just indicated. The distinction is that between *chrematistics* and *economics*.

Economics is the art of managing the goods of the *oikos*, the home, the family, the hearth, and even the city (nation or state), the technics necessary for acquiring or exchanging these goods in proportion to needs that are determinable and finite in principle. *Chrematistics* is not familiar with these limits. It refers to the art of acquiring goods or wealth *for themselves*, through commerce or speculation, according to the law of the market, without limit and behaving *as if* (this is, Aristotle tells us, the artificial, nonnatural, denaturing illusion of the chrematistic drive). Chrematistics behaves *as if* true wealth consisted in a quantity of money. And it is also the beginning of what will be called, starting in the eighteenth century, and by analogy, the *fetishism of money*. Chrematistics, were one to oppose it in this context or according to this convention to economics, and if one held it to be an art or a science, would be precisely that which forms both the spirit of the market [*l'esprit du marché*] and the market spirit [*l'esprit de marché*], everything in the market that exceeds—infinitely—the limits of need, of the useful, the natural, the reasonable, the calculable, the stable relation between production and consumption, between the *chez soi* and the *chez l'autre*, etc. My hypothesis here is that this limit between *need* and *desire*, and even the opposition between the two, like the opposition between the economic or purely monetary market and the spirit of the market—or the market spirit—is traversed from the moment there is the least exchange, the least trace, from the moment of the first need. And—to remain in the realm of money or currency—as soon as there is money, monetary sign, substitution, and repetition, the border between the economic and the chrematistic is already crossed over—as is the border of all related oppositions.

The inevitable, undeniable—and, I would say, originary—crossing of this limit has incalculable consequences, consequences *of* the incalculable, and this in all realms, but exemplarily with regard to everything that touches on money, everything that touches money. This is no doubt what allows for speculation, the labor without labor of capital, the accumulation, the fetishism of the commodity and the monetary sign, but it is also what allows one to pass beyond need, as one assumes is done by desire; which also allows one to pass beyond economic calculation, as should be done by the gift, if it is possible and if ever there is a gift.

In the beginning we said: one must sacrifice, one must save, time, first of all. And here we are lacking the time to conclude. Rushing things then, let us refer in conclusion to the time limits that we are given. Around this theme, time, I would organize several points which, although I will not treat them here, I would like to submit for discussion.

In the idiomatic expression that I recalled a moment ago, *le temps, c'est de l'argent*, and that can be translated into English at least ("time is money"), perhaps one must hear something other than what one generally hears in it, namely, that time measures a labor and production capacity and is therefore equivalent to the process of creation and acquisition of wealth—and wealth is in principle accountable or translatable, for economics or rhetoric, by metonymy, as money. In such a way that, according to this popular interpretation, *le temps, c'est de l'argent*, would by implication signify that work, labor as production, plays a mediating role between time and money. Labor would be a conjunction between time and money, or again the "copula," the industrial dowel of the statement *le temps, c'est de l'argent*, because it is the time of labor, even the immobile work of capital (and, as we know, Marx was not the only economist to be especially interested in the interpretation of time and the relations among time, labor, production, and money). Such would be the popular interpretation—and largely justified, moreover—of a proverb in circulation. A proverb is, furthermore, also a sort of money [*monnaie*] in circulation, both precious and without value, hard-wearing and devalued, the inheritance of a patrimony as *common* as the language. Nothing is at once more and less common than a proverb—or than money.

But if one wanted to displace or reevaluate the proverb, could it not be said that money is time? No longer because time allows us to earn [*gagner*] money, as I have just recalled, either because it represents a time of labor or because it causes money itself "to labor"; but conversely because money allows us to win [*gagner*] time? As substitute or equivalent in general, it begins by economizing on the time of exchange of things and goods; it accelerates circulation to infinity: not only by supplying substitutes but by first substituting its principle to the principle of barter. By opening the reign of repetition, of substitution, that is, of the neutralization that erases the individual characteristics of the things exchanged and the subjects of the exchange, it supplies an element of quantification or mathematization of value that is first an extraordinary neutralization of time. This is why, let it be said along the way, the saving of time that the technology of communication secures for the market, for the activity of the stock exchange, for the movements of chrematistic speculation, is not a secondary or accidental benefit; it is, one might say, the very deployment of the essence of money as time (money is time), as the acceleration of social time, as quantification and economy of time. Money is time won, time saved (we said, in the beginning, that one had to save time) or non-time in time, a *dead time* that allows one to win time. Between "the spirit of the market" and technics there is not an exteriority as one might be tempted to assume. The law of their movement is the same. This economy of time as quantification is also a spatialization of time according to its measure. Money is, in this regard, *an economy of time*, not only as currency but as spirit of the market, as movement of a chrematistic desire that carries itself beyond the economy—in the narrow sense that Aristotle gives it—*an economy of time*, a clock that technology, and in particular the technology of communication, supposing one could distinguish it from technics in general, ends up serving not only as instrument but that which technology carries off as its own movement.

From these few preliminary remarks, I will retain, again for the sake of economy, *two problems* (problems necessarily tied to *ethics* on the one hand, to the *signature* on the other) whose headings, as it were, I will do no more than schematize; both depend on the essential concepts of *substitution, repetition*, and *neutralization* that I have just mentioned. These three predicates have this in common: that they signify a certain *indifference*. Money is indifferent because its signs must be equal and similar (there is no difference between two ten-franc coins or two ten-franc bills: essential indifference, conventionality, nonnaturality, arbitrariness of the sign, thus repetition, iterability and substitutability, movement of universalization). The same thing holds for the origin or the holder [*porteur*] of money: Money, as they say, has no smell [*l'argent . . . n'a pas d'odeur*]. These three predicates of indifference (substitution, repetition, neutralization) are indissociable here—and indispensable to any concept of money: as quantifiable value, as monetary sign or figure of the desirable, of the infinitely desirable, be it simple or ambivalent.

Hence the problems of *ethics* and of *signature*.

1. Taking *ethics* in the broad sense, the first problem would be at once moral, juridical, and political. *Indifferent* to singularity, the experience of money would favor substitution, repetition, neutralization. Because of this indifference, combined with everything that associates money to nonvalue (money as waste, excrement, object of fetishistic desire, avarice, or anal retention—but "odorless"!), moral, juridical, or political reason should thus rise above money: not only above economics, above monetary calculability, but also and perhaps especially, above the

spirit of the market. Often *unavowable*, money would thus belong, according to Freud, to a *series* of substitutable objects: excrement, child, penis, weapon, gift. Figuring among these other terms, it also marks, it seems to me, the equivalence, therefore the indifference, that allows for serial substitution. Insisting from the very beginning on the necessity of payment in the cure, Freud also reminds us that civilized nations treat money as they do things sexual, with as much hypocrisy as inconsistency.

But there is a contradiction at work in this contempt for money. And what is more, this contradiction produces ideological denegations and hierarchical poses: the landed lord pretends to rise above the merchant, the speculator, or the usurer, who is often represented in the Christian West by the figure of the Levantine or the Jew (Shylock). These splits divide the community of philosophers: there are those who speak of money and those who pretend not to be interested in it. Concerning the great discourses that have opposed morality to the principle of the market, let us recall the Kantian distinction between two related but heterogeneous meanings, *dignity* and *price*, *Würde* and *Preis*. Dignity is an *unconditional* value. Absolute respect for it obeys an imperative law, which is, in truth, its cause, the origin of moral feeling. This law is not negotiable, it stands above the marketplace. Unlike dignity as *incalculable* worth, *price* is conditional, hypothetical, negotiable, calculable.

"In the kingdom of ends," says Kant, "everything has either a price [*Preis*] or a dignity [*Würde*]. Whatever has a price can be replaced by something else as its equivalent [*Äquivalent*]; on the other hand, whatever is above all price [*über allen Preis erhaben*] and therefore admits of no equivalent, has a dignity [*Würde*]." In other words, above all price, dignity is of the order of what is called the *priceless* [sans prix]. What is absolutely precious, the other in his or her dignity, has no price. And reciprocally: everything in the other (or in myself as other and absolute singularity) that is *absolutely precious* and worthy of respect, nonnegotiable, defines the order of dignity as end in itself. But what would this be, in the other, in the I [*le moi*] of the other or in me as other? This incalculable trait remains the most difficult to determine. Is it an "I"? Is it the most secret or the most universal element? What of singularity? Must one determine as subject, and subject of reason, that which transcends thus the price of the market? Or else, on the contrary, is the subject the very thing that, as identity that is calculable, accountable, etc., can become a commodity?

Kant continues: "Whatever has reference to general human inclina-
tions and needs has a *market price* [Marktpreis: the price of the market,
thus]; whatever, without presupposing any need, accords with a certain
taste—i.e., a delight in the mere unpurposive play of our mental powers—
has an *affective price* [Affectionspreis]; but that which constitutes the condition under which alone something can be an end in itself [*Zweck an sich
selbst*] has not merely a relative worth [*einen relativen Werth*], i.e., a price,
but has an intrinsic worth [*einen innern Werth*], i.e., a *dignity* [Würde]."

A terrifying problem is ushered in by this fundamental distinction,
which we signaled by raising the question of the subject: if the calculability of price, the market or money, threatens the notion of dignity (for example, the dignity of humanity, of rational beings, but also of any end in
itself—and the right of humanity is in Kant's eyes only the best example
of this), it is also, as *principle* of equivalence and substitution, that which
ensures the equality between all singularities, and thus the impossibility,
and even the moral prohibition, of choosing between two absolute ends,
between two singularities: two human beings, *for example*, have an equal
moral, juridical, political *dignity* whatever their differences in all other respects (social, economic, biological, sexual, psychical, or intellectual, etc.).
Between these two equivalences, these two neutralizations, these two heterogeneous indifferences, the choice is indispensable but also critical: radically threatened, most often impossible or aporetic.

It is here that *one must* negotiate the nonnegotiable. This necessity is
not an empirical last resort: In its very undecidability, it is an imperative.
It opens the space of decision and thus of responsibility (moral, juridical,
or political). And it opens this space even before any negotiation between
the imperative and the hypothetical, the unconditional and the conditional, the nonnegotiable and the negotiable. For it is the very possibility
of money, price, i.e., the principle of equivalence, that *also* allows one to
neutralize differences to arrive at pure singularity as dignity or universal
right. The access to the dignity of the other is the access to the singularity
of the other's absolute difference, certainly, but this is only possible by
means of *a certain indifference*, by means of a neutralization of differences
(social, economic, ethnic, sexual, etc.). Exceeding all knowledge and objective determination, this neutralization alone allows one an access to dignity, that is, to the fact that everyone, *every one* is worth as much as *the
other*, precisely beyond all value: *priceless*. The rejection of money or its
principle of abstract indifference, the contempt for calculation may be

complicit with the destruction of morality, of right—and for example of electoral democracy, that counts on "voices" or votes, etc.

The aporia always makes one think and decide: as much as we do money or commodity fetishism, is it not incumbent on us to analyze their contraries? Endlessly, and with the same vigilance?

2. The other problem, that of the *signature*, also touches on the time of absolute singularity. It is the problem of the growing disappearance not of money but of the monetary sign in its so-called material form. I say "in its so-called material form": one would have to analyze closely here, in effect, everything that renders the word *matter* problematic; especially when one says, and it has so happened, that I myself have used this ambiguous expression on occasion, that we are witnessing a dematerialization of the currency (credit card, computerization of exchanges, etc.). This time the problem of absolute singularity passes by way of the experience of the *signature*. In the history of the circulation of monetary signs, *l'argent* (the gold or silver coin, or the paper money that cannot be converted into gold—as was often the case after the First World War—or the paper money whose convertibility is ensured, sometimes by the state, or again as legal tender) belongs in principle to the subject as holder or *bearer* [porteur] of the currency, and as anonymous bearer, as a currency bearer who bears no name. The invention of the bill of exchange and the check still made an essential appeal to the bearer of the name who has to sign, in person, presently, here, now. Even if this signature can be delegated or imitated, delegation and imitation refer in principle, by right, and in an essential or structural way to the attestation of the bearer of the name in the act by which he commits himself, presently, to honor the engagement, the payment, the recognition of the debt, etc. Without restoring the anonymity of the bearer, the dematerialization of currency, that is, the system of coins and bank notes, appeals to a *coded* [chiffrée] signature, without proper name written by the hand of the subject; it substitutes this coded signature both for the noncoded signature and for the monetary sign, on its paper or metal support. What we call *dematerialization* does not mean the disappearance or the spiritualization of matter (moreover, one could show that there was also an ideality of currency whose medium was said to be *material*—let us leave this), but the passage from one medium to another, from the visible medium of the sort of substance that is held in one's hand or in the pocket of the *holder* [porteur]

(the metal or the paper) to an electronic medium that keeps a register that the subject does not *carry* [porte] as such, directly, on him. Although the authority [*instance*] of the name, of the present and personal attestation is preserved in a certain place of the system and remains an axiom of electronic currency (the difference being but one displacement, since somewhere one has to sign with his "own" hand to guarantee the secret and the use of the coded cipher), these phenomenal differences, these discrepancies in the phenomenality of exchanges cannot not have phenomenal effects—and let it be understood that these are enormous—on individual or social subjectivity; on the experience of subjectivity or even the experience of intersubjectivity; on everything that passes by way of the experience of the present; on the experience of the body proper, the experience of clothing, of the hand, of what one gives and receives in general. This cannot be without effect on the experience of the proper name itself, henceforth replaceable by a secret cipher, etc.

Having already taken advantage of the time I have been given, having given myself as a rule not to return or refer to the book I have just published on the gift and currency, I will content myself with recounting in the form of an elliptical epilogue, a true story. Something that recently happened to me at a train station. It made me and continues to make me think. I will tell it without commentary, but we can return to it in the discussion.

It is not a story about a bank credit card. Nor is it a question of those coded cards with which we are able to draw bills from walls after having shown one's credentials to cash distributing machines. It is about a telephone card, already partially used, but used to a degree that I could neither measure nor calculate. I had just called, using this card, from the Gare du Nord around midnight, having returned from Lille. A young English couple next to me was in front a telephone machine that took coins. The machine wasn't working, and the English couple didn't have a card. Having dialed the number for them with my card, I left it with them, and just as I was walking away, the young Englishman offered to pay me, without knowing how or how much: I made a gesture with my hand to signify no, that it was a gift and that, in any case, I didn't want any money. The whole thing lasted several seconds and I asked myself, and I think the answer is not possible for a thousand reasons that I will not go into, whether I had given something, and what, or how much, how much money, by helping them to do not just anything—but simply call someone far away by telephone. And for the same reasons, which I do not have time to develop, just as I did not have time to think at the Gare du Nord, there is no way to answer the question of knowing if there was something for which one ought to be congratulated, narcissistically, for having given, whether out of generosity or not, something, money or not. And to whom.

If we had time for a discussion, I would try to convince you that there cannot be and, what is more, that there *should not* be, an answer to satisfy these questions.

And thus one cannot, and should not, know—whether there was a gift. Into the bargain [*par-dessus le marché*].

The Right to Philosophy from a Cosmopolitan Point of View

The problem that structures the charter of our international meeting should lead us to consider, at least by way of example, two types of relation:

1. The *interinstitutional* relation between universities or research institutes on the one hand, the international institutions of culture (governmental or nongovernmental) on the other hand;

2. The special *interdisciplinary* relation among philosophy, the arts, the sciences, and the "humanities," "philosophy" naming here both a discipline that is a part of the "humanities" and the discipline that claims to think, elaborate, critique the axiomatic of the "humanities," and in particular the problem of its humanism or its alleged universalism.

The question of these two "relations" will remain in the background of the modest, preliminary reflections that I would like to propose to you today.

—I will begin with the question, "Where?"

Not directly with the questions, "Where are we?," "Where are we *at?*" but "Where does the question of the right to philosophy take place?" which immediately translates as, "Where should it take place?"

Where does it find its most appropriate place today?

The very form of this question about a question, namely, "Where, in what place can a question take place?", assumes that between the question and the place, between the question of the question and the question of the place, there is a sort of implicit contract, an assumed affinity, as if a question always had to be authorized beforehand by a place, legitimated in advance by a determined space that gave it both right and meaning, making it thus possible and necessary at the same time, both legitimate and inevitable.

According to the French idiom—and already the use of this idiom, the de facto authority of this idiom returns us to the question of the cosmopolitan, indeed the idiom alone would enjoin us to raise this question—one might say that there are places where *it is appropriate* [il y a lieu] to ask this question, that is, places where this question is rightfully [*en droit*] not only possible and authorized but necessary, or even prescribed. In such places, such a question, the question for example of the right to philosophy from a cosmopolitan point of view, can and must take place.

For example: UNESCO may in fact be this privileged place—I say this without convention and not at all out politeness for our hosts—perhaps the only possible place in which to truly deploy the question that brings us together today and whose authority carries, in some sense, within its very form, the seal of this institution, receiving from it, in principle, both its response and its responsibility. As if, in a word, UNESCO and, within UNESCO in a way that was privileged, its department of philosophy, were, if I can say this, the singular *emanation* of something like *philosophy* as "a right to philosophy from a cosmopolitan point of view," an emanation that was singular because it was circular, as if a source, and an emanation always comes from a source, were returning to the source. UNESCO perhaps arose from the position of a right to philosophy from a cosmopolitan point of view. It would be up to UNESCO exclusively [*en propre*] to answer for this right by responding to this question. UNESCO would bear both the response and the responsibility for this question.

Why? Why would UNESCO—in its specific purpose, in the mission it assigned itself—be the institution par excellence today whose vocation it was to ask this question, to do justice [*faire droit*] to this question in turn, to elaborate it and draw practical instruction from this elaboration?

My title makes a transparent allusion to the famous title of a great little text of Kant, the *Idee zu einer allgemeinen Geschichte in weltbürgerlicher Absicht* (1784), *Idea* [in view of] *a Universal History with a Cosmopolitan Purpose*. As we know, this brief and difficult text belongs to the writings of

Kant about which one can say that they *announce,* that is, both predict, prefigure, and prescribe a certain number of international institutions that have only come into existence in this century and for the most part after the Second World War. These institutions, like the idea of international law that they try to implement, are already *philosophemes.* They are philosophical acts and archives, philosophical productions and products, not only because the concepts that legitimate them have an ascribable *philosophical history* and thus a philosophical history that finds itself inscribed in the charter or the constitution of UNESCO; rather because, at the same time, and for this reason, such institutions imply the sharing of a culture and a philosophical language, committing themselves consequently to making possible, by means of education: first of all, the access to this language and to this culture. All of the states that adhere to the charters of these international institutions have committed themselves in principle, *philosophically,* to recognizing and to implementing in a way that is effective, something like philosophy and a certain philosophy of right, of the rights of man, of universal history, etc. To sign these charters is a philosophical act that engages one philosophically with philosophy. From this moment, whether they say it or not, know it or not, conduct themselves accordingly, these states and these peoples, by their adherence to these charters or by their participation in these institutions, make a philosophical commitment, and at the very least, thus, a commitment to maintain the culture or the philosophical education that is indispensable to the understanding and implementation of these commitments to these international institutions, which are, I will repeat, philosophical in essence (something that, let it be said in passing, some may interpret as an infinite opening, others as a limit to universality itself, if we consider for example that a certain concept of philosophy and even of philosophical cosmopolitanism, and even international law, is too European a thing—but this is a problem that will no doubt return in the course of our discussions).

What are the concrete stakes of this situation today? Why must the important questions concerning philosophical teaching and research, why must the imperative of the right to philosophy be deployed in their international dimension today more than ever? Why are the responsibilities that need to be taken no longer, and even less so today in the twenty-first century, simply national? What do "national," "cosmopolitan," "universal" mean here for, and with regard to, philosophy, philosophical research, philosophical education or training, or even for a philosophical question or practice that would not be essentially linked to research or education?

A philosopher is always someone for whom philosophy is not *a given,* someone who in essence must question the essence and the purpose of philosophy. And reinvent it. We must recall this fact even if it seems trivial or much too obvious; for what we have here are a situation and a duty that are more singular than it might appear, and this can lead to redoubtable practical consequences. The existence of places such as UNESCO, that is to say, international institutions that not only involve a philosophy, indeed the philosophy that is in the discourse and I would even say in the language of their charter, but have found it necessary to provide themselves with a department specialized in philosophy (something that is not at all obvious and recalls the whole debate opened by Kant's *Conflict of the Faculties*: why would an essentially philosophical institution need a philosophy department? Schelling thought, unlike Kant, that because the university was but a big philosophical institution through and through, because philosophy would therefore be everywhere present in it, there was no need [*il n'y avait pas lieu*] to contain it in a department). The existence, thus, of a properly philosophical place like UNESCO, the fact that UNESCO's mode of being is a mode of being that is a priori philosophical, this constitutes, it seems to me, an axiomatic of sorts, a system of values, norms, regulating principles in virtue of which, certainly, we are here, but which also prescribes that any philosopher question such a situation in concrete terms and not take it as an established fact, obvious, and without serious consequence.

Before drawing a few preliminary and less abstract consequences from these first axioms, let me remind you that Kant's text, even if it announces and prescribes a "universal cosmopolitan state" (state, *Zustand,* in the sense of the state of affairs, the situation, the real constitution, not in the sense of State with a capital *S*), even if Kant describes the hope (*Hoffnung*) at least, the hope that after many revolutions and transformations, "at last [*endlich*]" this cosmopolitanism will become a fact, even if Kant founds this hope (which remains a hope) on "the highest purpose of nature [*was die Natur zur höchsten Absicht hat*]," this hope is anything but the expression of a confident optimism or that of an abstract universalism. By briefly underlining a few of the *limitations* that give the Kantian discourse its form, its form that is the most positive, the most modern, the most pedagogically rich but also the most problematic, by insisting rather on the *difficulties,* I would like to give an introduction to the presentations and to the discussion that will follow, introduce and not, obviously, anticipate them, precede them, even less foresee or program them.

What are these difficulties? What do they prefigure of the tasks and the problems of our time? But also what do they not prefigure? And what in our times could, indeed, should exceed a discourse such as Kant's?

The Idea (in the Kantian sense) that brings us together here in the consciousness that the definition of a philosophical task and a right to philosophy must be posed in its cosmopolitan, thus international or inter-state dimension (and this is already a serious question, namely whether the cosmopolitan creates a link [*trace un trait d'union*] between cities, the *poleis* of the world as nations, as peoples, or as states), this Idea presupposes, Kant says it himself, a philosophical approach to universal history that is inseparable from a kind of plan of nature that aims for a total, perfect political unification of the human species (*die vollkommene bürgerliche Vereinigung in der Menschengattung*). Anyone who doubts such a unification and above all nature's plan would have no reason whatsoever to subscribe even to the sharing of a philosophical problem, an allegedly universal or universalizable problem of philosophy. For whoever questions this plan of nature, the entire project of writing a universal—thus philosophical—history, as well as that of creating institutions ruled by international—and thus philosophical—law, would be nothing but a fiction.

"*Roman* [novel]" is Kant's word. Kant remains so conscious of the risk that, on several occasions, he finds it necessary to discuss this hypothesis or this accusation, and to do this he must reaffirm that this philosophical idea, as extravagant as it might appear, is neither a fiction nor a fanciful history. Philosophy, in the body in formation of its institution, is above all not literature, he insists, nor more generally a fiction, in any case not a fiction of the imaginary. But the threat of literature, of the becoming-literature of philosophy is so pressing and so present to Kant that he names it and challenges it on several occasions. But to do this, he must both invoke the guiding thread of nature's design (the guiding thread, that is, a convenient instrument for representation [*Darstellung*], which is not the surest way of escaping the novelistic); and, on the other hand, he must take as his surest guiding thread, to follow this guiding thread, the history of European nations, first in its

Greek, then its Roman beginnings, as opposed to the so-called barbarian nations. Which makes this text whose spirit is cosmopolitan—according to a law that could be verified well beyond Kant—the most Eurocentric text there is, not only in its philosophical axiomatic, certainly, but in its retrospective reference to Greco-Roman history as well as in its prospective reference to the future hegemony of Europe, which, Kant says, "will probably legislate eventually to all other continents."

Because this difficult and crucial question of the European, indeed continental, model will keep coming up—as I suppose (and in truth I hope)—in the debate that awaits us, I would like to evoke several lines of Kant. They show that the only way of opposing philosophical reason to the novel or to an extravagant fiction is, at least in the eyes of Kant, to rely on the European history of reason and beginning with the Greco-Roman history of history. In his seventh proposition, Kant recalls that nature will have naturally and paradoxically used the natural unsociability of men (and here Kant is pessimistic in that he believes in this natural unsociability of man and in the natural or originary state of war between men) to drive them to contract artificial and institutional bonds and to enter into a Society of Nations:

Nature has thus again employed the unsociableness [*Ungeselligkeit, Unvertragsamkeit*] of men, and even the unsociableness of the large societies and political bodies that human beings construct, as a means of arriving at a state of calm and security through their inevitable antagonism. Wars, tense and unremitting preparation for war, and the resultant distress that every State must eventually feel within itself, even in times of peace—these are the means by which nature drives States to make initially imperfect attempts, but finally, after many devastations, upheavals, and even complete inner exhaustion of their powers, to take the step which reason could have suggested to them even without so many sad experiences—that of abandoning the lawless state of savagery and entering into a Society of Nations in which every State, even the smallest, could expect to derive its security and rights not from its own power or its own legal judgment, but solely from this great Society of Nations [of peoples: *Völkerbunde*] (*foedus amphictyonum*), from a united power and the law-governed decisions of the united will. However wild and fanciful [or more precisely, exalted, enthusiastic, *schwärmerisch*] this idea may appear—and it has been ridiculed as such when put forth by the Abbé St. Pierre or Rousseau (perhaps because they thought that its realization was so imminent)—it is nonetheless the inevitable outcome of the distress in which men involve one another. For this distress must force the States to make exactly the same decision.[1]

The logic of this teleology is that we must be grateful to nature—Kant says this literally—for having made us naturally, originally so unsociable and so unphilosophical that we are driven by culture, art and artifice (*Kunst*), as well as by reason, to bring to fruition the seeds of nature.

What seems like a fanciful history and is not one, what is in truth but the historicity of history, is this ruse of nature. Nature makes use of our primitive, thus natural, violence and unsociability to help reason and thus to bring philosophy into practice through a society of nations. However, and this is where today's debates may discover a paradoxical provocation, in this teleological ruse of nature, Greco-Roman Europe, Western—I would even dare say *continental*—philosophy and history play a driving, capital, exemplary role, as if nature, in its rational ruse, had charged Europe with this special mission: not only of founding history as such, and first as science, not only of founding philosophy as such, and first as science, but also of founding a rational (non-fanciful) philosophical history and of "legislat[ing] eventually" to all the other continents.

In his ninth proposition Kant recognizes for the second time that the philosophical attempt to treat universal history in function of a hidden design of nature and in view of a total political unification of humanity resembles a novel (and here he calls the novel by its name, *Roman*). But to contradict this novelistic hypothesis and to think human history beyond the novel as a system and not a plan-less aggregate without program, without providence, he refers to what he calls the *guiding thread* (Leitfaden) *of Greek history* (griechische Geschichte), "that in which all other earlier or contemporary histories are preserved or at least authenticated."

In other words, historicity and Greek historiographicity would be the sign, the indication, and thus the guiding thread that would allow us to think that a history is possible, a history that would bring together everything that touches on the universality of the human race. This Greek history (both in the sense of *Geschichte* and of *Historie,* of history in the sense of the event and in the sense of the narrative, of the documented relation, of historical science), one can follow its influence, says Kant, on the formation and decline of the political body of the Roman people as it "absorbed" the Greek *polis* and then set up the *cosmopolis* by influencing or colonizing the Barbarians who in turn destroyed Rome.

And Kant adds:

[A]nd if we finally add the political history of other peoples *episodically* [episodisch], insofar as knowledge of them has gradually come down to us from these enlightened nations, we shall discover a regular process of improvement in the political constitution of our continent [*in unserem Welttheile*] (which will probably legislate eventually to all others continents [*der wahrscheinlicher Weise allen anderen dereinst Gesetze geben wird*]).

The teleological axis of this discourse has become the tradition of European modernity. We find it intact, unchanged through variations as important as those that distinguish Hegel, Husserl, Heidegger, Valéry. We also find it, in its practical state, and at times through denial, in many European or global political-institutional discourses. Yet this Eurocentric discourse forces us to ask ourselves—and I will use a schematic word for it here in order not to go on too long—whether our reflection today on the limitless extension and the reaffirmation of a right to philosophy must not both *take into account and delimit* the assigning of philosophy to its origin or to its Greco-Roman memory. We cannot content ourselves with reaffirming a certain history, a certain memory of the origins or the Western history of philosophy (Mediterranean or central-European, Greco-Roman-Arab or Germanic), nor can we be content with opposing or opposing denial to this memory and to these languages; rather we must try to displace the fundamental schema of this problematic by carrying ourselves beyond the old, tiresome, wearing, wearying opposition between Eurocentrism and anti-Eurocentrism.

One of the conditions needed to reach this—and we will not reach it all at once; it will be the result of a long and slow historical labor that is in progress—is the active coming to consciousness of the fact that philosophy is no more determined by a program, an originary language or tongue [*langue*], the memory of which it would be enough to regain to discover its purpose, no more assigned at its origin or by its origin, thus, than it is simply, spontaneously, abstractly cosmopolitan or universal. More and more, we have the experience of modes of appropriation and transformation of the philosophical, in non-European languages and cultures, which return neither to the classical mode of appropriation— that consists in making one's own what belongs to the other (here to internalize the Western memory of philosophy and to assimilate it to one's own language)—nor to the invention of new modes of thought that, outside all appropriation, would no longer have any relation whatsoever to what we think we recognize under the name of philosophy.

What is happening today, and has been for some time, I think, are philosophical formations that will not let themselves be contained in this dialectic, which is basically cultural, colonial or neo-colonial, of appropriation and alienation. There are other ways [*voies*] of philosophy than those of appropriation as expropriation (losing one's memory by assimilating the memory of the other, the one opposing the other, as if an *ex-appropriation* were not possible, the only chance possible).

Not only are there other ways of philosophy, but philosophy, if there is such a thing, is the other way [*l'autre voie*].

And philosophy has always been the other way: philosophy has never been the responsible deployment of a single and originary assignation bound to a single language or to the place of only one people. Philosophy does not have just one memory. Under its Greek name and in its European memory, it has always been bastard, hybrid, grafted, multilinear, polyglot, and we must adjust our practice of the history of philosophy, of history and of philosophy, to this reality which was also a chance and which remains more than ever a chance. What I am saying here of philosophy can also be said, and for the same reasons, of right and democracy.

In philosophy as elsewhere, Eurocentrism *and* anti-Eurocentrism are symptoms of a missionary and colonial culture. A concept of cosmopolitanism still determined by this opposition would not only concretely limit the development of the right to philosophy but could not even give an account of what is happening in philosophy. To reflect in the direction of what is happening and can still happen under the name of philosophy (and this name is both very grave and altogether unimportant, depending on what one does with it), we must reflect on what could be the concrete conditions for respect and the extension of the right to philosophy.

1. *First title.* Whoever thinks that the right to philosophy from a cosmopolitan point of view must be respected, granted, extended will have to take into account the competition that exists and has always existed between several models, styles, philosophical traditions, linked to national or linguistic histories, even if they can never be reduced to effects of nationhood or language. To take the most canonical example, which is far from being the only example and which itself contains many subvarieties: the opposition between the tradition of what is called *continental* philosophy and what is called *analytic* or *Anglo-Saxon* philosophy can be reduced neither to national boundaries nor to linguistic givens. This is not only a

huge problem and an enigma for European or Anglo-American philoso-phers who have been trained in these traditions. A certain history, namely, but not only, a colonial history, has turned these two models into hege-monic references throughout the world. The right to philosophy not only passes through an appropriation of these two competing models and, ul-timately, of any model by all people [*par tous et par toutes*] (and when I say *toutes* it is not to be formally prudent as to grammatical categories; I will return to this in a moment), the right of all people also passes through re-flection, through the displacement and deconstitution of these hege-monies, through the access to places and philosophical events that are not exhausted either by these two dominant traditions or by these languages. These stakes are already intra-European.[2]

2. *Second Title.* The respect and extension of the right to philosophy to all people also presupposes—again I am saying this too quickly—the appropriation but also the overflowing of what are said to be, according to the schema that I challenged earlier, the founding or originary languages of philosophy—the Greek, Latin, Germanic, or Arabic languages. One must practice philosophy along paths that are not simply anamnesic, in languages that have no relation of filiation to these roots. If the extension (which is most often hegemonic) of such-and-such a language and in a way that is nearly all-powerful, I mean English, can serve as a vehicle for the universal penetration of the philosophical and of philosophical com-munication, philosophy at the same time requires, and for this very rea-son, that one free oneself of the phenomena of dogmatism and authority that the language may produce. It is not a matter of removing philosophy from language and from that which forever attaches it to the idiom; it is not a matter of promulgating an abstractly universal philosophical think-ing without inherence to the body of the idiom; but *on the contrary* of im-plementing it in a way that is original every time in a non-finite multi-plicity of idioms that produce philosophical events that are neither particularist and untranslatable nor abstractly transparent and univocal in the realm of some abstract universality. With only one language, one al-ways has a philosophy, an axiomatic of philosophical discourse and com-munication, that imposes itself without possible discussion. I would say something analogous, or in any case something that falls within the same logic, for science and technology. It is obvious that the development of sci-ence and technology (whether it be theoretical physics, astrophysics, or ge-

netics, computer technology or medicine, whether it be in the service of economics or of military strategy) is, for better and for worse, the opening of a cosmopolitan communication; as such, it clears the way, by the indirect means of scientific research but also of the epistemology or the history of science, to what in philosophy has always been in solidarity, will have been in solidarity, according to different modes, with the movement of science. The hypothesis or wish that I would be tempted to submit for discussion is the following: while taking account, or charge, of this progress of science, in the spirit of a new age of enlightenment for this new millennium (and in this regard I am still Kantian), a politics of the right to philosophy for all people should be, not only a politics of science and technology, but also a politics of *thought* that does not yield either to positivism or to scientism or to epistemologism and rediscovers, on the basis of new stakes, in its relation to science but also to religion, also to law and ethics, an experience that is an experience of provocation or reciprocal respect but also of *irreducible autonomy.* In this regard, the problems are always traditional and always new, be it a matter of ecology, of bioethics, of artificial insemination, of organ transplant, of international law, etc. They all touch on the concept of properness [*du propre*], of property, of the relation to self and other in the values of subject and object, of subjectivity, of identity, of personhood, that is, on all the fundamental concepts of the charters that govern international relations and institutions, like international law, which is supposed to regulate them in principle.

Taking into account what links science to technology, to economics, to political-economic or political-military interests, the autonomy of philosophy with regard to science is as essential to the exercise of a right to philosophy as autonomy with regard to religions is essential for whoever wants access to philosophy not to be forbidden to anyone. I am alluding here to what in every cultural, linguistic, national, or religious domain may limit the right to philosophy for social, political, or religious reasons, because one belongs to a class, an age, a sex—or all of these things together.

I will take the risk here of asserting that—beyond what would tie philosophy to its Greco-Roman memory, or to European languages, beyond even what would link it to an already established Western model of what in Greek is called *democracy*—it seems impossible to me to dissociate the notion of the right to philosophy "from a cosmopolitan point of view," from the notion of a *democracy to come.* Without binding the concept of democracy to its past givens and even less to the events that have been classified under this name, and that preserve within them the trace of the hegemonies that I evoked earlier more or less directly, I do not think that the right to philosophy (a right for which an international institution such as this one must demand respect, and whose actualization [*effectivité*] it must extend) can be dissociated from an actual movement of democratization.

You can well imagine that what I am saying here is anything but an abstract wish and a conventional concession to some democratic consensus. The stakes have never been higher in the world today, and they are new stakes, calling for a new philosophical reflection on what democracy, and I insist on this, the *democracy to come,* might mean and be. Because I do not want this introduction to be too long, I will save what more I have to say on this subject for the discussion.

3. *Third title.* Although philosophy does not simply amount to its institutional or pedagogical moments, nonetheless the many differences of tradition, style, language, and philosophical nationality are translated or embodied in the institutional or pedagogical models, at times even produced by these structures (school, collège [middle school], lycée [high school], university, research institutions). Here are the places for debate, competition, war, or communication that we will discuss later; to conclude on this subject, however, I would like to turn one last time to Kant to situate what today may constitute the limit or crisis that is most common to all societies, whether Western or not, when they seek to implement a right to philosophy. Beyond the political or religious motivations, beyond what appear to be the philosophical motivations that compel one to limit the right to philosophy, or even to prohibit philosophy (to a social class, to women, to adolescents before a certain age, etc., to specialists of such a discipline or to the members of such a group), beyond even all the motivations of discrimination in this regard, philosophy suffers everywhere, in Europe and elsewhere, in its teaching and in its research, because of a limit that, although it does not always take the explicit form of an interdiction or censorship, amounts to much the same; philosophy suffers everywhere simply because the funds allotted for the support of philosophical teaching and research are limited. This limitation is motivated— I am not saying justified—as much in societies of the liberal capitalist sort, socialist or social-democratic societies, not to speak of authoritarian or totalitarian regimes, by budgetary concerns that give priority to research and

training that is said to be (and often rightly so) useful, profitable, urgent; to applied science, to techno-economic, or even scientific-military, imperatives. For me, it is not at all a matter of contesting all of these imperatives indiscriminately. But the more these imperatives impose themselves and sometimes for the best reasons in the world, and sometimes in view of developments without which the development of philosophy itself would not have a chance in the world, the more the right to philosophy becomes urgent, irreducible, as does the call to philosophy precisely to think and discern, evaluate, critique the philosophies, for they, too, are philosophies that, in the name of a techno-economic-military positivism, even "pragmatism" or "realism," tend to reduce, according to different modalities, the field and the chances of a philosophy that is open and without limit in its teaching and its research, in the actualizing [*effectivité*] of its international exchanges.

This is why—and I have finished for the moment—although I believed it necessary to mark some reservation with regard to the Kantian concept of the *cosmopolis* (that is both too naturalistic and too teleological-European), I will cite Kant again in conclusion. I will quote what he exemplarily calls an *example*. His short treatise on the *Idea for a Universal History with a Cosmopolitan Purpose* is obviously also, and it could not have been otherwise, a treatise on education. And in his eighth proposition, after having announced and greeted "the age of Enlightenment" and the "universal freedom of religion," Kant writes the following, which we must still reflect on today, almost without transposition.

If I had to give a title to this passage, it might be something like "Concerning Philosophy—the debt and the duty."

[T]his Enlightenment, and with it a certain sympathetic interest which the enlightened man invariably feels for anything good which he comprehends, must gradually ascend upwards towards the thrones and even influence their principles of government. But while, for example, the world's present rulers have no money to spare for public educational institutions or indeed for anything which concerns the world's best interests [*das Weltbeste*] (for everything has already been calculated out in advance for the next war), they will nonetheless find that it is to their own advantage at least not to hinder their citizens' private efforts in this direction, however weak and slow they may be. But eventually, war itself gradually becomes not only a highly artificial undertaking, extremely uncertain in its outcome for both sides, but also a very dubious risk to take, since its aftermath is felt by the State in the shape of a constantly increasing national debt (a modern invention [*Schuldenlast einer neuen Erfindung*]) whose repayment [repayment is *Tilgung*, cancellation, erasure of the debt, destruction, which Hegel distinguishes from *Aufhebung,* from the *subsumption* that erases while preserving] becomes interminable. And in addition, the effects which an upheaval in any State produces upon all the others in our continent, where all are so closely linked by trade, are so perceptible that these other States are forced by their own insecurity to offer themselves as arbiters, albeit without legal authority, so that they indirectly prepare the way for a great political body of the future, without precedent in the past. [This parenthesis not only raises the important question of the debt in its geopolitical determinants today for the future of the world, it opens the way to a reading that is less, let us say teleologist of Kant than the one I sketched out earlier.] Although this political body exists for the present only in the roughest of outlines, it nonetheless seems as if a feeling is beginning to stir in all its members each of which has an interest in maintaining the whole [*Erhaltung des Ganzen*]. And this encourages the hope that, after many revolutions, with all their transforming effects, the highest purpose of nature, *a universal cosmopolitan State, will at last be realized* as the matrix within which all the original capacities of the human race may develop.[3]

Perhaps the right to philosophy passes henceforth through a distinction between several regimes of the debt, between a finite debt and an infinite debt, an internal debt and an "external" debt, between debt and duty, a certain erasure and a certain reaffirmation of the debt—and sometimes a certain erasure in the name of reaffirmation.

As If It Were Possible, "Within Such Limits" . . .

In spite of the delay of what begins here, this will not, as one might suspect, be about the last word. A reader should certainly not expect any last word. It is excluded, all but impossible that I, for one, should dare to lay claim to a last word. Indeed, it would be necessary, another protocol of the contract, *not to* lay claim to a last word or to expect one.

Perhaps, the Impossible (Aphoristic I)

I no longer know how the declaration I have just ventured in very ordinary language can be read. Is it a sign of modesty or an expression of presumptuousness? "Does he mean, modestly, and perhaps with affected timidity, that he will be unable to propose, by way of an answer, anything at all that is certain and definitive, not even the least *last word*?" a reader might query. "Would he be so arrogant as to suggest that he still has so many answers in reserve that, instead of a *last word* and in place of a last word, is simply a *foreword*?" another might add. "But then, how does one interpret the possibility of these two interpretations of the *last word*?" a third might sigh. Then the fourth, sententiously: "Have you read Austin on "*the crux of the Last Word*" about ordinary language, in "A Plea for Excuses"? Or three times Blanchot,[1] in "Le dernier mot," "Le tout dernier mot," "Le dernier mot," about a certain *il y a* that resembles Levinas's *il y a* and that absolutely cannot be translated without remainder into irreducible ordinary language? Especially not as *there is* or *es gibt*?

Dare I add my voice to this concert of hypotheses and virtual utterances? I would perhaps, then, orient things otherwise. For example, toward an irreducible modality of the "perhaps." Which would cause the authority [*instance*] of the "*last word*" to tremble. Have I not tried elsewhere to analyze both the possibility and the necessity of this "perhaps"?[2] Its promise and its fatality, its implication in every experience, at the approach of *that* which arrives [ce *qui vient*], of (that, the other) *who* arrives [qui *vient*] from the future and gives place to what is called an *event*? But this experience of the "perhaps" would be that of the possible *and* the impossible *at the same time*, of the possible *as* impossible. If only what is already possible arrives, what can be thus anticipated and expected, it does not make an event. An event is only possible when it comes from the impossible. It arrives *as* the coming of the impossible, where a "perhaps" deprives us of all assurance and leaves the future to the future. This "perhaps" is necessarily allied to a "yes": yes, yes to whatever (whoever) arrives [(*ce*) *qui vient*]. This "yes" would be common to the affirmation and the response; it would even come before any question. A *peut-être* like "*perhaps*" (*it may happen*, rather than the insubstantial *vielleicht*, rather than the call to being or the ontological insinuation, the *to be or not to be* of a *maybe*) is perhaps that which, exposed to an event like the "yes," that is, to the experience of what arrives (*happens*) and of *who* then arrives, far from interrupting the question, allows it to breathe. How is one not to forsake the question, its urgency or its interminable necessity, without also turning the question, or still more the response, into a "last word"? This lies close to my heart and to my thinking, but it is perhaps no longer a question or a response. Perhaps something else entirely, we will get to this. The "perhaps" keeps the question alive, and perhaps ensures its sur-vival [*sur-vie*]. What does "perhaps" mean, then, at the disarticulated juncture of the possible and the impossible? Of the possible *as* impossible?

Of Ordinary Language: Excuses (Aphoristic II)

It has taken me too long to respond to the studies that we have read, as the authors are well aware. Is this forgivable?

And yet I ask forgiveness for it. Sincerely. Not without committing myself once again, however, to respond. Thus I promise to *do* something that is called *responding* and to *do* it as it is believed a response should always be done: by *speaking*. Not by joining the gesture to the speech, as one says in ordinary language, but by *doing* something *with words*, according to Austin's formulation. Why mention here the well-known inventor of a now familiar distinction? Although the pair of concepts performative/constative may have a relatively recent origin, it has become canonical. In spite of its author's bemused insistence on following only the model of "ordinary language," this pair will have changed a great many things in the less-ordinary language of philosophy and theory in this century. But—first paradox—this is a distinction in whose purity Austin himself often said he did not believe.[3] He even declared it at the moment of giving a talk (irrefutable in my eyes) on ordinary language and, precisely, as in my case, on the subject of excuses and forgiveness: "Certainly, then, ordinary language is *not* the last word [an expression he had used a little earlier, not without irony, but as a quotation from ordinary language, in capital letters: "Then, for the Last Word"]; in principle it can everywhere be supplemented and improved upon and superseded. Only remember, it [ordinary language] *is* the *first* word."[4]

At this point, at this allusion to the "*first* word," Austin adds a footnote. We recognize the singularity and effectiveness of his philosophical style: "And forget, for once and for a while, that other curious question 'Is it true?' May we?" I thought, for a moment, as a manner of excuse and by way of a response to all the magnificent texts I have read here, of proposing a sort of interpretation or *close reading* of "A Plea for Excuses."

I will not do this. But "for once and for a while": what prudence! what cunning! what wisdom! "For a while," this means "for the moment," a rather brief moment, and sometimes "for a rather long time," or even "for a very long time," perhaps forever, but not necessarily once and for all. For how much time, then? Perhaps the time of a talk or an article, for example of an article on excuses or forgiveness, "A Plea for Excuses." Without asking forgiveness and without making excuses, at least without doing it explicitly but nonetheless without forgetting to apologize for it, Austin begins his article by announcing with irony that he is not going to treat his subject. He is not going to answer the question, and what he is going to say will not correspond to the subject as previously announced: *excuses*. He may perhaps *respond* to his readers and his listeners, since he is addressing them, but perhaps without answering the question, their questions, or to their expectations. The first sentence:

"The subject of this paper, *Excuses*, is one not to be treated, but only to be introduced, within such limits." He excuses himself, thus, for not taking the excuse seriously and for remaining, or leaving his audience, ignorant on the subject of what it means *to excuse oneself*. And this at the moment when (performative contradiction?) he begins by excusing himself—by pretending to do it, rather, by excusing himself for not treating the subject of the excuse. Will he have treated it? Perhaps. It is for the reader to judge, for the addressee to decide. It is like a postcard whose virtual addressee will have to decide whether or not he will receive it and whether it is indeed to him that the card is addressed. The signature is left to the initiative, to the responsibility, to the discretion of the other. To work itself [*au travail*]. One will sign, if one signs, at the moment of the arrival at destination, not at the origin. (As for the hypothesis according to which Austin might have let himself be caught in a "performative contradiction," he too, already he, the one without whom we would not even be able to formulate such a suspicion, let us smile at this hypothesis along with the specter of Austin. As if it were possible to escape from every performative contradiction! As if it were possible to exclude the notion that Austin may have played at illustrating this inevitable trap!)

Would a great philosopher of tradition have dared to do this? Can one imagine Kant or Hegel admitting that he will not treat the proposed subject? Can one see them, for example excusing themselves for not doing justice to the excuse, to the subject, or to the proposed title, "A Plea for Excuses," "within such limits"?

"A Plea for Excuses" may always (perhaps) have been but the title naming this one singular gesture of Austin, that day, or the scene, in a word, that he, and no other, created, when he asked to be excused for not treating the subject. A title is always a name. Here, the referent of this name is what Austin does (he apologizes) and not what he is talking about, since he excuses himself for not talking about it. All he did, perhaps, was to introduce the subject by giving an example, his own, here and now: namely, that he excuses himself for not treating the subject. But as soon as he makes this introduction, he knows what he should be talking about, and he has thus already begun to talk about it, even as he says he is incapable of doing it "within such limits." I would very much like to take him as a model, that is to say, as an example, or as a pretext—or as an excuse. Let us remember Rousseau, who, in the famous episode of the stolen ribbon in his *Confessions* (Book II), says: "*Je m'excusai sur le premier objet qui s'offrit* [I took the first thing that offered itself for my excuse]."

To Respond—Analogies (Aphoristic III)

Moreover, if one responded without failing the other, if one responded precisely, fully, adequately, if one adjusted the response perfectly to fit the question, the demand or the expectation, would one still be responding? Would anything happen? Would an event arrive? Or only the accomplishment of a program, a calculable operation? To be worthy of this name, must a *response* not *surprise* us by some irruptive novelty? And thus by an anachronistic dis-adjustment? Must it not respond "beside the question [*à côté de la question*]," in short? *Precisely and right* [justement et juste] beside the question? Not just anywhere, or anyhow, or anything, but *right and just* [juste et justement] beside the question—but at the very moment that the response does everything to address the other, truly, to the expectation of the other, in conditions that have been consensually defined (contract, rules, norms, concepts, language, code, etc.) with the utmost *directness* [droiture]? These two conditions of the response are incompatible, yet equally incontestable, it seems to me. This is, perhaps, the impasse in which I find myself paralyzed. This is the aporia in which I have placed myself. I find myself placed here, in truth, even before installing myself here.

Were I able to discuss my subject and respond to so many virtual questions, I would perhaps be tempted to *retranslate*, at great risk, all the problematics that have been so powerfully elaborated as the essays that precede me here. I would be tempted to *reformulate* them as the question of ordinary language. To take just two examples, in the direction of the fine analyses of John Sallis and Karel Thein, who help us to rethink— differently but with equal force and necessity—our philosophical memory, where it is indebted to the Greek idiom: where is the border within a so-called natural language, one that is thus not totally formalizable, between ordinary usage and philosophical usage? How do we constitute it, for example, when words like *pharmakon* (poison and/or remedy, sometimes undecidably) or *khora* (ordinary place, locality, village, etc.) are used in everyday life in Greece, but also in Plato's works, versus the unique *khora* of the *Timaeus*, which, in spite of its many appearances, no longer bears any relation, even by analogy, to the other. (The question of *analogy* awaits us precisely in the place where Thein speaks of the "limits of analogy"; I will have to return to this, because it will undoubtedly govern all of my remarks; it will provide me with the most general form of my address to the authors of the articles collected here.) In a word, which will not be the last: how—according to what economy, what transaction—does one treat analogy? The analogy (1) between relations of analogy, and (2) between relations of heterology, between the maintenance and the breakdown of an analogy? Is the first analogy possible or impossible, legitimate or abusive? How does one explain that the relation (*logos*) of analogy is named by one of the terms of the relation of proportionality, for example, between *logos* and soul, *pharmakon* and body? This question has been remarkably elaborated by Thein. It will run through this whole discussion, more or less visibly. An analogous question seems to impose itself on the subject of the different uses of the word *khora*, in daily life and in philosophical discourse but also in philosophical contexts (for example, the *Republic* and the *Timaeus*) that are both common and heterogeneous. There seem to be relations of articulable analogy *and* of irreducible dissociation—aphoristic or diaphoristic, one might say— between these contexts; they remain radically untranslatable into one another, at least if one holds to the stability of what is called here a *discursive* context. In particular, in certain passages that have been discovered and rigorously analyzed by Sallis, where the word "khora" seems to have a different meaning from the one it has in the *Timaeus* (without relation to the Good and the *epekeina tes ousias*) but designates, rather, the place of the sun itself, "*where the good and the khora are brought into a very remarkable proximity.*"

And here already, caught in the ordinary language of several natural languages, lies the syntax of a first question, of a first problem. It is the supplementary problem a priori of a complement. The complement of a word that, in our language, is a verb: *to respond*, yes, it should be done, here now. Yes, one could attempt it, be tempted to attempt it, certainly, but to respond [*répondre*] to *whom* [à qui]? *before whom* [devant qui]? to answer [*répondre*] *for what* [de quoi]? *and what* [et quoi]? As for "responding," for the grammar of the verb and the pragmatism of the act, we must acknowledge *four complements and four syntaxes.*

1. Thus, the first response that is perhaps possible on the subject of response, beginning with the *first two complements* (*to whom? before whom?*): to respond *to* whoever, then, and *before* whoever has at least *read*—this is the first condition—*read*, and, of course, understood, analyzed, or even written the texts that precede my own here—that is to say a number of earlier works that they themselves discuss, for example, and please excuse the few, those of the great canonical tradition, from Plato and Aristotle to Kant, Hegel, Husserl, or Heidegger, etc., in their relation to science, but also the works that inherit from these today more or less legitimately and in a minor key, including my own, hypothetically: all of us here are bound by the contract that the director of the *Revue Internationale de Philosophie* proposed to us. Any reader is supposed to accept such a contract, as have those whose names appear in the table of contents.

2. The second response that is perhaps possible on the subject of the response, the one I believe I must choose in any case, this time concerning the *last two complements* (*for what* and *what?*): not to answer *for* what I have written (could I answer for it in any responsible way? do others not discuss it more clearly than I?) but perhaps to respond (and here is the *what*) by saying a few words, *within such limits*, about the questions, the difficulties, the aporias, the impasses—I no longer dare say "problems"—in the midst of which I am presently struggling and which will no doubt continue to occupy me for some time. I will borrow (to beg forgiveness or to present my apologies) one of the economic formulas of this predicament from a seminar I am currently giving on forgiveness, excuse, and perjury. Here it is, bare and very simple in appearance: one only forgives the unforgivable. By only forgiving what is already forgivable, one forgives nothing. Consequently, forgiveness is only *possible, as such,* where, faced with the unforgivable, it seems thus *impossible.* As I attempt to show elsewhere more concretely, in a manner that is less formal but more consequential, this enjoins us to think the *possible* (the *possibility* of forgiveness, but also of the gift, of hospitality—and the list is not contained, by definition; it is that of all the *unconditionals*) *as the impossible itself.* If the *possible "is"* the impossible here, if, as I have so often ventured to say along different lines but in a way that is thus relatively formalizable, the "condition of possibility" is a "condition of impossibility," how then must we rethink the thinking of the possible, the thinking that

comes to us from the depths of our tradition (Aristotle, Leibniz, Kant, Bergson, etc., as well as Heidegger, whose use of the words *mögen* and *Vermögen*, notably in *The Letter on Humanism*,[5] would call for a separate discussion here, etc.)?

How are we to understand or hear the word *possible*? How are we to read what affects it with negation around the verb "to be" such that the three words of this proposition "the possible '*is*' the impossible" are no longer associated by a simple word game, a playful paradox or dialectical facility? But how are we to understand that these words undermine, in a serious and necessary way, the very propositionality of this proposition of the *S is P* type (*the possible "is" the impossible*)? Furthermore, is this a *question* or a *problem*? And what kind of complicity is there between this thinking of the impossible possible and the instance of the "perhaps" that I was discussing earlier? Since it seems I have already put forward the distinction between "who" and "what" (respond to *whom*? before *whom*? but also for *what*? and *what*?), to make it tremble a little, allow me to say that, in my current work, and especially in my teaching (for example, in the last several years, on the subject of the gift, the secret, testimony, hospitality, forgiveness, the excuse, the oath, and perjury), I try to reach a place *from* which this distinction between "who" and "what" begins to appear and determine itself, in other words, a place "prior" to this distinction, a place "older" or "younger" than this distinction, also a place that at once compels determination but also makes possible the terribly reversible translation of "who" into "what." Why call this a *place*, a location, a spacing, an interval, a sort of *khora*?

Rules for the Impossible (Aphoristic IV)

I have taken off at top speed [*démarrage sur les chapeaux de roue*], as they say. I ask once more for forgiveness and begin again, otherwise.

To respond—if this is the right word—this is what Michel Meyer had generously asked me, or offered me, to do. I was imprudent enough to promise to do it and thus to risk perjuring myself. After several appreciative readings of these strong, lucid, and generous texts, my delay will only have been that of an anxious, feverish race, both slower and slower and faster and faster. Slower and faster at the same time: try to understand this. A haste then took over, and, as they say, I was heading for failure. I was headed for disaster, which I could see coming more and more clearly without being able to do anything about it. Quite obviously, I did not want the silence of a simple nonresponse to be interpreted—wrongly, of course—as haughtiness or ingratitude. But, as is also quite obvious, I could not, with a limited amount of time and such a proportionally reduced number of pages, "within such limits" (Austin), hope to respond to so many different texts, texts so different in their approach, in their style, in the works they discuss, the problematics they elaborate; to respond to so many addresses as demanding in the force and acuity [*acribie*] of their questions, the richness of their propositions and the depth of the concerns for which they assume responsibility. A philosophical irresponsibility of sorts would have added further to the insufficient sufficiency of a rapid or brief response.

Certainly I will escape neither the one nor the other. At least, perhaps, I will have begun by admitting the failure and the fault—and by asking for forgiveness. If only better to uphold—precisely on the subject of forgiveness—the statement I made a moment ago. From the moment that the *possibility* of forgiveness, if there is one, consists in a certain *impossibility*, must one conclude that it is necessary to do the impossible? And to do it with words, only with words? Must one do the impossible for forgiveness to arrive as such? Perhaps, but this could never be established as a law, a norm, a rule, or a duty. There should not be any *il faut* for forgiveness. Forgiveness "must" always remain unmotivated and unpredictable. One never gives or forgives "in accordance with duty" (*pflichtmässig*), or even "from duty" (*eigentlich aus Pflicht*), to use the good Kantian distinction. One forgives, if one forgives, beyond any categorical imperative, beyond debt and obligation. And yet one *should* [il faudrait] forgive. What is, in fact, presupposed by infinite forgiveness, a "hyperbolic" thus unconditional forgiveness, the forgiveness from which the "commandment" seems to come to us, by inheritance from the Abrahamic tradition and taken up in different ways by Saint Paul and by the Koran? Does it presuppose as its condition (the condition of unconditionality itself, thus) that forgiveness be asked for and the fault avowed, as Jankelevitch so forcefully reminds us?[6] But then it would no longer be unconditional. Conditional once again, it would no longer be pure forgiveness, it would become impossible again, otherwise impossible. Or perhaps it cannot be unconditional and thus possible *as unconditional*, without forgiving the unforgivable (thus becoming possible *as* impossible)? Can it be what it must be—unconditional—if and only when it no longer requires this avowal or this repentance, this exchange, this identification, this economic horizon of reconciliation, redemption, and salvation? I would be tempted to think this, both *within and against* this powerful tradition. What would it mean to "inherit" a tradition under these conditions, from the moment one thinks on the basis of this tradition, in its name, certainly, but precisely *against it in its name*, against the very thing that tradition believed had to be saved to survive while losing itself? Again the possibility of the impossible: a legacy would only be possible where it becomes impossible. This is one of the possible definitions of deconstruction—precisely as legacy. I once suggested as much: deconstruction might perhaps be "the experience of the impossible."[7]

I must now—without deferring any further, without devoting any more space and time to introducing so many subjects that I will not discuss—present and justify, as much as possible, the rule that I thought I must choose to limit the seriousness of this long failure. I would not know how "within such limits" to respond in a detailed manner to each of the texts that we have read; it would require at least an article per page. But I cannot, nor do I wish to, organize my responses according to general themes, which would risk erasing the signed originality of each of the texts that I have read here. Finally, in none of the texts did I find anything to object to or anything that might make me want to defend my past work (this is another way of saying that these texts are not only courteous and generous, but, in my opinion, impeccable in their reading and the discussions they open). I therefore decided, finally, to put myself forward, me, in other words, to put forward, by following several rules, a more or less disconnected series of *quasi* propositions. Concerning my work in progress and the difficulties I am up against, these *quasi* propositions will resonate or reason "on the side [*à côté*]"; they correspond, by slightly displacing the consonance, to the anxieties, concerns, and questions of those who do me the honor of being interested in what I have written. Which is to say, as may already be clear, that these *quasi* propositions, limited as they are to a few rigorous pages, will remain, at least at a first glance, *aphoristic*. But can an argument ever be spared all discontinuity? It is true that there are leaps and that there are leaps. Certain hiatuses can be defended: some are worth more than others.

Such aphoristic *quasi* propositions are, and will remain, on the other hand, *oblique* in their relation to the texts to which I will always, nonetheless, try to keep them attuned. While doing everything to respond *precisely on the side* [justement à côté]. But this does not mean that I will yield to some *oratio obliqua* or that I will try to sidestep the issue. Even where it seems impossible, and there precisely, directness [*droiture*], as I said earlier, remains de rigueur. Inflexibly. If I have multiplied the detours and the contortions, including when I humbly asked for forgiveness and commiseration, it is because I am here, I am placed, I have placed myself, in an untenable position and before an impossible task. Forgiveness and pity: *mercy.*

Yes to Hospitality: (Aphoristic V)

The *problems* of the response and the delay have thus just presented themselves. Having read Michel Meyer, do I still have the right to refer to them in this way, to call them *problems*? And an instant ago I spoke imprudently of "propositions." To further call them, as I have, "*quasi* propositions," certainly draws attention to the problem of propositionalism underlined precisely by Meyer.[8] But this *quasi*, all by itself, does not get us very far. Another concept is needed. I have never found a concept that could hold in a word. Should we be surprised by this? Has there ever been a concept that is truly namable? I mean namable in one name or in one word? The concept always requires sentences, discourses, work, and process: text, in a word. For example, *khora* certainly does not designate the same concept in the *Timaeus* and in the *Republic* (516b, passage cited by Sallis). One could say that it is only a homonym, another word, almost. The consequences of this necessity (of what I take to be an irrecusable experience in any case) seem to me formidable yet inescapable. I sometimes have the impression of having done nothing else, ever, but try to be coherent in this regard. Perhaps I have simply wanted to take account of this necessity and to testify to it.

But it is certainly not fortuitous that the modality of "*quasi*" (or the logical-rhetorical fiction of "as if") has so often forced me to turn a word into a sentence, and initially, especially, as has often been noted and commented on, around the word *transcendental*. A question of problematic context and strategy, no doubt: one must unceasingly reaffirm *here* the question of the transcendental kind, and one must, almost simultaneously, also wonder *there* about the history and limits of what we call *transcendental*. But above all else, the essential possibility of an "as if" had to be taken into account, an "as if" that affects all language and all experience with *possible* fictionality, phantasmaticity, spectrality. The word *transcendental* is not merely an example among others. The category of the "quasi transcendental" has played a deliberately equivocal, yet determinant, role in a number of my essays. Rodolphe Gasché has proposed a powerful interpretation in this direction.[9] Of course, the use of "quasi" and of "ultra-transcendental"[10] to which I resigned myself, is still—it was already—a way of saving, even as I betrayed it, the legacy of philosophy, namely, the demand for the condition of possibility (for the a priori, for what is originary or the foundation, so many different forms of the same radical exigency of every philosophical "question"); to use these terms was also to engage in the task, without concealing the difficulty from oneself, of rethinking the meaning of the "possible," as well as that of the "impossible," and to do so in terms of the so-called condition of possibility, often shown to be the "condition of impossibility." Thus, what can be said about the condition of possibility is also valid, by analogy, for the "foundation," the "origin," the "root" of "radicality," etc.

Even before I began naming them to acknowledge my guilt, the joint *problems* of response and delay [*retard*] were discussed by at least three of my colleagues: by Michel Meyer (who returns to the question of the question, and therefore the question of the answer, of "*answer-hood*" which is equated with "*propositionality*"—"*answer-hood, i.e., propositionality*"—but also of "*problematological difference*" as "*différance . . . when we leave propositionalism*"—and *différance* is also a sort of originary delay); by Daniel Giovannangeli (who recalls everything that follows from belatedness or *Nachträglichkeit*, where this "anachrony," the "anachrony of time itself . . . encloses and exceeds philosophy");[11] finally by John Sallis (for whom the question or the answer of the return to things themselves, to philosophy *itself*, presupposes, like "the very opening in question," the opening of an interval that delays (and lags behind) [*retarde (sur)*] imminence itself: "to intend to begin, to be about to begin, is also to delay, to defer the very beginning that one is about to make"—which, as you might have suspected for some time now, I have been doing here, without complacency).

Response and delay, then: a response, at least according to good sense, is always second and secondary. It lags behind [*retarde sur*] the question or the demand, behind the expectation [*attente*], in any case. And yet everything begins with a response. If I had to summarize, using an elliptical paradox, the thinking that has unceasingly permeated everything that I say and write,[12] I would speak of an *originary response*: The "yes," wherever this indispensable acquiescence is implied (in other words, wherever one speaks and addresses oneself to the other, were it to deny, to argue, to oppose, etc.), this "yes" is first of all a response. To say *yes* is to respond. But nothing precedes this response. Nothing precedes its belatedness [*retard*]—and therefore its anachrony.

Coming *after* them, after the texts and the authors that have just been read, and without judging it possible or necessary to do anything other than listen to them, and ask that they be read and reread, I will simply describe the movement in which I feel myself engaged in this respect. Although I never limit the question to the propositional form (whose necessity I also believe in, of course), I have never felt that I had to (not that anyone ever could or should be able to) give up the question, any form of question, a certain "*primacy of questioning*" (Michel Meyer), or that which ties the question to the problem, to a *problematization*. Could there ever be a problem-free question, that is to say, a question free of all elaboration, of all syntax, of all articulable differentiality, on the one hand, but also, on the other hand, of all self-protection? For problematization is indeed the only *consequential* organization of a question, its grammar and its semantics, but problematization is also a first *apotropaic* measure used to protect oneself against the question that is the barest, at once the most intractable and the most powerless [*démunie*], the question of the other when it calls me into question the moment it is addressed to me. I have tried elsewhere to take into account this "shield" of the *problema*. The *problema* also designates "the substitute, the replacement, the prosthesis, the thing or the person that one *puts forward* in order to protect oneself by hiding, the thing (or person) [*ce(lui)*] that comes in the place or in the name of the other."[13]

Problematization is already an articulated organization of the response. This is the case everywhere, in particular in the history of philosophical or scientific configurations. By whatever name they go by, and however they are interpreted (paradigm, *epistémè*, *themata*, etc.), these historical configurations that serve as the foundation of questions are already possibilities of response. They pre-organize, they make possible the event, the apparent invention, the emergence and the elaboration of the questions, their problematization, the reappropriation that momentarily renders them determinable and treatable.

There is, it would seem to me, in the inevitability of the question, not just an essence of philosophy but an unconditional right and obligation, the joint foundation of philosophy as science and as right. Insofar as this unconditionality is recalled where it goes as if without saying, I must also specify the following: although I have never ceased to deploy everything I have written as a *question of the question*,[14] this very *necessity* cannot be reduced to the question. The double necessity, the double law of the inevitable and the imperative injunction (*il faut*), exceeds the question at the very moment that it reaffirms its necessity. By so often confirming that everything begins not with the question but with the response, with a "yes, yes,"[15] which is originarily a response to the other, it is not matter of putting this unconditionality into question once again, so to speak, but of thinking both its possibility and its impossibility, the one *as* the other.

Nearly thirty-five years ago, I was already worried about (would I say that at the time I was *questioning* myself on this subject?) "unanswerable questions":

By right of birth, and for one time at least, these are problems put to philosophy as problems philosophy cannot resolve.

It may even be that these questions are not *philosophical*, are not *philosophy's* questions. Nevertheless, these should be the only questions today capable of founding the community, within the world, of those who are still called philosophers; and called such in remembrance, at the very least, that these questions must be examined unrelentingly. . . . A community of the question, therefore, within that fragile moment when the question is not yet determined enough for the hypocrisy of an answer to have already *initiated* itself beneath the mask of the question, and not yet determined enough for its voice to have been already and fraudulently articulated within the very syntax of the question. . . . A community of the question about the possibility of the question. This is very little—almost nothing—but within it, today, is sheltered and encapsulated an unbreachable dignity and duty of *decision*. An unbreachable responsibility.

Why unbreachable? Because *the impossible has already occurred* . . . there is a history of the question . . . the question has already begun. . . . A founded dwelling, a realized tradition of the question remaining a question . . . correspondence of the question with itself.[16]

Please forgive me this long quotation from an old text. Will I say, once more, that I am excusing myself for it? Beyond the weakness of which I might stand accused, I wanted first to acknowledge a trajectory that at least cuts across—as it has for such a long time—many of the "problematological" motives that have been elaborated by Michel Meyer, in particular when he writes that "*problematicity is historicity.*" But, surprised myself (can I acknowledge it without seeming too naive or foolishly reassured in the face of what could be nothing but immobility and monotony?) by the insistence or the constancy of my remarks, and by the continuity of their displacement, I especially wanted to locate the new themes that—without interruption, because they have not ceased to occupy me in my seminars for the last few years—have not yet been touched on here in this collection of texts. Indeed, I had announced my wish—rather than *to respond* to all the essays in this volume—*to correspond* with them by situating certain difficulties of my work in progress. The words I just emphasized in the above quotation are, first of all, indications of this sort and paths for me. They point to the themes and problems that beset me today: another way of thinking the limit of the philosophical in the face of questions like *hospitality* (*invitation/visitation*, and a whole chain of associated topics: the *promise, testimony*, the *gift, forgiveness*, etc.), but also capable of withstanding [*à l'épreuve de*] an impossible that would not be negative. Such a test implies another thinking of the event, of the *avoir-lieu*: only the impossible takes place. The deployment of a potentiality or a possibility that is already there will never make an event or an invention. What is true of the event is also true of the decision, therefore of responsibility: a decision that I *am able* to make, the decision that is *in my power* and that indicates the passage to the act or the deployment of what is *already possible* for me, the actualization of my possible, a decision that only depends on me: would this still be a decision? Whence the paradox without paradox that I am trying to accept: the responsible decision must be this impossible possibility of a "passive" decision, a decision of the other-in-me who will not acquit me [*qui ne m'exonère*] of any freedom or any responsibility.

The Necessity of the Impossible (Aphoristic VI)

I have devoted many analyses of the aporetic kind to "the singular modality of this 'impossible.'" Of the *gift*, in particular, in *Given Time*:

[O]ne can think, desire, and say only the impossible, according to the measureless measure [*mesure sans mesure*] of the impossible. If one wants to recapture the proper element of thinking, naming, desiring, it is perhaps according to the measureless measure of this limit that it is possible, possible as relation *without* relation to the impossible. One *can* desire, name, think in the proper sense of these words, if there is one, *only* to the *immeasuring* extent [que *dans la mesure démesurante*] that one desires, names, thinks still or already, that one still lets announce itself what nevertheless cannot *present itself* as experience, to knowing: in short, here *a gift that cannot make itself* (*a*) *present* [un don qui ne peut se faire présent].[17]

The figure of "given time" had been invoked long before this, and emphasized.[18] It followed upon the development of the "possibility of the impossible," which was at the time another name for time: "But it has already been remarked that this impossibility, when barely formulated, contradicts itself, is experienced as the possibility of the impossible. . . . Time is a name for this impossible possibility."[19] Later, the concept of the invention obeyed the same "logic":

Invention is always possible, it is the invention of the possible. . . . Thus it is that invention would be in conformity with its concept, with the dominant feature of the word and concept "invention," only insofar as, paradoxically, invention invents nothing, when in invention the other does not come, and when nothing comes to the other or from the other. For the other is not the possible. So it would be necessary to say that the only possible invention would be the invention of the impossible. But an invention of the impossible is impossible, the other would say. Indeed. But it is the only possible invention: an invention has to declare itself to be the invention of that which did not appear to be possible; otherwise, it only makes explicit a program of possibilities within the economy of the same.[20]

In the interval, *The Post Card* . . . carries the same necessity in the direction of destination [*à destination de la destination*], of the very concept of destination. From the moment that a letter *cannot arrive* at its destination, it is impossible for it to arrive *fully*, or *simply*, at a single destination. The impossibility, the possible as impossible, is always bound to an irreducible divisibility that affects the very essence of the possible. Whence the insistence on the divisibility of the letter and of its destination:

The divisibility of the letter—this is why we have insisted on this key or theoretical safety lock of the Seminar [of Lacan]: the atomystic of the letter—is what chances and sets off course, without guarantee of return, the remaining [*restance*] of anything whatsoever: a letter does *not always* arrive at its destination, and from the moment that this possibility belongs to its structure one can say that it never truly arrives, that when it does arrive its capacity not to arrive torments it with an internal drifting.[21]

Why this allusion to *torment?* It names a suffering or a passion, an affect that is both sad and joyous, the instability of an anxiety proper to all possibilization. Possibilization allows itself to be haunted by the specter of its impossibility, by its mourning for itself: a self-mourning carried within itself that also gives it its life or its survival, its very possibility. This *im*possibility opens its possibility, it leaves a trace—chance and threat—*within* that which it makes possible. Torment signs this scar, the trace of this trace. But the same is also said in *The Post Card* of the "impossible decision," the decision that appears to be impossible insofar as it only falls to the other.[22] (This topic was largely elaborated in *Politics of Friendship*). We find it again in terms of Freud and the concept of *Bemächtigung*, of the limit or the paradoxes of the possible as power.

It is not at all fortuitous that this discourse on the conditions of possibility—even where its claim is obsessed with the impossibility of overcoming its own performativity—can be extended to all the places where some performative force occurs or makes occur (the event, the invention, the gift, forgiveness, hospitality, friendship, the promise, the experience of death—the possibility of the impossible, the impossibility of the possible, experience in general, etc. *Et cetera*, because the contagion is without limit; it eventually leads to all concepts and no doubt the concept of the concept, etc.).

Promising to respond in all rightness [*dans la droiture*], thus *right beside* [juste à côté] the question: the impossible possible. Recalling that everything I have written in the name of *destinerrance* has been written on the untenable line of this impossible possible and that it has always been at the crossing of many of the trajectories that have been sketched out and reinterpreted by the texts assembled here. The risk of misunderstandings, the errancy of a response beside the question: this is what must always remain possible in the exercise of rightness [*droiture*]. There would be no rightness [*droiture*], no ethics of discussion otherwise. (But what I am proposing here is not meant to suggest—any more than were my earlier allusions to responsibility, hospitality, the gift, forgiveness, testimony, etc.—some *"ethical turn,"* as some have said. I am simply trying to pursue with some consequence the thinking that for years has been engaged with the same aporias. The question of ethics, of rights and politics has not sprung forth unexpectedly, as from a bend in the road. Furthermore, the way in which this question is discussed is not always reassuring as far the "moral" is concerned—perhaps because it asks too much of it.

The *possibility* of this evil (the misunderstanding, the miscomprehension, the mistake) is, in its own way, a chance. It gives time. Thus there must be the *il faut* of the fault [*Il faut donc le "*il faut*" du défaut*], and adequation must remain *impossible*. But there is nothing negative, ontologically, in this "*il faut du défaut* [there must be fault].*"* There must be [*il faut*], or if one prefers—*in*adequation must *always* remain *possible* for interpretation in general, and the response in turn, to be *possible*. This is an example of the law that binds the possible to the impossible. An interpretation that was without flaw, a self-comprehension that was completely adequate would not only mark the end of a history exhausted by its very transparency. By prohibiting the future, it would make everything *impossible*, both the event and the coming of the other, the coming to the other—and thus the response, the "yes" of the response, the "yes" *as* response. The response can only be adjusted in exceptional fashion, and we still have no preliminary and objective criterion to assure ourselves of it, to assure us that the exception does indeed take place *as* exception.

Perhaps the haunting of the exception indicates the passage, if not the way out. I say *haunting*, because the spectral structure is the law here, both of the possible and the impossible, and of their strange intertwining. The exception is always de rigueur. This applies, perhaps, to the stubbornness of the "perhaps," in its ungraspable modality that is irreducible to any other, fragile and yet indestructible. "Quasi" or "as if," "perhaps," "spectrality" of the *phantasma* (which also means ghost): these are the components of another thinking of the virtual, of a virtuality that is no longer organized according to the traditional notion of the possible (*dynamis, potentia, possibilitas*). When the impossible *makes itself* possible, the event takes place (possibility *of* the impossible). This is, irrecusably, the paradoxical form of the event: if an event is only possible, in the classic sense of the word, if it is inscribed in conditions of possibility, if it does no more than make explicit, unveil, reveal, accomplish what was already possible, then it is no longer an event. For an event to take place, for an event to be possible, it must be, as event, as invention, the coming of the impossible. This is weak evidence, evidence that is nothing less than evident. It is what has unceasingly guided me, between the possible and the impossible. It is also what has so often inspired me to talk about the *condition of impossibility*. What is at stake, then, is nothing less than the powerful concept of the *possible* that runs through Western thought from Aristotle to Kant and to Husserl (and then otherwise to Heidegger), with all of its virtual or potential significations: the being-in-power, precisely, *dynamis*, virtuality (in its classical and modern, pretechnological and technological forms), but also power, ability, anything that makes one able or capacitates, etc. Indeed, the choice of this topic possesses a strategic value, but it also carries with it a forward-going movement, beyond all calculable strategy. It carries what is called *deconstruction* toward a question that provokes trembling, tormenting it thus from the inside: deconstruction, at once the most powerful and the most precarious axiom (impotent in its very potency) of the dominant thinking of the possible in philosophy (enslaved in the power of its very dominance).

But how is it possible, one will ask, that that which makes possible makes impossible the very thing that it makes possible, thus, and introduces—as its chance—a non-negative chance, a principle of ruin into the very thing it promises or promotes? The *im-* of the im-possible is indeed radical, implacable, undeniable. But it is not simply negative or dialectical: it *introduces* the possible; it is its *gatekeeper today*; it makes it come, it makes it turn either according to an anachronic temporality or according to an incredible filiation—which is, moreover, also the origin of faith. For it exceeds knowledge and conditions the address to the other, inscribes all theorems into the space and time of a testimony ("I am talking to you, believe me"). In other words—and this is the introduction to an aporia without example, an aporia of logic rather than a logical aporia—here is an impasse of the undecidable through which a decision cannot not pass. All responsibility must pass through this aporia that, far from paralyzing it, puts in motion a new thinking of the possible. It ensures its rhythm and its breathing: diastole, systole, and syncope, the beating of the *im*possible possible, of the impossible as condition of the possible. From the very heart of the impossible, one hears, thus, the pulsion or the pulse of a "deconstruction."

Hence, the condition of possibility gives the possible a chance but by depriving it of its purity. The law of this spectral contamination, the impure law of this impurity, this is what must be constantly re-elaborated. For example, the possibility of failure is not only inscribed as a preliminary risk in the condition of the possibility of the success of a performative (a promise must *be able not to* be kept, it must risk not being kept or becoming a threat to be a promise that is freely given, and even to succeed;[23] whence the originary inscription of guilt, of confession, of the excuse and of forgiveness in the promise). The possibility of failure must continue to mark the event, even when it succeeds, as the trace of an impossibility, at times its memory and always its haunting. This impossibility is therefore not the simple opposite of the possible. It only seems opposed to it but it also gives itself over to possibility: it runs though possibility and leaves in it the trace of its withdrawal [*enlève-ment*]. An event would not be worthy of its name; it would not make anything arrive, if it did nothing but deploy, explain, actualize what was already possible, that is to say, in short, if all it did was to implement a program or apply a general rule to a specific case. For there to be an event, the event has to be possible, of course, but there must also be an exceptional, absolutely singular interruption in the regime of possibility; the event must not *simply* be possible, it must not reduce itself to the explanation, the unfolding, the acting out of a possible. The event, if there is one, is not the actualization of a possible, a simple acting out, a realization, an effectuation, the teleological accomplishment of a power, the process of a dynamic that depends on "conditions of possibility." The event has nothing to do with history, if by history one means a teleological process. The event must interrupt in a certain manner this kind of history. It is according to these premises that I spoke, particularly in *Specters of Marx*, of messianicity without messianism. *It is imperative* [il faut], thus, that the event also announce itself as impossible or that its possibility be threatened.

But then why this *il faut*, one may ask? What is the status of this necessity, of this apparently contradictory yet doubly obligatory law? What is the *double bind* on the basis of which the possible *must* still be rethought as *im*possible?

Perhaps it is a necessity that escapes from the habitual regime of necessity (*ananké, Notwendigkeit*), from necessity understood as natural law or law of freedom. For one cannot think the possibility of the impossible *otherwise* without rethinking necessity. I have attempted analyses of the event or the performative, the scope of which has been recalled here, in an analogous manner over the course of the last fifteen years, in particular in terms of destination, testimony, invention, the gift, forgiveness, which is also that which binds hospitality to the impossible promise, to the pervertibility of the performative in general, etc.—and above all, in terms of death, the aporicity of the aporia in general. This pervertibility is less transcendental in that it does not affect the classical reflection on the transcendental, on the transcendental "condition of possibility" in all of its forms: medieval ontotheology, criticism or phenomenology.[24] It does not delegitimize transcendental questioning, it de-limits and questions its original historicity. For nothing can discredit the right to the transcendental or ontological question. This question is the only force that resists empiricism and relativism. In spite of appearances, and the hasty philosophers who often rush to them, nothing is less empiricist or relativist than a certain attention to the multiplicity of contexts and discursive strategies that they govern: a certain insistence on the fact that a context is always open and cannot be saturated; a taking into account of the "perhaps" and the "quasi" in a thinking of the event, etc.

Transaction and Event (Aphoristic VII)

There is something like a *transaction* in this insistent displacement of the strategy and the non-strategy (that is, of the vulnerable exposure to what arrives). One negotiates, one compromises *with*, and *on*, the limit of philosophy as such. This limit takes the double form of a différantial logic of analogy: on one hand, the "quasi," the "as if," of a différance that maintains the delay, the relay, the return or the term in the economy of the same; and on the other hand, the rupture, the event of the impossible, différance as *diaphora*, the aphorismic experience of absolute heterogeneity. On one hand, the concatenation of syllogistic sequences, on the other—but "at the same time"—the seriality of aphoristic sequences.

Karel Thein is therefore correct to guide his rich analysis of the analogy in "Plato's Pharmacy" to the point where the question refers—precisely with the insistence [*instance*] of the decision—to what he calls *the conditions and the limits of the analogy as such*. The interpretation that I am proposing of the *khora* disturbs the regime of the analogy. As John Sallis so rightly notes (in our ongoing dialogue that has meant so much to me over the years around this text of Plato, a text whose power of implosion we both feel to be kept in reserve), this is also true of what, in the definition of Good and the *epekeina tes ousias* as what-is-beyond-being, would remain in a sort of ana-onto-logy. It is about another excess. The "other time" that Sallis notes is also what carries all the trials of which I spoke earlier (the impossible, the passive decision, the "perhaps," the event as absolute interruption of the possible, etc.). All of Sallis's questions certainly seem legitimate to me, as do the answers he brings to them ("Can there be, then, a metaphorizing of the khora? If not, then how is one to read the passage of the khora of the sun . . .? How is the khora itself—if there be a khora itself—to be beheld? What is the difference marked by the as [in the hypothesis in which *khora* is perceived 'as in a dream']?") But these legitimate responses fall under the law of the philosophical; the latter is dominated by the necessity of the ana-onto-logy (which are that of ontology but also of phenomenology, that is, of the appearance as such of the *as such*, of the *as*). Yet the rupture that is important to me in the reading of the *khora*, the reading that I have ventured, is that *khora* becomes the name of that which never allows itself to be metaphorized, in spite the fact that *khora* both can and cannot not give rise to so many analogical figures. It does not seem to me that the *khora* of the sun in the *Republic* could be a metaphorical value of the *khora* of the *Timaeus*. Nor, for that matter, could the reverse be true. Although the word clearly designates a "site" or a "locality" in both cases, there is no analogy, no possible commensurability, it seems to me, between these two places. The word *place* itself has such a different semantic value in the two cases that what we are dealing with—I believe this and I suggested it earlier—would be a relation of homonymy rather than one of figurality or synonymy. It is on the basis of this conviction that, rightly or wrongly, I treated *khora* in the *Timaeus* as a *quasi* proper noun. If *khora* eludes all metaphors, it is not to remain inaccessible in its proper properness [*sa propre propriété*], in its ipseity, in the itself of what it is. Rather, earlier [*plutôt, plus tôt*], because what is there is not the *khora* itself. There is no *khora* itself (as John Sallis rightly supposes when he writes "*if there be a khora itself*"). I will concede that this seems very disconcerting. This unicity without property initiates a crisis, for example, here and not necessarily elsewhere, in any distinction between figure and non-figure, and therefore in this distinction between *literal reading* and *figural reading*, which Michel Meyer is certainly correct, in other cases, to dissociate into two "steps." There is, here, in the singular case of *khora* (but also in the case of its analogs that still remain absolutely singular and different), a name without a referent, without a referent that would be a thing or a being [*étant*] or even a phenomenon appearing *as such*. Thus this possibility disorganizes the whole regime of the philosophical kind of question (ontological or transcendental) without giving in to a pre-philosophical empiricism. It only announces itself in the figure of the impossible that is no longer a figure and that, as I have tried to show, never appears as such.[25] It throws the "as such" off track and deprives it of its status as a phenomeno-ontological criterion. I am trying to get at the necessity of this singular naming, as well as at its contingency, and at what we inherit here: a noun from a natural language in its ordinary usage (*khora*), a noun both replaceable and irreplaceable. To be replaceable in its very irreplaceability, this is what happens to every singularity, to every proper noun, even and especially when what it names "properly" has no relation of indivisible properness [*propriété*] to itself, to some self that would properly be what it is *as such*, to some intact ipseity. Prosthesis of the proper noun that comes to signify (without any ontic referent, without anything that appears as such, without corresponding object or being, without a meaning in the world or out of the world), to call forth some "thing" that is not a thing and entertains no relation of analogy to anything at all. This naming is an event (at once impossible and decisive, which we may or may not decide to inherit). But is every inaugural naming not an event? Is the giving of a name not the performative par excellence?

Savoir-penser: Inheriting "The Critical Mission of Philosophy" (Aphoristic VII)

Without being a "program" in the least, what does *différance* "say" or "do"? (It "is" neither a word nor a concept, I once said[26] in obvious denegation, but whose traces remain, in some sense—to the point of making denegation of denegation as legitimate as it is inoperative, as if there were many of us who suspected that this untenable denegation must have wanted to affirm, through its very inconsistency, "something" that still deserved to be taken seriously.) What announced itself thus as "différance" had this singular quality: that it simultaneously welcomed, but without dialectical facility, the same and the other, the economy of analogy—the same only deferred, relayed, delayed—*and* the rupture of all analogy, absolute heterology. Yet one could also, in this context, retreat this question of *différance* as a question of legacy. The legacy would consist here in remaining faithful to what is received (and *khora* is also that which receives, it is the enigma of what "receptacle," *endekhomenon*, might mean and do in the place where *khora* says nothing and does nothing), while breaking with the particular figure of what is received. One must always break out of faithfulness—and in the name of a legacy that is fatally contradictory in its injunctions. For example, in what concerns the gift, forgiveness, hospitality, etc., in the name of the Abrahamic legacy that requires of me a certain hyperbolic unconditionality, I must be ready to break with all the economic and conditional reappropriations that constantly compromise the said legacy. But this break itself will still have to conduct transactions and define the necessary conditions—in history, law, politics, economics (and economics means economics in the strict sense but also the economy among these different fields)—to make this legacy of hyperbole as effective as possible. On the basis of this paradoxical yet largely formalizable necessity, from this break (that is *still* economic) with economy, from this heterogeneity that interrupts analogy (though *still* lending itself to analogy to be understood), I would be tempted to interpret all of the gestures that, even here, elaborate so clearly and against so many prejudices, the engagement of deconstruction, insofar at least as I try to practice and interpret it, from the point of view of science, of technology, of reason and the Enlightenment. I am thinking here in particular of the demonstrations of Christopher Johnson, Christopher Norris, and Arkady Plotnitsky.

For a long time, now, we have been able to follow Norris's work— so original, so persistent and so incisive—against countless misunderstandings and a host of prejudices as tenacious as they are crudely polemical (deconstruction as "relativist," "skeptical," "nihilist," "irrationalist," "the enemy of the Enlightenment," "the prisoner of verbal language and rhetoric," "ignorant of the difference between logic and rhetoric, philosophy and literature," etc.). It is no accident that Norris so often calls for a reexamination of the status of the *analogy* in my work, as he does here again, and for the reelaboration of the problem concept/metaphor. I find particularly judicious a strategy that is often privileged in his texts, and here again (a certain passage through "White Mythology"—in its relation to Nietzsche, but also to Canguilhem and to Bachelard—and "The Supplement of the Copula"); and particularly effective the re-situation of the demonstrative levers that he proposes with respect to the Anglo-American developments that he has for a long time helped me to read and to understand (Davidson, for example). I am not shocked, even if it makes me smile, to see myself defined by Norris in a deliberately provocative and ironic way as a "transcendental realist." Earlier, I explained why I did not believe it was necessary to give up the transcendental motif. The deconstruction of logocentrism, of linguisticism, of economism (of the proper, of the at-home [*chez-soi*], *oikos*, of the same), etc., as well as the affirmation of the impossible are always put forward *in the name of the real*, of the irreducible reality of the real— not of the real as attribute of the objective, present, perceptible or intelligible *thing* (*res*), but of the real as the coming or event of the other, where the other resists all reappropriation, be it ana-onto-phenomenonological appropriation. The real is this non-negative impossible, this impossible coming or invention of the event the thinking of which is not an onto-phenomenology. It is a thinking of the event (singularity of the other, in its unanticipatible coming, *hic et nunc*) that resists reappropriation by an ontology or a phenomenology of presence as such. I am attempting to dissociate the concept of event and the value of presence. This is not easy, but I am trying to demonstrate this necessity, like the necessity of thinking the event-without-being. Nothing is more "realist," in this sense, than a deconstruction. It is (what-/who-)ever arrives [(*ce*) *qui arrive*]. And there is no fatality about the *fait accompli*: neither empiricism nor relativism. Is it empiricist or relativist to seriously take into account what arrives—differences of every order, beginning with the difference of contexts?

Without wanting to reduce the richness and the many paths of his demonstrations, I also find it rather remarkable that, when *he, too*, follows the thread of the analogy without analogy, Christopher Johnson first sets the word *metaphor* apart. ("The metaphor of writing, as it is articulated with the genetic and the biological in Derrida's texts, is not simply metaphor.") Having proposed "a more discriminating vocabulary"—here the word *isomorphism*—he reorients in a way that I find very clear and very confident the very premise of this choice toward another logic or toward another structure, that of the "metaphorical catastrophe" that changes the entire scene and forces us to reconsider the structure of a semantic inversion or of a conceptual classification. For example: "not only is the term a germ, but the germ is, in the most general sense, a term" (an analysis it might perhaps be fruitful to cross with Karel Thein's discussion of "strong" and "weak" "germs" and of the *sperma athanaton*). One should certainly take into account the fact that this remarkable analysis finds its privileged horizon in the so-called life sciences, biology and cybernetics (without, however, yielding to vitalism, as Johnson rightly points out). But is this merely Johnson's choice (which did not prevent him from opening a rich and diversified field of questioning)? Or else, taking account of what he says at the end of his discussion about the "open" system and its limit, about the necessity of including his own discourse as an example of the system described ("and more than an example," he adds, and I would have liked to ask him to help me think this "more than an example"), could one, then, extend what he demonstrates to other sciences, to sciences that would no longer be sciences of the living? For example, in the direction indicated by the article and so many other decisive works of Arkady Plotnitsky on the subject of the relations between deconstruction and the physical or mathematical sciences? (In the course of this impressive reflection on the folds, positions, points, and counterpoints of a certain Hegelian "legacy" of deconstruction, we will indeed have noted Plotnitsky's insistence on what he has long held[27] to be a "conceptual" proximity between quantum mechanics—such, in particular, as it has been interpreted by Niels Bohr—and a certain theoretical strategy, a certain relation to calculated risk in deconstructive practice. The attention paid to the notion of "strategy" here is, I believe, justified and determinant.)

I also wonder—without making any objection to it—how one can determine the "outside" of science about which Johnson talks, and what name one is to give to that which he calls a *"position* outside *of science."* When he recognizes, and rightly attributes to me, the intention of taking a step beyond a certain boundary of scientific discourse "by taking the notion of the open system to its logical limit, including his own discourse as an example, and more than an example, of the system he describes," is this still a philosophical gesture, as Johnson seems to think, "the critical mission of philosophy?" Or is this a gesture that also passes beyond the closure of philosophy, such that philosophical discourse would find itself on the same side as scientific discourse? I admit that I have no simple, stable answer to this question. And this is also due to the somewhat invaginated structure of this limit, of this form of boundary that includes without integrating, so to speak, the outside in the inside. Plotnitsky nicely sets out the paradoxes of the limit in this respect. At times it is in the name of classical philosophical exigencies (transcendental, phenomenological, ontological) that I find it necessary to determine certain limits to scientific discourse. More often, it is in the name of something that, for the sake of convenience, I call *the thinking* [la pensée] (at the same time distinct from knowledge, from philosophy, and from faith) that I search for this position of exteriority. But the word *thinking* does not satisfy me completely, for several reasons. In the first place, it recalls a Heideggerian gesture (*Das Denken* is neither philosophy nor science nor faith) that certainly interests me very much and whose necessity I clearly see but to which I do not completely subscribe, in particular when he makes such declarations as "science does not think." Neither does the traditional semantics of the word *thinking* [pensée], its figure or its etymological values (*la pesée* [weighing], *l'examen* [examining] etc.) satisfy me without reservation. Finally, I attempted long ago to justify, in a way that was less simple than certain hasty readers may have believed, the statement according to which "In a certain manner, 'la pensée' does not mean anything. . . . This thinking [*pensée*] has no weight. It is, in the play of the system, the very thing that never has weight."[28] Yes, "in a certain manner," at least.

As one might suspect, it is not simply a matter of a label, a title, or a terminology here. When Johnson is forced to use three words (*thought, philosophy, science*)[29] to situate the most obscure border difficulties, he clearly designates the burdensome effort I insist on imposing on myself to mark *and pass* over these borders: pass over them in the sense that *to pass* is to exceed and pass to the other side, to exceed the limit by confirming it, by taking it into account, but also in the sense that *to pass* is not to let oneself be detained at a border, not to take a border for a border, for an impassable opposition between two heterogeneous domains. This double "logic" of the limit is what I wanted to try to formalize here by way of the "responses" sketched out, from one aphoristic sequence to the other. Thus, I believe that the orders of thought and philosophy, even if they cannot be reduced to the order of scientific knowledge, are not simply external to it either, both because they receive from it what is essential and because they can, from the other side of the limit, have effects on the inside of the scientific field (elsewhere I have tried to articulate the order of "faith" here, as well[30]). Scientific progress or inventions also respond to questions of the philosophical "type." This is why these *différantial* limits never signify oppositional limits or exclusions. This is why I will never say that "science does not think." How can we not be extremely grateful to Johnson, Norris, and Plotnitsky, for having not simply understood, argued, elaborated, but for having deployed this gesture in a way that is novel every time? As all the authors of this collection have done, they have carried and explored the necessity of this gesture well beyond any point that I could ever lay claim to myself.

Translated by Benjamin Elwood with Elizabeth Rottenberg

Globalization, Peace, and Cosmopolitanism

I want to begin by expressing my profound gratitude to Mr. Federico Mayor and to my friends at UNESCO for the invitation with which they have honored me. Jerôme Bindé can testify to the many hesitations I had to overcome. To address the enormous, formidable, and urgent tasks—under the three concepts that are on the program for this session, "globalization [*mondialisation*]," "peace," and "cosmopolitanism," and in twenty minutes (seven for globalization, seven for peace, no more than six for cosmopolitanism)—to expose oneself thus before a large, diverse, and demanding audience is a wager, not to say a torture, that, out of respect for the rights of man, should not be imposed on any human being, and especially not within these confines. On this point, at least, it would be easy to find consensus between, on the one hand, the believers in the natural universality of the rights of man and, on the other, those who would be tempted, with or without cultural relativism, with or without historicism, to see the rights of man and international law in general, as still marked by their European or Greco-Roman-Abrahamic (by which I mean their Greek, Roman, Jewish, Christian, and Islamic) origin, insofar as they are rooted in a history, in particular languages and archives, even where their uprooting is the constitutive law of their history, their vocation, and their structure.

As you see, I have already gained a little time. And even gained a certain angle on my topic. For, although one must never impose on a human being, and especially one whose profession is philosophy, an exercise such as this one and thus the failure he must inevitably face . . . well then, my only recourse will be to run faster and faster toward the inescapable failure and not lose a second more in protocols or in protests of inadequacy, as sincere and non-rhetorical as they may be.

Thus, allow me to proceed, in a way that is brutally direct, straight to a series of statements. I submit them for discussion less as theses or hypotheses than as professions of faith, in some sense. These quasi professions of faith will be declared through aporias, contradictory and apparently incompatible injunctions, which are (and this is the first point that I bring up for debate), according to me, the only situations in which, forced to obey two apparently antinomical imperatives, I literally do not know what to do, what I would prefer to do, what to privilege, and I must then *take* what is called a *decision* and a *responsibility*, a responsible decision; I must give myself, I must invent for myself a rule of transaction, of compromise, of negotiation that is not programmable by any knowledge, not by science or consciousness. Even if I had at my disposal, or could acquire all knowledge, all possible science or consciousness on this matter—as must in fact be done, this is a duty—an infinite leap still remains before me, because a responsible decision, if it is to be the event of a decision in the face of two contradictory imperatives, cannot simply be dictated, programmed, prescribed by knowledge as such. This is why I am tempted to speak of a *profession of faith*.

Having posed this axiom, let us take the word *mondialisation*, the French word *mondialisation* that should resist, according to me and I will say why, its translation and its alleged English or German equivalents: *globalization* or *Globalisierung*. The term *mondialisation* has become, and the statistics would bear this out, the site of the most symptomatic uses and abuses of our time, especially in the last decade. The inflation, even the rhetorical turgidity that affect the term, and not only in political discourse and the media, often conceal one of the contradictions with which I would like to begin and with regard to which a true cultural critique, the *contract* of a new education or reeducation, is no doubt necessary. This, both against the beatific celebration and the demonization of the phenomenon of the aforementioned *mondialisation*. Celebration and demonization often hide interests and strategies that we must learn to detect.

On the one hand, as is well known, a certain number of unprecedented and irrecusable phenomena justify this concept. The effects of globalization [*mondialisation*] are essentially conditioned by techno-science (a techno-science that is, furthermore, unequally, unfairly distributed in the world in its production and its benefits), and they involve—we know this and I will say it very quickly—the rhythms and the scope of transportation and telecommunication in the electronic age (computerization, E-mail, Internet, etc.), the circulation of persons, commodities, modes of production, and socio-political models on a market that is being opened in a more-or-less regulated way. As for the (altogether relative) opening of borders (which, at the same time, has rarely given rise to so many inhospitable acts of violence, so many prohibitions, so many exclusions, etc.), as for the progress of legislation and especially the practice of international law, as for the limitations or the displacements of sovereignty that the concept of globalization calls forth, globalization depends less than ever on *fact* or techno-scientific knowledge-power [*savoir-pouvoir*] as such. Indeed, it calls for ethical-political decisions and political-economic-military strategies. Here the ideal or euphoric image of globalization as homogenizing opening must be challenged seriously and with unfailing vigilance. Not only because the said homogenization, where it is produced or would be produced, contains in itself both a chance and chance's double—a terrifying risk (too obvious for me to have to spend time on it)—but also because the apparent homogenization often hides old and new inequalities and hegemonies (what I call *homo-hegemonizations*) that we must learn to detect behind their new features—and fight. International institutions—governmental and nongovernmental—are in this regard privileged places, both as revelation, as fields of analysis or experimentation, and as battlefields or as places of palpable confrontation. These are also privileged places for the organization of resistance to these imbalances, the most visible and massive of which are linguistic. These imbalances are all the more difficult to challenge—and this is another contradiction—because, on the one hand, this hegemony is very useful for universal communication (thus equivocal in its effects); and, on the other, because the linguistic-cultural hegemony (obviously I am alluding to the Anglo-American hegemony), which increasingly asserts itself or imposes itself on all modes of techno-scientific exchange, the Web, the Internet, academic research, etc., promotes powers that are either national and sovereign states, or supranational states, this time in the sense of corporations or new figures of the concentration of capital. Since all of this is well known, I will only insist here on the aporetic contradiction in which responsible decisions must be made—and contracts framed. If a linguistic-cultural hegemony (and everything that comes with it: ethical, religious, legal models) is at the

same time, as integrating homogenization, the positive condition and democratic pole of a desired globalization, enabling access to a common language, to exchange, to techno-science, and to an economic and social
progress for communities, national or not, communities that would not
otherwise have access to them and would find themselves, without Anglo-
American, deprived of their participation in the global forum, then how
does one fight this hegemony without compromising the broadening of exchange and distribution [*partage*]? It is here that a transaction must be
sought at every moment, in every singular set of circumstances. It is here
that the transaction must be invented, reinvented without prior criteria and
without assured norms. One must, and this is the formidable responsibility of the decision, if ever there is one, reinvent the norm itself, the very
language of the norm for such a transaction. This inventiveness, this reinvention of the norm, even if it must be inaugural, different, without precedent and without prior guarantee, without available criteria every time,
must not for all that yield to relativism, empiricism, pragmatism, or opportunism. It must justify itself by producing its principle of universalization in a universally convincing way, by validating its principle through its
very invention. In this way, I am formulating (and I am perfectly aware of
it) a task that appears contradictory and *impossible*. Impossible at least for
a response that would be instantaneous, simultaneous, immediately
coherent, and identical to itself. But I maintain that only the impossible
arrives and that there is no event, and thus no irruptive and singular decision except where one does more than deploy the possible, a possible
knowledge—where exception is made to the possible.

Instead of pursuing the analysis directly, I will, for lack of time, try to
illustrate it with an analogy that is not just any analogy, but precisely an
analogy of the example of the concepts of world [*monde*] and *mondialisation*. If I maintain the distinction between these concepts and the concepts
of *globalization* or *Globalisierung* (and it should be noted that the word *globalization* is itself becoming global to the point of imposing itself more and
more, even in France in the rhetoric of politicians and the media), it is because the concept of world gestures toward a history, it has a memory that
distinguishes it from that of the globe, of the universe, of Earth, of the *cosmos* even (at least of the cosmos in its pre-Christian meaning, which Saint
Paul then christianized precisely to make it say *world* as *fraternal* community
of human beings, of fellow creatures, brothers, sons of God and neighbors
to one another). For the world begins by designating, and tends to remain,

in an Abrahamic tradition (Judeo-Christian-Islamic but predominantly Christian) a particular space-time, a certain oriented history of human brotherhood, of what in a Pauline language—the language that continues to structure and condition the modern concepts of the rights of man or the crime against humanity (horizons of international law in its actual form to which I would like to return, a form that conditions, in principle and by right, the becoming of globalization [*mondialisation*])—of what in this Pauline language one calls *citizens of the world* (*sympolitai*, fellow citizens [*concitoyens*] of the saints in the house of God), brothers, fellow men, neighbors, insofar as they are creatures and sons of God.

If you grant me, for lack of time, that it is possible in principle to demonstrate the Abrahamic filiation, Christian predominantly or par excellence, of the concept of world and all the ethical-political-juridical concepts that tend to regulate the process of globalization [*mondialisation*], the becoming-world of the world—especially through international law and even international criminal law (in its most interesting, most promising, most turbulent becoming), through the difficulties of international cosmopolitan institutions and even the felicitous crises of national state sovereignty—then responsibility, the most necessary task and the most risky wager would consist in doing two things at once, without giving up either one. On the one hand, it would consist in analyzing rigorously and without complacency all of the genealogical features that lead the concept of world, the geopolitical axioms and the assumptions of international law, and everything that rules its interpretation, back to its European, Abrahamic, and predominantly Christian, indeed Roman, filiation (with the effects of hegemony implicit and explicit that this inherently involves). On the other hand, it would consist in never giving up—through cultural relativism or a facile critique of Eurocentrism—the universal, universalizing exigency, the properly revolutionary exigency that tends irresistibly to uproot, to de-territorialize, to dehistoricize this filiation, to contest its limits and the effects of its hegemony (all the way to the theological-political concept of sovereignty that is experiencing a sea change in terms of the borders of war and peace and even, at these borders, between a cosmopolitanism that assumes, as does citizenship of the world, the sovereignty of states, and another, democratic International beyond the nation state, even beyond citizenship). Therefore, one must not give up rediscovering, inventing, inventing this time in the sense of inventing as discovering what is already there potentially, namely, in this filiation itself, the principle of its excess, of its bursting outside itself, of its auto-deconstruction. Without ever yielding to empiricist relativism, it is a matter of accounting for what in this genealogy, let us say *European* to go quickly, gets carried away, exceeds itself by exporting itself (even if this exportation did and can still imply an infinite violence, whether we use more or less worn-out words to talk about it—imperialism, colonialism, neo-colonialisms, neo-imperialisms—or modes of domination that are more refined, trickier, more virtual, less identifiable in the future under the names nation-states or national states' gathering).

The task of the philosopher here, such as I see it assigned and implied by the new "world contract" that we are thinking about, would also be that of whoever tends to assume political or legal responsibilities in this matter: to account for what in this heritage of the concept of the world and in the process of globalization makes possible and necessary—by assuming it, with a profession of faith—an actual universalization, which frees itself of its own roots or historical, geographical, national state limitations at the same moment that, out of faithfulness (and faithfulness is an act of faith), it implements the best memory of this heritage and fights against the effects of inequality and hegemony, of homo-hegemonization that this same tradition did and can still produce. For it is also from the depths of this heritage that certain themes themselves arise, themes that today, particularly through the mutations of international law and its new concepts—about which I will say a word in a moment—have the potential to universalize and thus to split, or if one prefers, to expropriate the Euro-Christian heritage.

Instead of remaining at this level of abstraction within the short time I have left, I would like to indicate, or at least name, the four related examples—thus putting these statements into practice—with which I would have liked to orient the discussion. The titles of these four examples, all of which are linked, would successively be: *work, forgiveness, peace,* and *the death penalty.* The common premises with which I will bring these four themes together in a single problematic are all taken in the process of a globalization that has been accelerated in its rhythm, driven to the point of a true mutation, i.e., of a rupture whose juridical events, which are more than indications here, would be as follows:

1. The renewed reaffirmation in its many declarations of the constantly enriched "rights of man."

2. The performative production in 1945 of the concept of crime against humanity, which, together with the war crime, the crime of geno-

cide and the crime of aggression, transformed the global public space and opened the way for international criminal agencies. We can foresee and hope that they will develop irreversibly, thereby limiting national state sovereignties. The four crimes that I have just listed define the jurisdiction of the International Court of Criminal Law.

3. Consequently, the putting into question (very unequal, it is true, and indeed problematic, but altogether crucial and irreversible) of the barely secularized theological principle of the sovereignty of nation states.

A few words, thus, on work and then a telegraphic question to begin the discussion about forgiveness, peace, and the death penalty.

1. *Work.* Let us say or make as if the world began where work ended, as if the globalization of the world had both as its horizon and its origin the disappearance of what we call *work*, this old word, painfully charged with so much meaning and history, work, *labor, travail,* etc., and which still means actual, effective, and not virtual, work.

When we say *as if,* we are neither in the fiction of a possible future, nor before the resurrection of a historical or mythical past, the past of a revealed origin. The rhetoric of this "as if" belongs neither to the science fiction of a utopia to come (a world without work, "in the end without end," *in fine, sine fine* of an eternal sabbatical, of a Sabbath without night, as in Augustine's *City of God*); nor does it belong to the poetics of nostalgia that would hark back to a golden age or a paradise on Earth, to the moment in Genesis before sin when the sweat of work had not yet begun to flow, neither from the labor and toil [*la labeur et le labour*] of man nor from the childbirth of women. In these two interpretations of "as if," science fiction or memory of the immemorial, it would be as if, in effect, the beginnings of the world originally excluded work: work would be not-yet or no-longer. It would be as if, between the concept of world and the concept of work, there were no originary harmony, and thus no given accord or possible synchrony. Original sin would have introduced work into the world, and the end of work would announce the terminal phase of an expiation. One would have to choose between the world and work, whereas, according to common sense, it is hard to imagine a world without work or work that would not be of the world or in the world. The Christian world and the Pauline conversion of the concept of the Greek cosmos introduces—among many other associated meanings—the assignation of expiatory work. The concept of work is burdened with meaning, history, and equivocation; it is difficult to think it beyond good and evil. For, even if it has always been associated at the same time with dignity, life, production, history, goods, and freedom, it nonetheless just as often connotes evil, suffering, penalty, sin, punishment, oppression. No. This "as if" points in the present to two common places on which to test them: on the one hand, one often speaks about the end of work, and on the other hand, and just as often, of a globalization of the world [*mondialisation du monde*], about a becoming-global of the world [*devenir-mondial du monde*]. And one always associates one with the other. I am borrowing the expression "end of work" from the title of the well known book by Jeremy Rifkin, *The End of Work: The Decline of the Global Labor Force and the Dawn of the Post-Market Era*. This book brings together a sort of widespread doxa about a "third industrial revolution" that, according to him, would be "a powerful force for good and evil," given that "new information and telecommunication technologies have the potential to both liberate and destabilize civilization." I do not know if it is true, as Rifkin says, that we are entering a "new phase in world history": "fewer and fewer workers," he says, "will be needed to produce the goods and services for the global population." *The End of Work*, he adds, thus naming his book, "examines the technological innovations and market-directed forces that are moving us to the edge of a near workless world."

To know if these statements are "true," one would have to agree on the meaning of each of these words (end, history, world, work, production, goods, etc.). I do not have the time here, nor therefore the intention, to discuss this serious and enormous problematic further, in particular the concepts of world and work that are brought into play in it. Something serious is indeed happening [*arrive*], is in the process of arriving or is at the point of arriving, to what we call *work, tele-work, virtual work*, and to what we call *world*—and thus to the being-in-the-world of what is still called *man*. It depends, in large part, on the techno-scientific mutation that, in the cyberworld, in the world of the Internet, of E-mail, and of cellular phones, is affecting tele-work, time, and the virtualization of work; a mutation that, at the same time that it is affecting the communication of knowledge, all forms of making common and all "community," is also affecting the experience of place, of taking place, of the event and the production [*œuvre*]: of what arrives.

The problematic of the aforementioned "end of work" was not absent from certain texts of Marx or Lenin—Lenin, who associated the gradual shortening of the work day to a process that would lead to the complete disappearance of the state. For Rifkin, the third technological revolution inscribes an absolute mutation. The two first revolutions, that of the steam engine, coal burning, steel, and textiles (in the nineteenth century), that of electricity, gasoline, and the automobile (in the twentieth century) did not radically affect the history of work. This is because both isolated a sector that the machine had not penetrated and where human work, non-machinal, nonreplaceable by a machine, was still available. After these two technical revolutions came: ours, the third, that of cyberspace and microcomputing and robotics. Here, it seems, there is no fourth zone in which to put the unemployed to work. A saturation by machines leads to the end of the worker, thus a certain end to work. (End of *der Arbeiter* and his era, as Jünger would say). Rifkin's book leaves room, however, for what it calls the *knowledge sector* in this mutation in progress. In the past, when new technologies replaced workers in different sectors, new spaces emerged to absorb those who had lost their jobs. Today, however, while agriculture, industry, and services send millions of people into unemployment owing to the progress of technology, the only category of worker that is spared is the category of "knowledge," an elite of industrial innovators, scientists, technicians, computer programmers, teachers, etc. But this remains a narrow space, one that is incapable of absorbing the vast numbers of unemployed. Such would be the dangerous singularity of our time.

I am not going to address the objections that one might make to these remarks, neither the objections one might make to the said "end of work" nor those to the said *globalization* [mondialisation]. In both cases, which, furthermore, are closely linked, I would begin by distinguishing—were I to discuss them head-on—between the incontestable mass phenomena registered by these words and the use one makes of these concept-less words. In fact, no one will deny it: something is happening to work in this century, to the reality and to the concept of work—active or actual work. What is happening to work is, in fact, an effect of techno-science, with the virtualization and globalizing dislocation of tele-work. (Even though, as Le Goff has shown, these contradictions concerning the time of work began very early in the Christian Middles Ages.) What is happening [*arrive*] indeed underscores a certain tendency to shorten asymptotically the time of work, as work in real time and localized in the same place as the body of the worker. All of this affects work in its classical forms, those forms we inherit; it affects work through our new experience of borders, of virtual communication, of the speed and range of information. This evolution is moving in the direction of a certain globalization; it is irrecusable and well known. But these phenomenal indices remain partial, heterogeneous, unequal in their development; they call for a fine-tuned analysis and no doubt for new concepts. On the other hand, between these obvious indices and their doxic usage—others would say ideological inflation, the rhetorical and often hazy complacency with which one yields to these words, "end of work" and "globalization"—there is a gap. And I think that those who forget this gap should be severely criticized. Because they are then trying to hide or hide from themselves the zones of the world, the populations, nations, groups, classes, individuals who in their massive majority are the excluded victims of this movement of the said "end of work" and "globalization." These victims suffer either because they do not have the work they need or else because they work too much for the salary they receive in exchange for their work on a world market that is so violently non-egalitarian. This capitalistic situation (where capital plays an essential role between the actual and the virtual) is more tragic in absolute numbers than it has ever been in the history of humanity. Humanity has perhaps never been further from the globalizing or globalized homogeneity, from the "work" and the "without work" that is often cited. A large part of humanity is "without work" when it wants to work, more work, and another part has too much work when it wants to have less, or even to put an end to work that is so poorly paid on the market. Any eloquent disquisition on the rights of man that does not take into account this economic inequality is threatened with chatter, formalism, or obscenity (here one would have to speak of GATT, the IMF, the external debt, etc.). This history began a long time ago. Intertwined with it is the real and semantic history of the words *trade* [métier] and *profession*. Rifkin is aware of the tragedy that might be provoked by an "end of work" that would not have the sabbatical or restful meaning it has in the Augustinian *City of God*. But in his moral and political conclusions, when he comes to define the responsibilities that must be assumed in the face of the "technological storm clouds on the horizon," in the face of a "new era of globalization and automation," he rediscovers, and I think that this is neither fortuitous nor acceptable without examination, the Christian language of "fraternal bonds," of virtues "not easily reducible to . . . machines," the "renewed meaning" of life, the "resurrection" of the service sector, the "rebirth of the human spirit"; he even imagines new forms of charity, for example, the payment of "shadow wages" to volunteers, a "value-added" tax on high-tech products and services "to be used exclusively to guarantee a social wage for the poor in return for . . . community service," etc.; he then rediscovers, in a way that is a little incantatory, the accents (and more than just the accents) of the discourse that I was talking about earlier when I said that it called for a complex genealogical analysis, but without complacency.

If I had had the time to retrace this genealogy with you, I would certainly have insisted more on the time of work, drawing my inspiration from the work of my colleague Jacques Le Goff. In the chapter "Time and Work" in *Another Middle Ages*, he shows how, in the fourteenth century, the demands for a lengthening and the demands for a shortening of the work day were already coeval. We have here the premises of a right of work and of a right to work, such as they will later come to be inscribed in the rights of man. The figure of the humanist is a response to the question of work. The humanist is someone who, in the theology of work that governed this period and is certainly not dead today, begins to secularize both the time of work and the use of monastic time [*l'emploi du temps monastique*]. Time, which is no longer simply a gift of God, can be calculated and sold. In the iconography of the fourteenth century, the clock sometimes represents the attribute of the humanist . . . this clock that I am forced to watch over and that strictly watches over the secular worker that I am here. Le Goff shows how the unity of the world of work, faced with the world of prayer and the world of war, did not last very long, if it ever existed. Following the "contempt for work [*métiers*]," "a new border of contempt established itself, one that passed right through the middle of the new classes, right through the middle of the work force [*professions*]." Although he does not distinguish (it seems to me) between "métier" and "profession" (as I think should be done), Le Goff also describes the process that, in the twelfth century, gave rise to a "theology of work" and to the transformation of the tripartite schema (*oratores, bellatores, laboratores*) into "more complex" schemas, which can be explained by the differentiation of economic and social structures and by a greater division of work.

2. *Forgiveness*. Today there is a globalization, a global dramatization of the scene of repentance and of asking forgiveness. It is conditioned both by the ground swell of our Abrahamic heritage and the new position of international law, and thus the new figure of globalization that has been produced since the last war by the transformed concepts of the rights of man, the new concepts of crime against humanity and genocide,

of war and aggression—the chief accusations of these auto-accusations. It
is hard to make out the scope of this question. Too often in the world
today, especially in political debates that reactivate and displace this notion, one maintains the ambiguity. One often confuses, sometimes in a
calculated way, forgiveness with a large number of related themes: excuse,
regret, amnesty, prescription, etc., many different themes, some of which
have to do with law, with criminal law; forgiveness must remain irreducible to all of them. As mysterious as the concept of forgiveness may
be, the scene, the figure, the language with which one tries to accommodate it belong to Abrahamic heritages (Judaism, Christianities, and
Islams). Yet, however differentiated and even conflictual this tradition
may be, it is both singular and on the way to universalization, precisely
through what this theater of forgiveness brings to light. Consequently,
the dimension of forgiveness tends to be erased in the course of this globalization and, with it, all measure, all conceptual limit. In all of the scenes
of repentance, confession, forgiveness, or excuse that have increasingly
appeared on the geopolitical scene since the last war, and in an accelerated way over the last few years, we are seeing not only individuals but
whole communities, professional guilds, representatives of ecclesiastical
hierarchies, sovereigns, and heads of state ask for "forgiveness." They do
it in a language that is not always that of the dominant religion in their
society (in the case of Japan or Korea, for example). This language
thereby becomes the universal idiom of law, politics, economics, and
diplomacy: both the cause and the significant symptom of this internationalization. The proliferation of these scenes of repentance and asking
"forgiveness" no doubt signifies, among other things, an *il faut* of anamnesis, an *il faut* without limit: a debt without limit toward the past.
Without limit, because this act of memory, which is also the subject of
the auto-accusation, of the "repentance," of the [court] appearance [*com-
parution*], must be carried beyond both legal and national state authority.
Thus, one wonders what is happening when the dimensions are such as
these. As for the reflection elicited by this phenomenon, one path regularly leads back to a series of events without precedent: those events that,
after and during the Second World War, made possible, "authorized" at
any rate, with the Nuremberg Trials, the international institution of a
legal concept such as "crime against humanity." A "performative" event
took place there whose reach is still hard to measure, and yet terms like
crime against humanity seem so common and intelligible to everyone

today. This mutation was itself provoked and legitimated by an international authority at a date, and according to a figure, determined by its history. This history is inseparable from a reaffirmation of the rights of man, of a new Declaration of the Rights of Man, even if it cannot be reduced to it. A sea change of this sort structures the space in which the grand pardon, the great world scene of repentance is being played out—sincerely or not. It often makes one think of a great convulsion. It would be indecent—and needlessly provocative—to say that this convulsion often resembles an irrepressible and very obscure compulsion, ambiguous in its unconscious roots. For it also obeys, fortunately, what one might call a *positive* movement. But it is true—and we should never forget it—that the sham, the forced ritual, sometimes the excess of falsehood in the confession itself, calculation or mimicry, are often there, as well. They corrupt this moving ceremony of guilt from the inside: an entire humanity shaken by the gesture of a unanimous confession! Nothing less than the human race would suddenly come and accuse itself publicly, dramatically, of all the crimes that have indeed been committed by it against itself, "against humanity." Were one to take inventory, while asking for forgiveness, of all the past crimes against humanity, there would be no innocent person left on earth. Who, then, would be in the position of judge or arbiter? All humans are the heirs, at least, of people or of events that were marked, in an indelible way, by "crimes against humanity." A supplementary but essential paradox: those events of the past, which at times gave rise to organized exterminations, and at other times took the form of great revolutions ("legitimate" and, in any case, still celebrated today by national or universal memory), have allowed for the emergence, and the gradual refinement, of legal pronouncements like the rights of man, the crime against humanity, genocide, the crime of aggression, etc.

Today this convulsion looks like a conversion. An "objective" conversion and one that tends to exceed all national limits: on the way to globalization. For, if the concept of crime against humanity is the chief accusation of this auto-accusation and of this request for forgiveness; if, furthermore, only a sacredness of the human can, in the last instance, justify this incrimination (no evil, no wrong is worse, according to this logic, than a crime against the humanity of man and against the rights of man); if the sacredness of the human finds its most legible, if not its only source of meaning, in the memory of the religions of the book and in a Jewish, but above all Christian, interpretation of the "neighbor" or the "fellow creature"; if, consequently, any crime against humanity touches what is most sacred in the living, and thus already touches the divine in man, some God-become-man or some man-become-God-by-God (the death of man and the death of God would betray the same crime here); then the "globalization [*mondialisation*]" of forgiveness resembles a huge process in progress, an endless procession of repentants, thus a virtually Christian convulsion-conversion-confession, a "work" of Christianization that no longer even needs the church or missionaries. This "work" sometimes looks like atheism, humanism, or triumphant secularization. But the difference is not important. Humanity would be ready as one man to accuse itself of a crime against humanity. To testify on its own behalf against itself, that is, and with good reason, to accuse itself as an other. This is terribly economical.

Whether one sees enormous progress here, a historical rupture, and/or a concept whose limits are still blurry, precarious in its foundations (and one can do both at the same time—this is my *temptation*, if I can still use this word in confessing), one fact remains irrecusable: the concept of crime against humanity governs the whole geopolitics of forgiveness. It gives it its code and its justification. Let us think of the extraordinary Commission for Truth and Reconciliation in South Africa. A unique phenomenon in spite of several South American precedents, particularly in Chili. Well then, what conferred the declared legitimacy on this commission was the definition of apartheid as a crime against humanity by the international community in its UN representation. One could take a hundred other examples, they all return to this reference in the form of a security.

3. *Peace.* Because I will not be able devote to peace the time necessary for an analysis that would be more appropriate and worthy of this great topic, which is in the contract of this session, I will say just a word that is directly inspired by the title of these large discussions, a new world contract. It seems to me that if there is a lesson to be learned from the most recent phenomena, which one hardly dares to call *wars* anymore (because of the semantic mutations that precisely imply the ambiguous role of the state in such "interventions")—the aforementioned Gulf War, Rwanda, the Congo, Kosovo, Timor, etc., phenomena all very different in their logic of sovereignties—the lesson is that, late or not, well-run or not, these interventions, in the name of the universal rights of man, with the prospect of judging chiefs of state and military commanders before inter-

national criminal courts, have indeed successfully challenged the sacred principle of state sovereignty, but have often done so in disturbing ways. As Arendt notes, only small states ever see their sovereignty contested and disputed by powerful states, even when it is in the name of universal principles. Not only would these powerful states never allow their own sovereignty to be challenged, but, what is more, they orient or preempt the decisions, and sometimes even the deliberations, of the recognized international agencies, in view of their own political-military-economic strategy because they are the only ones who have the economic and techno-military power to implement decisions. A world contract to come would have to acknowledge this fact: as long as these international agencies do not have an autonomy of deliberation, of decision-making, and especially of military intervention, as long as they do not have the force of law it is their mission to represent, well then, all the infractions of sovereignty in the name of the rights of man, which should be just in principle, will be suspect and contaminated by strategies before which vigilance will always remain de rigueur.

4. The serious question of *the death penalty* in the world cannot be dissociated from what I have just said. For, without going through the long abolitionist struggles that have developed over the centuries and even in the United States, one must remember this fact at least: since the last world war, a long series of conventions and international declarations of the rights of man, the right to life and the prohibition, hardly compatible with the death penalty, of cruel treatments (declarations that I do not have the time to cite, but almost all of them emanate from the UN) have created, directly or indirectly, a supra-state pressure to which a great number of democratic countries have been, let us say, sensitive at the moment they abolished the death penalty. It is always an international and supra-state agency, transcending the sovereignty of the state, that enjoins the states (both the death penalty and the right of pardon have always been the eminent signs of state sovereignty) to abandon the death penalty (seemingly on their own but, in fact, by international obligation). This is obviously the case in Europe, in France for the last twenty years, and in fifty-or-so other countries around the world. One may find, in accordance with certain jurists, that this growing tendency to abolish the death penalty is becoming what in English is called a *customary norm of international law* and in Latin a norm of *jus cogens*. Yet we know that among the countries that

386   ETHICS AND POLITICS TODAY

resist this tendency, among the nation states that present themselves as great Western democracies in the Christian-European tradition, the United States is today, to the best of my knowledge, the only country that, in the aftermath of the death penalty's turbulent history (an ancient and recent history that I do not have time to recall), not only has not abolished the death penalty but makes use of it massively, increasingly, cruelly, and, it must be said, in a way that is discriminatory when it is not blind—as many recent examples have shown. With other international associations, with the International Parliament of Writers, to which I have the honor of belonging (and which will be discussed tomorrow, I think, in connection with refuge-cities and the engagement of UNESCO on their behalf), in the name of these institutions, thus, and in my own name, I ask that the question of the death penalty be inscribed in the form of a solemn appeal in any text about a new "world contract." I will spare you my other professions of faith. Thank you.

Notes

INTRODUCTION

1. Jacques Derrida, "'Eating Well,' or the Calculation of the Subject: An Interview with Jacques Derrida," trans. Peter Conor and Avital Ronell, in *Who Comes after the Subject?*, eds. Eduardo Cadava, Peter Connor, Jean-Luc Nancy (New York and London: Routledge, 1991), 118.

2. Jacques Derrida, "'En ce moment même dans cet ouvrage me voici," *Psyché: Inventions de l'autre* (Paris: Galilée, 1987), 159–202; "At This Very Moment in This Work Here I Am" in *Re-Reading Levinas*, eds. Robert Bernasconi and Simon Critchley, trans. Ruben Berezdivin (Bloomington: Indiana University Press, 1991), 11–48.

3. Immanuel Kant, *Metaphysics of Morals*, trans. Mary Gregor (Cambridge: Cambridge University Press, 1991), 110–111.

4. For another break with Kant's moral heritage, see Derrida's discussion of duty and debt in *Passions* (Paris: Galilée, 1993), notes 3 and 11, 75 passim; *On the Name*, ed. Thomas Dutoit, trans. David Wood, John P. Leavy, and Ian McLeod (Stanford: Stanford University Press, 1995), notes 3 and 12, 132 passim.

NEGOTIATIONS

This interview was conducted by Deborah Esch and Tom Keenan in 1987 in view of this collection. It appears here for the first time in any language.

1. In 1974 Derrida wrote the *Avant-projet pour la fondation du Groupe de recherches sur l'enseignement philosophique* (GREPH), and the group was founded one year later. The Report to which Derrida refers here is the "Rapport" that was presented to M. Jean-Pierre Chevènement, Minister of State, Minister of Research and Industry, on 30 September 1982 by François Châtelet, Jacques Derrida, Jean-Pierre Faye, and Dominique Lecourt. The Collège International de Philosophie was founded in 1984. For more information concerning the activities of these groups, see *Du droit à la philosophie* (Paris: Galilée, 1990).

LETTER TO JEAN GENET (FRAGMENTS)

This unsent letter was written in response to Jean Genet's appeal on behalf of George Jackson, whose letters from prison, *Soledad Brother*, had just been published (New York: Coward-McKann, 1970) with a preface by Genet. The project to publish a collection of texts on Jackson was never realized; Jackson was shot and killed in San Quentin Prison on 21 August 1971. Derrida's letter appears here for the first time in any language.

DECLARATIONS OF INDEPENDENCE

This translation first appeared in *Caucus for a New Political Science* 15, Summer 1986, 7–15. "Déclarations d'Indépendance" was published in French in *Otobiographies: L'enseignement de Nietzsche et la politique du nom propre* (Paris: Galilée, 1984), 13–32. Most of the material contained in *Otobiographies* had previously been published in Canada under the title *L'oreille de l'autre: otobiographies, transferts, traductions*, eds. Claude Lévesque and Christie V. McDonald (Montréal: VLB Editeur, 1982). The latter has been translated into English by Peggy Kamuf and Avital Ronell as *The Ear of the Other: Otobiography, Transference, Translation*, ed. Christie V. McDonald (New York: Schocken Books, 1985). "Déclarations" was not included in *L'oreille* and was thus not translated in *The Ear of the Other*. "Déclarations" was first delivered as a public lecture at the University of Virginia in Charlottesville in 1976.

1. "Shortly" refers the reader to the discussion of Nietzsche's birthday ("anniversaire") in the French text.

2. Here the text of *Otobiographies* continues, following a chapter break, with the reading of Nietzsche that has been translated in *The Ear of the Other*.

WHAT I WOULD HAVE SAID . . .

The colloquium in question here, "Création et développement," was held in Paris at the Sorbonne on 12–13 February 1983 and was organized by the French Ministry of Culture. Derrida's unspoken contribution, "Ce que j'aurais dit . . . ," was published in *Le complexe de Léonard ou la société de la création*: Actes de la Rencontre internationale de la Sorbonne, février 1983 (Paris: Les Editions du *Nouvel Observateur*/J.-C. Lattès, 1984). It appears here in English for the first time.

1. William Bennett, "The Shattered Humanities," *The Wall Street Journal*, 31 December 1982. Mr. Bennett writes: "Increasingly, we read or try to read self-isolating vocabularies that abound within sub-disciplines. There seems to be a competition for complete unintelligibility. A popular movement in literary criticism called *deconstruction* denies that there are any texts at all. If there are no texts, there are no great texts, and no argument for reading."

ECONOMIES OF THE CRISIS

"Economies de la crise" was first published in *La Quinzaine littéraire* 399, 1–31 August 1983 in a special issue on "the crisis." It appears here in English for the first time.

EVENTS? WHAT EVENTS?

"Les événements? Quels événements?" was first published in *Le Nouvel Observateur* 1045, November 1984. It appears here in English for the first time.

"PARDON ME FOR TAKING YOU AT YOUR WORD"

"Pardonnez-moi de vous prendre au mot" was first published in *La Quinzaine littéraire* 459, 16–31 March 1986, in an issue marking the twentieth anniversary of the journal. It appears here in English for the first time. To celebrate the occasion of its twentieth anniversary, *La Quinzaine* wrote to "certain of its well-known friends," inviting them to contribute to a special anniversary issue. The following invitation, to which Derrida refers, was published in the same issue:

> On March 15th, 1966, the first issue of *La Quinzaine littéraire* appeared. We are going to celebrate its twentieth anniversary. We would be happy if you would accept to attend this celebration.
>
> Over the last twenty years, intellectual life in France has seen a wealth of events. In the special issue that we are planning for March 15, 1986, our regular contributors will evoke these events while trying to measure the place that our journal has had in them. This will be an opportunity for them and for our readers to become more acutely aware of today's situation as concerns creativity and knowledge, and to see along what probable lines of force the future is taking shape.
>
> Your own research and work encourage us to ask you what connections you maintain with the present intellectual situation, one which *La Quinzaine littéraire* has tried to and continues to try to reflect. Which events during these twenty years have seemed important to you, and which ones seem so to you today? To what degree do any of these seem to you to prefigure the future?
>
> It may be that this theme of reflection is far from your present preoccupations. In that case, we would be grateful if you would entrust us with a short extract, along with your commentary, from your work in progress.
>
> For the Editorial Board,
> Maurice Nadeau

1. This celebration of *La Quinzaine* ought to have been extended by publishing anonymous responses and asking the reader, in exchange for a gift subscription, to recognize the authors. Or else *La Quinzaine* could have mixed up the signatures and then asked the reader to put them back in order; in short, what could never have been written by *X*? Why must *Y* have written this and nothing else?

THE DECONSTRUCTION OF ACTUALITY

This interview was conducted by Brigitte Sohn, Cristina de Peretti, Stéphane Douailler, Patrice Vermeren, and Emile Malet for the monthly review *Passages* in August 1993 to mark the publication of *Spectres de Marx* (Paris: Galilée, 1993); *Specters of Marx: The State of the Debt, the Work of Mourning, and the New International,* trans. Peggy Kamuf (Routledge: New York, 1994). It appeared in French in *Passages* 57, September-October 1993, 60–75. It first appeared in English in *Radical Philosophy* 68, Autumn 1994, 28–41. It has been retranslated here.

1. See especially *Donner le temps 1: La fausse monnaie* (Paris: Galilée, 1992); *Given Time: 1. Counterfeit Money,* trans. Peggy Kamuf (Chicago: University of Chicago Press, 1992); and "Force of Law: 'The Mystical Foundation of Authority'" (bilingual text), in *Deconstruction and the Possibility of Justice*, Cardozo Law Review (New York, July-August 1990); English text reprinted in *Deconstruction and the Possibility of Justice*, ed. Drucilla Cornell et al. (Routledge: New York, 1992), 3–67.

2. Emmanuel Levinas, *Totalité et Infini: Essai sur l'extériorité* (The Hague: Martinus Nijhoff, 1961), 62; *Totality and Infinity,* trans. Alfonso Lingis (Pittsburgh: Duquesne University Press, 1969), 89.

TAKING SIDES FOR ALGERIA

"Parti Pris pour l'Algérie" was first published in *Les Temps Modernes* 580, January-February 1995, 233–41. It appears here in English for the first time. The occasion of this text was a public meeting held at the Sorbonne (in the great amphitheater) on 7 February 1994 at the initiative of CISIA (Comité International de Soutien aux Intellectuels Algériens [the International Committee for the Support of Algerian Intellectuals]) and la Ligue des droits de l'homme [the League for the Rights of Man] following an appeal for civil peace in Algeria. Following are two excerpts from the appeal to which Derrida refers in his intervention:

> It is for the Algerians alone to bring political solutions to the crisis that is sweeping through Algeria today. These solutions, however, cannot arise from the isolation of the country.
>
> We recognize the complexity of the situation: differing analyses and perspectives may legitimately be expressed concerning the origins and development of this situation. Nonetheless, an agreement can be reached on several points of principle.

Above all, to reaffirm that any outcome must be a civil one. Recourse to armed violence in order to defend or conquer power, terrorism, repression, the practice of torture and executions, assassinations and kidnappings, destruction, threats against the life and security of persons can only ruin the possibilities that Algeria still has at its disposal to establish its own democracy and the conditions of its economic development.

[. . .]

It is the condemnation by all of acts of terrorism and repression that will thus begin to carve out a space for the confrontation of individual analyses, in the respect for differences.

Efforts will be made in order to multiply the acts of solidarity in France and in other countries. Initiatives will be undertaken without delay in order to sensitize opinion to the Algerian drama, to underline the responsibility of governments and international financial institutions, to increase support for the Algerian democratic exigency.

FOR MUMIA ABU-JAMAL

This text is a transcription of the remarks made by Derrida at a press conference held at the United Nations Educational, Scientific and Cultural Organization (UNESCO) by the International Parliament of Writers on 1 August 1995. It was published on page one of *Le Monde* on 9 August 1995, where it was entitled "Pour Mumia Abu Jamal." It was then published as the "Preface" to the French translation of Mumia Abu-Jamal's book *En direct du couloir de la mort*, trans. Jim Cohen (Paris: Editions la Découverte, 1996), 7–13. It is published here in English for the first time. *Live from Death Row* by Mumia Abu-Jamal appeared in March 1995 and was published by Addison-Wesley (Reading, Massachusetts).

OPEN LETTER TO BILL CLINTON

This letter, which was received by the "Federal Priority Issues Office" at the White House, remains unanswered to this day. It first appeared in *Les Temps Modernes* 592, February-March 1997, 179–82.

DERELICTIONS OF THE RIGHT TO JUSTICE

This text is the transcription of Derrida's improvised intervention at the Théâtre des Amandiers on 21 December 1996, during a demonstration in support of the "sans-papiers." The transcription was originally published as "Manquements du droit à la justice (mais que manque-t-il donc aux 'sans-papiers'?)" in *Marx en jeu* (Paris: Descartes & Cie, 1997), 73–91. It appears here in English for the first time. The "sans-papiers"—literally those who are "without papers"—refers, as the text itself will make clear, to what in the United States are called *undocumented aliens*.

POLITICS AND FRIENDSHIP

This interview was conducted by Michael Sprinker in April 1989 at the University of California at Irvine. It was first published in *The Althusserian Legacy*, eds. E. Ann Kaplan and Michael Sprinker (London-New York: Verso, 1993), 183–231. A related article, indirectly referred to in this text, is Jacques Derrida, "The Politics of Friendship," *Journal of Philosophy* 11 (November 1988).

THE AFOREMENTIONED SO-CALLED HUMAN GENOME

"La norme et son suspens," "La norme doit manquer," "Vers une reconstruction du concept juridique de l'humain'?", "Même l'autre," and "Décidément garder l'éveil" were delivered by Derrida in the context of a multidisciplinary colloquium organized by the Association Descartes under the patronage of the French Ministry of Research and Space, UNESCO, and the Commission for Education of the French Republic in December 1992. The proceedings of the colloquium, "Analysis of the Human Genome: Freedoms and Responsibilities," were later published in a book entitled *Le génome et son double*, ed. Gérard Huber (Paris: Editions Hermes, 1996). Derrida's interventions appear here in English for the first time.

NIETZSCHE AND THE MACHINE

This interview was conducted by Richard Beardsworth in 1993. It first appeared in English in *Journal of Nietzsche Studies* 7, Spring 1994, 7–66. Beardsworth had prepared thirteen questions for Derrida in advance of the interview, and in *Journal of Nietzsche Studies* they appear *en bloc* before the interview. I have preferred to present the questions within the interview itself (thus the reader will have both question and response in close succession).

1. Jacques Derrida, *Otobiographies: l'enseignement de Nietzsche et la politique du nom propre* (Paris: Galilée, 1984), 98.

2. Friedrich Nietzsche, *The Will to Power*, trans. W. Kaufmann and R. Hollingdale (New York: Vintage Books, 1968), Book Two, note 343, 189.

3. Jacques Derrida, *Of Grammatology*, trans. Gayatri Spivak (Baltimore: Johns Hopkins University Press, 1974), 140.

4. Jacques Derrida, *Of Spirit: Heidegger and the Question*, trans. Geoffrey Bennington and Rachel Bowlby (Chicago: University of Chicago Press, 1989), 39–40.

5. Jacques Derrida, *Writing and Difference*, trans. Alan Bass (New York: Routledge, 1978), note 21, 313.

6. Jacques Derrida, "Psyche: Invention of the Other," trans. Catherine Porter, in *Reading de Man Reading*, eds. Lindsay Waters and Wlad Godzich (Minneapolis: University of Minnesota Press, 1989), 60.

7. Because *Specters of Marx* came out after Derrida had received Beardsworth's interview questions, it was thought best to retain the original form of these questions and to discuss *Specters of Marx* directly in the interview.

"DEAD MAN RUNNING": SALUT, SALUT

This letter appeared (along with its notes) in the fiftieth anniversary issue of *Les Temps Modernes* 587, March-April-May 1996, 7–54. It appears here in English for the first time.

1. "Writing for One's Age [*Ecrire pour son époque*]," trans. Bernard Frechtman, *"What Is Literature?" and Other Essays* (Cambridge: Harvard University Press, 1988), 239. I will in what follows refer at greater length to the context of this expression, which resonates very differently today but which at the time [*époque*] precisely defined the age [*époque*], the Sartrian concept of age [*époque*].

2. These are the first words of "Ecrire pour son époque," at the very beginning of the issue I have before me and whose paper has suffered greatly, for I must have bought it in Algeria at a time when I had not yet set foot in what was then called the *Metropolis*. How could I not enjoy remembering this? And I am pleased that one of only two texts that I have recently published in *Les Temps Modernes* is a "Taking sides for Algeria" in an issue that is in the best tradition of *Les Temps Modernes* (*Algérie, La guerre des frères* 580, January-February 1995) in which you reaffirm so accurately the "bounds [*cap*] of non-infidelity" and maintain—*saving* them thus—those fine words that are brand new and that I will mention again later, "commitment and resistance." I very much like this prudent and tormented expression, the "bounds of non-infidelity." It does not say "fidelity" (which would be too much and too impossible) but the renewed oath not to betray, which returns without returning to the same and takes into account what comes at us from the future, where one does not expect it: hence the impossibility of the promise that one nevertheless renews and whose bounds [*cap*] one maintains, for lack of all the rest. What more can one ever promise than the bounds of non-infidelity through all the changes of direction, complete turnarounds, even, at times perjuries, but never repudiations or renunciations?

3. *Nausea*, trans. Lloyd Alexander (New York: New Directions, 1964), 117. The emphasis is mine, naturally, and in this letter, in the end, I am simply retracing the way of freedom as the way of salvation, underlining passages as I go.

4. In "Introducing *Les Temps Modernes*" [trans. Jeffrey Mehlman, *"What Is Literature?" and Other Essays*], this critique of the ideology of fraternity is, in fact, directed at the "analytic cast of mind" as the "defensive weapon" of "bourgeois democracy": "All men are *brothers*: fraternity is a passive bond among distinct molecules, which takes the place of an active or class-bound solidarity that the analytic cast of mind cannot even imagine" (256). In multiplying the questions about the authority of this fraternalist scheme and everything it implies in our

culture, recently, in *Politics of Friendship*, I forgot that—in a way that is certainly different in all regards—Sartre had already challenged the rhetoric of fraternity. This forgetting, which happens to me more often that I can acknowledge, often, belatedly, is at bottom the theme of this letter: a strange transaction between amnesia and anamnesis in the legacy that makes us what we are and has already made us think what we have not yet thought, as if our inheritance were always a specter to come, a ghost that runs *before us, after which* we breathlessly follow, in turn running ourselves to death, to death and loss of breath . . .

5. "Introducing *Les Temps Modernes*," 265. Sartre underlines "delivered."

6. "Introducing *Les Temps Modernes*," 261. Sartre underlines "liberation."

7. I am tempted to think exactly the opposite, namely that one writes for the dead or for the in-nate, even though this is, in fact, "too easy" and "too difficult." I remember that Genet said the same (i.e., that he wrote for the dead); and I would dare to say that those who are not yet living, "not yet born" are also the spectral addressees, irrecusable as well, of everything we address, of all our letters . . . Would the author of *Shoah* contradict me? Better yet, I think that Sartre himself did not say anything and above all did not do anything, though saying it, everywhere, except the opposite of what he says here. If "an era, like a man, is first of all a future" (already cited, "Introducing *Les Temps Modernes*," 253), then we write, and do everything we do as if magnetized by what no longer is or is not yet living—and this is life itself, at least if memory, date, and anniversary are possible in it. As the "bounds of non-infidelity." Which will always remain, I will admit, a question and the stakes of a bet.

What is more, I am not sure that the Sartrian thinking of salvation, as I would like to reconstitute it here, is absolutely pure of any memory of "Christian belief," which Sartre will nonetheless immediately denounce. I am not sure this is possible, that such a purification is possible, possible in a way that is pure or in general.

8. I read "What Is Literature?" almost half a century ago. And I had not opened it again since. At first this text was important to me; then I found I had to distance myself from it, undoubtedly because I judged it very inadequate and even spoke publicly of its limits as to what *happens and is done*, according to me, with and by "literature," or its limits as to what literature "is" in its supposed essence. It does not matter whether I was right or wrong, this is not the place or the moment to return to it. But given that all virtual discussion remains suspended today, the time of this letter, I want to say this, that when I reread this text in *Situations II*, I find "What Is Literature?" of an admirable and impressive lucidity, "topical," as they say, almost intact, at times even advancing us, exemplary and not only as an exercise and program of the "sociology of literature" (I will perhaps return to this in a moment).

9. I am using this strange word here, synonymous to a certain degree with "safe [*sauf*]" and "unharmed [*indemne*]," even with sacred and saintly (*heilig*,

holy), to put this argument in an important relation (at least I hope to do this) with the logic of immunology and above all of auto-immunology that I tried to formalize elsewhere (in "Foi et savoir," in *La religion*, Seuil 1996, for example, or in *Résistances—de la psychanalyse*, Galilée 1996). I have already said that self-contradiction was what interested and touched me the most in Sartre. Here the desire for immunological salvation always tragically contradicts itself according to an auto-immunological necessity that loses its own protection and goes so far as to ruin its most elementary defenses.

10. Rereading myself, I suddenly remembered that the first of my only two contributions to the *T.M.*, classified at the time under the rubric *Correspondance*, contained the word *sidelines* [écart] in its title ("D'un texte à l'écart" ["From a Text on the Sidelines"], *Les Temps Modernes* 284, March 1970). It concerned, twenty-five years ago, a nasty quarrel, and I notice, as I reread this polemical text, that I did not content myself with refuting a given article or author but that I challenged an "altogether Parisian form of guerrilla warfare," even going so far as to say that "I will keep to myself certain hypotheses concerning the ideological strategy of *Les Temps Modernes*" (1552).

11. The figure is so tempting! It is thus not necessary to inscribe this rhetoric in a filiation, in the trajectory of a loan or an unconscious plagiarism. Nonetheless, Sartre's cemetery, a library, still resembles the enlargement of a reminiscence. Is he not already resuscitating another cemetery, the cemetery of *A la Recherche du Temps Perdu* (III, 903), a cemetery-book this time and not a library? This would make the Sartrian library a cemetery of cemeteries. Proust: "A book is a large cemetery where on most of the tombstones one can no longer read the names that have been erased." A pretext for entitling the fantasy of a book to come on the French literary tradition of the twentieth century: "A Question of Taste, from Proust to Sartre." Or again: "The Book of Life and the Book of the Dead." Or again: "In Search of Lost Taste: Between Time and Epoch."

12. Sartre himself, as he often does (this is the "rhetoric" or the "logic" of contradiction that is so important to me), takes the opposite side of this assurance about eternity: it is not a matter, he says in "What Is Literature?" of "testifying before eternity."

13. "Introducing *Les Temps Modernes*," 250. It is true that he adds "it was honorable." Visibly, however, he no longer wants anything to do with the poet who "took himself to be a prophet." On the other hand, it is hard to find fault with Sartre when he concedes that "it was honorable." Not just anyone can take himself or allow himself to be taken for a prophet, supposing that, and this is the whole question, one has a concept that is a little rigorous, a little more refined than the current *doxa* of what prophesy is, and what the relation is between prophet, prophesy, and prophetism. Besides the boredom, deadly, which I will not mention, what would happen if everything that resembled a prophetic function were to

be banished from discourse and especially, as Sartre himself seems to want, from poetry? Fortunately, I believe that an annihilation of *all prophetic dimension* is impossible. One can only watch over its content (this is always necessary, especially in politics, and the prophets themselves sometimes invite us to do it) or weaken its tension (one is then dealing with boring little prophets, prophesies of low intensity that enthrall or convince no one). But however necessary and preliminary it remains here, the thinking of prophesy—and, still more, messianicity in general (I am not saying prophetism or messianism), is something that is too difficult for a letter, an anniversary . . .

14. Anna Boschetti, *Sartre et "Les Temps Modernes,"* (Paris: Editions de Minuit, 1985).

15. Sartre et *"Les Temps Modernes,"* 149. The analogy not only performs miracles, in a way, between "Hebraic prophetism" and the prophetism of S. and the *T.M.* Rather, it is invoked, one might say, between the latter and other prophetisms, often very close to it in history, without one being able to see how "prophetism" constitutes the *specific* and thus determining feature with which to identify—analytically, precisely—this or that, the former or the latter. Anna Boscetti admits in passing, without worrying about the demarcation of her object, that, before Sartre, Romain Rolland, just like Zola, very famous and very much discussed, rediscovers political prophetism in a sentence in which "art for art's sake" triumphs again unreservedly in the literary field after the parentheses devoted to Dreyfus (31). Thus, if one can speak of "prophetism" in general, if indeed "political prophetism" is recurrent, it is because this concept of prophetism does not define anything singular for a given historical or political "field," at a given epoch, as long as it itself is not defined otherwise. And what if all the "intellectuals," all the "philosophers," "poets," writers," "ideologues," "politicians," "scientists" (I am stopping here arbitrarily) were never to escape the "prophetic function"? What if they could only inflect it and translate it, what would one have to conclude then? And would this be a bad thing in itself? But how bored we would be, and how tasteless things would become otherwise! In short: as long as I have not been shown an "intellectual" (and even a "speaking subject" in general) whose speech is free of all "prophetism" (revolutionary reference to the future— to what comes, to good and evil, to justice—promise and performativity, inspiration that comes from the other, etc.) and also of all messianicity, I do not know what one is speaking about, what it is being opposed to, or that from which it is being distinguished when one speaks to me of a "prophetism" produced by the state of the field. I do not know above all what "field" one is speaking to me about because there is "prophetism" in every field, at the determining center of any "field," a priori, and even in the zone of a field that wants to be or calls itself *scientific*—which makes the designation of a field, however useful it may sometimes be, a gesture that is often more "knowing [*savant*]" than purely scientific. As such, it calls (*ad infinitum*) for a new effort at "objectivation."

16. See above, p. 258.

ETHICS AND POLITICS TODAY

This text is the transcription of an intervention that took place at a forum at the Collège International de Philosophie in the Spring of 1987. It is published here for the first time in any language. Following Derrida's talk is a question and answer session; unfortunately, many of the questions could not be transcribed fully and have been rendered here by sentence fragments or paraphrase. Georges Ibrahim Abdallah, a Lebanese Christian, was the founder (1979) of the Fractions armées révolutionnaires libanaises (FARL, or LARF in English), which was responsible for a number of terrorist attacks in France. In October 1984, Abdallah was arrested in Lyon; he was put on trial in 1987, where his lawyer was Jacques Vergès—the celebrated defender of the indefensible, including Klaus Barbie and Carlos the Jackal. Abdallah was convicted on 28 February 1987, and sentenced to life in prison for murder. There were a number of bombings in Paris associated with his capture and trial.

ON THE "PRICELESS," OR THE "GOING RATE" OF THE TRANSACTION

"Du 'sans prix', ou le 'juste prix' de la transaction" first appeared in *Comment penser l'argent?: Troisième Forum Le Monde Le Mans,* ed. Roger-Pol Droit (Paris: Editions Le Monde: 1992), 386–401. It appears here in English for the first time.

1. Marc Shell informed me after this conference that, according to the Oxford English Dictionary, *silver* can also sometimes mean *money in general,* but that even if the quotations used to support this definition go back to the ninth century, they remain, as one can well imagine, "ambiguous." In Canada, today still, *silver* can sometimes mean *small change* or "monnaie," money back.

2. Immanuel Kant, *Grounding for the Metaphysics of Morals,* trans. James W. Ellington (Indianapolis/Cambridge: Hackett Publishing Company, 1981), 40.

THE RIGHT TO PHILOSOPHY FROM A COSMOPOLITAN POINT OF VIEW

"Le droit à la philosophie du point de vue cosmopolitique" was first delivered as an introduction to an international conference organized by M. Sinaceur under the auspices of UNESCO on 23 May 1991. It was published as a fifty-page book by the Editions Unesco/Verdier in 1997. It appears here in English for the first time.

1. Immanuel Kant, "Idea for a Universal History with a Cosmopolitan Purpose," *Political Writings,* ed. Hans Reiss, trans. H.B. Nisbet (Cambridge: Cambridge University Press, 1991), 47–48.

2. These themes are further elaborated in the texts published by GREPH, the Collège International de Philosophie (in particular in its founding report) and in

certain of my essays, for example, *Du droit à la philosophie* (Galilée, 1990), and *L'Autre Cap: La démocratie ajournée* (Minuit, 1991).

3. "Idea for a Universal History with a Cosmopolitan Purpose," 51.

AS IF IT WERE POSSIBLE "WITHIN SUCH LIMITS" . . .

"Comme si c'était possible 'within such limits' . ." first appeared in the *Revue Internationale de Philosophie* 3/1998, number 205, 497–529, an issue devoted to the work of Jacques Derrida. It appears here in English for the first time.

1. See "The Last Word" and then "The Very Last Word" on Kafka in *Friendship*, trans. Elizabeth Rottenberg (Stanford: Stanford University Press, 1997) and "Le dernier mot" (1935–36) in *Après coup* (Paris: Editions de Minuit, 1983): ". . . the echo of the word *il y a*. There, without a doubt, is the last word I thought as I listened to them" (66).

2. See in particular chapters 2 and 3 of *Politics of Friendship*, trans. George Collins (London: Verso, 1997), following this "dangerous perhaps" that Nietzsche said was the thinking of the philosophers of the future [*de l'à-venir*]. For example (and I will underline certain words although I will take the following precaution from the outset: the quotations that I may happen to make from certain of my texts are intended only to open the space of a discussion here. I want only to extend this discussion beyond certain limits in which it must—for lack of space—remain contained and constrained. I quote myself although I find it distasteful and at the risk, a risk that is deliberately run, of being accused of complacency; these quotations are to my mind neither arguments of authority nor abusive exhibitions, nor are they reminders for the authors of the articles published here. These authors are in no need of reminders. I would simply like, in a brief and economical way, to address myself, by means of these quotations or references, to the reader who, interested in pursuing the exchange that is begun here, would like to consult the texts in question):

> "Now the thought of the 'perhaps' perhaps engages the only *possible* thought of the event—of friendship to come and friendship for the future. For to love friendship, it is not enough to know how to bear the other in mourning; one must love the future. And there is no more just category for the future than that of the '*perhaps*.' Such a thought conjoins friendship, the future, and the *perhaps* to open on to the coming of what comes—that is to say, necessarily in the regime of a *possible* whose *possibilization* must prevail over the *impossible*. For a possible that would only be *possible* (*non-impossible*), a *possible* surely and certainly *possible*, accessible in advance, would be a poor *possible*, a futureless *possible*, a *possible* already set aside, so to speak, life-assured. This would be a program or a causality, a development, a process without an event. The *possibilization of the impossible possi-*

ble must remain at one and the same time as undecidable—and therefore as decisive—as the future itself" (29).

"Without the opening of an absolutely undetermined *possible*, without the radical abeyance and suspense marking a *perhaps*, there would never be either event or decision. Certainly. But nothing takes place and nothing is ever decided without suspending the *perhaps* while keeping its 'living' *possibility* in living memory. If no decision (ethical, juridical, political) is *possible* without interrupting determination by engaging oneself in the *perhaps*, on the other hand, the same decision must interrupt the very thing that is its *condition of possibility*: the perhaps itself" (67 passim).

The quotation marks around the word *living* signal the necessary connection between the risky aporetic of the *impossible possible* and a thinking of spectrality (*neither* living *nor* dead, but living *and* dead).

3. For example, in *How to Do Things with Words* (Cambridge: Harvard University Press, 1962). On this impurity, understood otherwise, I, too, have attempted to draw some consequences (in *Limited Inc* and elsewhere). I could, given the time and space for such an exercise, connect this idea to almost all of my thinking.

4. J.L. Austin, "A Plea for Excuses," *Philosophical Papers* (Oxford: Oxford University Press, 1961), 175.

5. One would have to reconstitute and problematize the context in which propositions such as the following appear:

"To take charge [*annehmen*] of a 'thing' or a 'person' in its essence means to love it: to favor it [*sie lieben: sie mögen*]. Thought in a more original way this favoring [*dieses Mögen*] means to bestow essence as a gift [*das Wesen schenken*]. . . . Being as the enabling-favoring [*als Vermögend-Mögende*] is the possible [*das Mögliche*]. As the element, Being is the 'quiet power' of the favoring-enabling [*des mögende Vermögens*], that is, of the possible [*das heißt, des Möglichen*]. Of course, our words *möglich* and *Möglichkeit* under the dominance of 'logic' and 'metaphysics,' are thought solely in contrast to 'actuality [*Wirklichkeit*]': that is, they are thought on the basis of a definite—the metaphysical—interpretation of Being as *actus* and *potentia*, a distinction identified with the one between *extentia* and *essentia*."

Martin Heidegger, "Letter on Humanism" in *Basic Writings*, trans. David Farrell Krell (New York: Harper and Row, 1977), 196. On these problems, see Richard Kearney's remarkable work *La poétique du possible* (Paris: Vrin, 1984). As for a certain thinking of the "more impossible [*plus impossible*]" or of the "more than impossible [*plus qu'impossible*]" as possible ("*Das überunmöglischste ist möglich*," Angelus Silesius), I will allow myself to refer to *Sauf le nom* (Paris: Galilée, 1993),

32 ff. All the aporias of the impossible-possible or of the more-than-impossible would be thus "lodged" but also dislodged "on the inside" of what is quietly called favor, love, the movement toward the Good, etc.

6. For example in *Le pardon* (Paris: Aubier Montaigne, 1967), 204; and "Nous a-t-on demandé pardon?" in *L'imprescriptible* 1948–1971 (Paris: Seuil, 1986), 47 ff.

> 7. "[T]he most rigorous deconstruction has never characterized itself as either foreign to literature or, especially, as something that is *possible* . . . it loses nothing by admitting its own impossibility, and those who might be given to premature celebration will not lose anything by waiting. The danger for the deconstructive task would be, rather, *possibility*, and to become a collection of regulated procedures, methodological practices, and accessible formulas. If the force and the desire of deconstruction have a significance, it is a certain experience of the impossible . . . the experience of the other as the invention of the impossible, or in other words, the only possible invention."

"Psyche: Inventions of the Other" in *Reading de Man Reading*, trans. Catherine Porter, ed. Lindsay Waters and Wlad Godzich (Minneapolis: University of Minnesota Press, 1989), 36.

8. "We should be more *radical* than deconstruction, and completely leave the realm of propositionalism. Derrida's thought *invites* us to do so." I have underlined the two words here.

1. On one hand I emphasize the word *invite* for reasons that will become clear later on, I hope. Must one say that unconditional hospitality, hospitality that is both pure and impossible, responds to a *logic of invitation* (when the ipseity of the at-home [*chez-soi*] welcomes the other into its own horizon, when it poses its conditions, claiming thus to know whom it wants to receive, to expect and to invite, and *how, up to what point, whom* it is *possible* to invite, etc.?) or does it respond to *a logic of visitation* (the host then says *yes* to the coming or to the *unexpected and unpredictable* event of whoever comes, at any moment, too early or too late, in absolute anachrony, without being invited, without being announced, without any horizon of expectation: like a messiah so difficult to identify and so difficult to anticipate that the very name of messiah, the figure of the messiah, and especially of messianism, would again reveal a haste in putting invitation before visitation). How does one conform to the meaning of *what* we call an *event*, namely the unanticipatible coming of *what*ever comes [ce *qui vient*] and of *who*ever comes [qui *vient*], the meaning of the event being none other than the meaning of the other, the meaning of absolute alterity? The *invitation* maintains control and receives within the limits of the possible; it is not thus pure hospitality, it rations hospitality, it still belongs to the order of the judicial and the political; *visitation*, on the other hand, appeals to a pure and unconditional hospitality that welcomes whatever arrives as impossible. The only possible hospitality, as pure

hospitality, must thus do the impossible. How would such an impossible be possible? How would it become possible? What is the best transaction—economic and aneconomic—between the logic of invitation and the logic of visitation? Between their analogy and their heterology? What is experience then, if it is this becoming-possible of the impossible as such? I am not sure that I have practiced or preferred invitation, to the waitless-wait [*l'attente sans attente*] of visitation, but I will not swear to anything.

2. On the other hand, I emphasize the word *radical*, namely, the powerful metaphysical notion of radicality, the necessity of which this word recalls. One thinks of the figures of the root, of depth, of the origin said to be radical, etc., from Aristotle (for whom causes are "roots") to Husserl—and of all the "foundation-alisms," as they say in the world of Anglo-Saxon thought, in the course of debates to which I have never been able, I admit, to adjust my premises. Feeling myself to be both foundationalist *and* anti-foundationalist, from one problematic context to another, from one interrogative strategy to another, I do not know how to use this "word" *in general*: in general I am and I remain a "*quasi* foundationalist." This notion of radicality, as figure and as irrecusable injunction, is it not precisely [*justement*] what is subject to the turbulence of a deconstruction? Deconstruction has never laid claim to radicalism and in any case has never consisted in raising the stakes of radicality. The fact remains that an excess in this direction can certainly do no harm (indeed radicalism is to be recommended to all philosophy and is no doubt philosophy itself) but it might not change its ground, change the ground that is subject to the seismic turbulence I have just mentioned. This is why, just above, in the place where this note is called for in the text, I underline the cumbersome "quasi" that I take on so often. On *deconstruction and radicality*, and for the sake of brevity, within such limits, I will allow myself to refer, among my most recent texts, to *Spectres de Marx* (Paris: Galilée, 1993), 148 ff.

9. In particular in *The Tain of the Mirror, Derrida and the Philosophy of Reflection* (Cambridge: Harvard University Press, 1986).

10. *De la grammatologie* (Paris: Editions de Minuit, 1967), 90.

11. Beyond his luminous readings with which, for some years Giovannangeli has recalled me to a Sartrian legacy that I can, thanks to him, reinterpret—see in particular his book *La passion de l'origine* (Paris: Galilée, 1995) and his articles in *Le passage des frontières* (Paris: Galilée 1994) and *Passions de la littérature* (Paris: Galilée 1996)—I would have liked to pursue here, in this connection, the discussion of the impossible-possible as law of desire or love (in Heidegger and in relation to another thinking of *Ereignis*—whether or not one translates this word by "event"). I would do so, given the time and space, by taking into account what Giovannangeli develops in terms of the *possibility of an unconscious affect*.

12. To say or to write is at the same time to assume the legacy of natural language and ordinary language *and to formalize them*, by bending them to this formalizing abstraction whose power they carry originally: the use of a word or

phrase, however simple and ordinary they may be, the putting into play of their power, is already, by identification of iterable words, a formalizing idealization. Thus there is no *purely* ordinary language just as there is no *purely* philosophical, formal or, in any sense of the word, extraordinary language. In this sense, if it is true, as Austin says, that there is no "last word," it is hard to say, as he does, that ordinary language is the "first word," a word that is simply and indivisibly "first."

13. *Passions* (Paris: Galilée, 1993), 26 ff. and 81 ff. I also examined the Foucauldian notion of "problematization" in "Etre juste avec Freud" in *Résistances—de la psychanalyse* (Paris: Galilée 1996), 142–43.

14. See in particular *De l'esprit, Heidegger et la question* and the discussion of the promise, the *yes* prior to any opposition of *yes* and *no*—and especially what comes "before any question" (Galilée: Paris, 1987), 147 ff. See also *Politics of Friendship*.

15. On the repetition of this "yes, yes," I will allow myself to refer to *Ulysse Gramophone, Deux mots pour Joyce* (Paris: Galilée, 1987), 132 passim, as well as "Nombre de oui" in *Psyché* (Paris: Galilée, 1987), 639 ff.

16. "Violence and Metaphysics" in *Writing and Difference*, trans. Alan Bass (Chicago: The University of Chicago Press, 1978), 79 ff.

17. *Given Time: I. Counterfeit Money*, trans. Peggy Kamuf (Chicago: University of Chicago Press, 1992), 29 passim.

18. "Ousia and Grammè: Note on a Note from *Being and Time*" in *Margins of Philosophy*, trans. Alan Bass (Chicago: University of Chicago Press, 1982), 29.

19. "Ousia and Grammè," 55.

20. "Psyche: Inventions of the Other," 60.

21. *The Post Card*, trans. Alan Bass (Chicago: University of Chicago Press, 1987): 489.

22. *The Post Card*, 30.

23. On this impossible possibility, this *im*possibility as pervertibility, as the permanent possibility of the perversion of the promise into a threat, see "Avances," Preface to Serge Margel, *Le tombeau du Dieu artisan* (Paris: Minuit, 1995).

24. Some time ago, in the space of Husserlian phenomenology, I analyzed in analogous fashion an apparently negative possibility of form, an impossibility, the impossibility of full and immediate intuition, the "essential possibility of non-intuition," the "possibility of crisis" as a "crisis of the logos." But this possibility of the impossibility, as I said at the time, is not simply negative; the trap also becomes a chance: "for Husserl, this possibility [of crisis] remains connected to the very movement of truth and to the production of ideal objectivity: ideal objectivity has in fact an essential need for writing." See *Of Grammatology*, trans. Gayatri Spivak (Baltimore: Johns Hopkins University Press, 1974), 40; and especially *Introduction à l'origine de la géométrie de Husserl* (Paris: PUF, 1962).

25. "The ultimate aporia is the impossibility of the aporia *as such*." *Apories* (Paris: Galilée, 1993), 137. Another way of saying that there is no question with-

out a problem, and no problem that does not hide or protect itself behind the possibility of an answer.

26. "Différance" (1967) in *Margins of Philosophy*, trans. Alan Bass (Chicago: University of Chicago Press, 1982).

27. One could refer here to many of the admirable works of Plotnitsky, in particular *In the Shadow of Hegel: Complementarity, History and the Unconscious* (Gainesville: Florida University Press, 1993), *Complementarity: Anti-epistemology after Bohr and Derrida* (Durham, NC: Duke University Press, 1994), as well as to his masterful, most recent interventions around the so-called Sokal Affair. Moreover, Christopher Norris has just published (in the perspective of his article here) an important work in which he devotes a chapter to quantum mechanics; the interested reader will find in this book a friendly discussion of certain aspects of Plotnitsky's interpretation with which Norris is basically in agreement. Norris regrets that Plotnitsky's interpretation is at times, here and there, "*more postmodernist than deconstructive*," though he nonetheless pays Plotnitsky the homage he is due: *Against Relativism, Philosophy of Science, Deconstruction and Critical Theory* (London: Blackwell, 1997), 113. Although I do not share Norris's reservations, the space of this problematic and this discussion, it seems to me, is of great necessity today. As for myself, I always learn a great deal about all of these crossings: between deconstruction and the sciences, certainly, but also between two very different approaches—that of Norris and that of Plotnitsky—whom I would like to acknowledge here. No one today has done more or succeeded better than these two philosophers in dispelling the tenacious prejudices ("deconstruction" is foreign or hostile to "science," to "reason"; deconstruction, as we noted earlier, is "empiricist," "skeptical," or "relativist," "playful" or "nihilist," "anti-humanist," etc.). No one demonstrates better than they the necessity and richness of the co-implications between "deconstructive" and "scientific" problematics that are too often separated. Both in discussions and in institutions.

28. *Of Grammatology*, 93

29. I am underlining the passages that refer here to these three instance—thought, philosophy and science: "Derrida's work reflects or mediates aspects of contemporary science. It deals of course with only one dimension of his work, but it does show a *thinker open to the implications of science.*" And Johnson goes on to say the following, which I would like to underline precisely because it suspends the prejudice according to which "science does not think" (Heidegger): "*open to the implications of science, of what science gives us to think.*" How does science "give" one to think? Beyond "*such limits,*" I would have liked to develop this analysis in terms of this "give [*donne*]" and this "gift [*donation*]".

30. See in particular "Foi et savoir: Les deux sources de la 'religion' aux limites de la simple raison," in *La religion*, ed. J. Derrida and G. Vattimo (Paris: Editions du Seuil, 1996).

GLOBALIZATION, PEACE, AND COSMOPOLITANISM

"La mondialisation, la paix et la cosmopolitique" was first delivered as a talk on 6 November 1999, at UNESCO headquarters in Paris as part of the "Discussions of the Twenty-first Century." The general theme of the day was "The New World Contract" that was being drawn up by Federico Mayor, then Director General of the Institution. Derrida's intervention took place in the context of a debate on "Globalization and the Third Industrial Revolution." It was transcribed and published in the journal *Regards* 54, February 2000, 16–19. It appears here in English for the first time.

Cultural Memory | *in the Present*

Jacques Derrida, *Negotiations: Interventions and Interviews, 1971–2001*

Brett Levinson, *The Ends of Literature: Post-transition and Neoliberalism in the Wake of the "Boom"*

Timothy J. Reiss, *Against Autonomy: Global Dialectics of Cultural Exchange*

Hent de Vries and Samuel Weber, eds., *Religion and Media*

Niklas Luhmann, *Theories of Distinction: Re-Describing the Descriptions of Modernity*, ed. and introd. by William Rasch

Johannes Fabian, *Anthropology with an Attitude: Critical Essays*

Michel Henry, *I Am the Truth: Toward a Philosophy of Christianity*

Gil Anidjar, *"Our Place in al-Andalus": Kabbalah, Philosophy, Literature in Arab Jewish Letters*

Hélène Cixous and Jacques Derrida, *Veils*

F. R. Ankersmit, *Historical Representation*

F. R. Ankersmit, *Political Representation*

Elissa Marder, *Dead Time: Temporal Disorders in the Wake of Modernity (Baudelaire and Flaubert)*

Reinhart Koselleck, *Timing History, Spacing Concepts: The Practice of Conceptual History*

Niklas Luhmann, *The Reality of the Mass Media*

Hubert Damisch, *A Childhood Memory by Piero della Francesca*

Hubert Damisch, *A Theory of /Cloud/: Toward a History of Painting*

Jean-Luc Nancy, *The Speculative Remark: (One of Hegel's Bons Mots)*

Jean-François Lyotard, *Soundproof Room: Malraux's Anti-Aesthetics*

Jan Patočka, *Plato and Europe*

Hubert Damisch, *Skyline: The Narcissistic City*

Isabel Hoving, *In Praise of New Travelers: Reading Caribbean Migrant Women Writers*

Richard Rand, ed., *Futures: Of Jacques Derrida*

William Rasch, *Niklas Luhmann's Modernity: The Paradoxes of Differentiation*

Jacques Derrida and Anne Dufourmantelle, *Of Hospitality*

Jean-François Lyotard, *The Confession of Augustine*

Kaja Silverman, *World Spectators*

Samuel Weber, *Institution and Interpretation: Expanded Edition*

Jeffrey S. Librett, *The Rhetoric of Cultural Dialogue: Jews and Germans in the Epoch of Emancipation*

Ulrich Baer, *Remnants of Song: Trauma and the Experience of Modernity in Charles Baudelaire and Paul Celan*

Samuel C. Wheeler III, *Deconstruction as Analytic Philosophy*

David S. Ferris, *Silent Urns: Romanticism, Hellenism, Modernity*

Rodolphe Gasché, *Of Minimal Things: Studies on the Notion of Relation*

Sarah Winter, *Freud and the Institution of Psychoanalytic Knowledge*

Samuel Weber, *The Legend of Freud: Expanded Edition*

Aris Fioretos, ed., *The Solid Letter: Readings of Friedrich Hölderlin*

J. Hillis Miller / Manuel Asensi, *Black Holes / J. Hillis Miller; or, Boustrophedonic Reading*

Miryam Sas, *Fault Lines: Cultural Memory and Japanese Surrealism*

Peter Schwenger, *Fantasm and Fiction: On Textual Envisioning*

Didier Maleuvre, *Museum Memories: History, Technology, Art*

Jacques Derrida, *Monolingualism of the Other; or, The Prosthesis of Origin*

Andrew Baruch Wachtel, *Making a Nation, Breaking a Nation: Literature and Cultural Politics in Yugoslavia*

Niklas Luhmann, *Love as Passion: The Codification of Intimacy*

Mieke Bal, ed., *The Practice of Cultural Analysis: Exposing Interdisciplinary Interpretation*

Jacques Derrida and Gianni Vattimo, eds., *Religion*